RAVINE™

created by

STJEPAN ŠEJIĆ

written by

STJEPAN ŠEJIĆ & RON MARZ

illustrated by

STJEPAN ŠEJIĆ

lettered by

TROY PETERI

•••••

production by

PHIL SMITH & VINCENT KUKUA

•••••

published by

image® & TOP COW® PRODUCTIONS, INC.

~DEDICATION~

To my wife Linda, because all this began
that day in college when I decided to
draw you wearing armor.

-STJEPAN ŠEJIĆ

To my wife Kirsten, because without you
there is no us, and without us, there is no
anything.

-RON MARZ

IMAGE COMICS, INC.
Robert Kirkman - chief operating officer
Erik Larsen - chief financial officer
Todd McFarlane - president
Marc Silvestri - chief executive officer
Jim Valentino - vice-president

Eric Stephenson - publisher
Ron Richards - director of business development
Jennifer de Guzman - pr & marketing director
Branwyn Bigglestone - accounts manager
Emily Miller - accounting assistant
Jamie Parreno - marketing assistant
Emilio Bautista - sales assistant
Susie Giroux - administrative assistant
Kevin Yuen - digital rights coordinator
Tyler Shainline - events coordinator
David Brothers - content manager
Jonathan Chan - production manager
Drew Gill - art director
Jana Cook - print manager
Monica Garcia - senior production artist
Vincent Kukua - production artist
Jenna Savage - production artist
www.imagecomics.com

For Top Cow Productions, Inc.:
Marc Silvestri - Chief Executive Officer
Matt Hawkins - President and Chief Operating Officer
Bryan Rountree - Managing Editor
Elena Salcedo - Operations Manager
Betsy Gonia - Production Assistant

RAVINE Volume 1 Trade Paperback,
AUGUST 2013. SECOND PRINTING. ISBN: 978-1-60706-722-1. $14.99 USD.
Published by Image Comics, Inc. Office of Publication: 2001 Center St., 6th Floor, Berkeley, CA 94704. RAVINE © 2013 Stjepan Sejic and Ron Marz. "RAVINE,"
the RAVINE logos and the likeness of all featured characters are trademarks of Stjepan Sejic and Ron Marz. All rights reserved. Image Comics and its logos
are registered trademarks of Image Comics, Inc. Any resemblance to actual persons (living or dead), events, institutions, or locales, without satiric intent, is
coincidental. No portion of this publication may be reproduced or transmitted, in any form or by any means, without the express written permission of Image
Comics. PRINTED IN SOUTH KOREA.

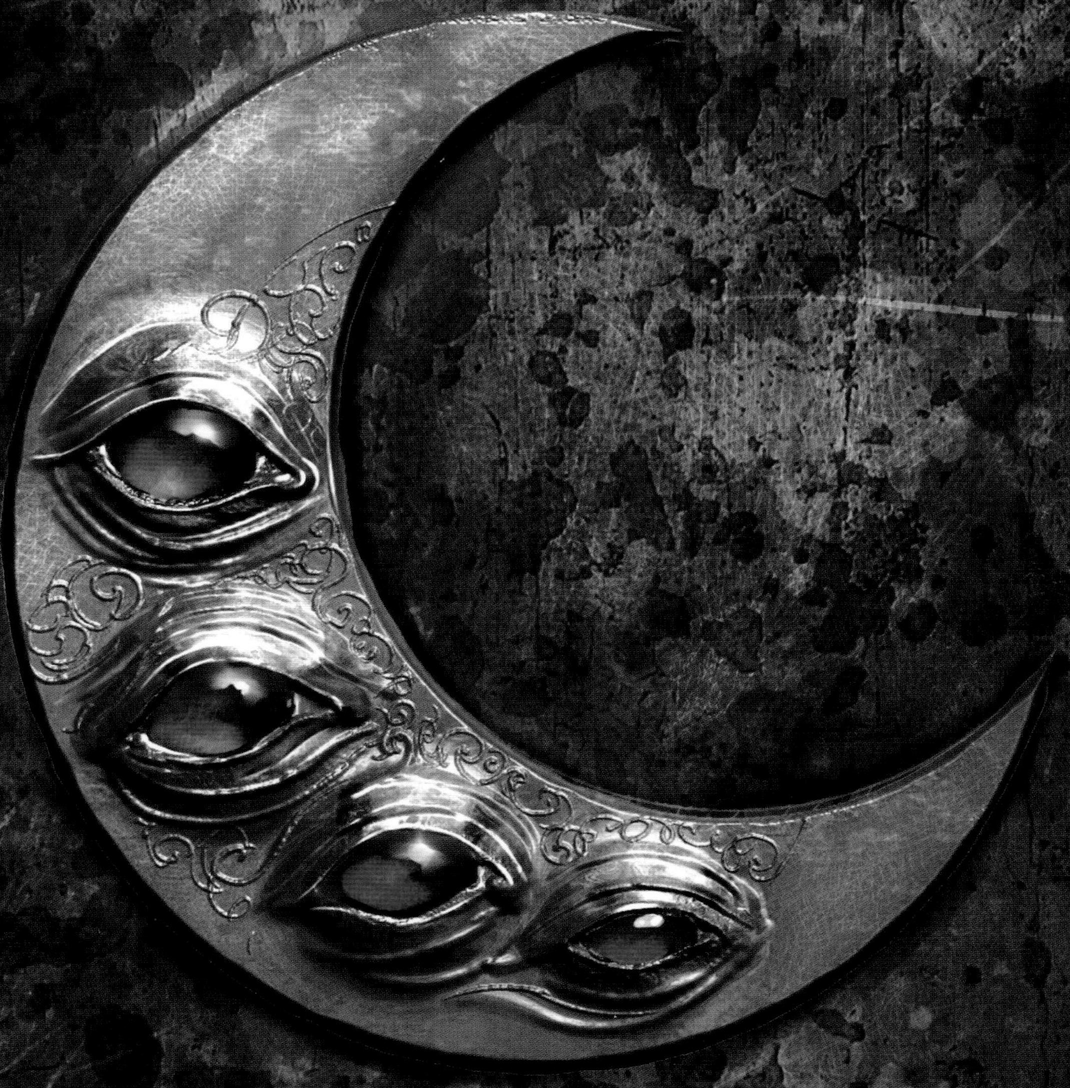

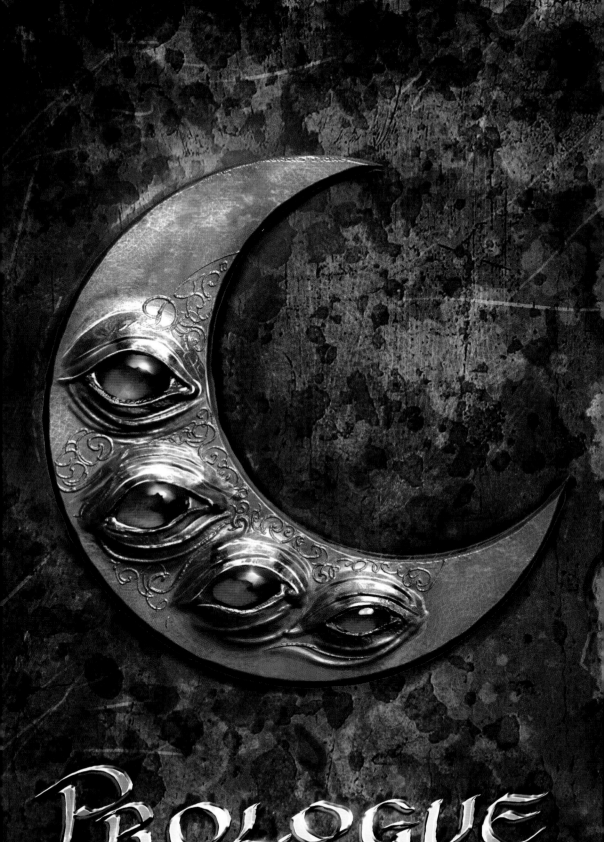

PROLOGUE

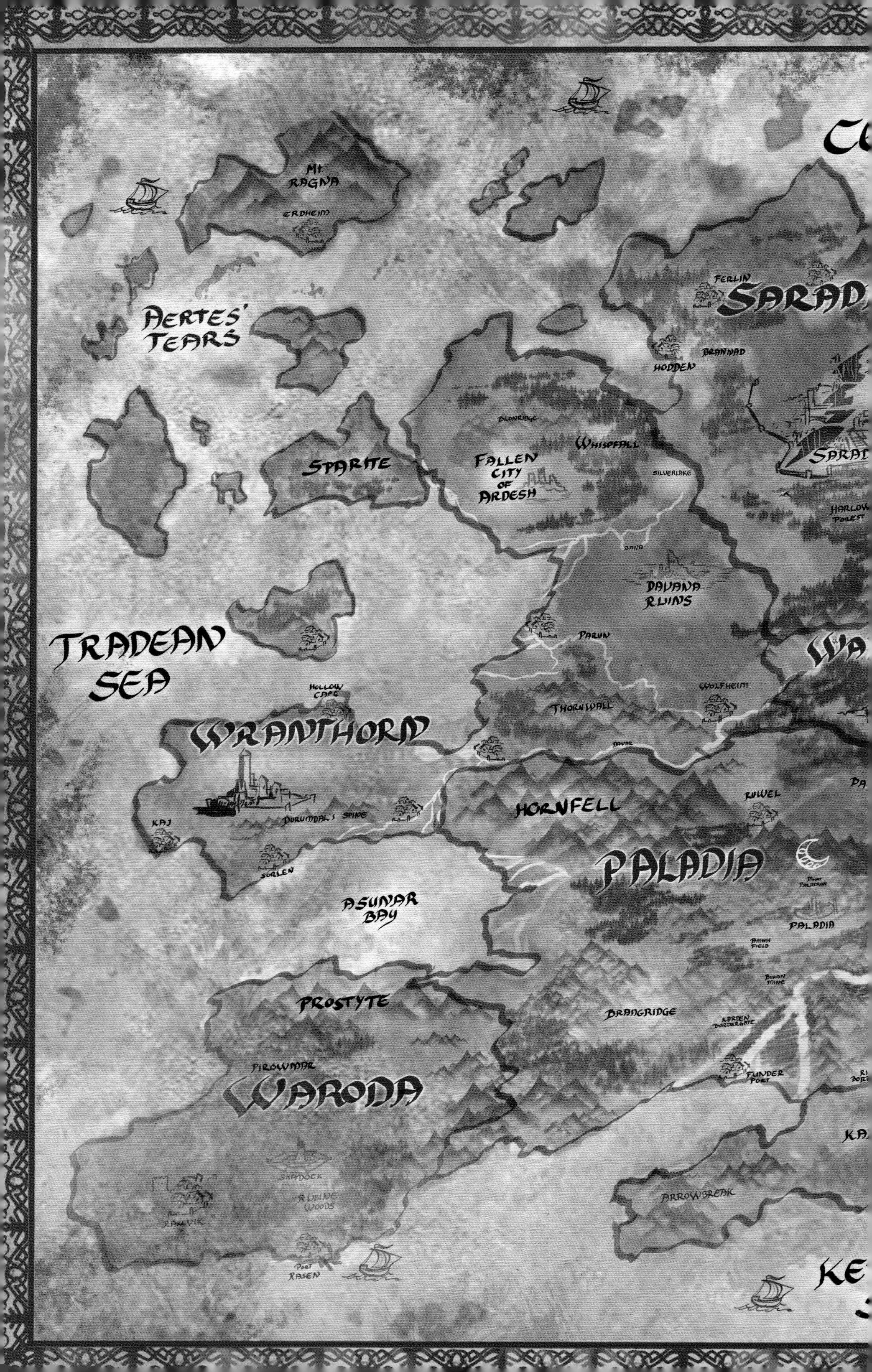

Mt. RAGNA
ERDHEIM
AERTES' TEARS
SPARITE
FALLEN CITY OF ARDESH
BLONRIDGE
WHISPFALL
SILVERLAKE
FERLIN
HODDEN
BRANNAD
HARLOW FOREST
BANA
DAVANA RUINS
PARUN
THORNWALL
WOLFHEIM
DAVAR
TRADEAN SEA
HOLLOW CAPE
WRANTHORN
KAJ
DURUMDAL'S SPINE
SORLEN
HORNFELL
RUWEL
PALADIA
PALADIA
ASUNAR BAY
PROSTYTE
BRANGRIDGE
KARDEN BORDERGATE
FUNDER PORT
PIROWMAR
WARODA
SHADOCK
ARROWBREAK
PORT RASEN

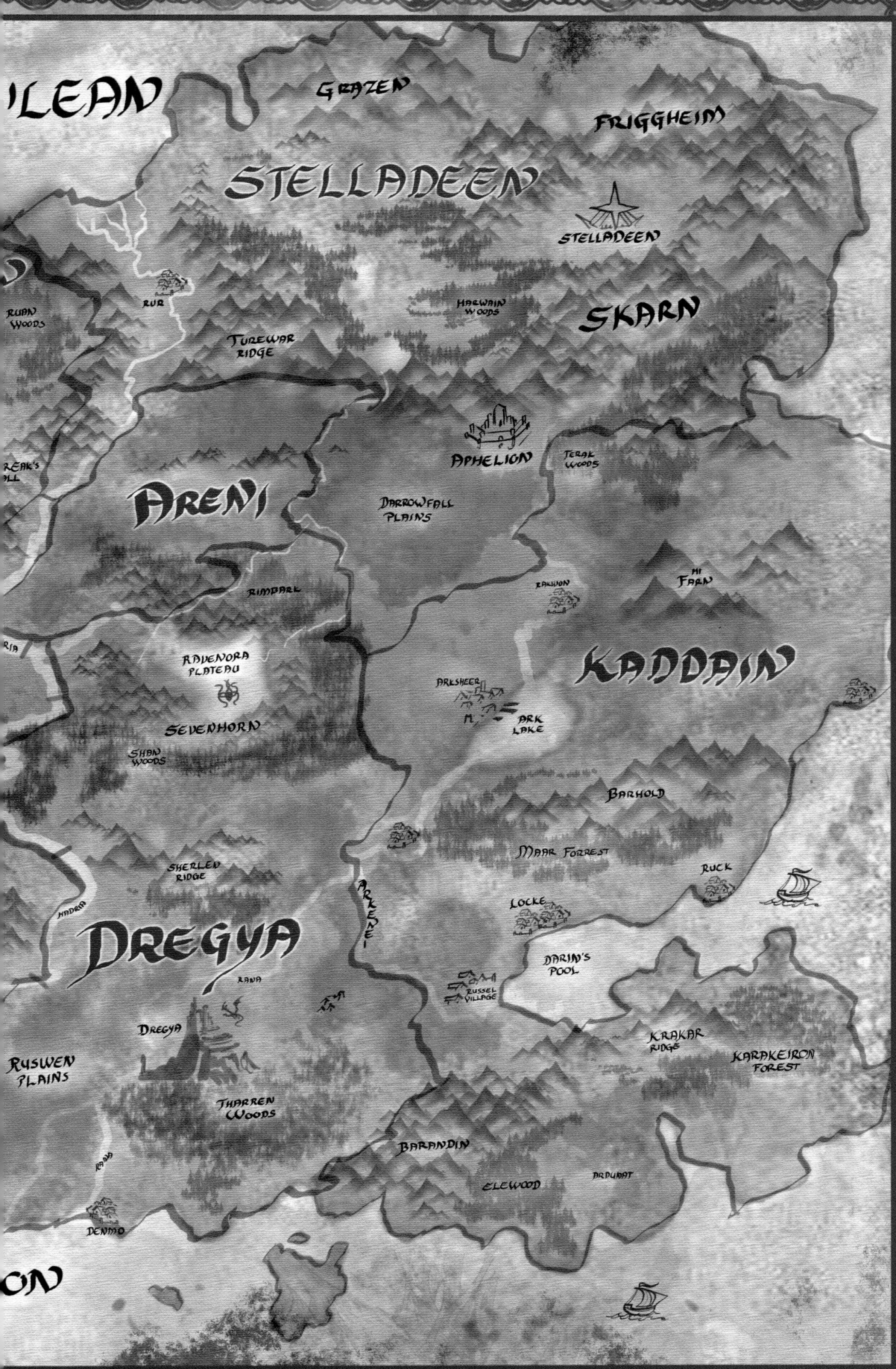
GRAZEN
FRIGGHEIM
STELLADEEN
STELLADEEN
RUR
RUAN WOODS
HARWAIN WOODS
SKARN
TUREWAR RIDGE
APHELION
TERAK WOODS
ARENI
DARROWFALL PLAINS
RIMBARK
RAKWON
MI FARN
RAVENORA PLATEAU
KADDAIN
ARKSHEER
ARK LAKE
SEVENHORN
SHAN WOODS
BARHOLD
MAAR FORREST
SHERLEN RIDGE
ARKENEI
RUCK
HADRA
LOCKE
DREGYA
DARIN'S POOL
RANA
RUSSEL VILLAGE
DREGYA
KRAKAR RIDGE
KARAKEIRON FOREST
RUSWEN PLAINS
THARREN WOODS
BARANDIN
ELEWOOD
ARDUNAT
DENMO

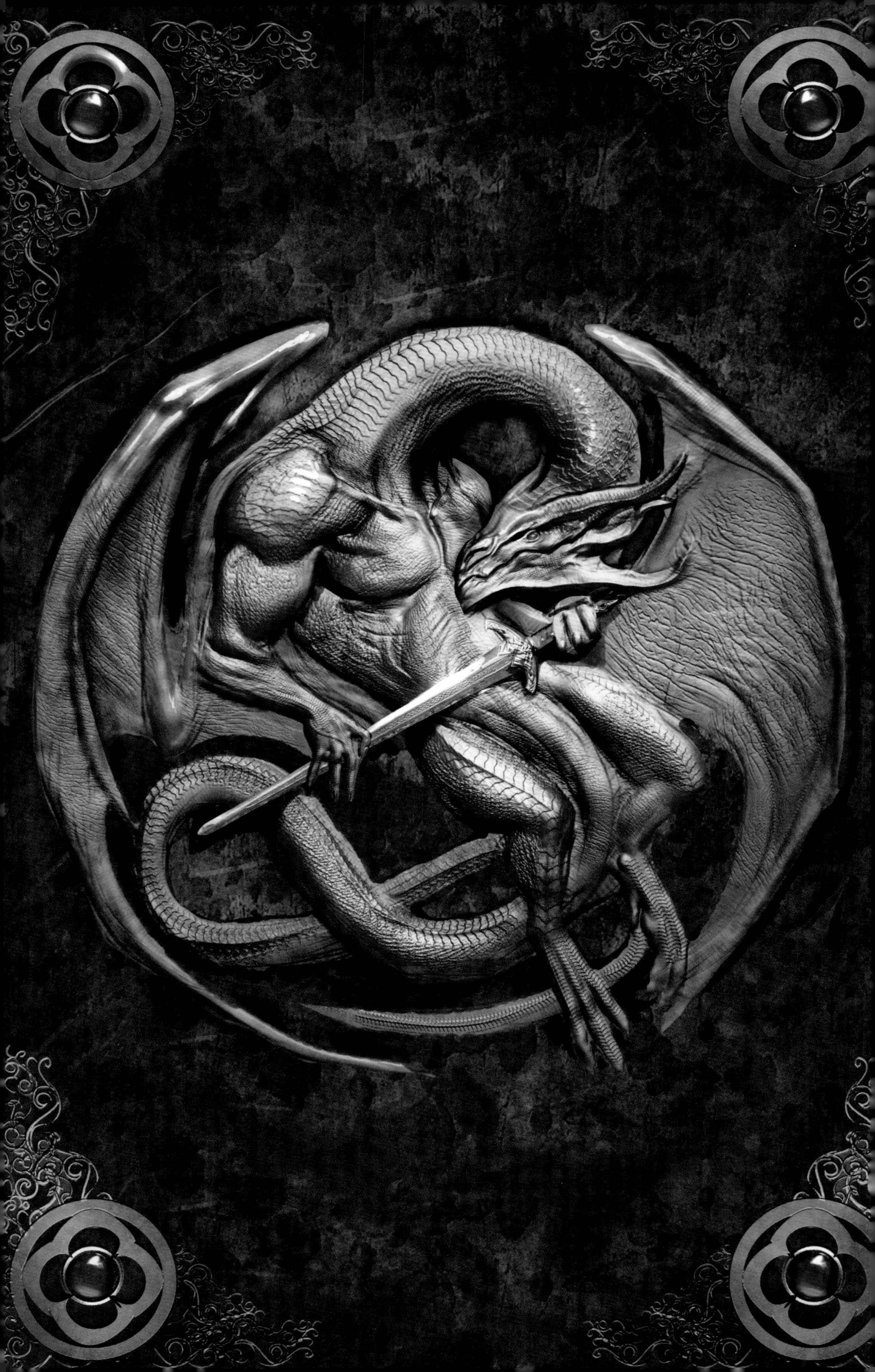

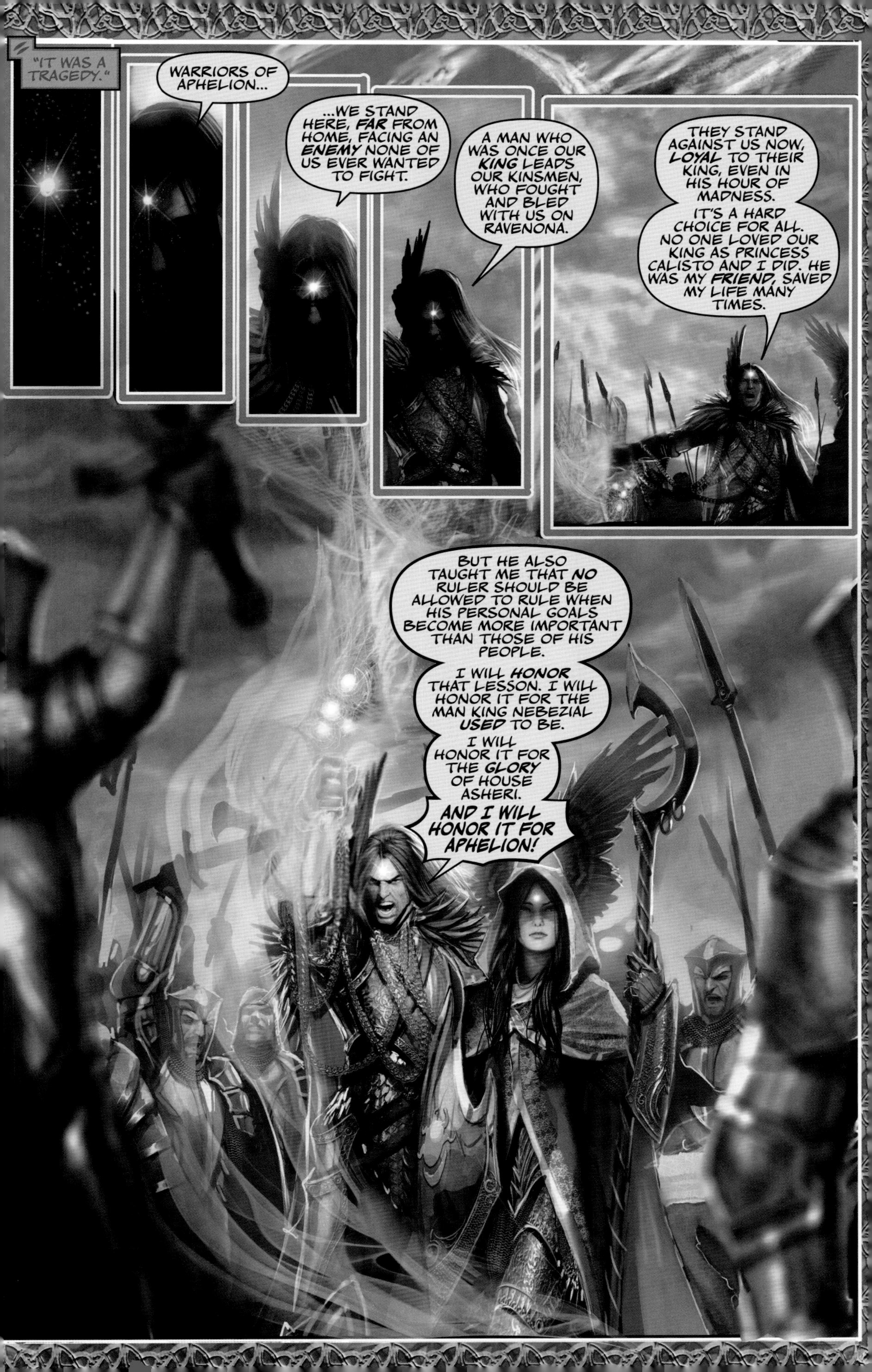
"IT WAS A TRAGEDY."
WARRIORS OF APHELION...
...WE STAND HERE, FAR FROM HOME, FACING AN ENEMY NONE OF US EVER WANTED TO FIGHT.
A MAN WHO WAS ONCE OUR KING LEADS OUR KINSMEN, WHO FOUGHT AND BLED WITH US ON RAVENONA.
THEY STAND AGAINST US NOW, LOYAL TO THEIR KING, EVEN IN HIS HOUR OF MADNESS.
IT'S A HARD CHOICE FOR ALL. NO ONE LOVED OUR KING AS PRINCESS CALISTO AND I DID. HE WAS MY FRIEND, SAVED MY LIFE MANY TIMES.
BUT HE ALSO TAUGHT ME THAT NO RULER SHOULD BE ALLOWED TO RULE WHEN HIS PERSONAL GOALS BECOME MORE IMPORTANT THAN THOSE OF HIS PEOPLE.
I WILL HONOR THAT LESSON. I WILL HONOR IT FOR THE MAN KING NEBEZIAL USED TO BE.
I WILL HONOR IT FOR THE GLORY OF HOUSE ASHERI.
AND I WILL HONOR IT FOR APHELION!

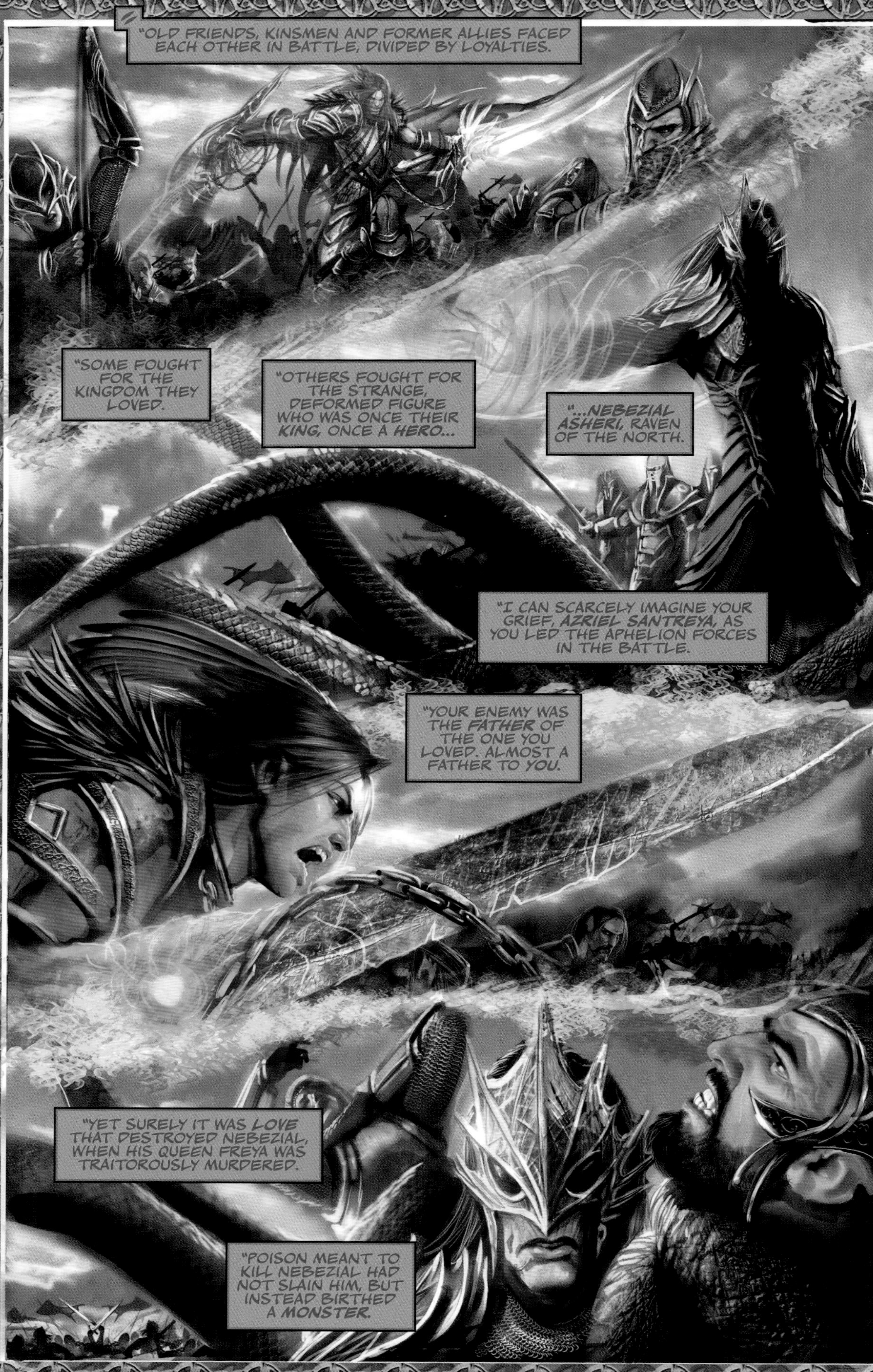
"OLD FRIENDS, KINSMEN AND FORMER ALLIES FACED EACH OTHER IN BATTLE, DIVIDED BY LOYALTIES.
"SOME FOUGHT FOR THE KINGDOM THEY LOVED.
"OTHERS FOUGHT FOR THE STRANGE, DEFORMED FIGURE WHO WAS ONCE THEIR KING, ONCE A HERO...
"...NEBEZIAL ASHERI, RAVEN OF THE NORTH.
"I CAN SCARCELY IMAGINE YOUR GRIEF, AZRIEL SANTREYA, AS YOU LED THE APHELION FORCES IN THE BATTLE.
"YOUR ENEMY WAS THE FATHER OF THE ONE YOU LOVED. ALMOST A FATHER TO YOU.
"YET SURELY IT WAS LOVE THAT DESTROYED NEBEZIAL, WHEN HIS QUEEN FREYA WAS TRAITOROUSLY MURDERED.
"POISON MEANT TO KILL NEBEZIAL HAD NOT SLAIN HIM, BUT INSTEAD BIRTHED A MONSTER.

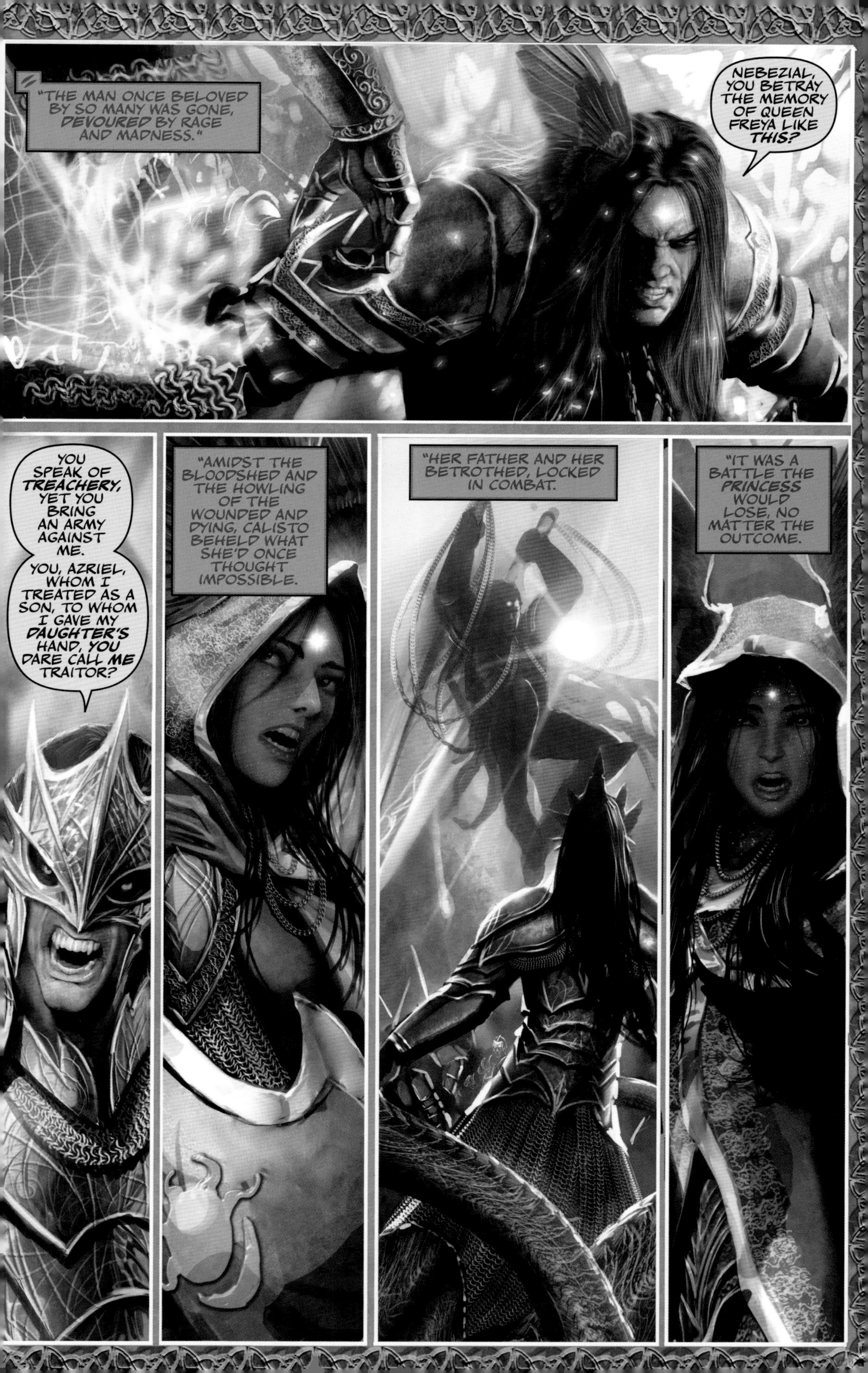
"THE MAN ONCE BELOVED BY SO MANY WAS GONE, DEVOURED BY RAGE AND MADNESS."
NEBEZIAL, YOU BETRAY THE MEMORY OF QUEEN FREYA LIKE THIS?
YOU SPEAK OF TREACHERY, YET YOU BRING AN ARMY AGAINST ME.
YOU, AZRIEL, WHOM I TREATED AS A SON, TO WHOM I GAVE MY DAUGHTER'S HAND, YOU DARE CALL ME TRAITOR?
"AMIDST THE BLOODSHED AND THE HOWLING OF THE WOUNDED AND DYING, CALISTO BEHELD WHAT SHE'D ONCE THOUGHT IMPOSSIBLE.
"HER FATHER AND HER BETROTHED, LOCKED IN COMBAT.
"IT WAS A BATTLE THE PRINCESS WOULD LOSE, NO MATTER THE OUTCOME.

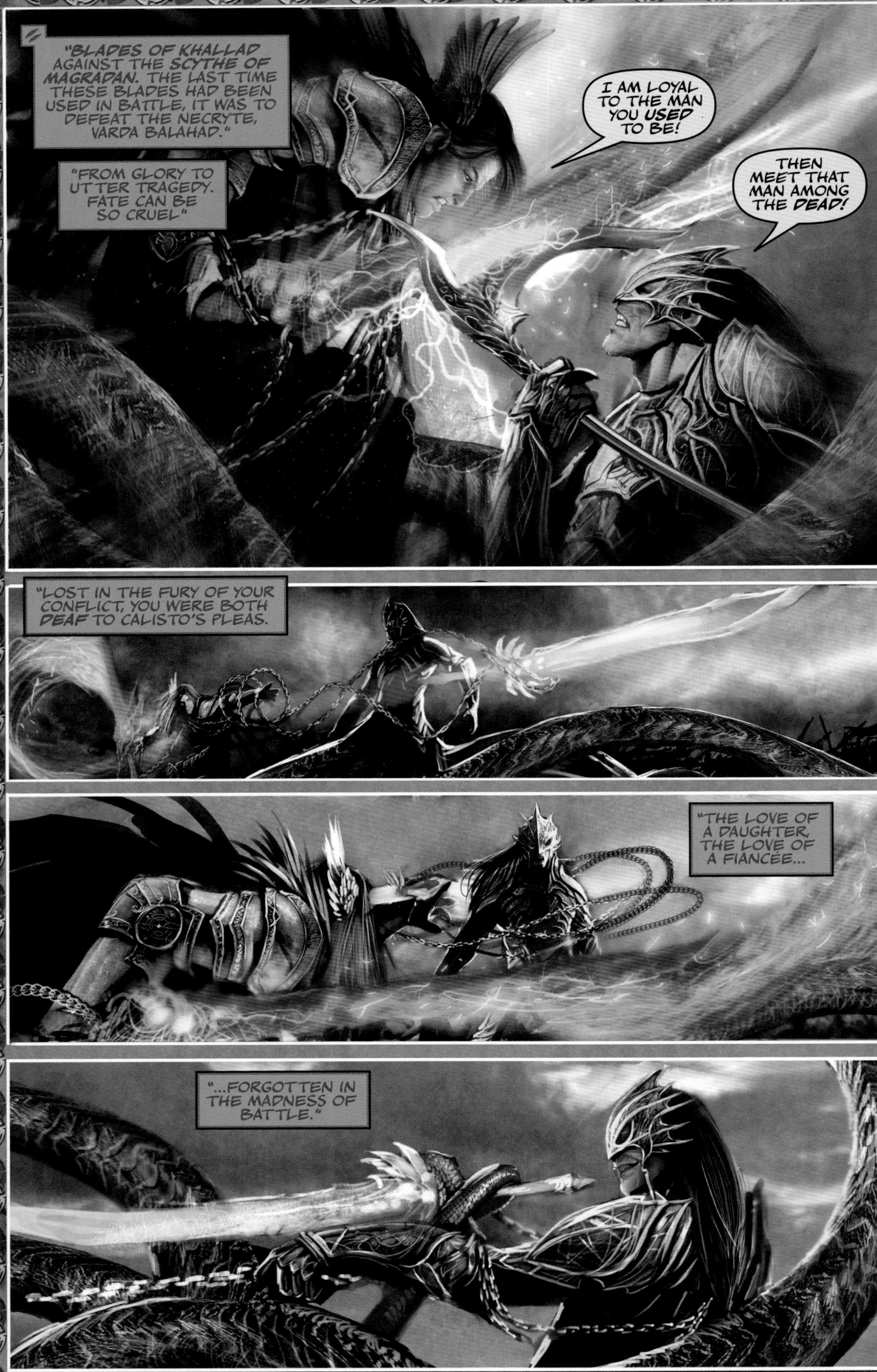
"BLADES OF KHALLAD AGAINST THE SCYTHE OF MAGRADAN. THE LAST TIME THESE BLADES HAD BEEN USED IN BATTLE, IT WAS TO DEFEAT THE NECRYTE, VARDA BALAHAD."
"FROM GLORY TO UTTER TRAGEDY. FATE CAN BE SO CRUEL"
I AM LOYAL TO THE MAN YOU USED TO BE!
THEN MEET THAT MAN AMONG THE DEAD!
"LOST IN THE FURY OF YOUR CONFLICT, YOU WERE BOTH DEAF TO CALISTO'S PLEAS.
"THE LOVE OF A DAUGHTER, THE LOVE OF A FIANCÉE...
"...FORGOTTEN IN THE MADNESS OF BATTLE."

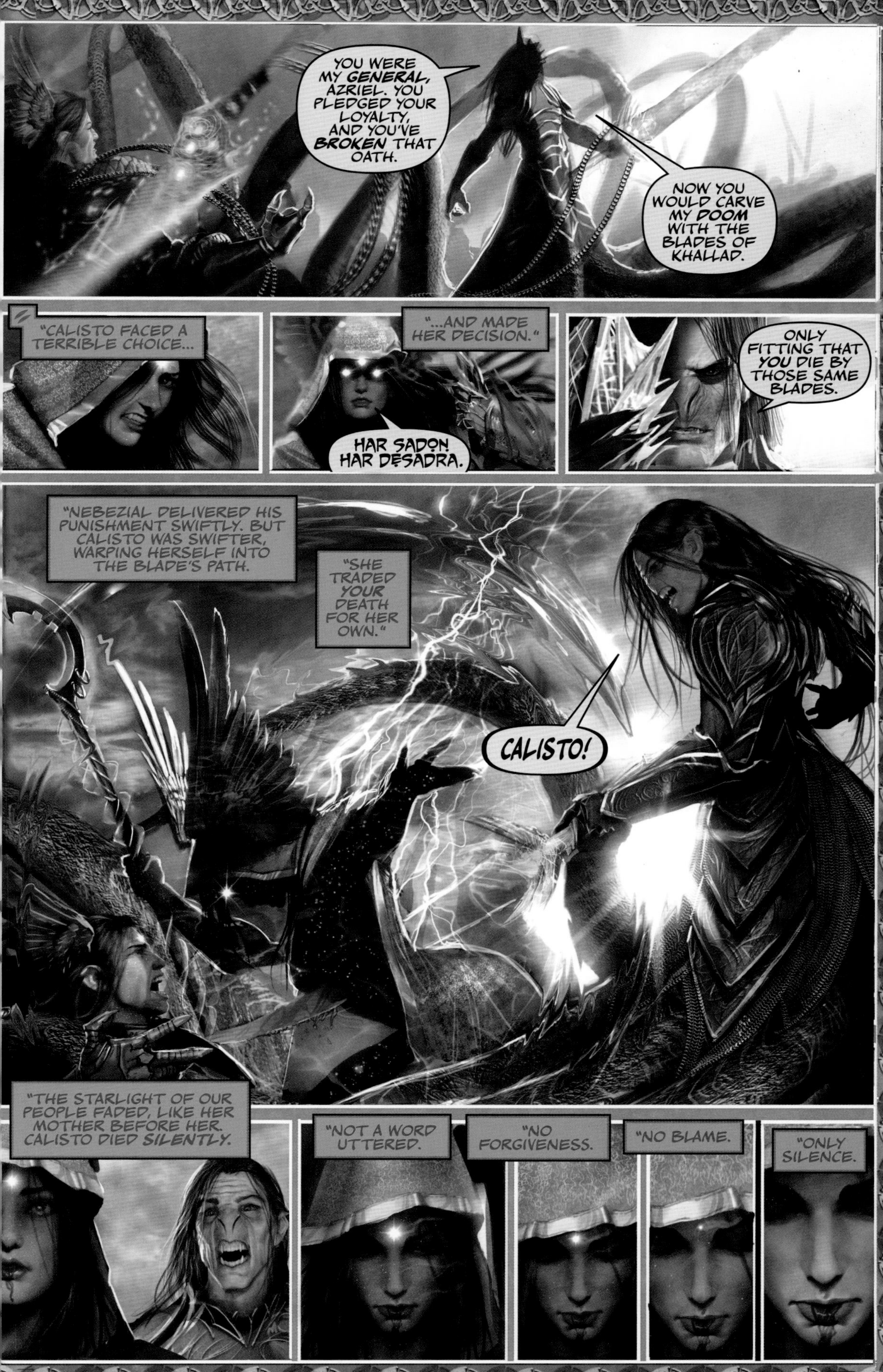
YOU WERE MY GENERAL, AZRIEL. YOU PLEDGED YOUR LOYALTY, AND YOU'VE BROKEN THAT OATH.
NOW YOU WOULD CARVE MY DOOM WITH THE BLADES OF KHALLAD.
"CALISTO FACED A TERRIBLE CHOICE...
"...AND MADE HER DECISION."
HAR SADON. HAR DESADRA.
ONLY FITTING THAT YOU DIE BY THOSE SAME BLADES.
"NEBEZIAL DELIVERED HIS PUNISHMENT SWIFTLY. BUT CALISTO WAS SWIFTER, WARPING HERSELF INTO THE BLADE'S PATH.
"SHE TRADED YOUR DEATH FOR HER OWN."
CALISTO!
"THE STARLIGHT OF OUR PEOPLE FADED, LIKE HER MOTHER BEFORE HER. CALISTO DIED SILENTLY.
"NOT A WORD UTTERED.
"NO FORGIVENESS.
"NO BLAME.
"ONLY SILENCE.

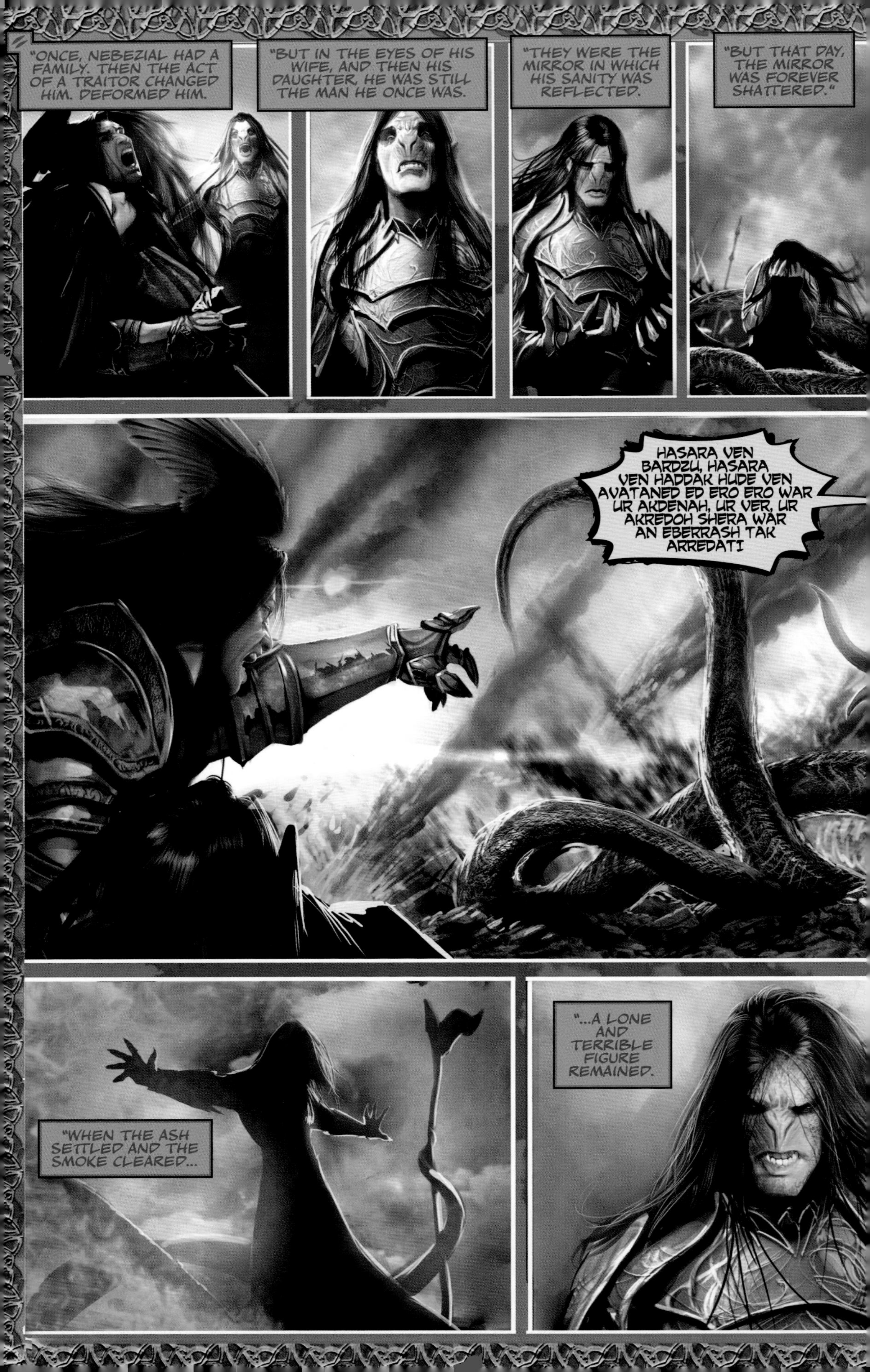
"ONCE, NEBEZIAL HAD A FAMILY. THEN THE ACT OF A TRAITOR CHANGED HIM. DEFORMED HIM.
"BUT IN THE EYES OF HIS WIFE, AND THEN HIS DAUGHTER, HE WAS STILL THE MAN HE ONCE WAS.
"THEY WERE THE MIRROR IN WHICH HIS SANITY WAS REFLECTED.
"BUT THAT DAY, THE MIRROR WAS FOREVER SHATTERED."
HASARA VEN BARDZU, HASARA VEN HADDAK HUDE VEN AVATANED ED ERO ERO WAR UR AKDENAH, UR VER, UR AKREDOH SHERA WAR AN EBERRASH TAK ARREDATI
"WHEN THE ASH SETTLED AND THE SMOKE CLEARED...
"...A LONE AND TERRIBLE FIGURE REMAINED.

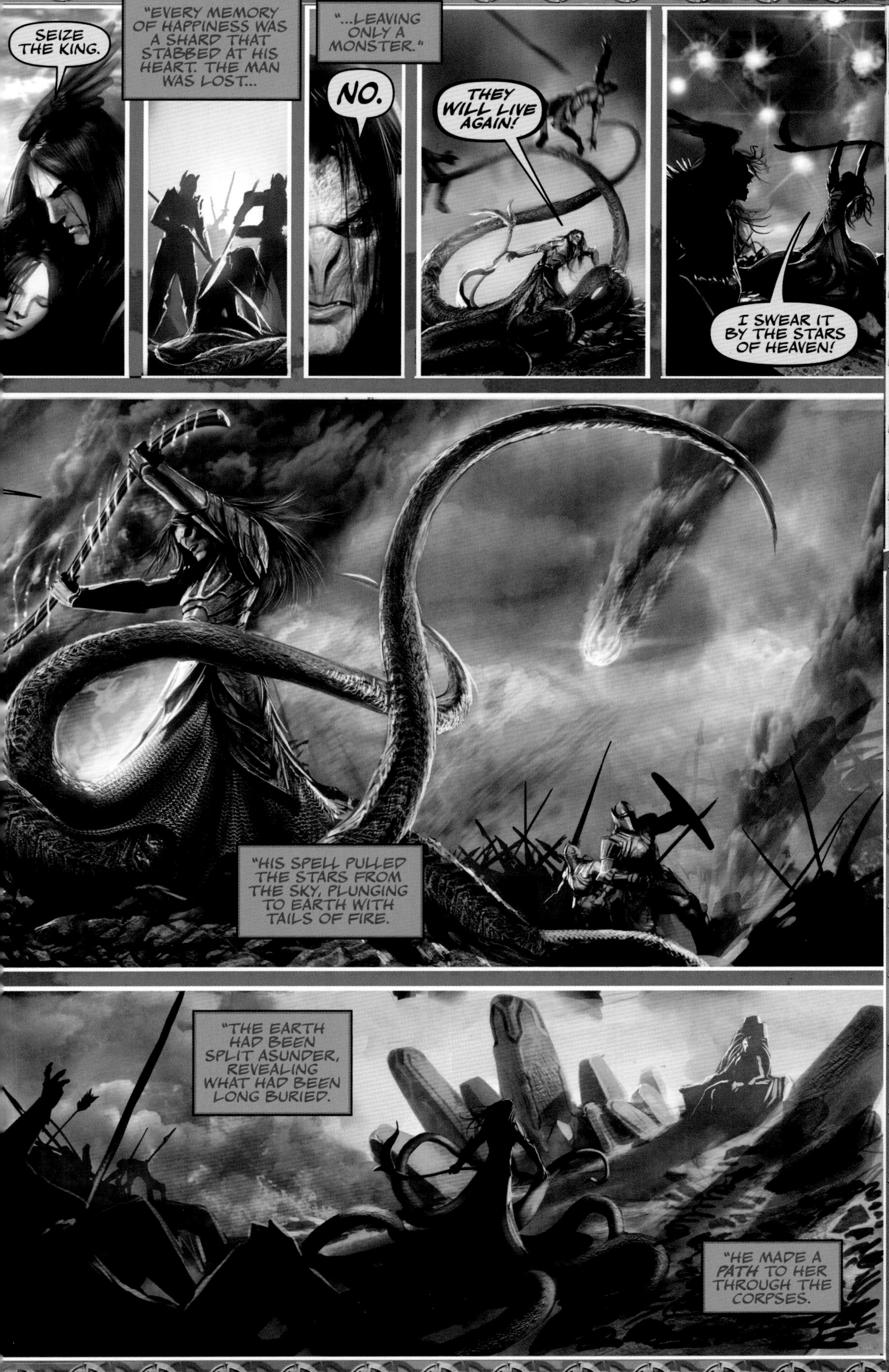
SEIZE THE KING.
"EVERY MEMORY OF HAPPINESS WAS A SHARD THAT STABBED AT HIS HEART. THE MAN WAS LOST...
"...LEAVING ONLY A MONSTER."
NO.
THEY WILL LIVE AGAIN!
I SWEAR IT BY THE STARS OF HEAVEN!
"HIS SPELL PULLED THE STARS FROM THE SKY, PLUNGING TO EARTH WITH TAILS OF FIRE.
"THE EARTH HAD BEEN SPLIT ASUNDER, REVEALING WHAT HAD BEEN LONG BURIED.
"HE MADE A *PATH* TO HER THROUGH THE CORPSES.

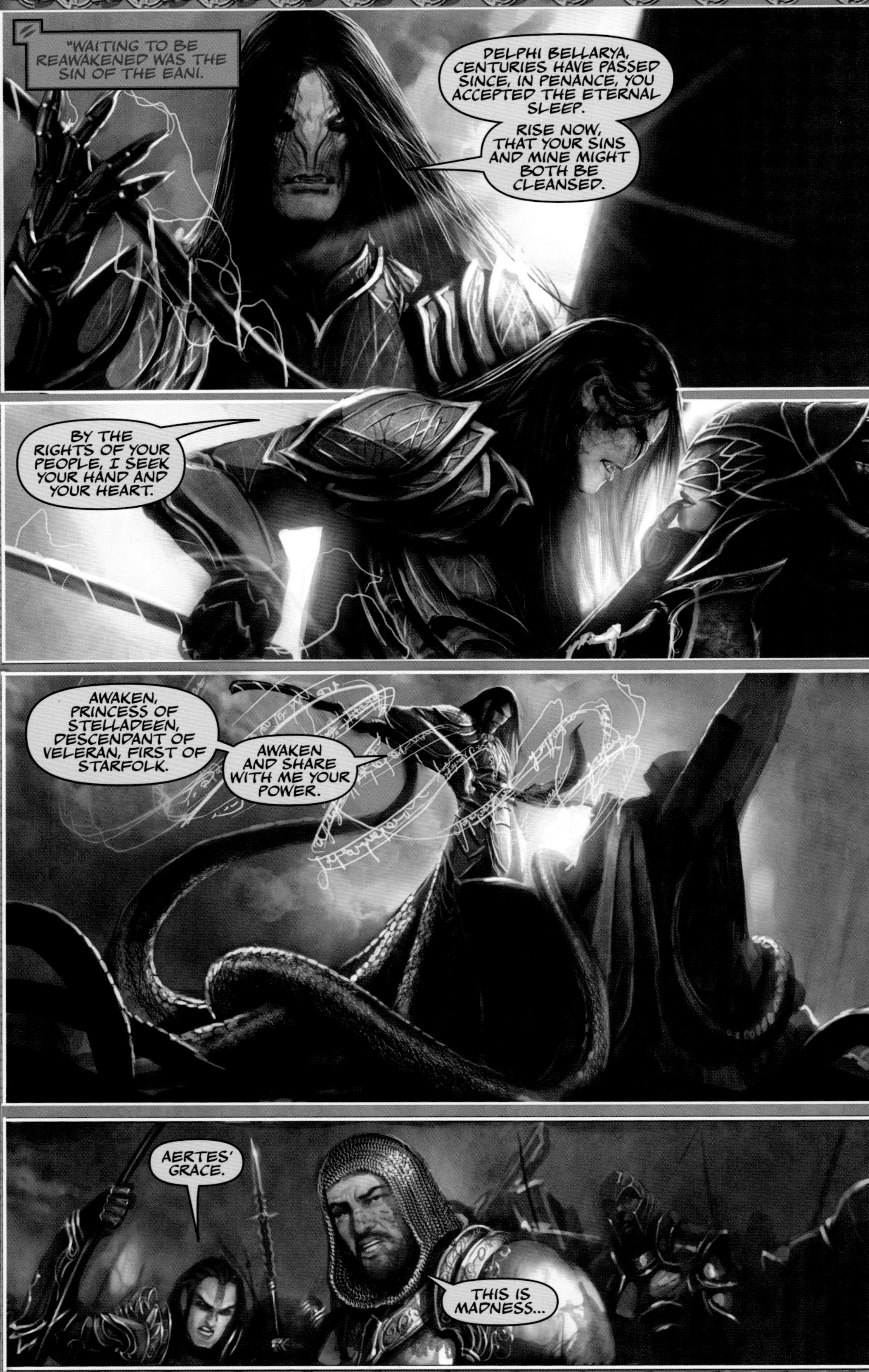
"WAITING TO BE REAWAKENED WAS THE SIN OF THE EANI.
DELPHI BELLARYA, CENTURIES HAVE PASSED SINCE, IN PENANCE, YOU ACCEPTED THE ETERNAL SLEEP.
RISE NOW, THAT YOUR SINS AND MINE MIGHT BOTH BE CLEANSED.
BY THE RIGHTS OF YOUR PEOPLE, I SEEK YOUR HAND AND YOUR HEART.
AWAKEN, PRINCESS OF STELLADEEN, DESCENDANT OF VELERAN, FIRST OF STARFOLK.
AWAKEN AND SHARE WITH ME YOUR POWER.
AERTES' GRACE.
THIS IS MADNESS...

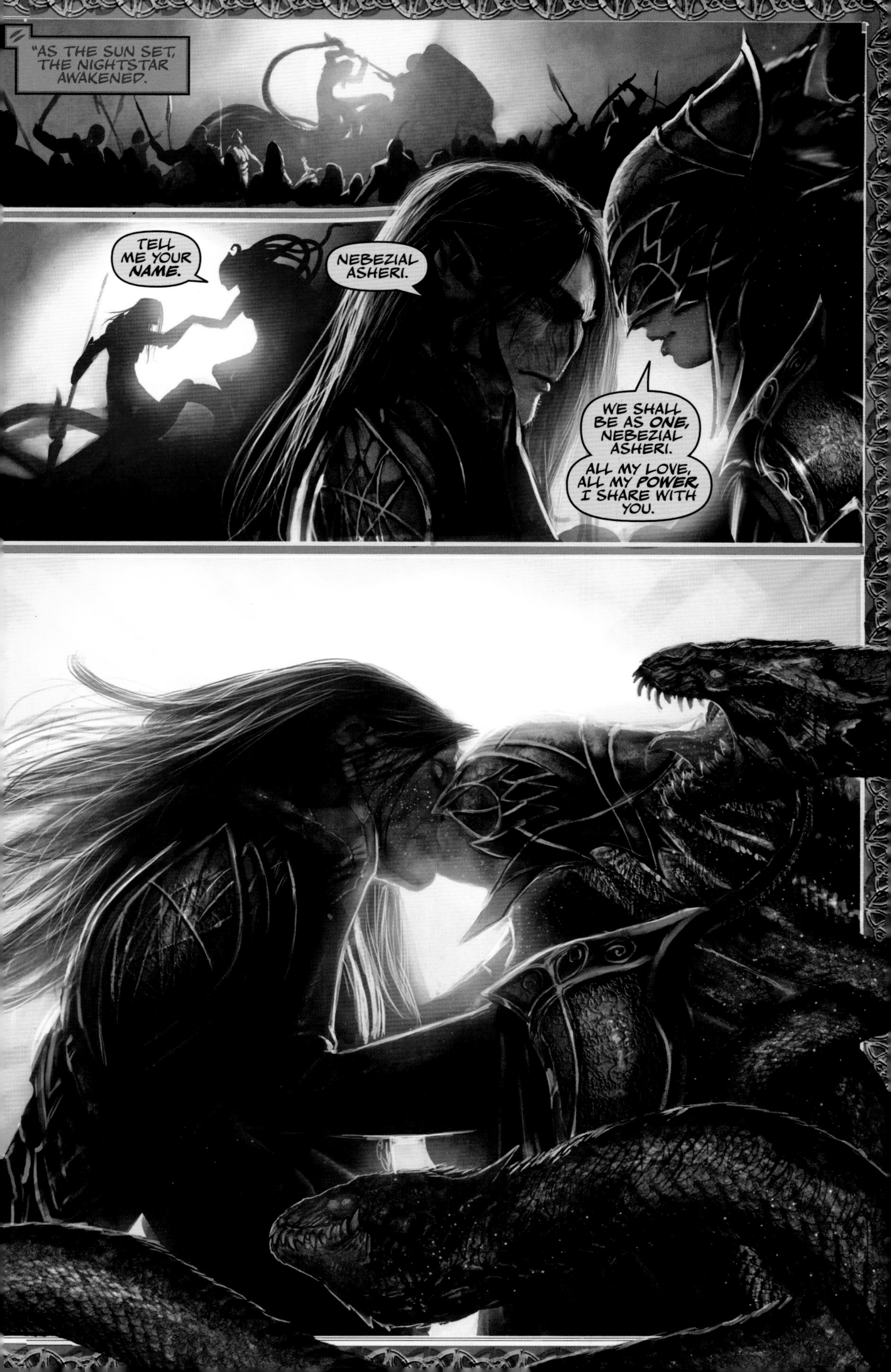
"AS THE SUN SET, THE NIGHTSTAR AWAKENED.
TELL ME YOUR NAME.
NEBEZIAL ASHERI.
WE SHALL BE AS ONE, NEBEZIAL ASHERI.
ALL MY LOVE, ALL MY POWER, I SHARE WITH YOU.

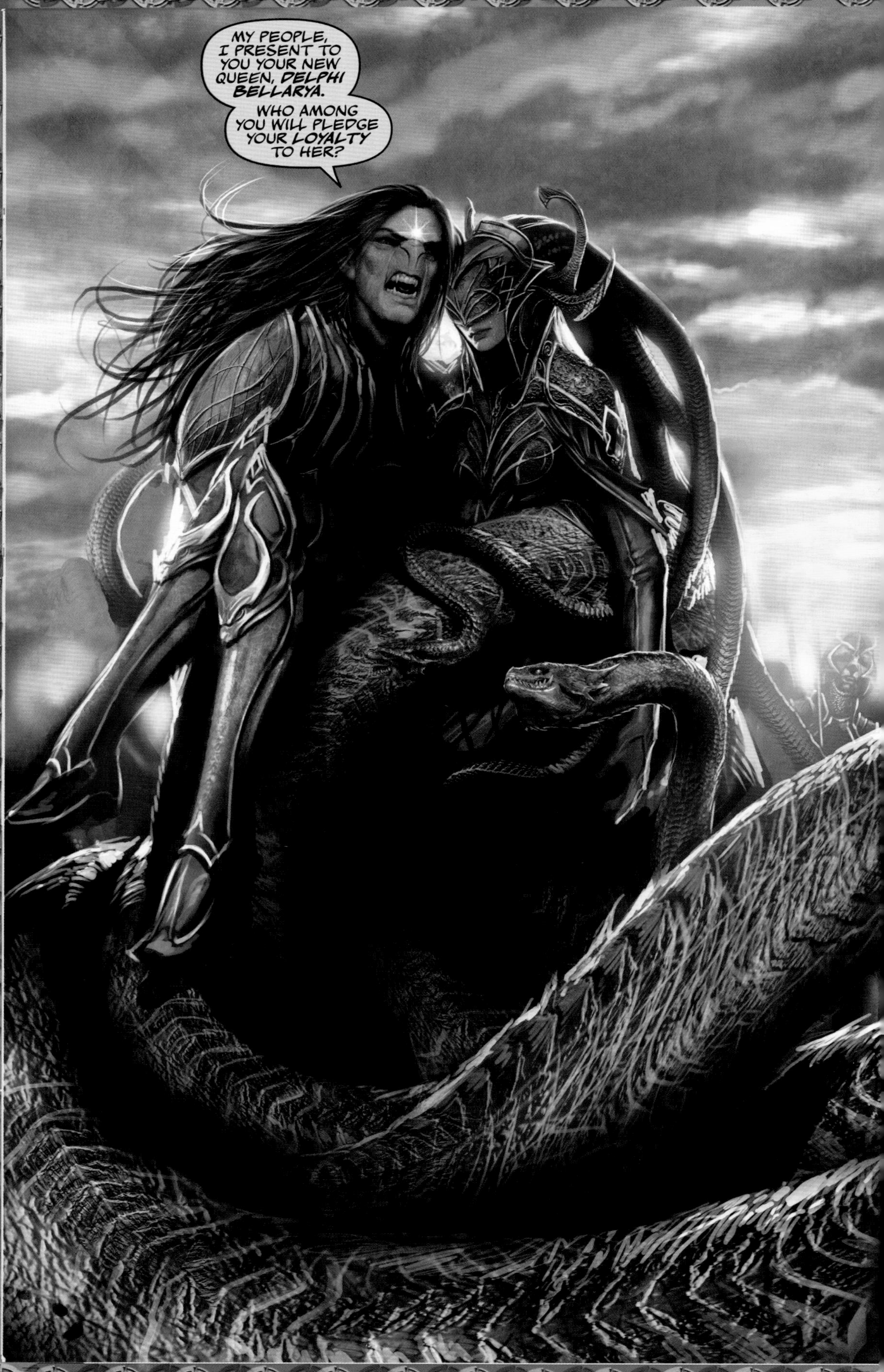
MY PEOPLE, I PRESENT TO YOU YOUR NEW QUEEN, DELPHI BELLARYA.
WHO AMONG YOU WILL PLEDGE YOUR LOYALTY TO HER?

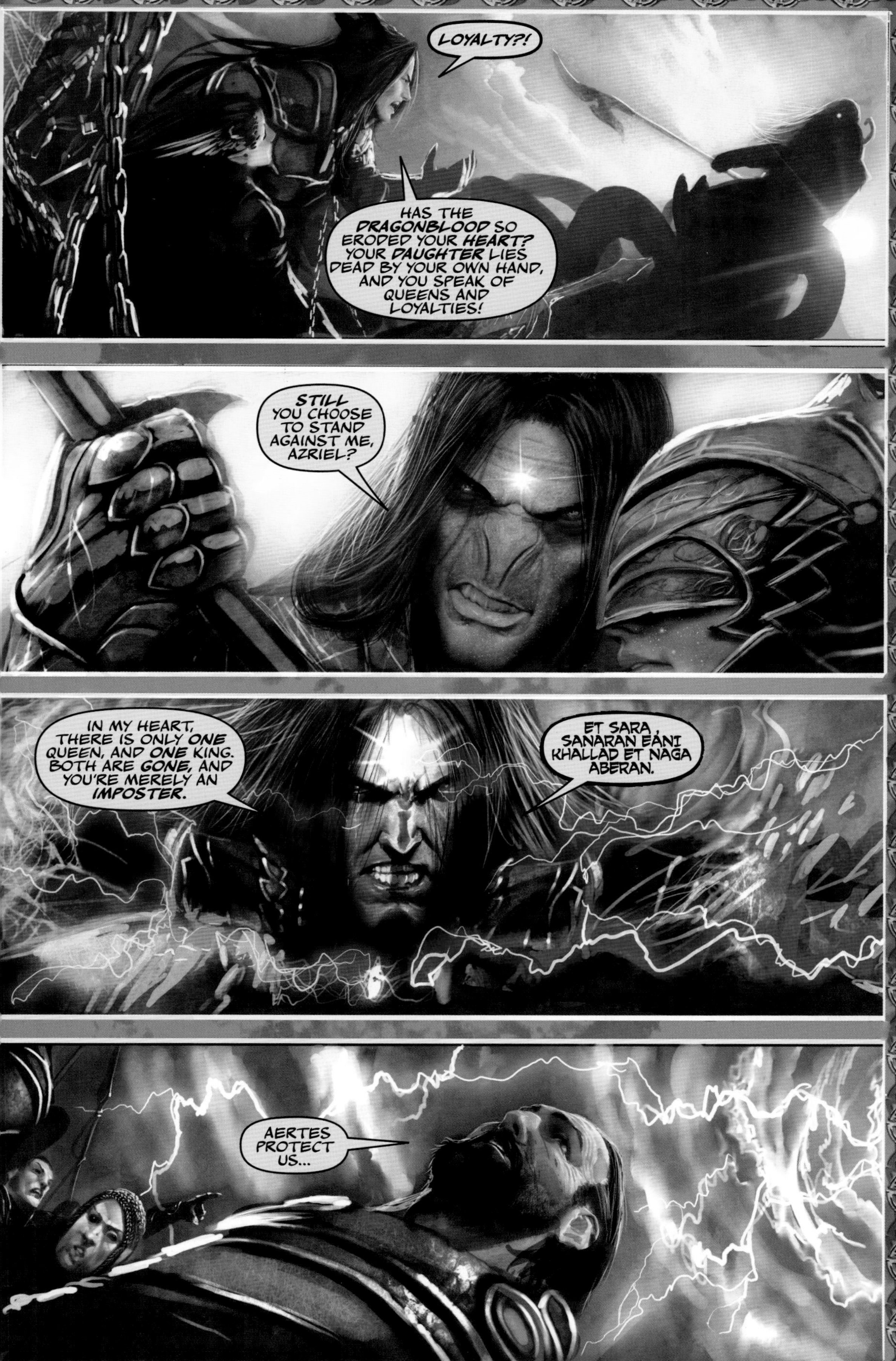
LOYALTY?!
HAS THE DRAGONBLOOD SO ERODED YOUR HEART? YOUR DAUGHTER LIES DEAD BY YOUR OWN HAND, AND YOU SPEAK OF QUEENS AND LOYALTIES!
STILL YOU CHOOSE TO STAND AGAINST ME, AZRIEL?
IN MY HEART, THERE IS ONLY ONE QUEEN, AND ONE KING. BOTH ARE GONE, AND YOU'RE MERELY AN IMPOSTER.
ET SARA, SANARAN EANI KHALLAD ET NAGA ABERAN.
AERTES PROTECT US...

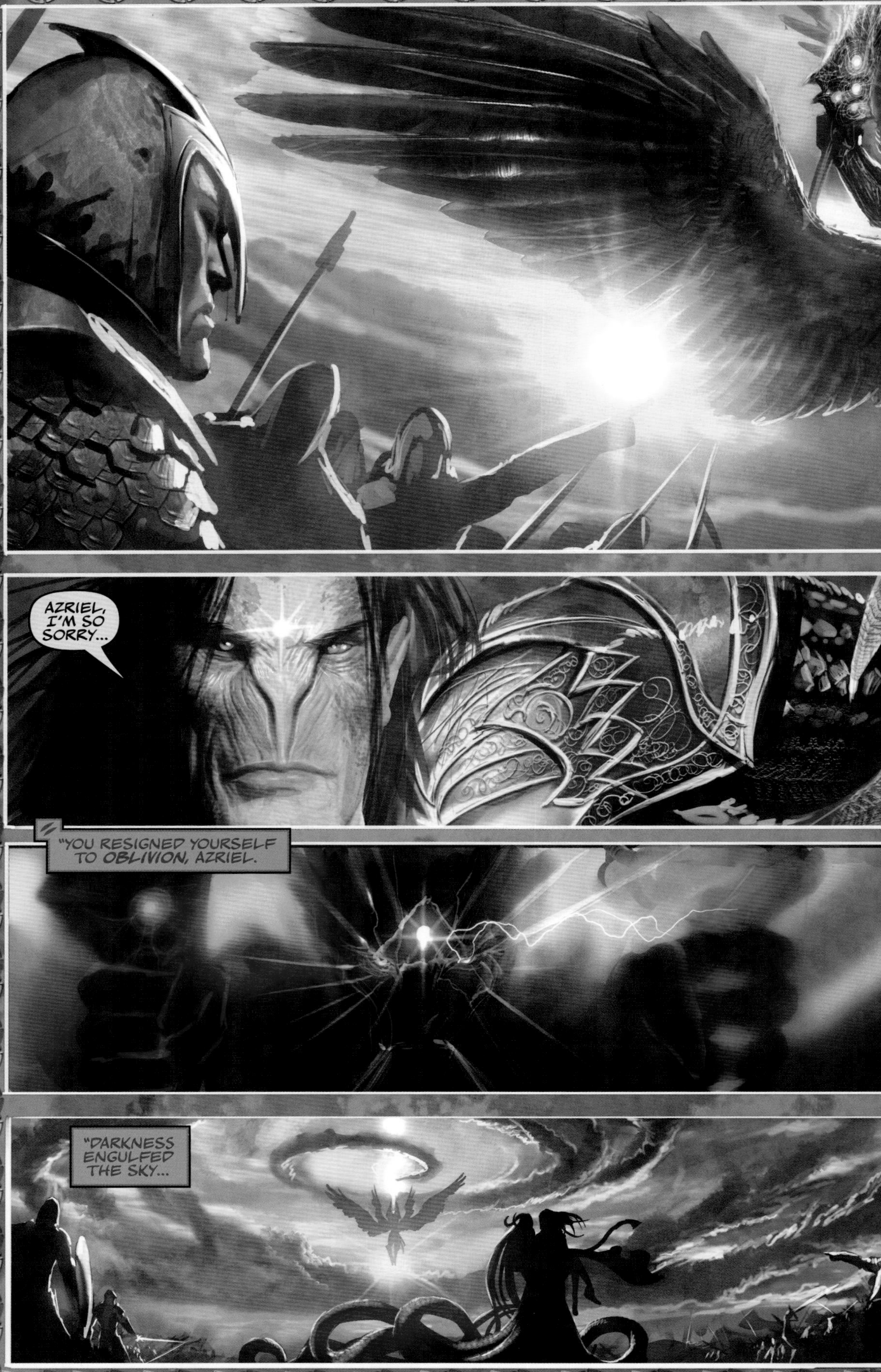
AZRIEL, I'M SO SORRY...
"YOU RESIGNED YOURSELF TO OBLIVION, AZRIEL.
"DARKNESS ENGULFED THE SKY...

SARAD MADA RABONAS BAR ET ADRA DAROM OGDERAN.

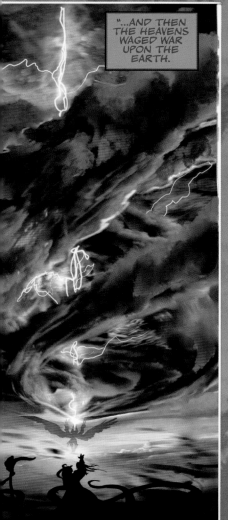

"...AND THEN THE HEAVENS WAGED WAR UPON THE EARTH."

"EVERMOOR PLATEAU VANISHED IN A SEARING FLASH OF DESTRUCTION."

"NOTHING REMAINED, SAVE THE POWER THAT HAS BEEN UNLEASHED. KING NEBEZIAL WAS GONE..."

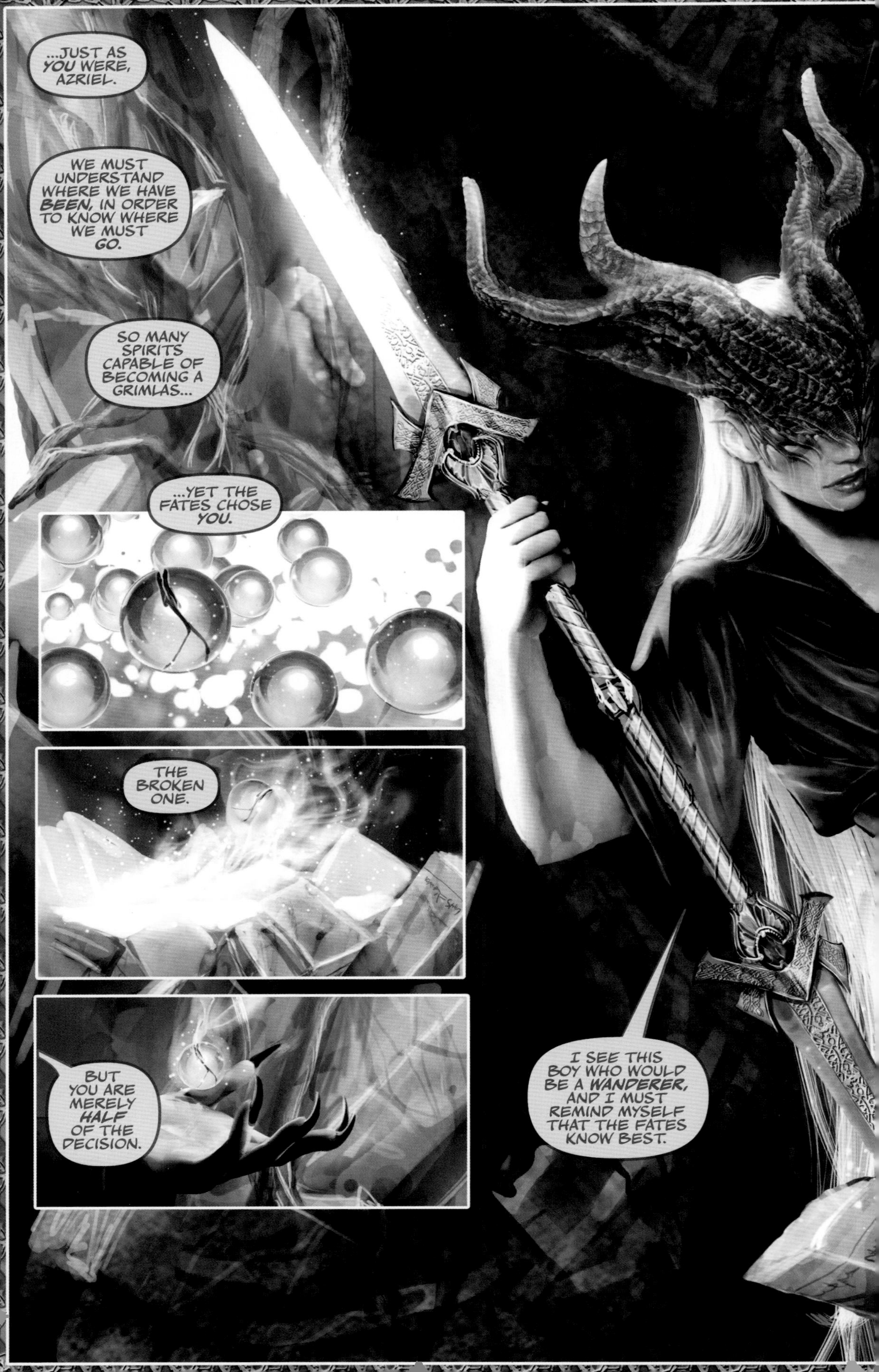
...JUST AS YOU WERE, AZRIEL.
WE MUST UNDERSTAND WHERE WE HAVE BEEN, IN ORDER TO KNOW WHERE WE MUST GO.
SO MANY SPIRITS CAPABLE OF BECOMING A GRIMLAS...
...YET THE FATES CHOSE YOU.
THE BROKEN ONE.
BUT YOU ARE MERELY HALF OF THE DECISION.
I SEE THIS BOY WHO WOULD BE A WANDERER, AND I MUST REMIND MYSELF THAT THE FATES KNOW BEST.

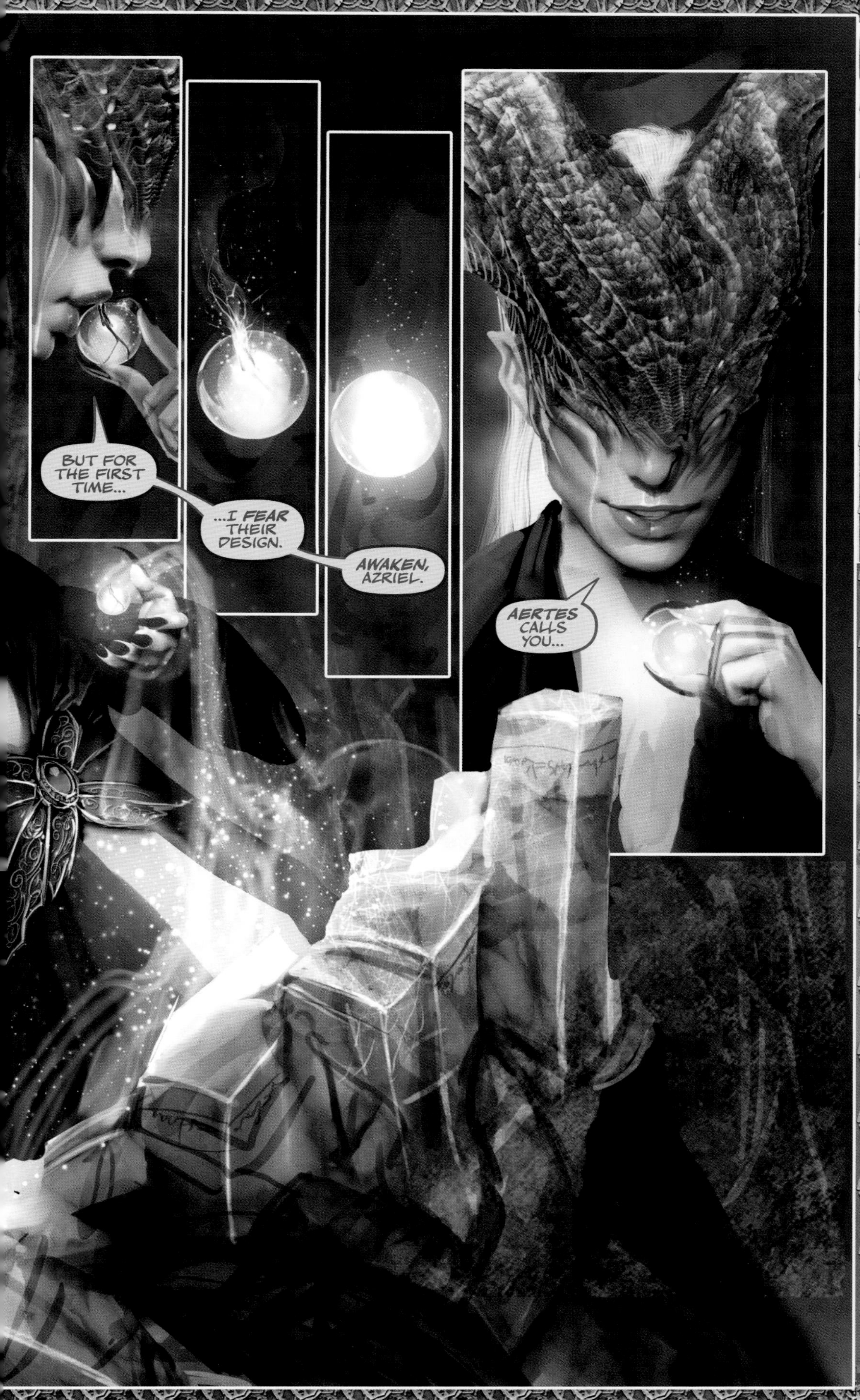
BUT FOR THE FIRST TIME...
...I FEAR THEIR DESIGN.
AWAKEN, AZRIEL.
AERTES CALLS YOU...

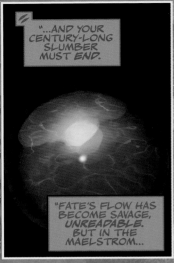

"...AND YOUR CENTURY-LONG SLUMBER MUST *END*.

"FATE'S FLOW HAS BECOME SAVAGE, *UNREADABLE*. BUT IN THE *MAELSTROM*...

"...I SEE A YOUNG MAN OF GREAT IMPORT."

MY LADY *AERTES*, I'M *UNWORTHY* TO BE A *GRIMLAS*.

"PERHAPS YOU ARE. BUT IF *MADNESS* SLIPS INTO THIS WANDER'S MIND, HE COULD BRING *RUIN* TO THE WORLD. SUCH IS THE *POWER* HE WIELDS."

ARE YOU...ARE YOU SAYING HE'S *NECRYTE*?

"A *TERROR* OF THE OLD WORLD, EVIL *WE* UNLEASHED UPON THE HUMANITY. AND HE WILL NEED A *GUIDE*."

A *NECRYTE* WITH A *GRIMLAS* WEAPON...

BUT HOW AM I TO HELP *HIM*? A *NECRYTE* CAN'T GIVE ME *FORM*.

"*HE* WILL HEAR YOUR THOUGHTS, AS *YOU* WILL HEAR HIS.

"THIS WILL BE YOUR *LIMIT*, AND THE PRICE OF YOUR *REDEMPTION*.

"REMEMBER AZRIEL, HE WILL NEED YOUR *FRIENDSHIP* FAR MORE THAN YOUR *POWER*.

"GO NOW, BECOME A *GRIMLAS AVENDATI*...

"...AND GUIDE THE WANDERER."

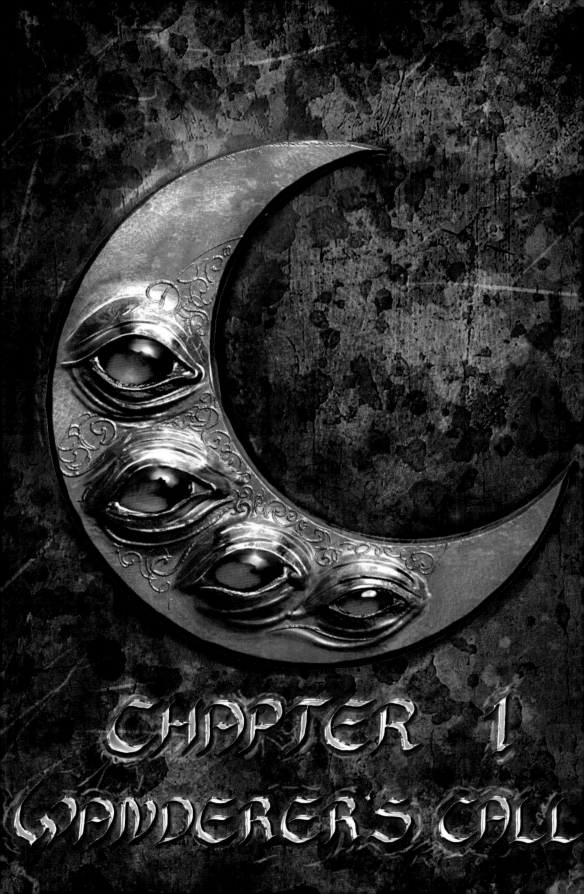

CHAPTER 1
WANDERER'S CALL

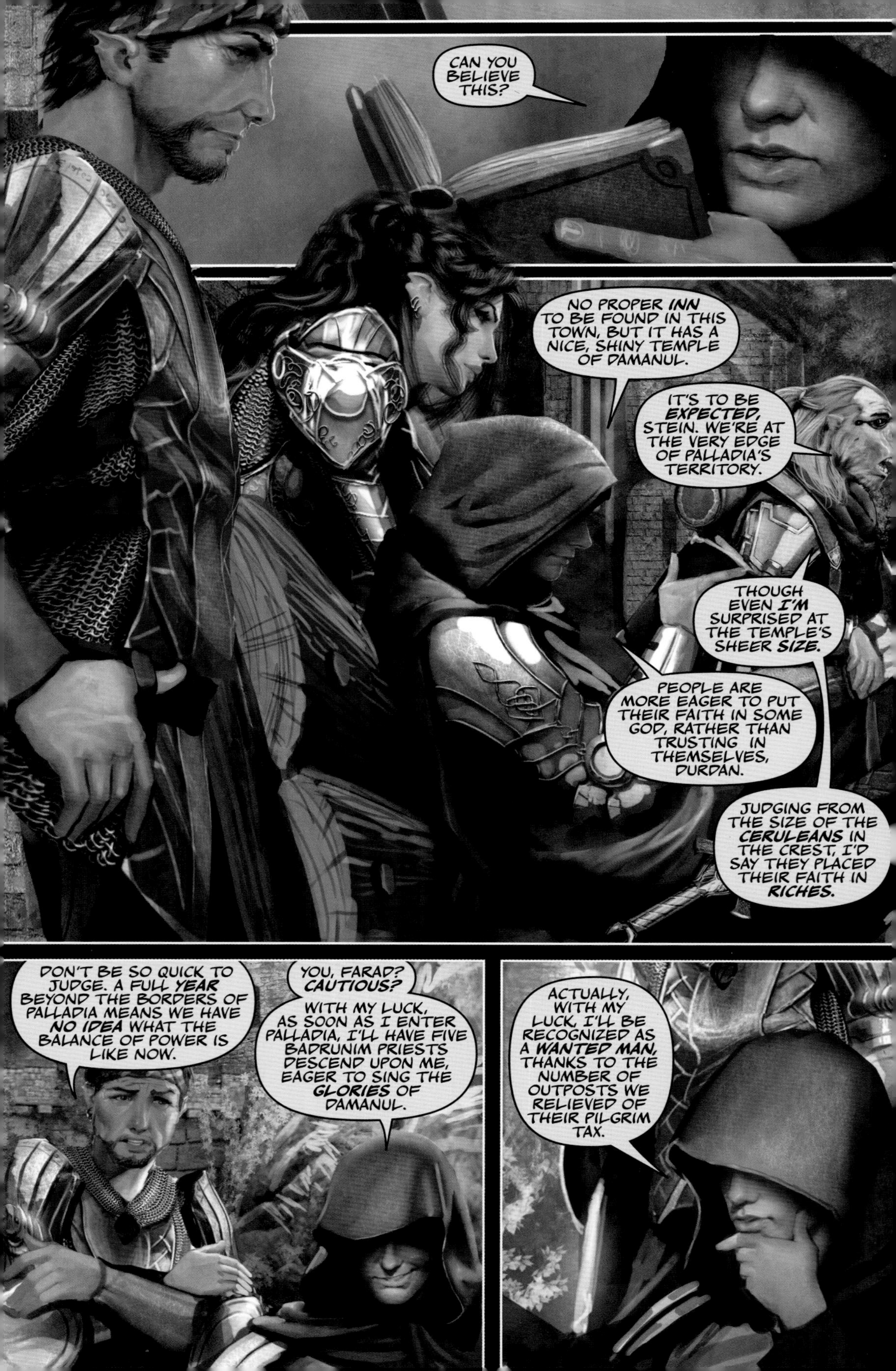
CAN YOU BELIEVE THIS?
NO PROPER INN TO BE FOUND IN THIS TOWN, BUT IT HAS A NICE, SHINY TEMPLE OF DAMANUL.
IT'S TO BE EXPECTED, STEIN. WE'RE AT THE VERY EDGE OF PALLADIA'S TERRITORY.
THOUGH EVEN I'M SURPRISED AT THE TEMPLE'S SHEER SIZE.
PEOPLE ARE MORE EAGER TO PUT THEIR FAITH IN SOME GOD, RATHER THAN TRUSTING IN THEMSELVES, DURDAN.
JUDGING FROM THE SIZE OF THE CERULEANS IN THE CREST, I'D SAY THEY PLACED THEIR FAITH IN RICHES.
DON'T BE SO QUICK TO JUDGE. A FULL YEAR BEYOND THE BORDERS OF PALLADIA MEANS WE HAVE NO IDEA WHAT THE BALANCE OF POWER IS LIKE NOW.
YOU, FARAD? CAUTIOUS?
WITH MY LUCK, AS SOON AS I ENTER PALLADIA, I'LL HAVE FIVE BADRUNIM PRIESTS DESCEND UPON ME, EAGER TO SING THE GLORIES OF DAMANUL.
ACTUALLY, WITH MY LUCK, I'LL BE RECOGNIZED AS A WANTED MAN, THANKS TO THE NUMBER OF OUTPOSTS WE RELIEVED OF THEIR PILGRIM TAX.

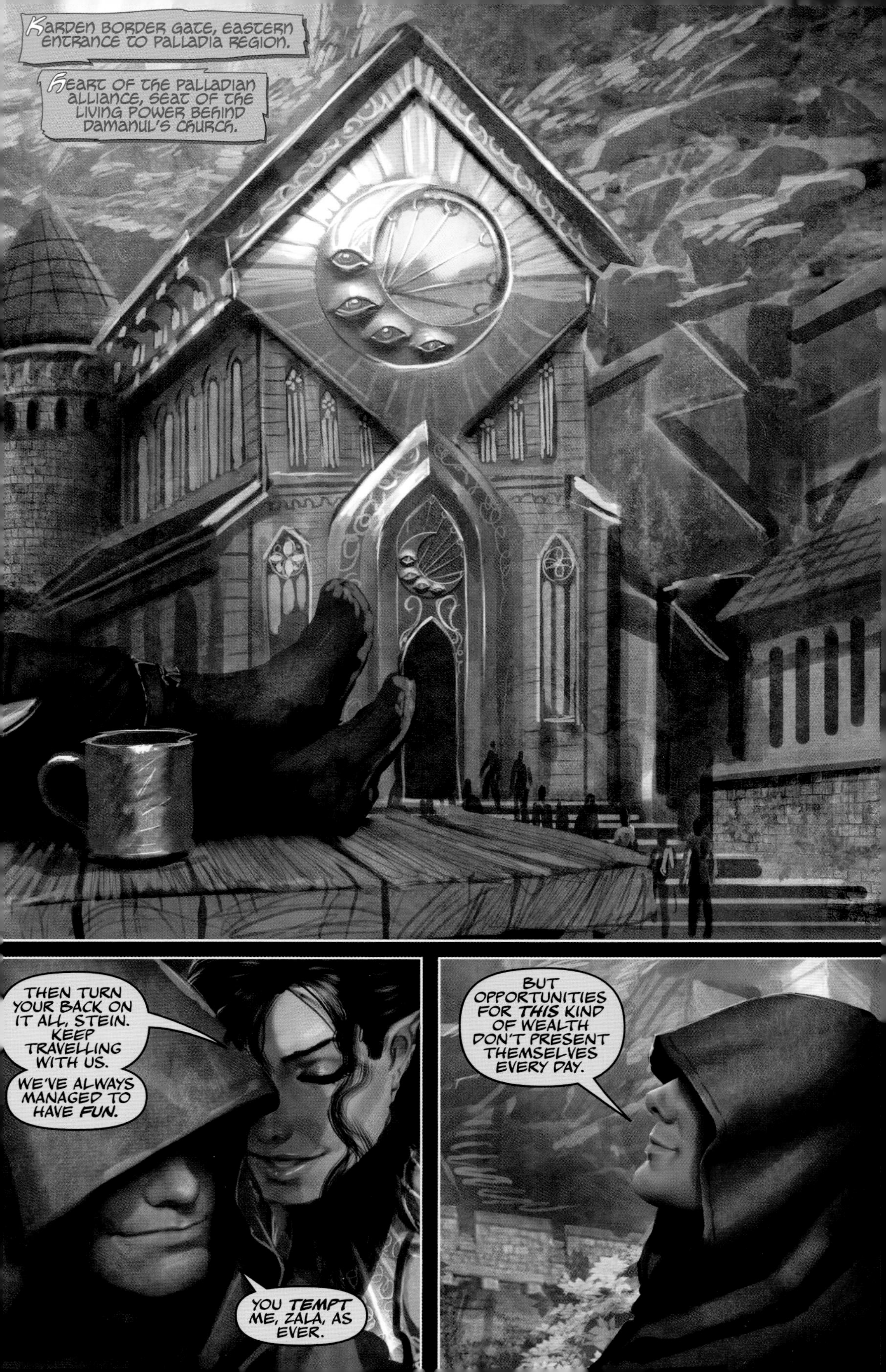
Karden border gate, eastern entrance to Palladia region.
Heart of the Palladian alliance, seat of the living power behind Damanul's church.
THEN TURN YOUR BACK ON IT ALL, STEIN. KEEP TRAVELLING WITH US.
WE'VE ALWAYS MANAGED TO HAVE FUN.
YOU TEMPT ME, ZALA, AS EVER.
BUT OPPORTUNITIES FOR THIS KIND OF WEALTH DON'T PRESENT THEMSELVES EVERY DAY.

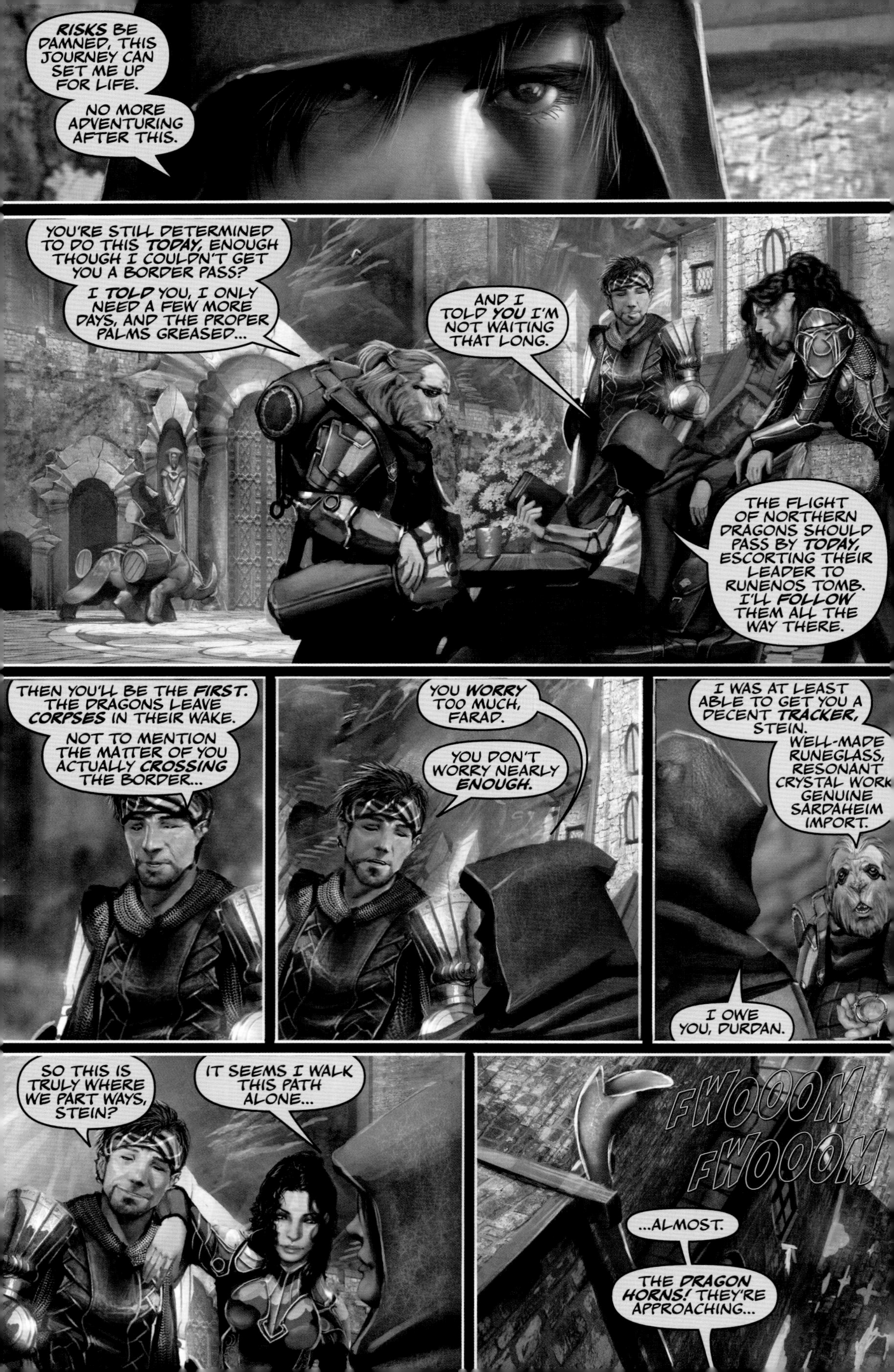
RISKS BE DAMNED, THIS JOURNEY CAN SET ME UP FOR LIFE.
NO MORE ADVENTURING AFTER THIS.
YOU'RE STILL DETERMINED TO DO THIS TODAY, ENOUGH THOUGH I COULDN'T GET YOU A BORDER PASS?
I TOLD YOU, I ONLY NEED A FEW MORE DAYS, AND THE PROPER PALMS GREASED...
AND I TOLD YOU I'M NOT WAITING THAT LONG.
THE FLIGHT OF NORTHERN DRAGONS SHOULD PASS BY TODAY, ESCORTING THEIR LEADER TO RUNENOS TOMB. I'LL FOLLOW THEM ALL THE WAY THERE.
THEN YOU'LL BE THE FIRST. THE DRAGONS LEAVE CORPSES IN THEIR WAKE.
NOT TO MENTION THE MATTER OF YOU ACTUALLY CROSSING THE BORDER...
YOU WORRY TOO MUCH, FARAD.
YOU DON'T WORRY NEARLY ENOUGH.
I WAS AT LEAST ABLE TO GET YOU A DECENT TRACKER, STEIN.
WELL-MADE RUNEGLASS, RESONANT CRYSTAL WORK GENUINE SARDAHEIM IMPORT.
I OWE YOU, DURDAN.
SO THIS IS TRULY WHERE WE PART WAYS, STEIN?
IT SEEMS I WALK THIS PATH ALONE...
FWOOOM
FWOOOM
...ALMOST.
THE DRAGON HORNS! THEY'RE APPROACHING...

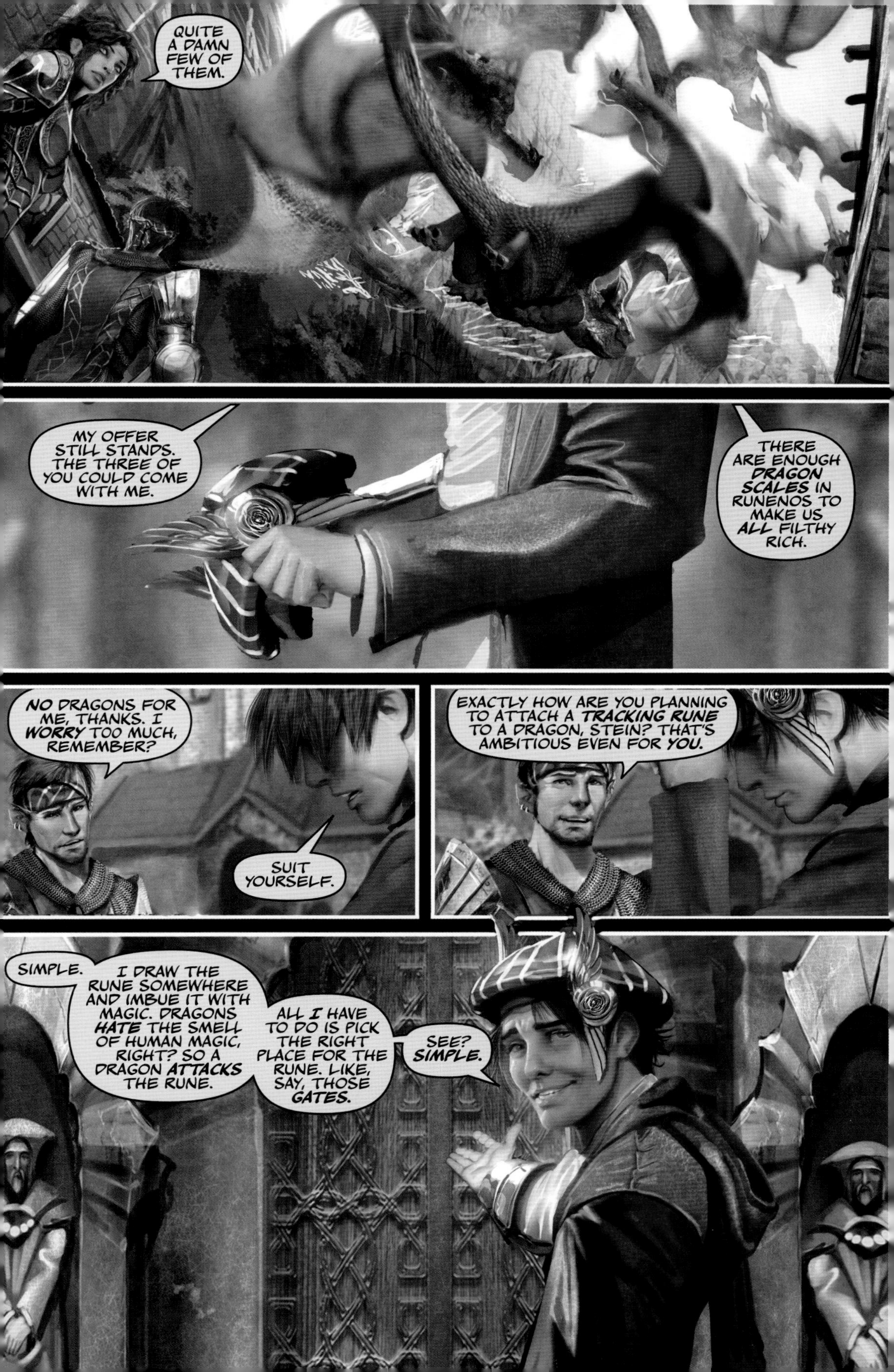
QUITE A DAMN FEW OF THEM.
MY OFFER STILL STANDS. THE THREE OF YOU COULD COME WITH ME.
THERE ARE ENOUGH DRAGON SCALES IN RUNENOS TO MAKE US ALL FILTHY RICH.
NO DRAGONS FOR ME, THANKS. I WORRY TOO MUCH, REMEMBER?
SUIT YOURSELF.
EXACTLY HOW ARE YOU PLANNING TO ATTACH A TRACKING RUNE TO A DRAGON, STEIN? THAT'S AMBITIOUS EVEN FOR YOU.
SIMPLE.
I DRAW THE RUNE SOMEWHERE AND IMBUE IT WITH MAGIC. DRAGONS HATE THE SMELL OF HUMAN MAGIC, RIGHT? SO A DRAGON ATTACKS THE RUNE.
ALL I HAVE TO DO IS PICK THE RIGHT PLACE FOR THE RUNE. LIKE, SAY, THOSE GATES.
SEE? SIMPLE.

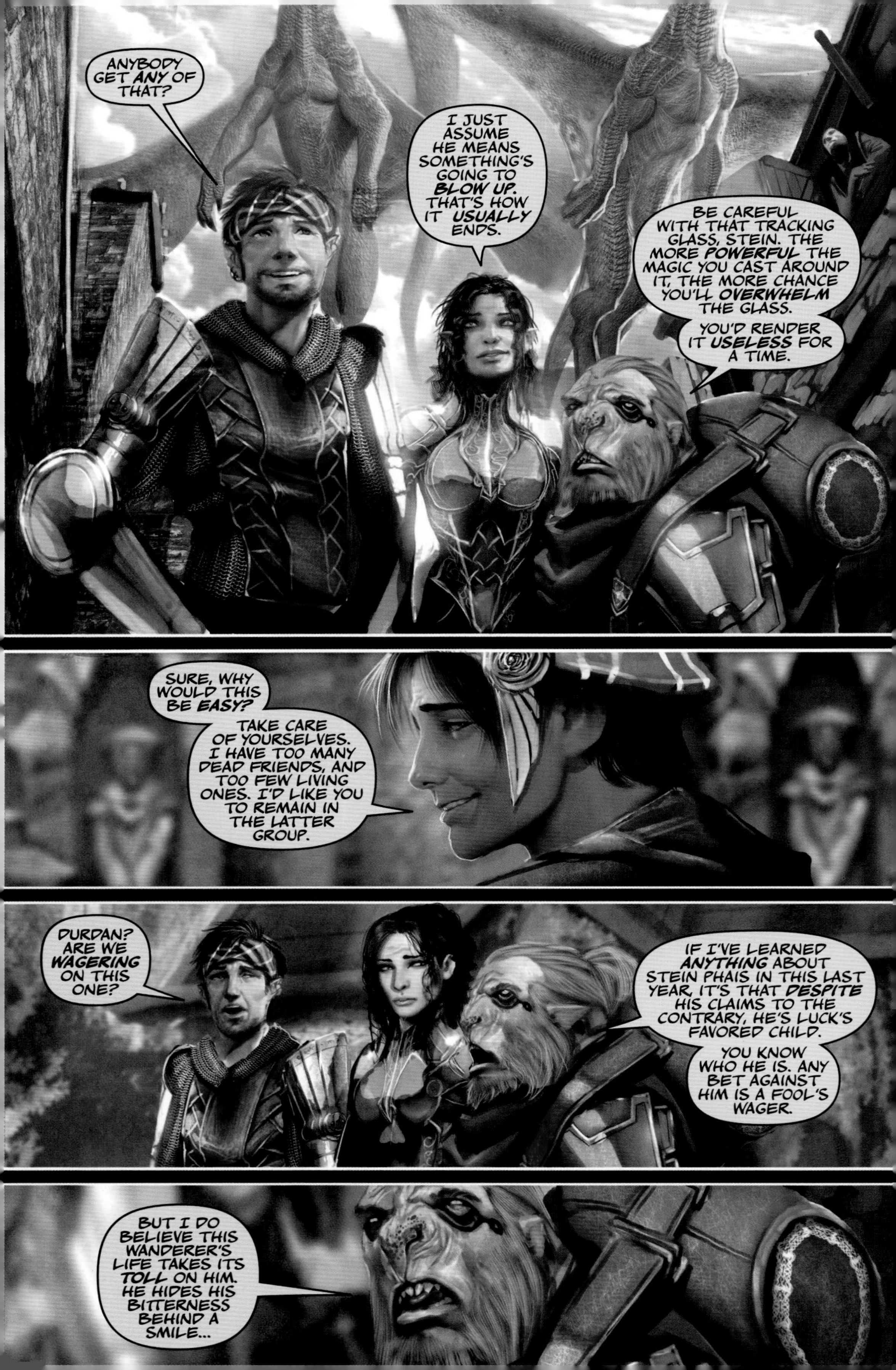
ANYBODY GET ANY OF THAT?
I JUST ASSUME HE MEANS SOMETHING'S GOING TO BLOW UP. THAT'S HOW IT USUALLY ENDS.
BE CAREFUL WITH THAT TRACKING GLASS, STEIN. THE MORE POWERFUL THE MAGIC YOU CAST AROUND IT, THE MORE CHANCE YOU'LL OVERWHELM THE GLASS.
YOU'D RENDER IT USELESS FOR A TIME.
SURE, WHY WOULD THIS BE EASY?
TAKE CARE OF YOURSELVES. I HAVE TOO MANY DEAD FRIENDS, AND TOO FEW LIVING ONES. I'D LIKE YOU TO REMAIN IN THE LATTER GROUP.
DURDAN? ARE WE WAGERING ON THIS ONE?
IF I'VE LEARNED ANYTHING ABOUT STEIN PHAIS IN THIS LAST YEAR, IT'S THAT DESPITE HIS CLAIMS TO THE CONTRARY, HE'S LUCK'S FAVORED CHILD.
YOU KNOW WHO HE IS. ANY BET AGAINST HIM IS A FOOL'S WAGER.
BUT I DO BELIEVE THIS WANDERER'S LIFE TAKES ITS TOLL ON HIM. HE HIDES HIS BITTERNESS BEHIND A SMILE...

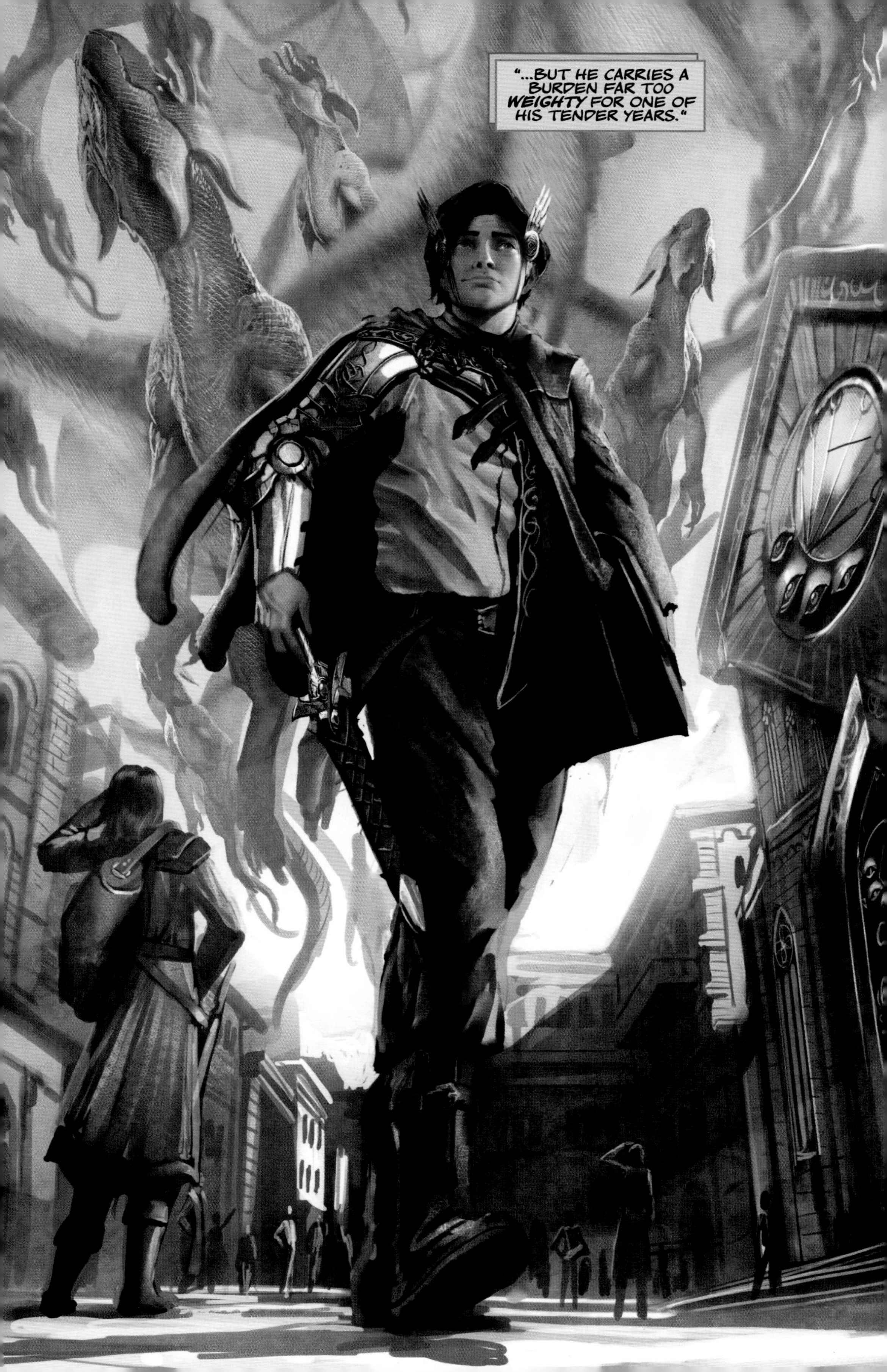
"...BUT HE CARRIES A BURDEN FAR TOO WEIGHTY FOR ONE OF HIS TENDER YEARS."

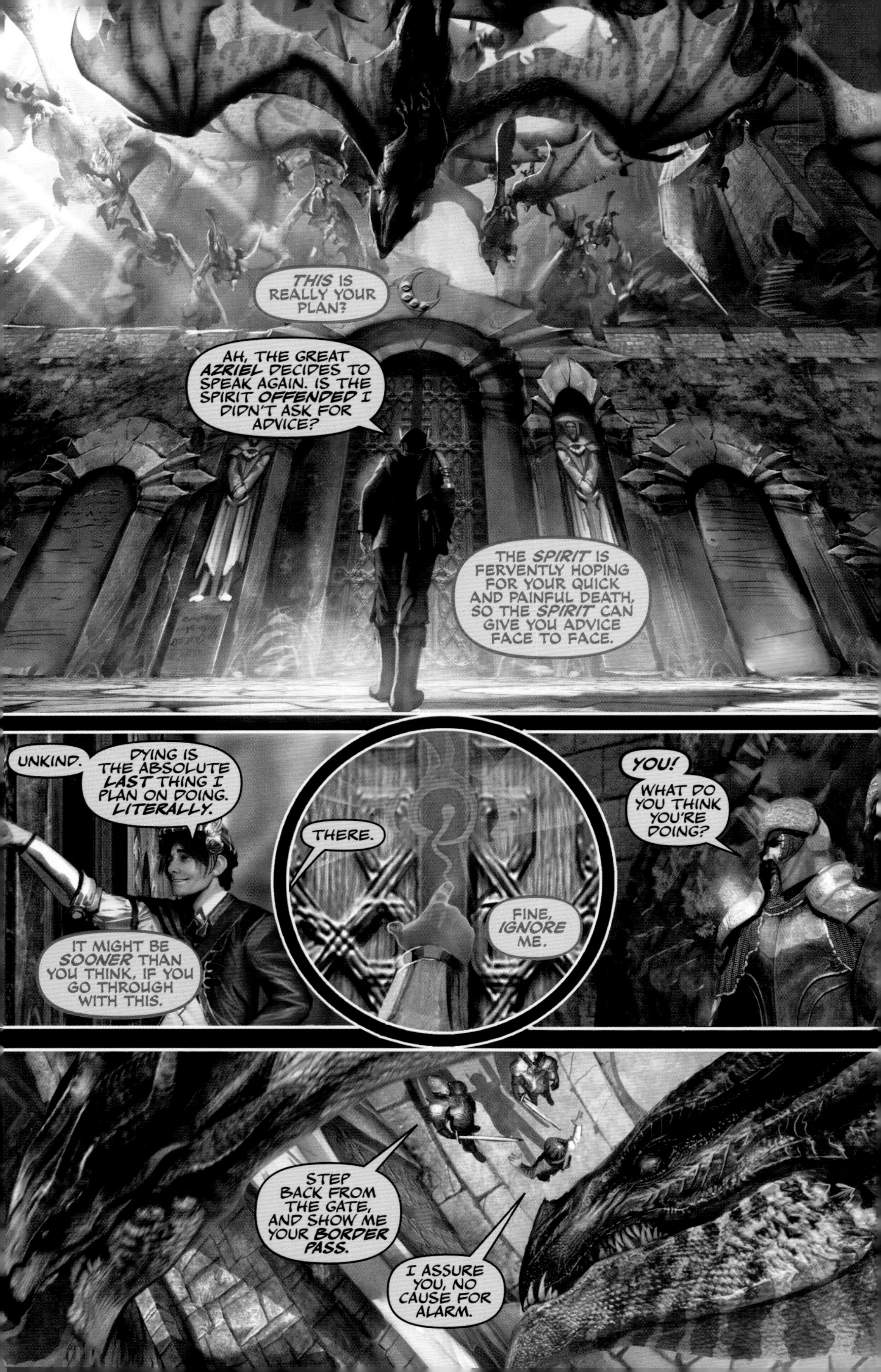
THIS IS REALLY YOUR PLAN?
AH, THE GREAT AZRIEL DECIDES TO SPEAK AGAIN. IS THE SPIRIT OFFENDED I DIDN'T ASK FOR ADVICE?
THE SPIRIT IS FERVENTLY HOPING FOR YOUR QUICK AND PAINFUL DEATH, SO THE SPIRIT CAN GIVE YOU ADVICE FACE TO FACE.
UNKIND.
DYING IS THE ABSOLUTE LAST THING I PLAN ON DOING. LITERALLY.
IT MIGHT BE SOONER THAN YOU THINK, IF YOU GO THROUGH WITH THIS.
THERE.
FINE, IGNORE ME.
YOU!
WHAT DO YOU THINK YOU'RE DOING?
STEP BACK FROM THE GATE, AND SHOW ME YOUR BORDER PASS.
I ASSURE YOU, NO CAUSE FOR ALARM.

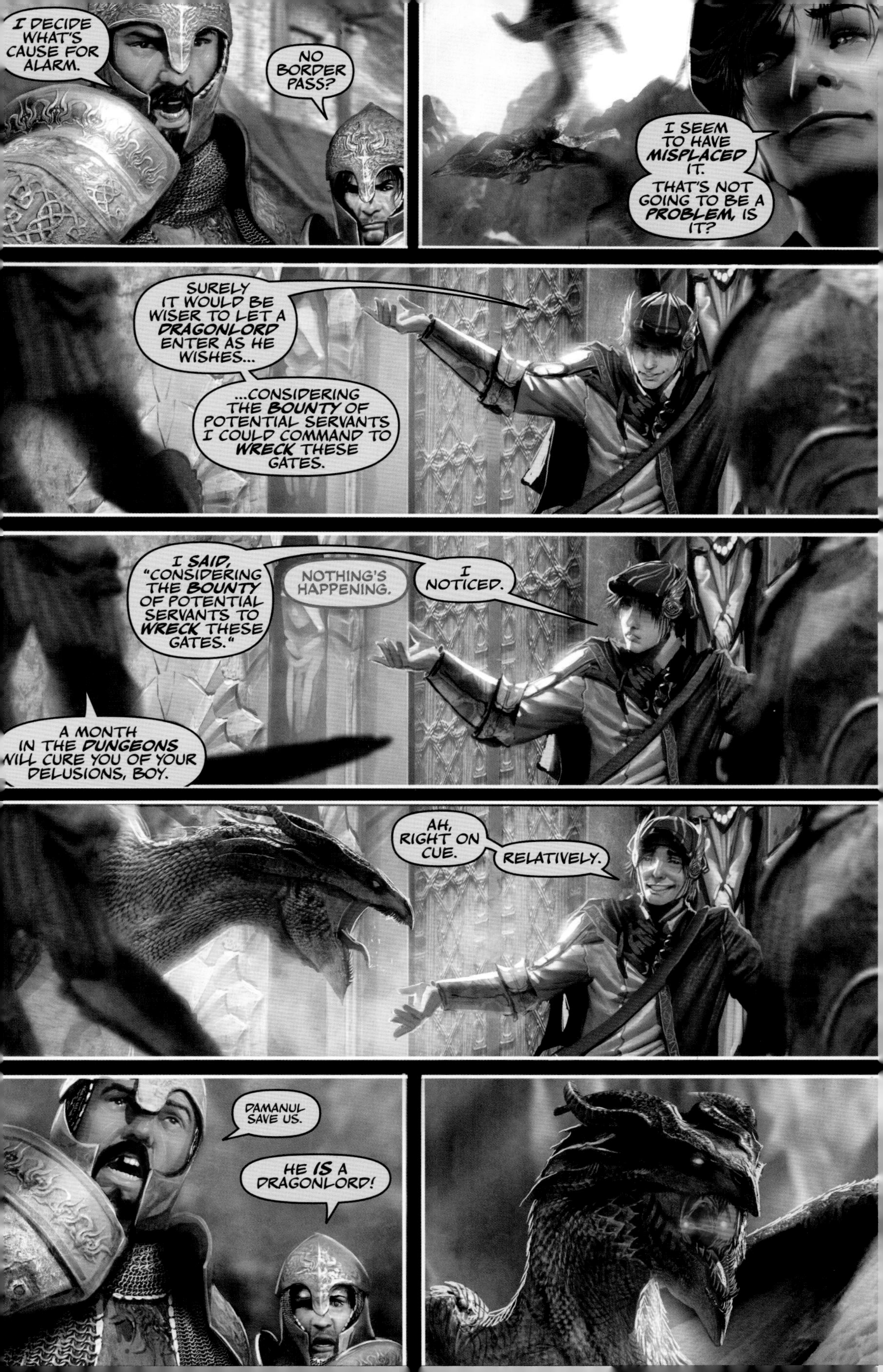
I DECIDE WHAT'S CAUSE FOR ALARM.
NO BORDER PASS?
I SEEM TO HAVE MISPLACED IT.
THAT'S NOT GOING TO BE A PROBLEM, IS IT?
SURELY IT WOULD BE WISER TO LET A DRAGONLORD ENTER AS HE WISHES...
...CONSIDERING THE BOUNTY OF POTENTIAL SERVANTS I COULD COMMAND TO WRECK THESE GATES.
I SAID, "CONSIDERING THE BOUNTY OF POTENTIAL SERVANTS TO WRECK THESE GATES."
NOTHING'S HAPPENING.
I NOTICED.
A MONTH IN THE DUNGEONS WILL CURE YOU OF YOUR DELUSIONS, BOY.
AH, RIGHT ON CUE.
RELATIVELY.
DAMANUL SAVE US.
HE IS A DRAGONLORD!

AND THE TRACKER ATTACHED.

IMPRESSIVE FOR AN IDIOT LIKE YOU.

THAT'S ME, AN IMPRESSIVE IDIOT.

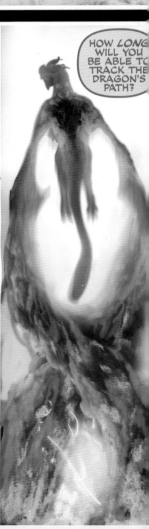

HOW LONG WILL YOU BE ABLE TO TRACK THE DRAGON'S PATH?

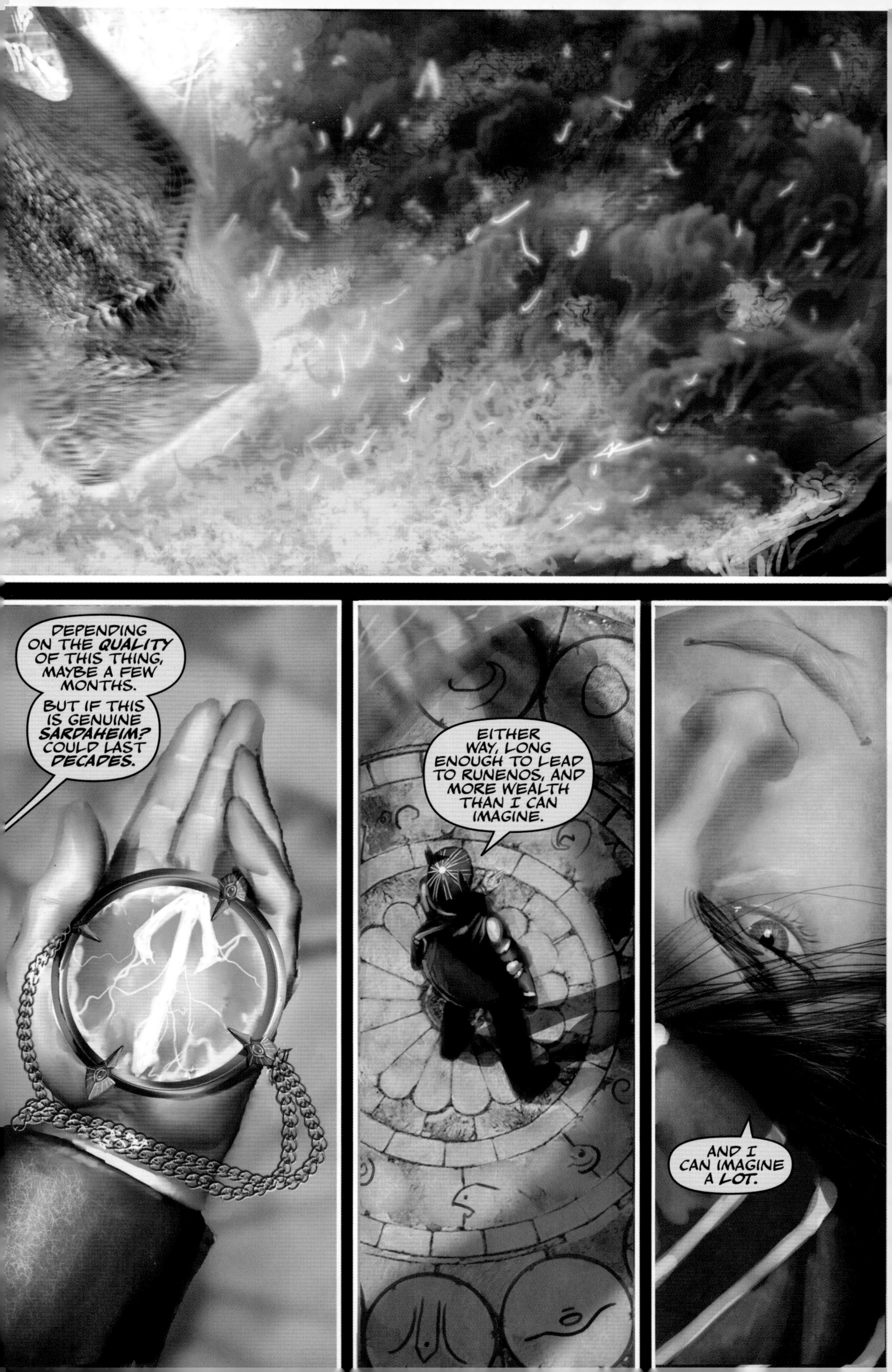
DEPENDING ON THE *QUALITY* OF THIS THING, MAYBE A FEW MONTHS.
BUT IF THIS IS GENUINE *SARDAHEIM?* COULD LAST *DECADES.*
EITHER WAY, LONG ENOUGH TO LEAD TO RUNENOS, AND MORE WEALTH THAN I CAN IMAGINE.
AND I CAN IMAGINE A *LOT*.

TIME FOR US TO GO, AZRIEL.

CAN I TRUST YOU TO REFRAIN FROM MAGIC, SO THE RUNEGLASS ISN'T COMPROMISED?

NO ATTACK SPELLS, AT LEAST...

CHIK

CHAK

...BUT I'LL HAVE NO NEED OF THOSE.

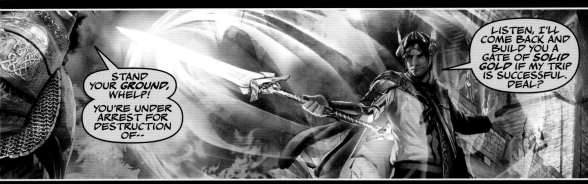

STAND YOUR GROUND, WHELP! YOU'RE UNDER ARREST FOR DESTRUCTION OF--

LISTEN, I'LL COME BACK AND BUILD YOU A GATE OF SOLID GOLD IF MY TRIP IS SUCCESSFUL. DEAL?

SHOOT HIM!

SO THAT'S A "NO," THEN?

SO BE IT. BUT HOW WILL YOU ARREST...

...ONE WHO IS SERVED BY THE WINDS THEMSELVES?

KAFF KAFF

WHERE...?

"...ONE WHO IS SERVED BY THE WINDS THEMSELVES"? OH, PLEASE.

SHUT UP. IT PLAYS WELL WITH RUBES.

IT'S EMBARRASSING.

I LIKED YOU MUCH BETTER WHEN YOU WERE SILENT.

I STOOD HERE AND WITNESSED IT, AND I'M STILL NOT SURE I BELIEVE IT.

WHAT WAS IT YOU CALLED HIM, DURDAN?

LUCK'S FAVORED SON.

CARE TO WAGER ON THE SIZE OF THE BOUNTY THEY'LL PLACE ON STEIN'S HEAD?

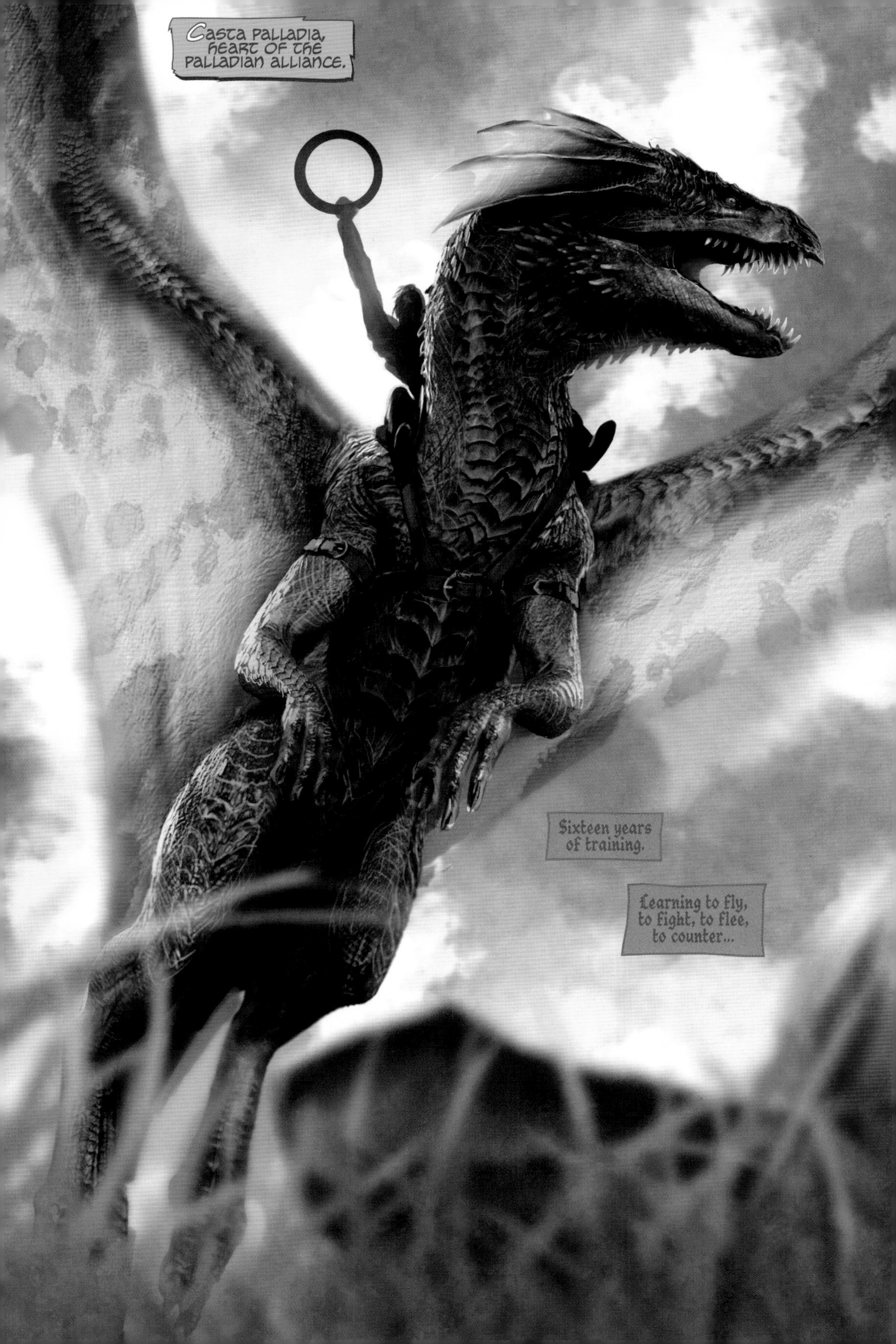
Casta Palladia, heart of the Palladian alliance.
Sixteen years of training.
Learning to fly, to fight, to flee, to counter...

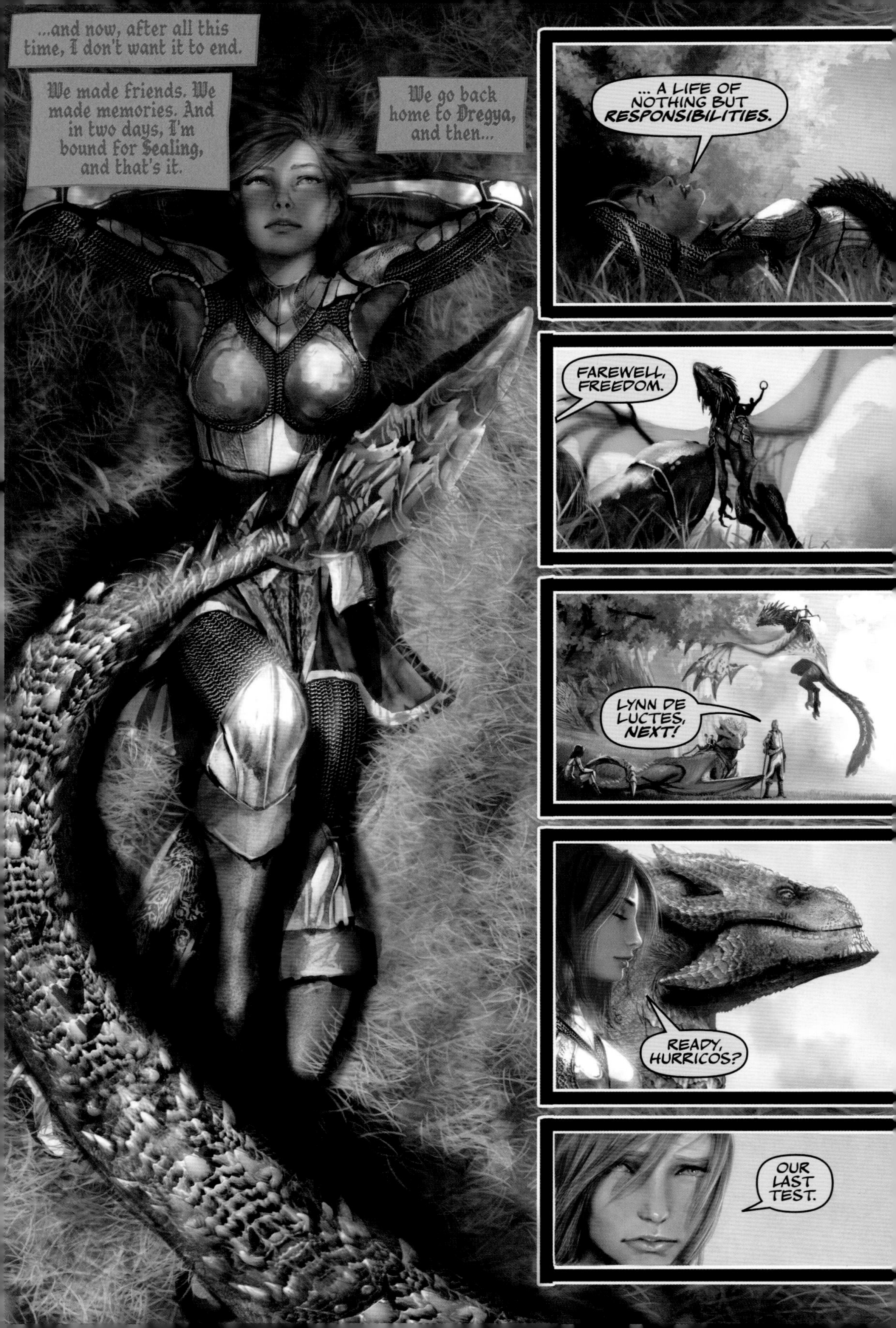
...and now, after all this time, I don't want it to end.
We made friends. We made memories. And in two days, I'm bound for Sealing, and that's it.
We go back home to Dregya, and then...
... A LIFE OF NOTHING BUT RESPONSIBILITIES.
FAREWELL, FREEDOM.
LYNN DE LUCTES, NEXT!
READY, HURRICOS?
OUR LAST TEST.

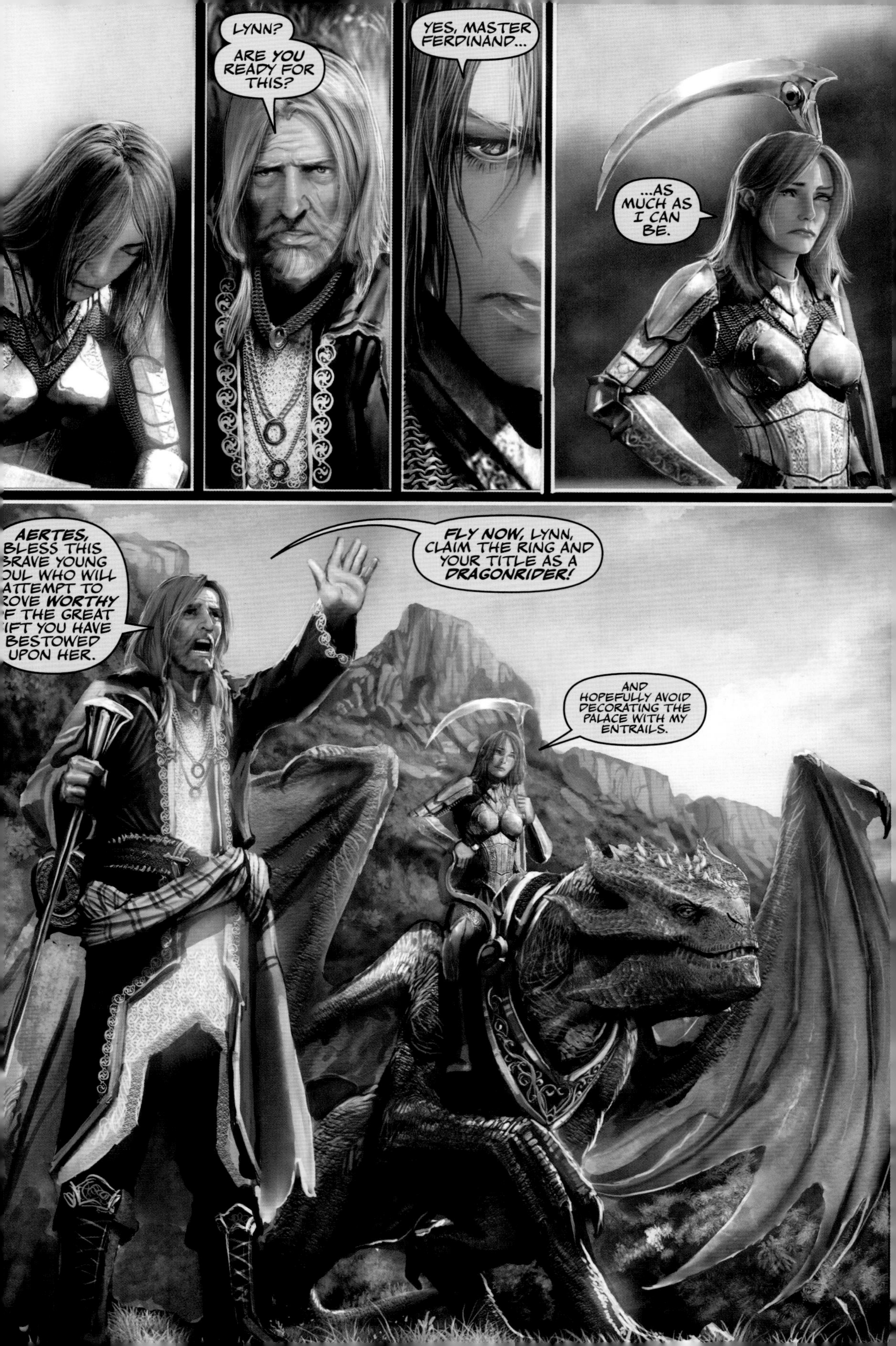
LYNN?
ARE *YOU* READY FOR THIS?
YES, MASTER FERDINAND...
...AS MUCH AS I CAN BE.
AERTES, BLESS THIS BRAVE YOUNG OUL WHO WILL ATTEMPT TO ROVE ***WORTHY*** F THE GREAT IFT YOU HAVE BESTOWED UPON HER.
FLY NOW, LYNN, CLAIM THE RING AND YOUR TITLE AS A ***DRAGONRIDER!***
AND HOPEFULLY AVOID DECORATING THE PALACE WITH MY ENTRAILS.

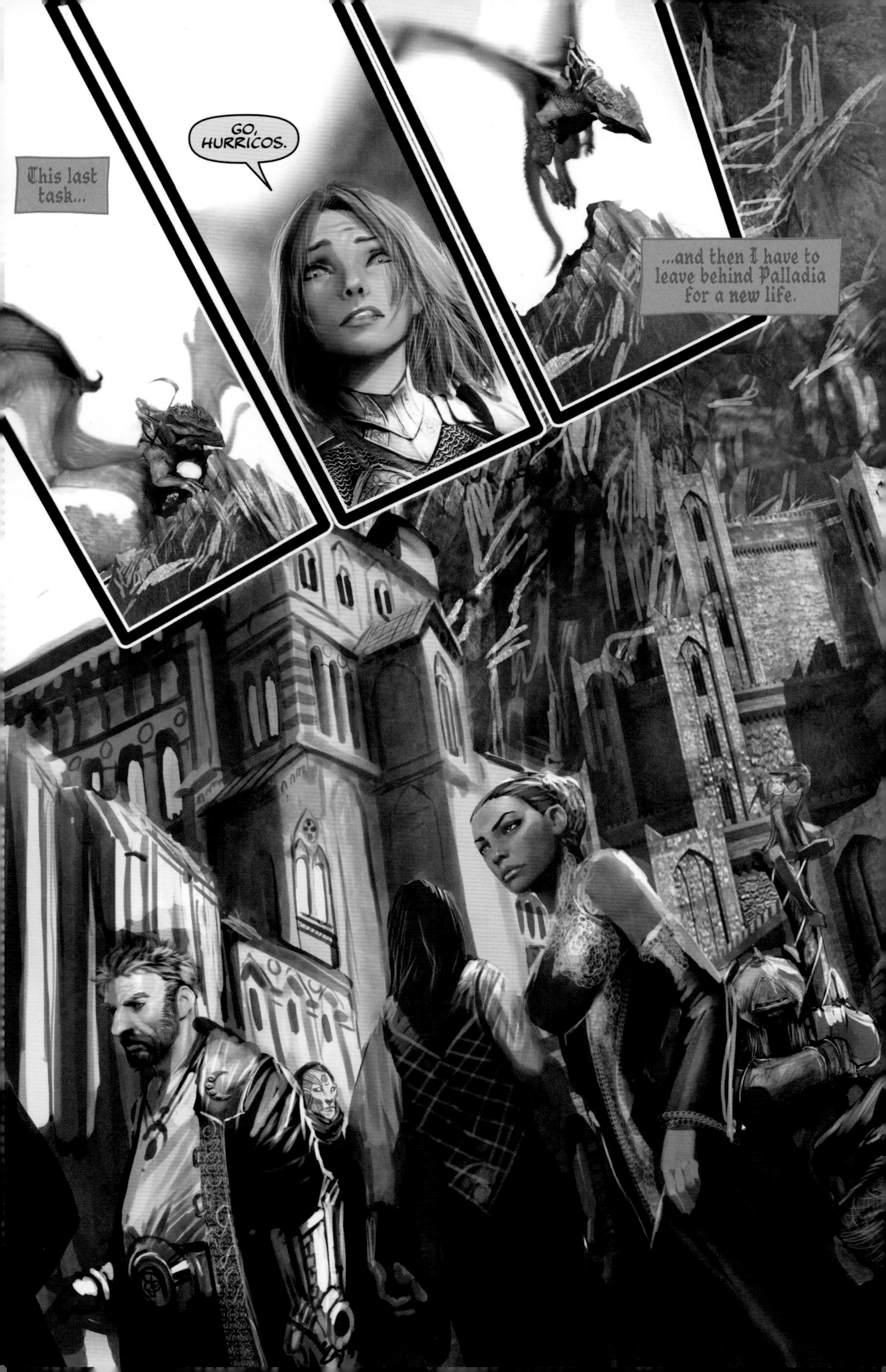
This last task...
GO, HURRICOS.
...and then I have to leave behind Palladia for a new life.

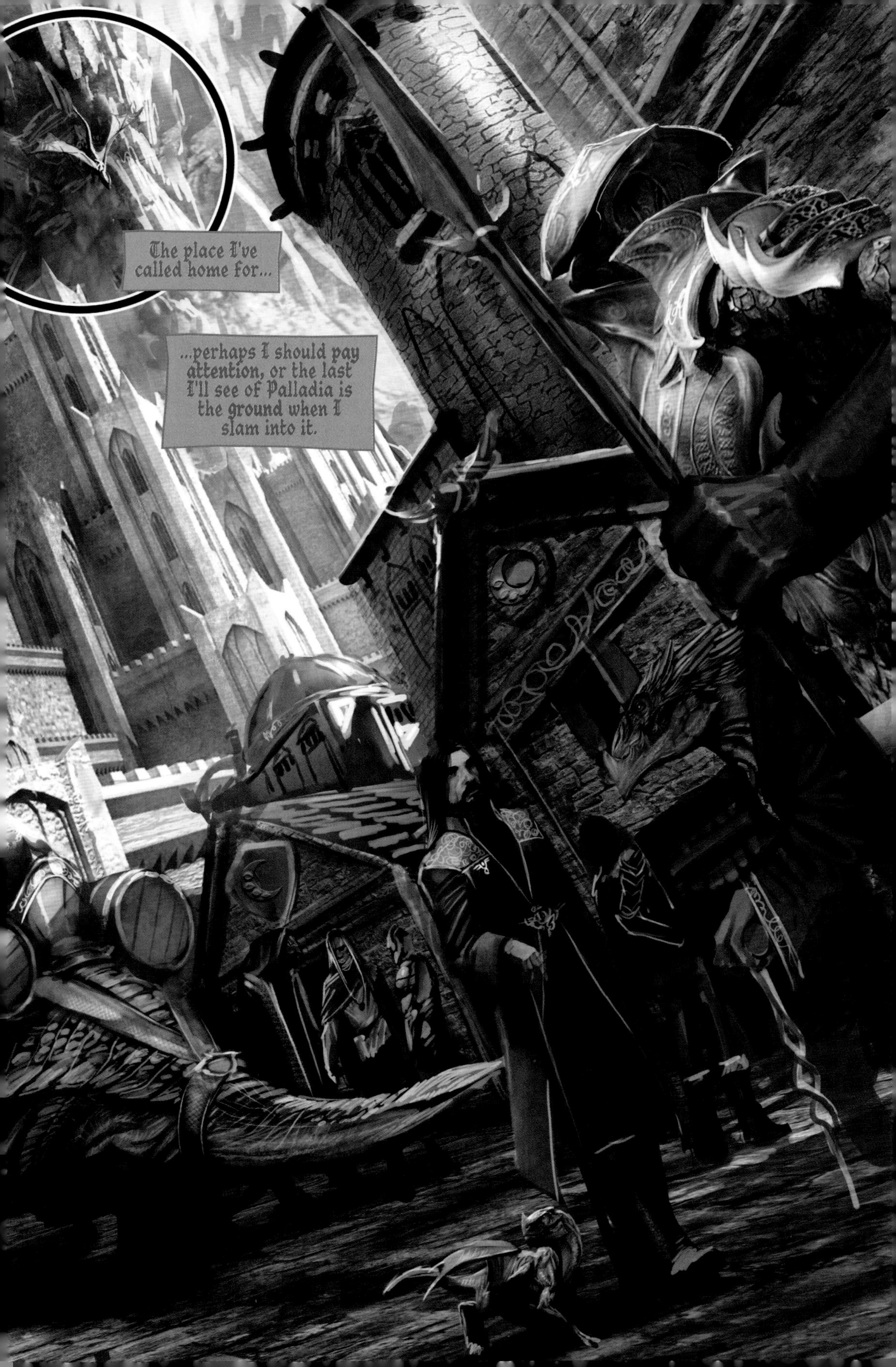
The place I've called home for...
...perhaps I should pay attention, or the last I'll see of Palladia is the ground when I slam into it.

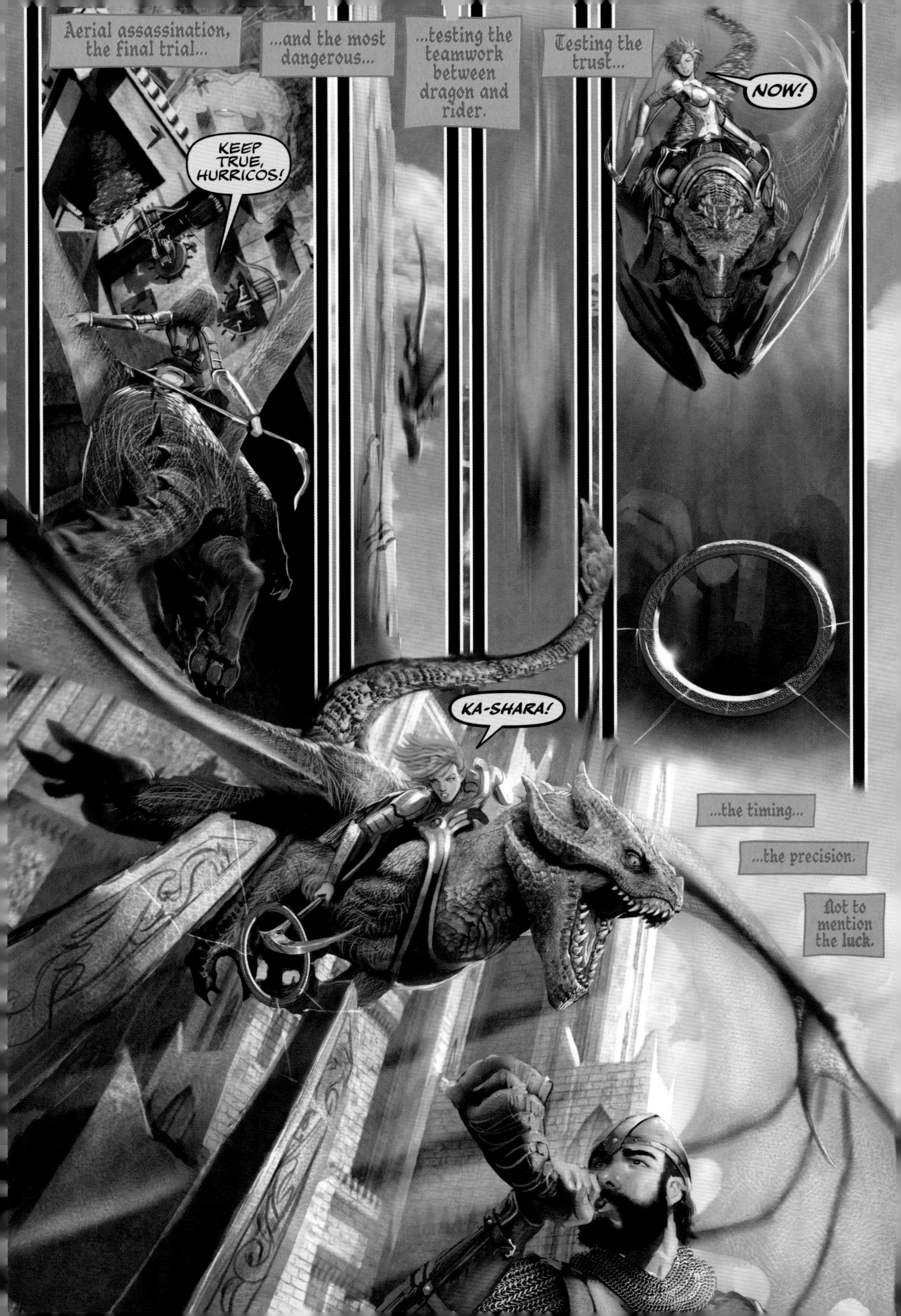
Aerial assassination, the final trial...
KEEP TRUE, HURRICOS!
...and the most dangerous...
...testing the teamwork between dragon and rider.
Testing the trust...
NOW!
KA-SHARA!
...the timing...
...the precision.
Not to mention the luck.

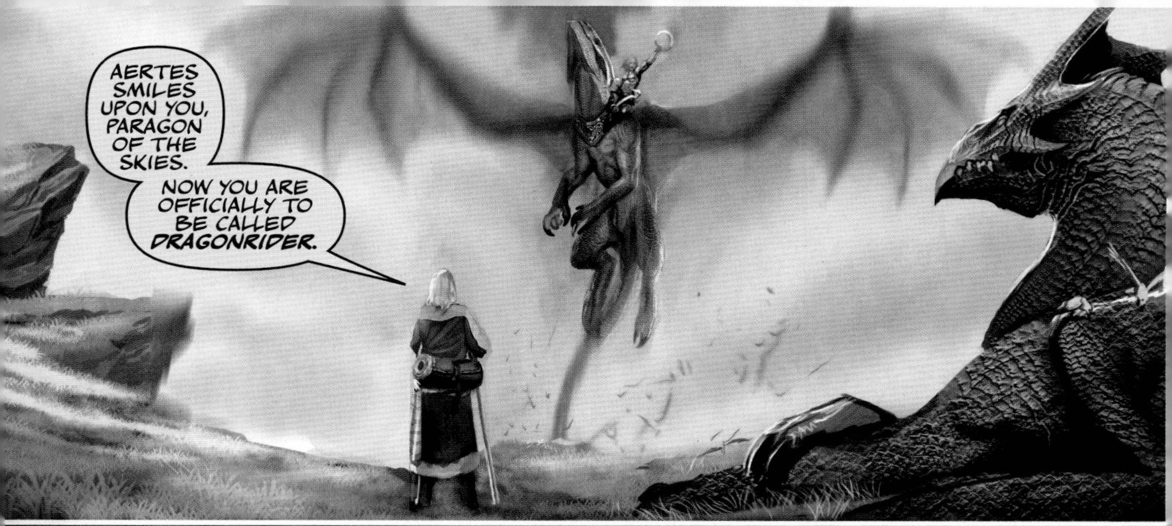
AERTES SMILES UPON YOU, PARAGON OF THE SKIES.
NOW YOU ARE OFFICIALLY TO BE CALLED **DRAGONRIDER.**

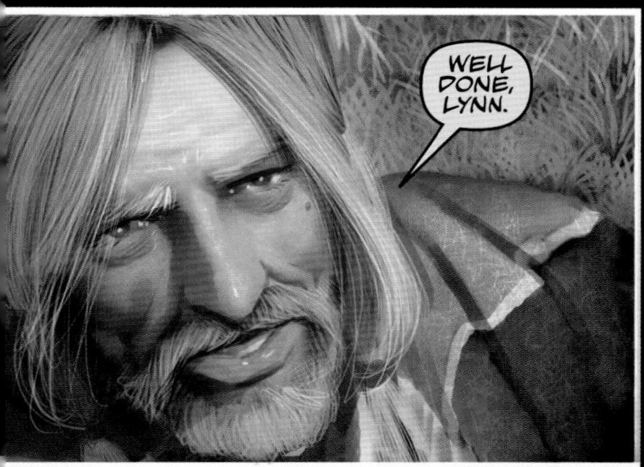
WELL DONE, LYNN.

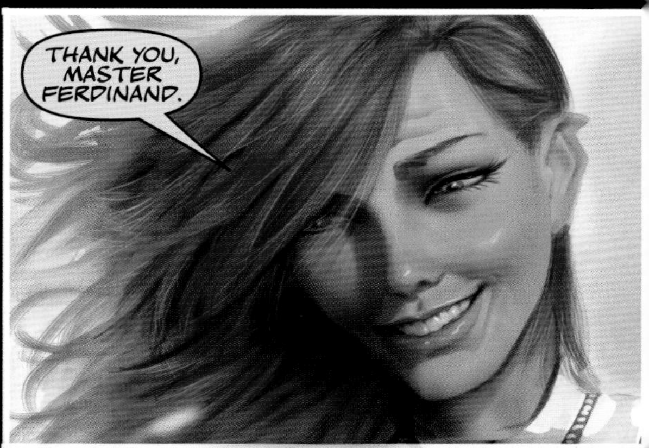
THANK YOU, MASTER FERDINAND.

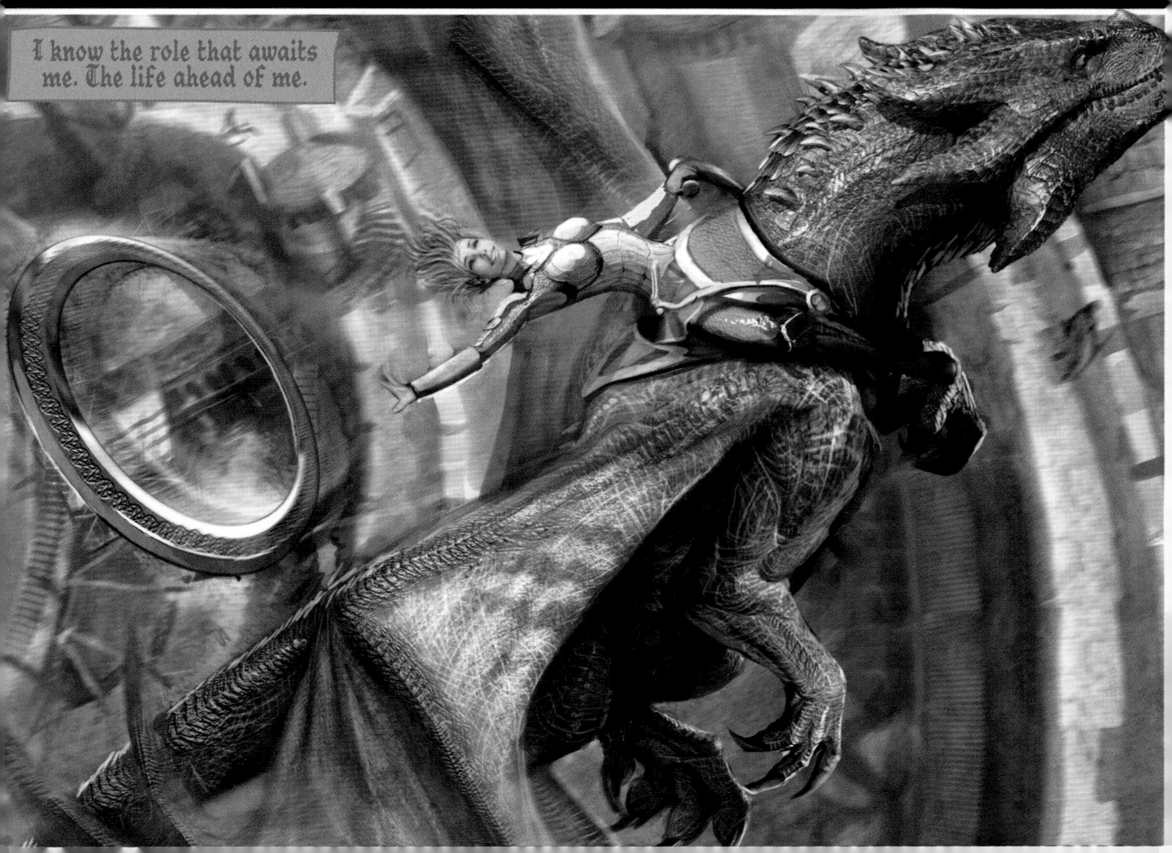
I know the role that awaits me. The life ahead of me.

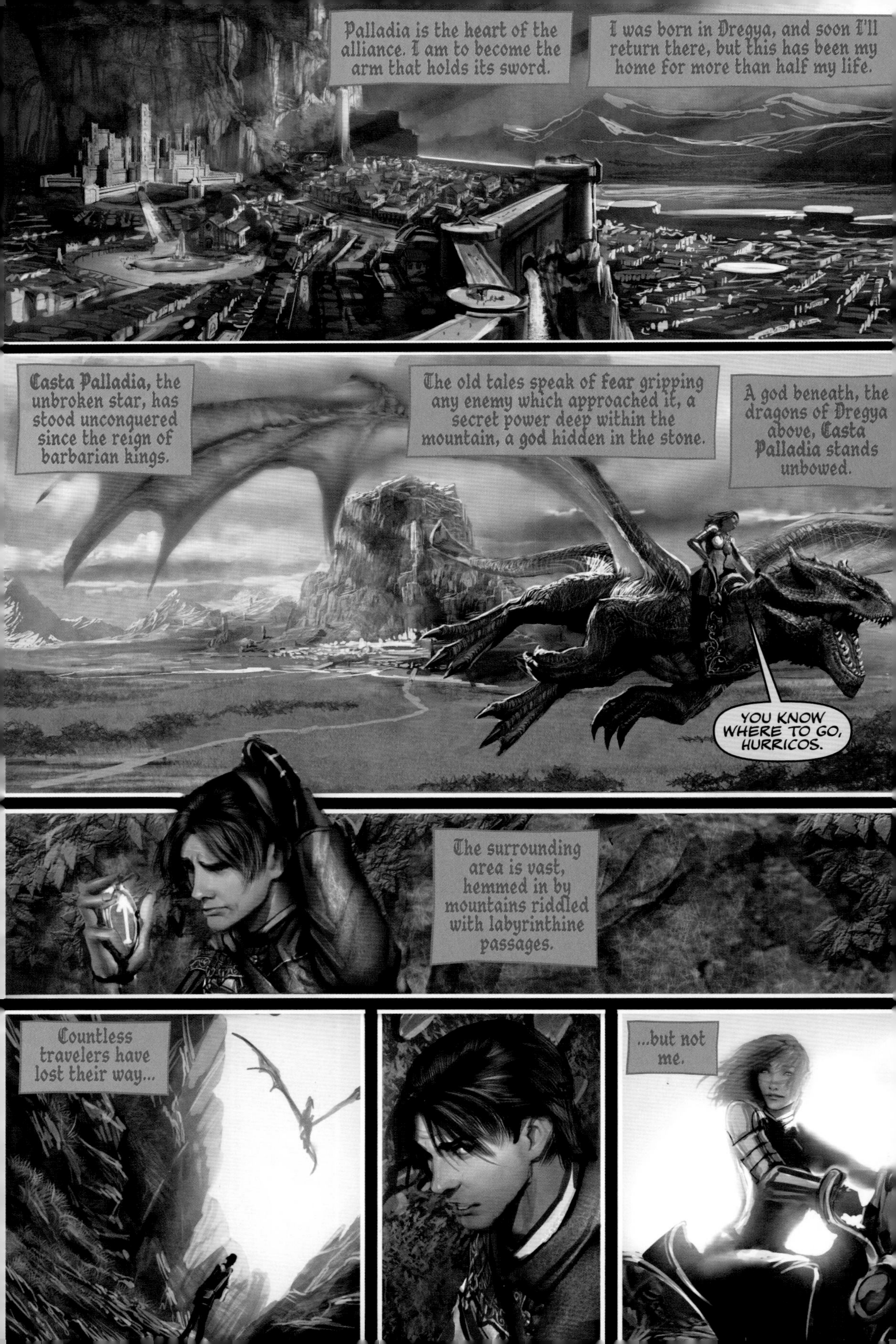
Palladia is the heart of the alliance. I am to become the arm that holds its sword.
I was born in Dregya, and soon I'll return there, but this has been my home for more than half my life.
Casta Palladia, the unbroken star, has stood unconquered since the reign of barbarian kings.
The old tales speak of fear gripping any enemy which approached it, a secret power deep within the mountain, a god hidden in the stone.
A god beneath, the dragons of Dregya above, Casta Palladia stands unbowed.
YOU KNOW WHERE TO GO, HURRICOS.
The surrounding area is vast, hemmed in by mountains riddled with labyrinthine passages.
Countless travelers have lost their way...
...but not me.

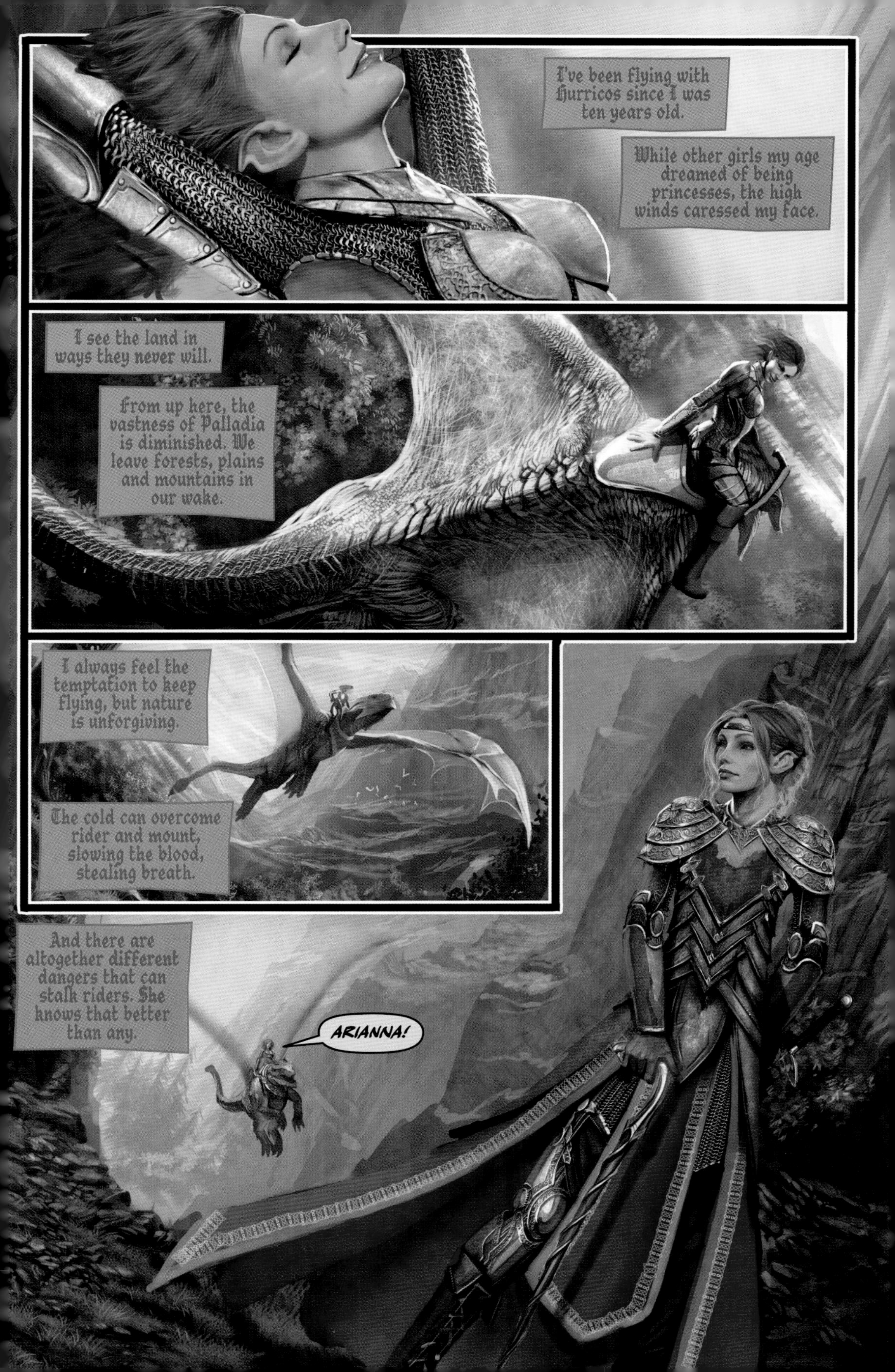
I've been flying with Hurricos since I was ten years old.
While other girls my age dreamed of being princesses, the high winds caressed my face.
I see the land in ways they never will.
From up here, the vastness of Palladia is diminished. We leave forests, plains and mountains in our wake.
I always feel the temptation to keep flying, but nature is unforgiving.
The cold can overcome rider and mount, slowing the blood, stealing breath.
And there are altogether different dangers that can stalk riders. She knows that better than any.
ARIANNA!

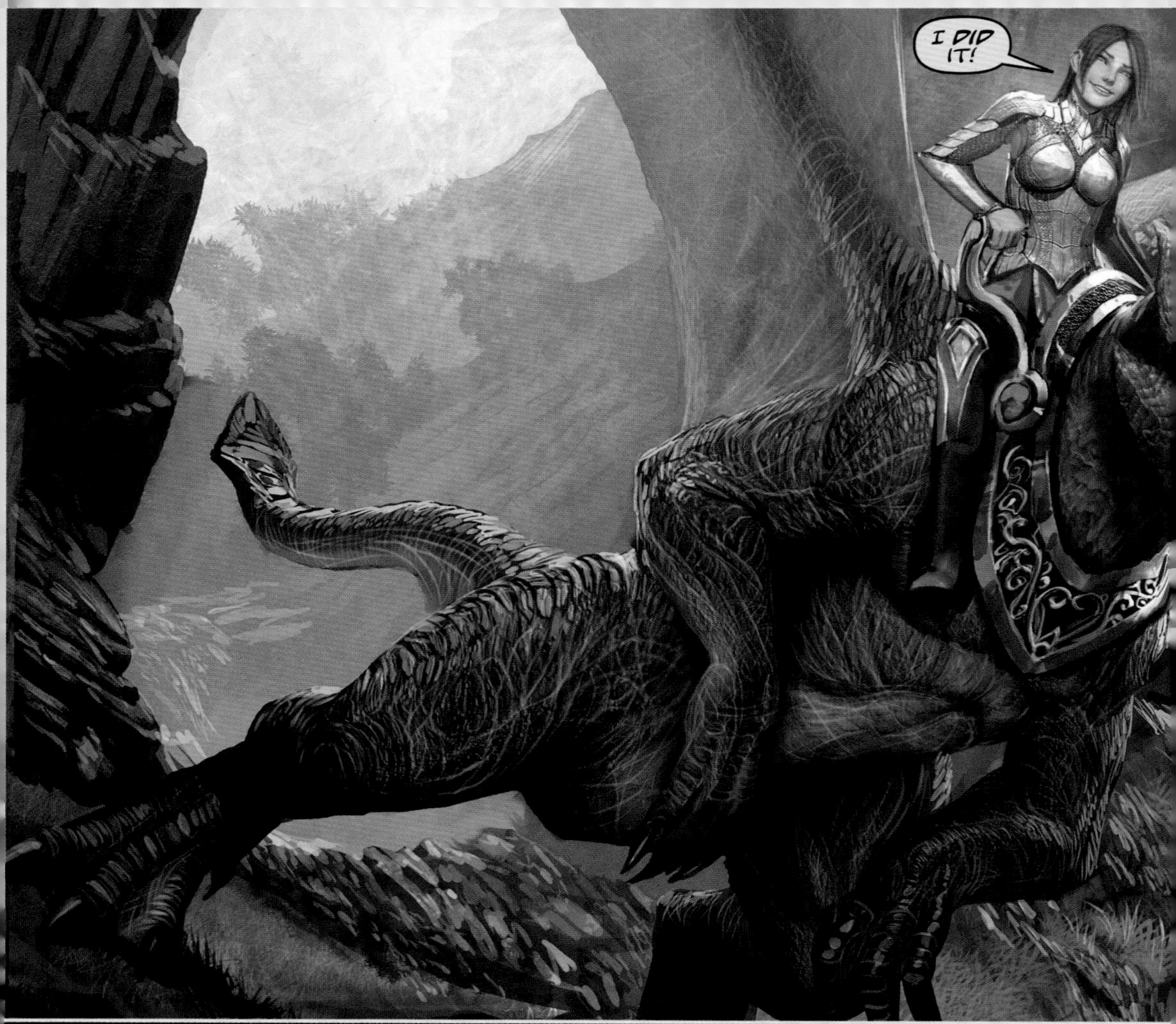
I DID IT!

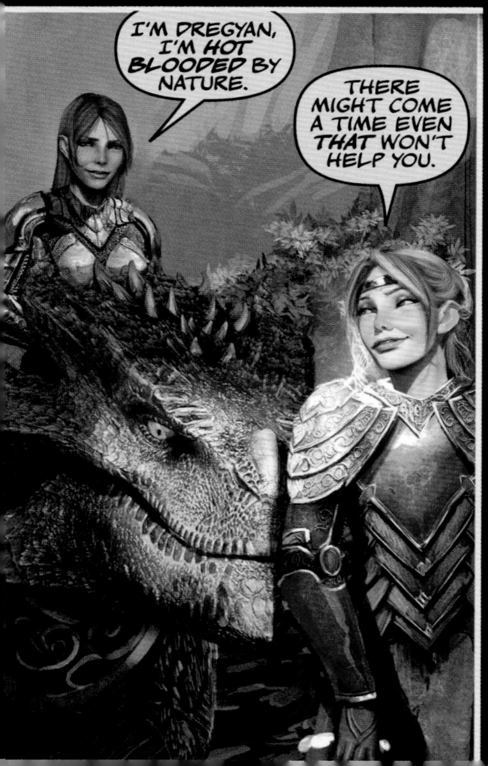
I'M DREGYAN, I'M HOT BLOODED BY NATURE.
THERE MIGHT COME A TIME EVEN THAT WON'T HELP YOU.

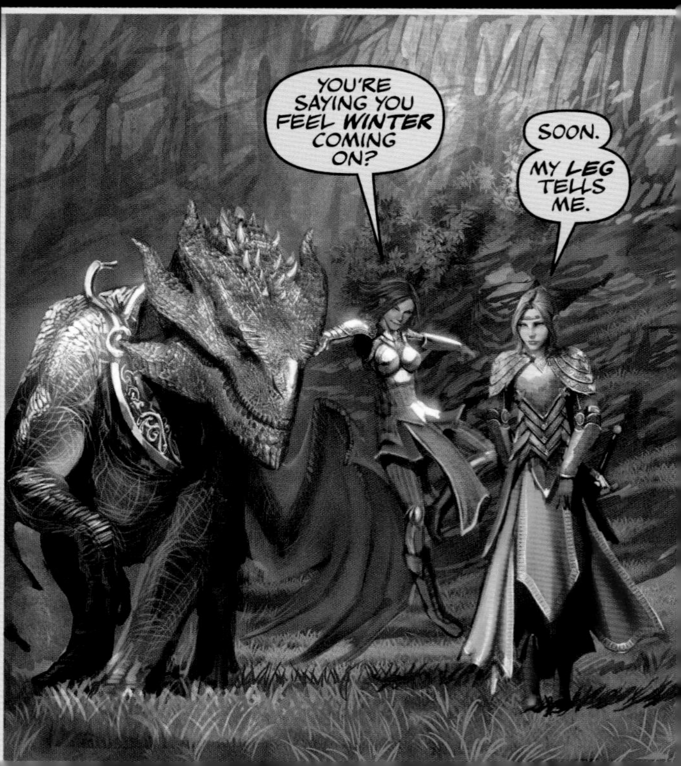
YOU'RE SAYING YOU FEEL WINTER COMING ON?
SOON.
MY LEG TELLS ME.

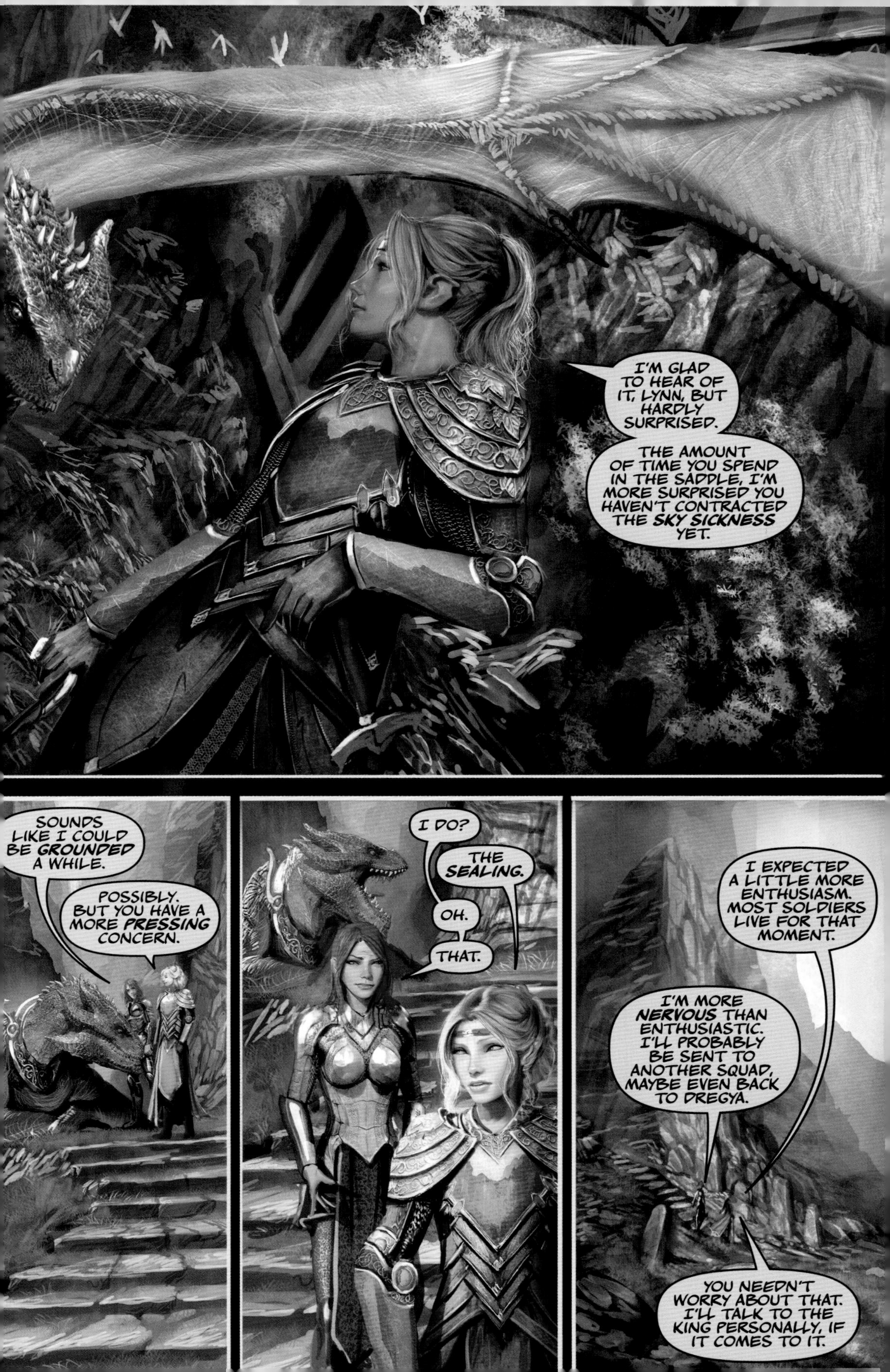
I'M GLAD TO HEAR OF IT, LYNN, BUT HARDLY SURPRISED.
THE AMOUNT OF TIME YOU SPEND IN THE SADDLE, I'M MORE SURPRISED YOU HAVEN'T CONTRACTED THE SKY SICKNESS YET.
SOUNDS LIKE I COULD BE GROUNDED A WHILE.
POSSIBLY. BUT YOU HAVE A MORE PRESSING CONCERN.
I DO?
THE SEALING.
OH.
THAT.
I EXPECTED A LITTLE MORE ENTHUSIASM. MOST SOLDIERS LIVE FOR THAT MOMENT.
I'M MORE NERVOUS THAN ENTHUSIASTIC. I'LL PROBABLY BE SENT TO ANOTHER SQUAD, MAYBE EVEN BACK TO DREGYA.
YOU NEEDN'T WORRY ABOUT THAT. I'LL TALK TO THE KING PERSONALLY, IF IT COMES TO IT.

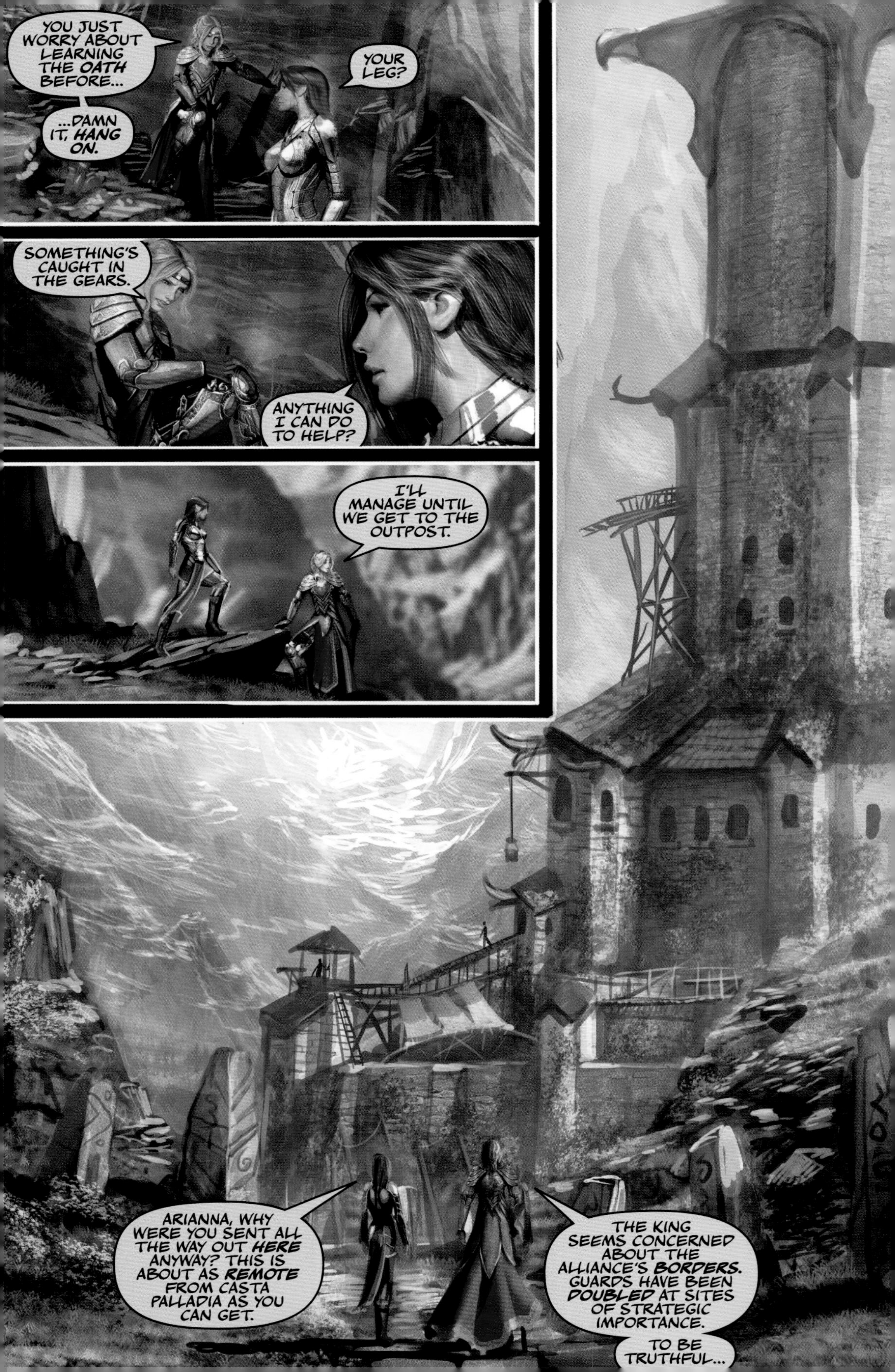
YOU JUST WORRY ABOUT LEARNING THE OATH BEFORE...
YOUR LEG?
...DAMN IT, HANG ON.
SOMETHING'S CAUGHT IN THE GEARS.
ANYTHING I CAN DO TO HELP?
I'LL MANAGE UNTIL WE GET TO THE OUTPOST.
ARIANNA, WHY WERE YOU SENT ALL THE WAY OUT HERE ANYWAY? THIS IS ABOUT AS REMOTE FROM CASTA PALLADIA AS YOU CAN GET.
THE KING SEEMS CONCERNED ABOUT THE ALLIANCE'S BORDERS. GUARDS HAVE BEEN DOUBLED AT SITES OF STRATEGIC IMPORTANCE.
TO BE TRUTHFUL...

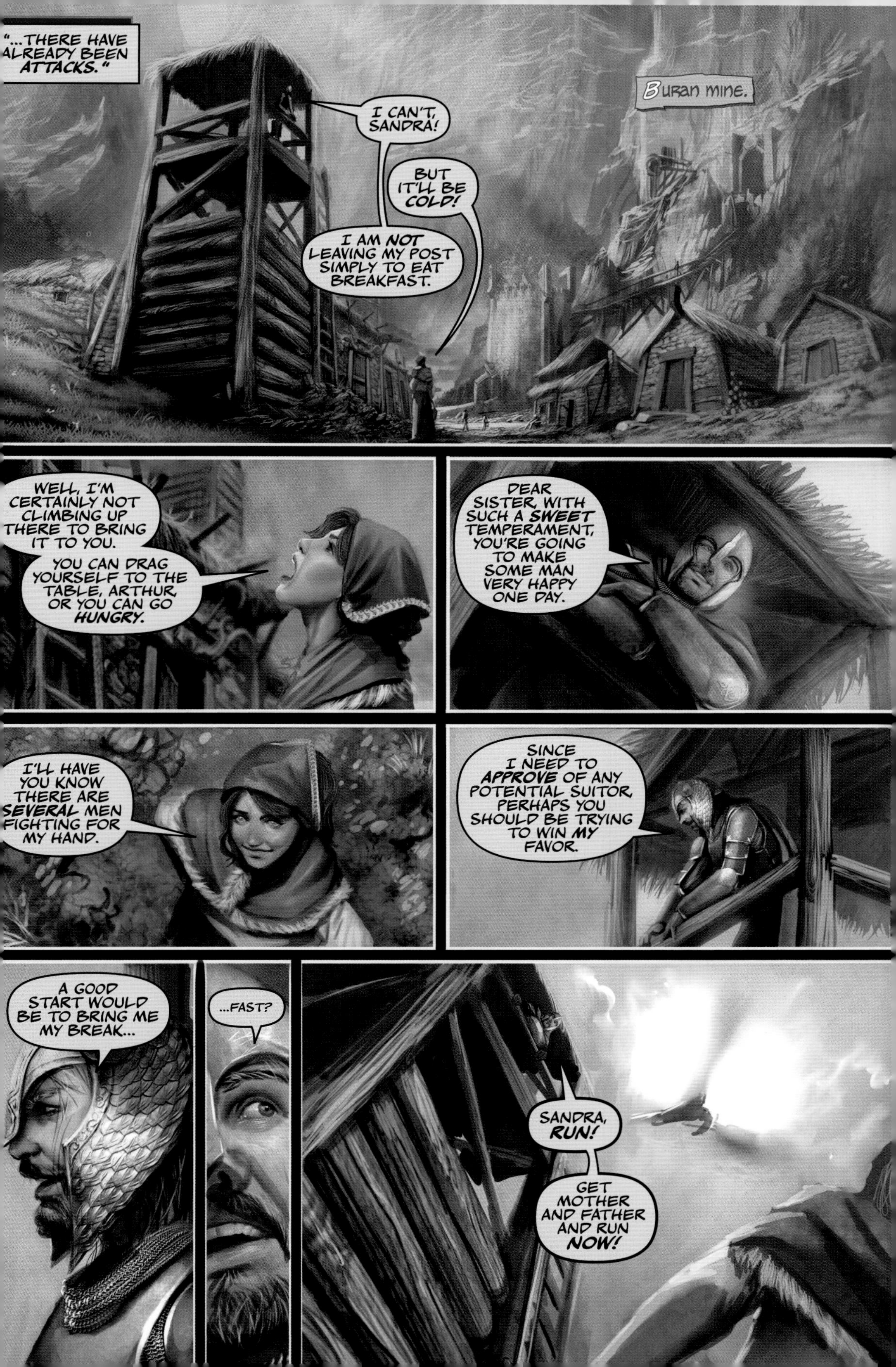
"...THERE HAVE ALREADY BEEN ATTACKS."
Buran mine.
I CAN'T, SANDRA!
I AM NOT LEAVING MY POST SIMPLY TO EAT BREAKFAST.
BUT IT'LL BE COLD!
WELL, I'M CERTAINLY NOT CLIMBING UP THERE TO BRING IT TO YOU.
YOU CAN DRAG YOURSELF TO THE TABLE, ARTHUR, OR YOU CAN GO HUNGRY.
DEAR SISTER, WITH SUCH A SWEET TEMPERAMENT, YOU'RE GOING TO MAKE SOME MAN VERY HAPPY ONE DAY.
I'LL HAVE YOU KNOW THERE ARE SEVERAL MEN FIGHTING FOR MY HAND.
SINCE I NEED TO APPROVE OF ANY POTENTIAL SUITOR, PERHAPS YOU SHOULD BE TRYING TO WIN MY FAVOR.
A GOOD START WOULD BE TO BRING ME MY BREAK...
...FAST?
SANDRA, RUN!
GET MOTHER AND FATHER AND RUN NOW!

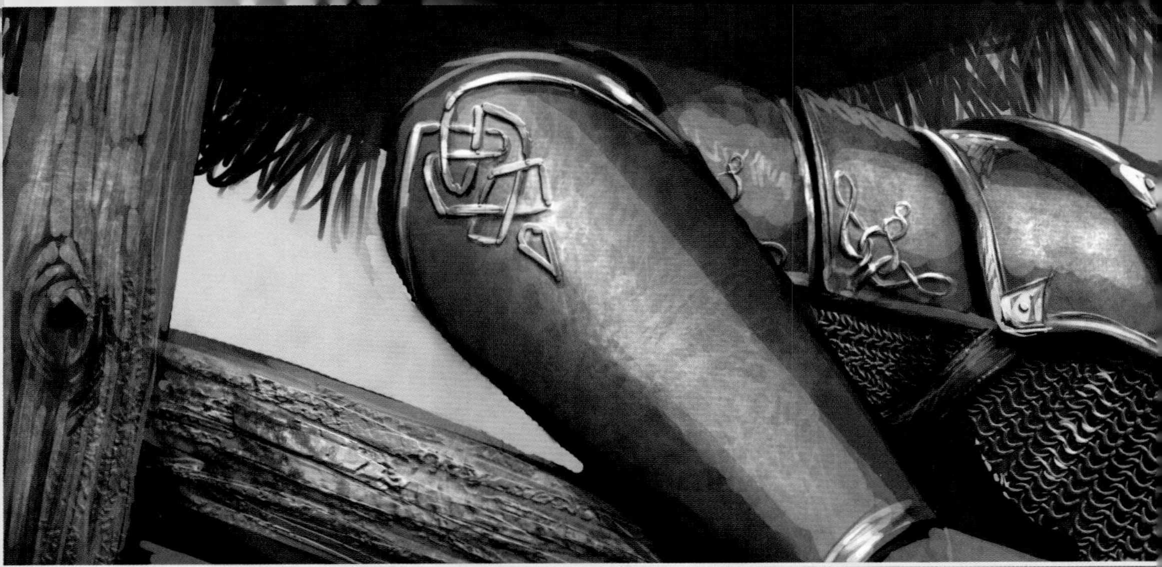

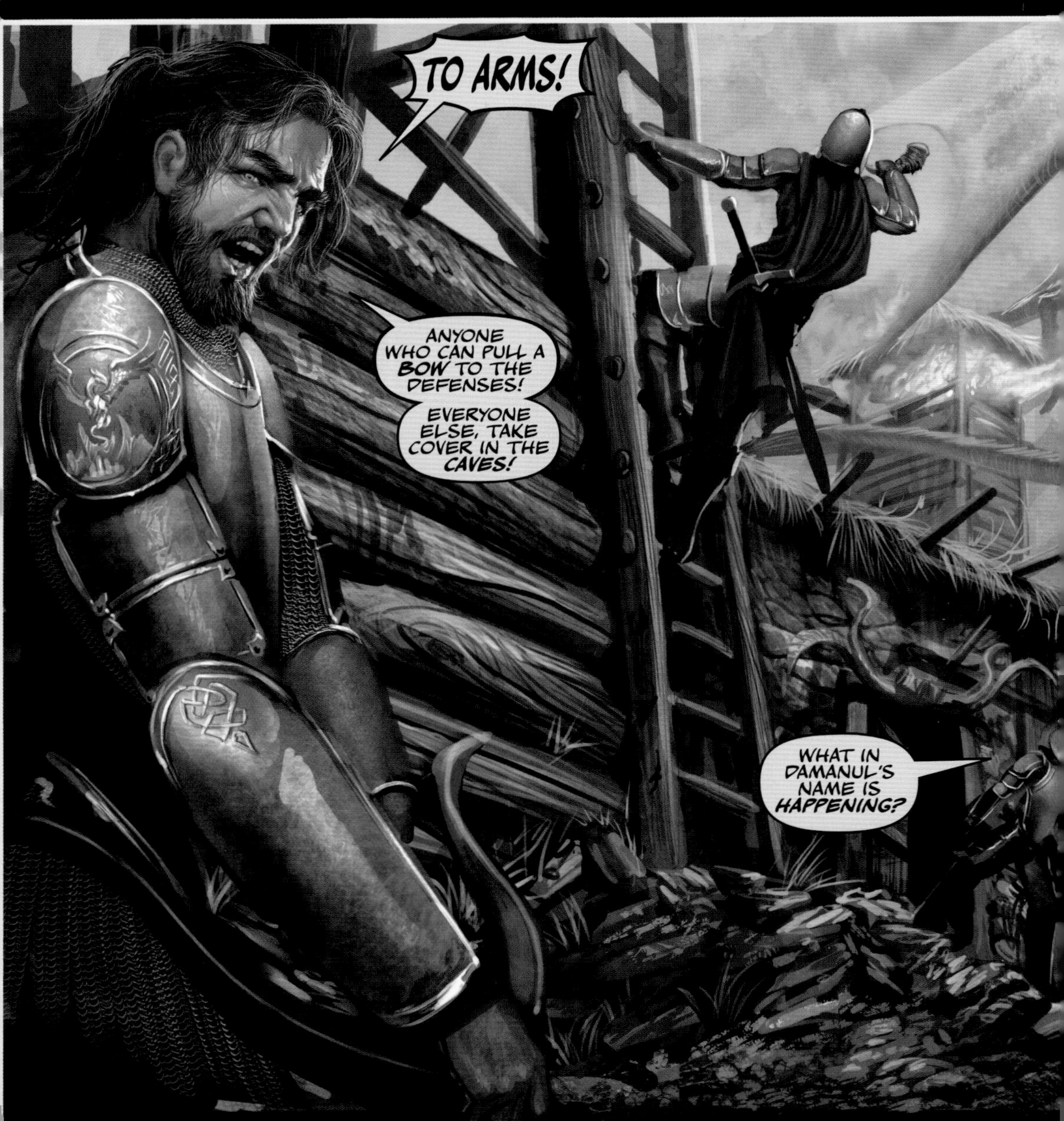
TO ARMS!
ANYONE WHO CAN PULL A BOW TO THE DEFENSES!
EVERYONE ELSE, TAKE COVER IN THE CAVES!
WHAT IN DAMANUL'S NAME IS HAPPENING?

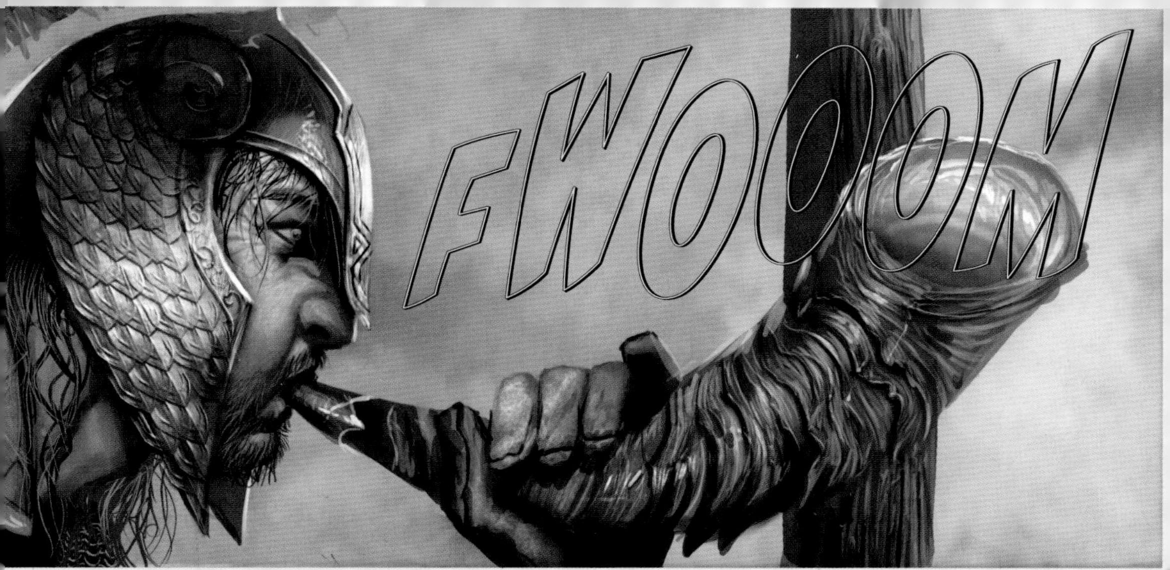
FWOOOM

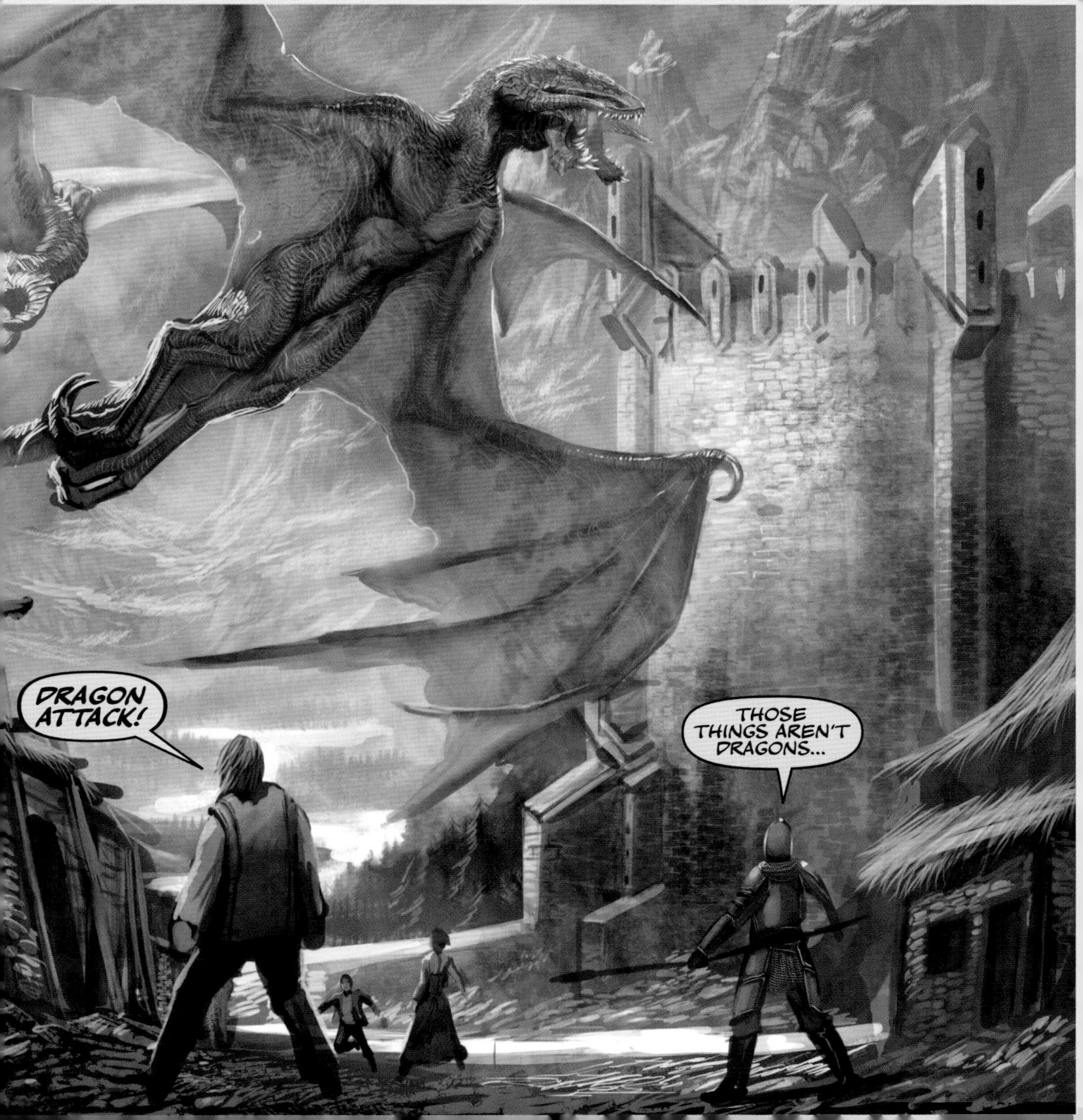
DRAGON ATTACK!
THOSE THINGS AREN'T DRAGONS...

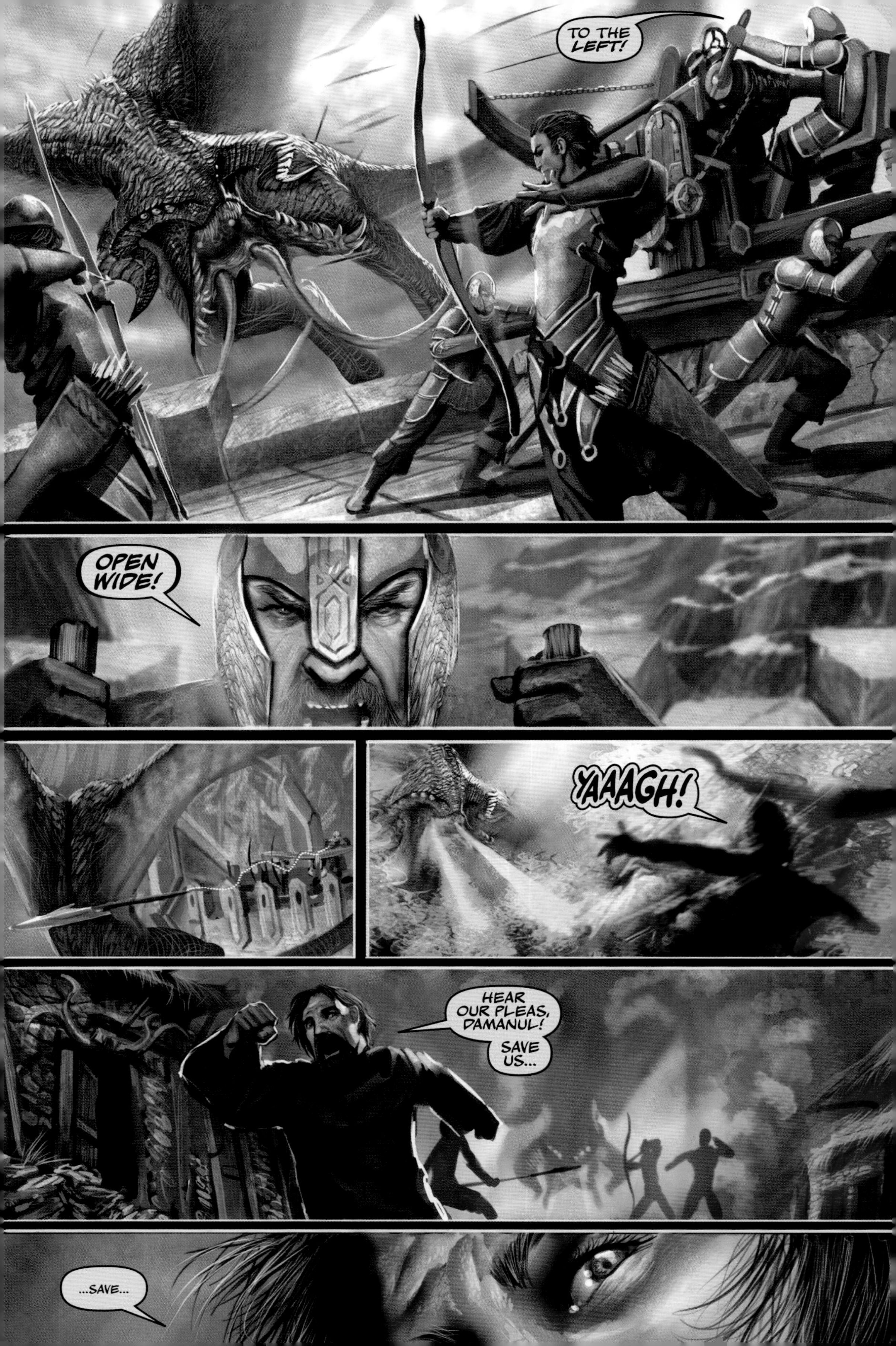
TO THE LEFT!
OPEN WIDE!
YAAAGH!
HEAR OUR PLEAS, DAMANUL!
SAVE US...
...SAVE...

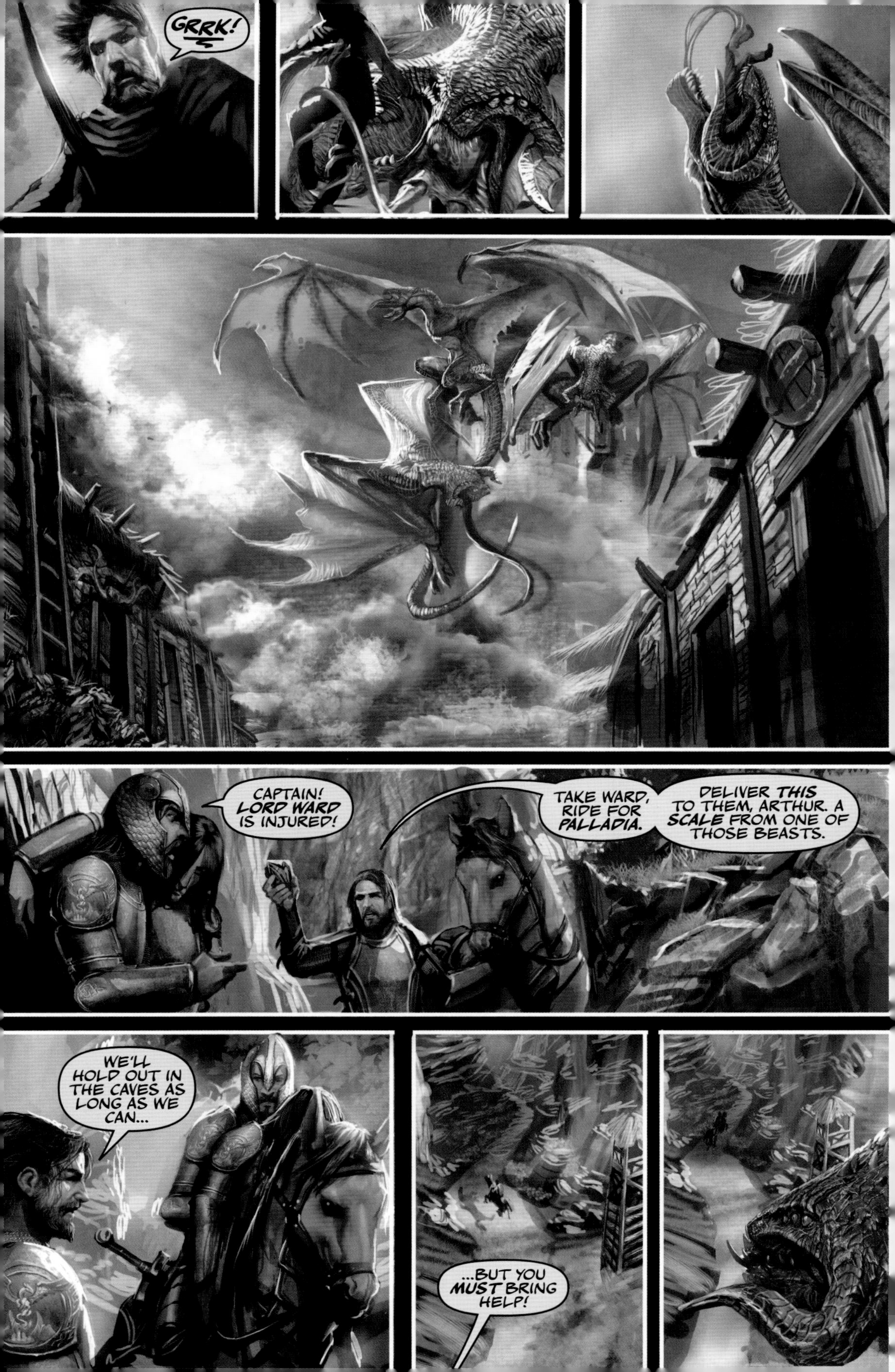
GRRK!
CAPTAIN! LORD WARD IS INJURED!
TAKE WARD, RIDE FOR PALLADIA.
DELIVER THIS TO THEM, ARTHUR. A SCALE FROM ONE OF THOSE BEASTS.
WE'LL HOLD OUT IN THE CAVES AS LONG AS WE CAN...
...BUT YOU MUST BRING HELP!

WE'RE STUCK.

THOUGHT OUT THIS PLAN QUITE *THOROUGHLY*, DID YOU?

YOU'RE NOT HELPING.

I'M NOT HERE TO HELP. I'M MERELY SUPPOSED TO BE A *GUIDE*.

IT DIDN'T OCCUR TO YOU THAT FOLLOWING A CREATURE OF THE *AIR* MIGHT MEAN AN INCONVENIENT PATH ON THE *GROUND*?

IT OCCURRED TO ME...

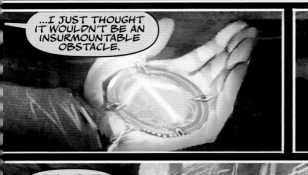

...I JUST THOUGHT IT WOULDN'T BE AN INSURMOUNTABLE OBSTACLE.

BUT IT IS.

I NEED TO GET *OUT* OF THIS MOUNTAIN MAZE.

YOU *THINK*?

YOU'RE *ENJOYING* THIS.

MY OPPORTUNITIES FOR ENJOYMENT ARE FEW AND FAR BETWEEN, SO I TAKE THEM WHERE

SMOKE.

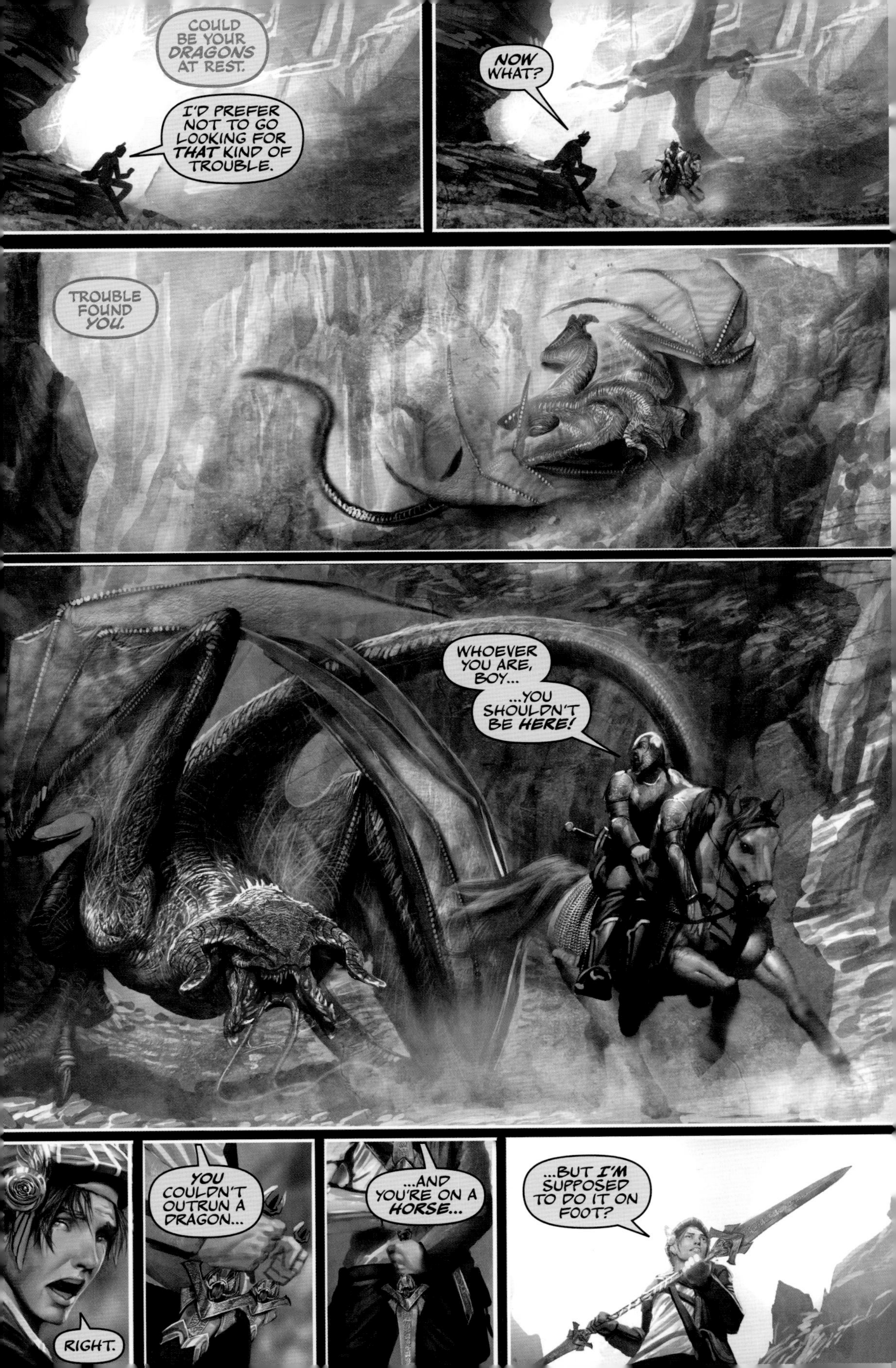
COULD BE YOUR DRAGONS AT REST.
I'D PREFER NOT TO GO LOOKING FOR THAT KIND OF TROUBLE.
NOW WHAT?
TROUBLE FOUND YOU.
WHOEVER YOU ARE, BOY...
...YOU SHOULDN'T BE HERE!
RIGHT.
YOU COULDN'T OUTRUN A DRAGON...
...AND YOU'RE ON A HORSE...
...BUT I'M SUPPOSED TO DO IT ON FOOT?

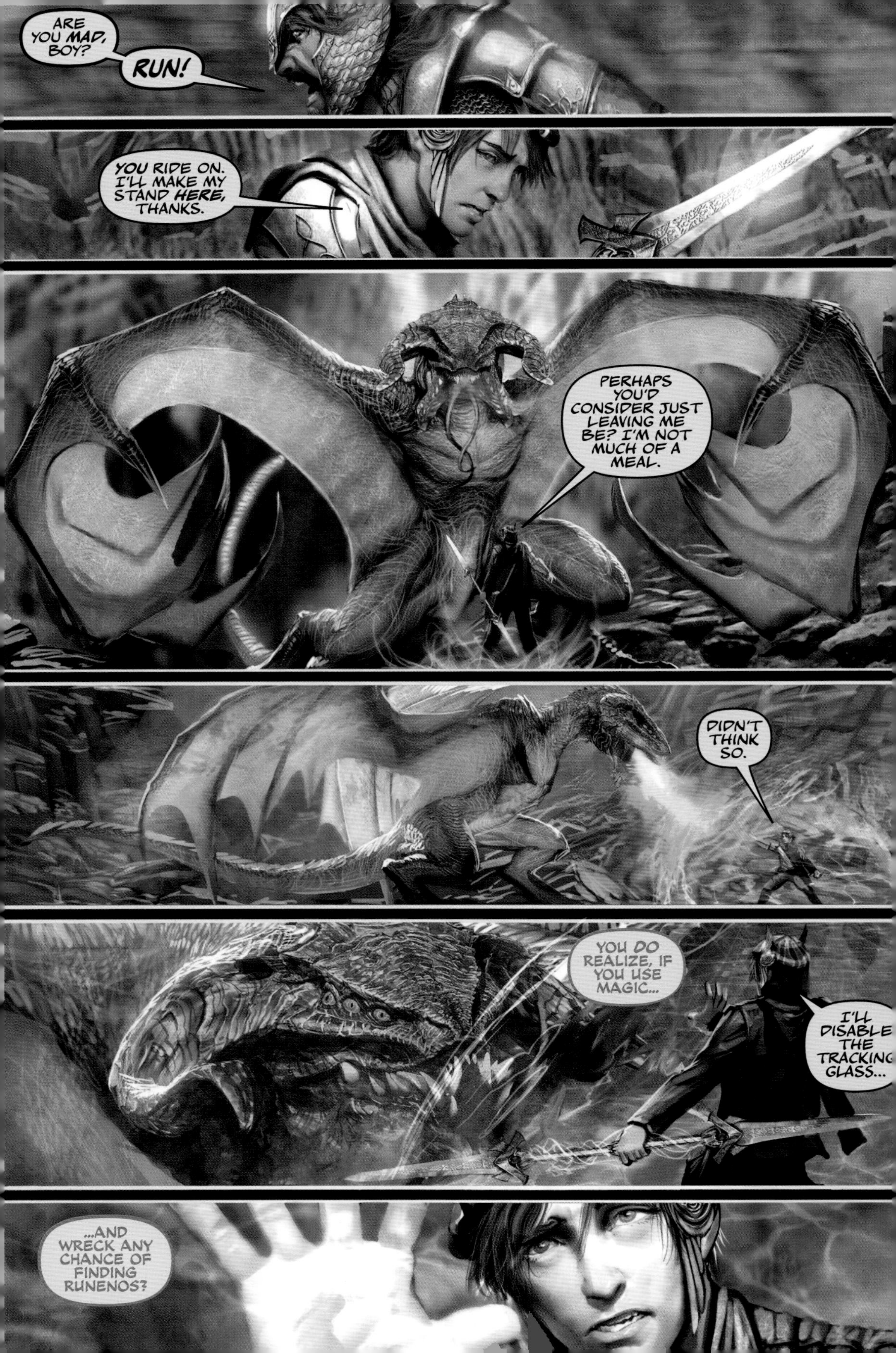
ARE YOU MAD, BOY?
RUN!
YOU RIDE ON. I'LL MAKE MY STAND HERE, THANKS.
PERHAPS YOU'D CONSIDER JUST LEAVING ME BE? I'M NOT MUCH OF A MEAL.
DIDN'T THINK SO.
YOU DO REALIZE, IF YOU USE MAGIC...
I'LL DISABLE THE TRACKING GLASS...
...AND WRECK ANY CHANCE OF FINDING RUNENOS?

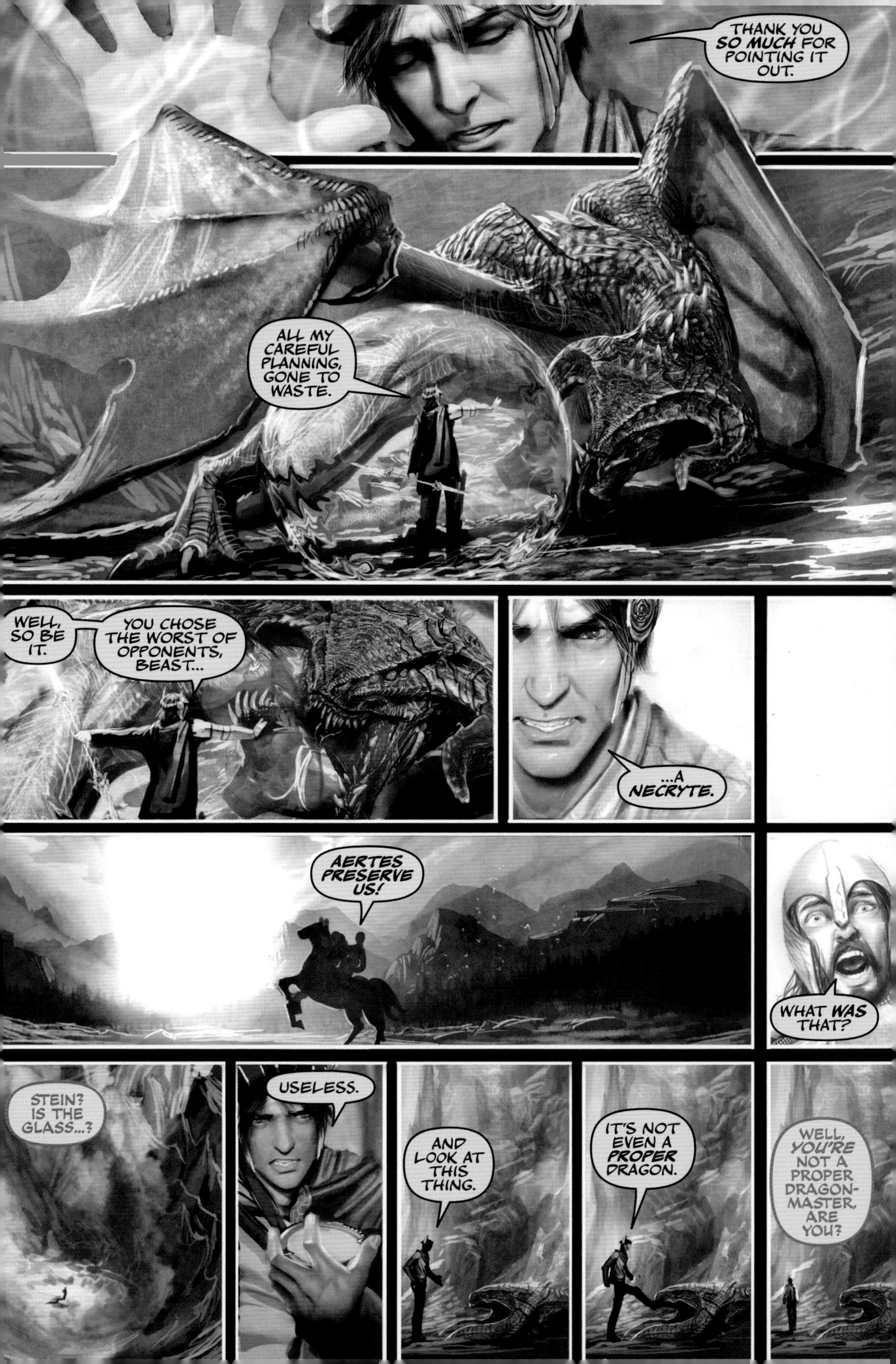

THANK YOU SO MUCH FOR POINTING IT OUT.
ALL MY CAREFUL PLANNING, GONE TO WASTE.
WELL, SO BE IT.
YOU CHOSE THE WORST OF OPPONENTS, BEAST...
...A NECRYTE.
AERTES PRESERVE US!
WHAT WAS THAT?
STEIN? IS THE GLASS...?
USELESS.
AND LOOK AT THIS THING.
IT'S NOT EVEN A PROPER DRAGON.
WELL, YOU'RE NOT A PROPER DRAGON-MASTER, ARE YOU?

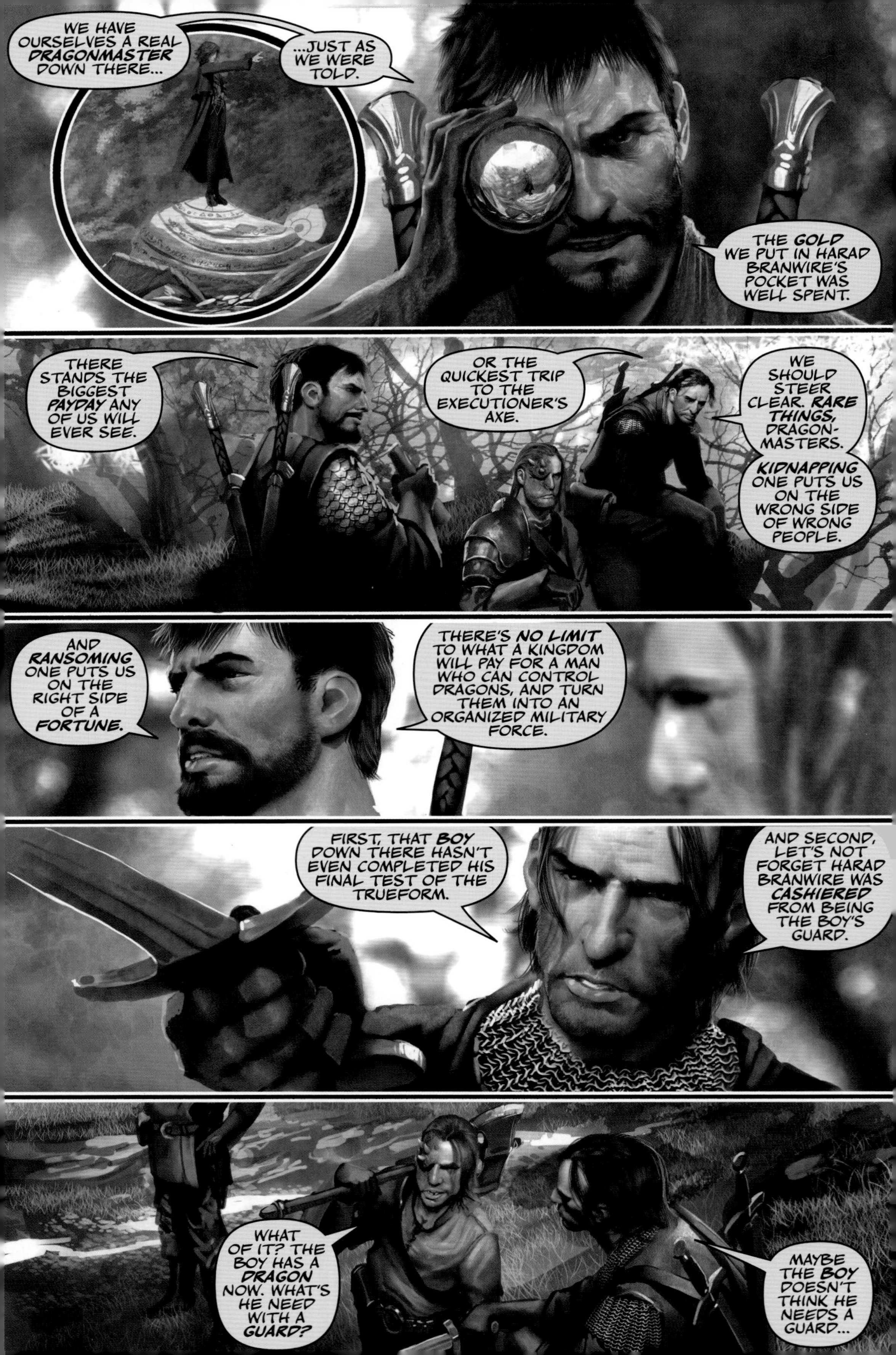
WE HAVE OURSELVES A REAL DRAGONMASTER DOWN THERE...
...JUST AS WE WERE TOLD.
THE GOLD WE PUT IN HARAD BRANWIRE'S POCKET WAS WELL SPENT.
THERE STANDS THE BIGGEST PAYDAY ANY OF US WILL EVER SEE.
OR THE QUICKEST TRIP TO THE EXECUTIONER'S AXE.
WE SHOULD STEER CLEAR. RARE THINGS, DRAGON-MASTERS.
KIDNAPPING ONE PUTS US ON THE WRONG SIDE OF WRONG PEOPLE.
AND RANSOMING ONE PUTS US ON THE RIGHT SIDE OF A FORTUNE.
THERE'S NO LIMIT TO WHAT A KINGDOM WILL PAY FOR A MAN WHO CAN CONTROL DRAGONS, AND TURN THEM INTO AN ORGANIZED MILITARY FORCE.
FIRST, THAT BOY DOWN THERE HASN'T EVEN COMPLETED HIS FINAL TEST OF THE TRUEFORM.
AND SECOND, LET'S NOT FORGET HARAD BRANWIRE WAS CASHIERED FROM BEING THE BOY'S GUARD.
WHAT OF IT? THE BOY HAS A DRAGON NOW. WHAT'S HE NEED WITH A GUARD?
MAYBE THE BOY DOESN'T THINK HE NEEDS A GUARD...

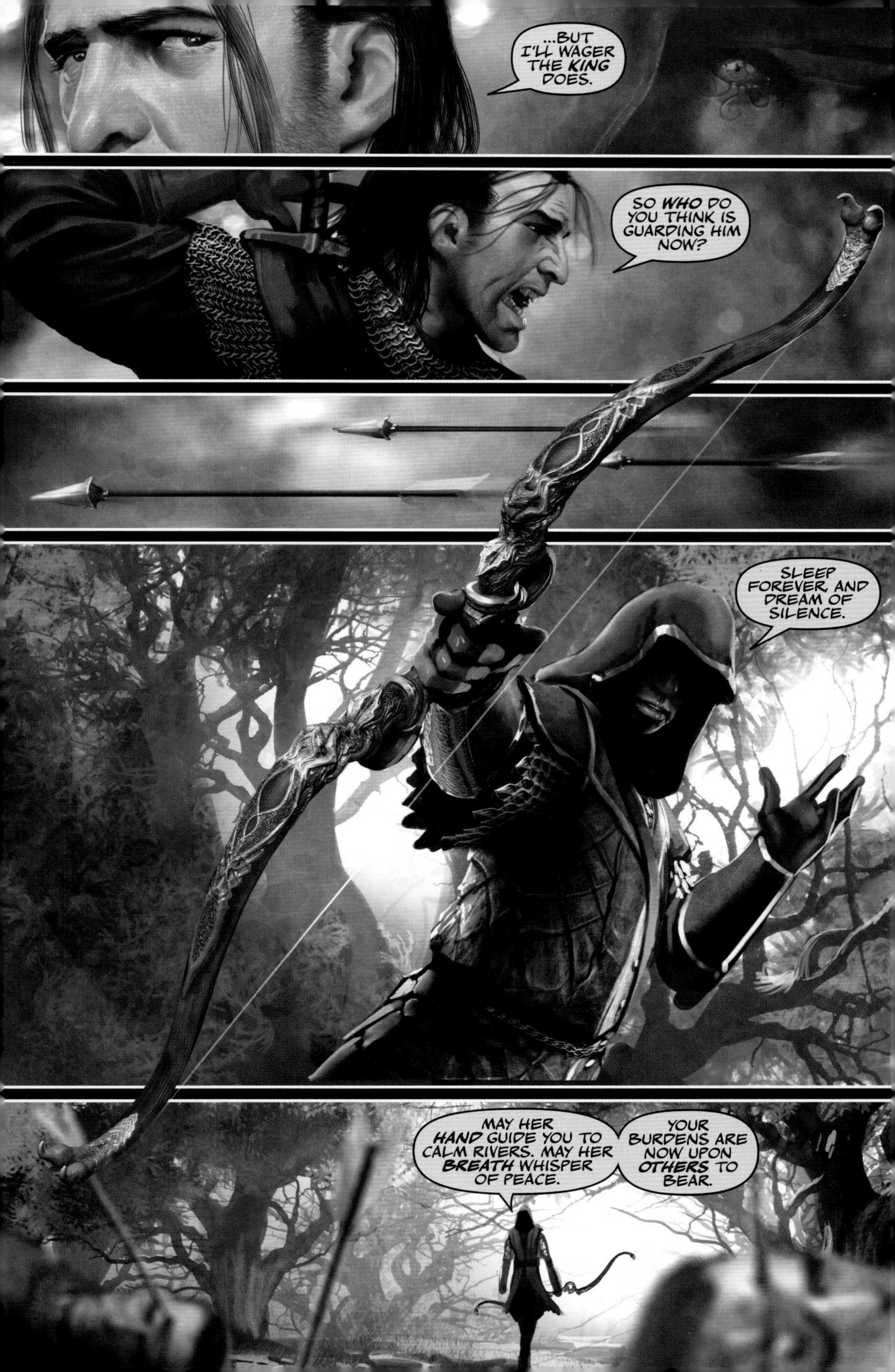
...BUT I'LL WAGER THE KING DOES.
SO WHO DO YOU THINK IS GUARDING HIM NOW?
SLEEP FOREVER, AND DREAM OF SILENCE.
MAY HER HAND GUIDE YOU TO CALM RIVERS. MAY HER BREATH WHISPER OF PEACE.
YOUR BURDENS ARE NOW UPON OTHERS TO BEAR.

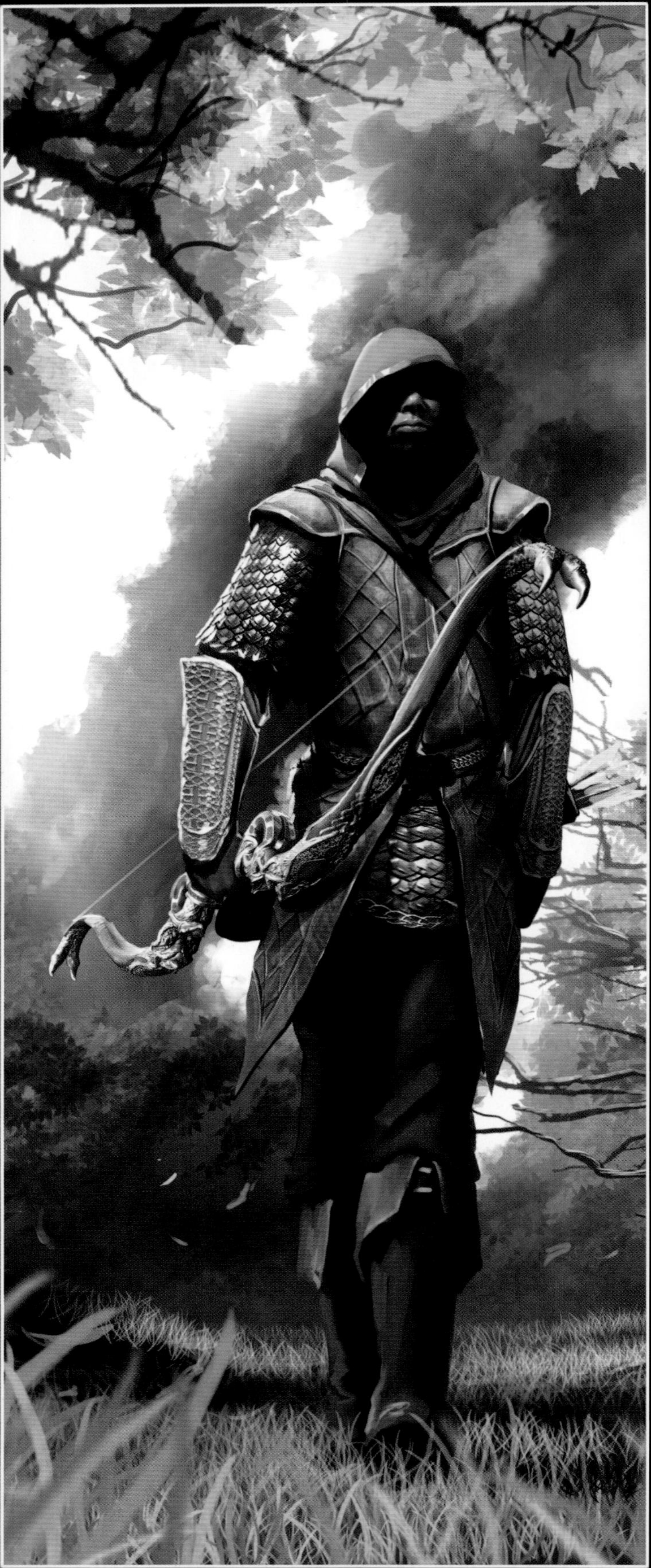

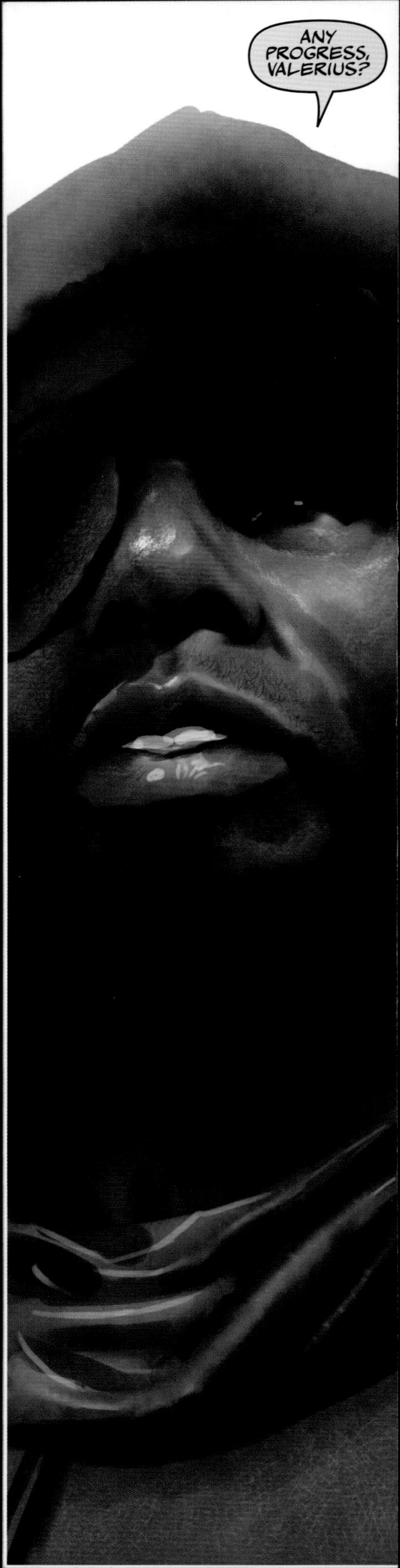
ANY PROGRESS, VALERIUS?

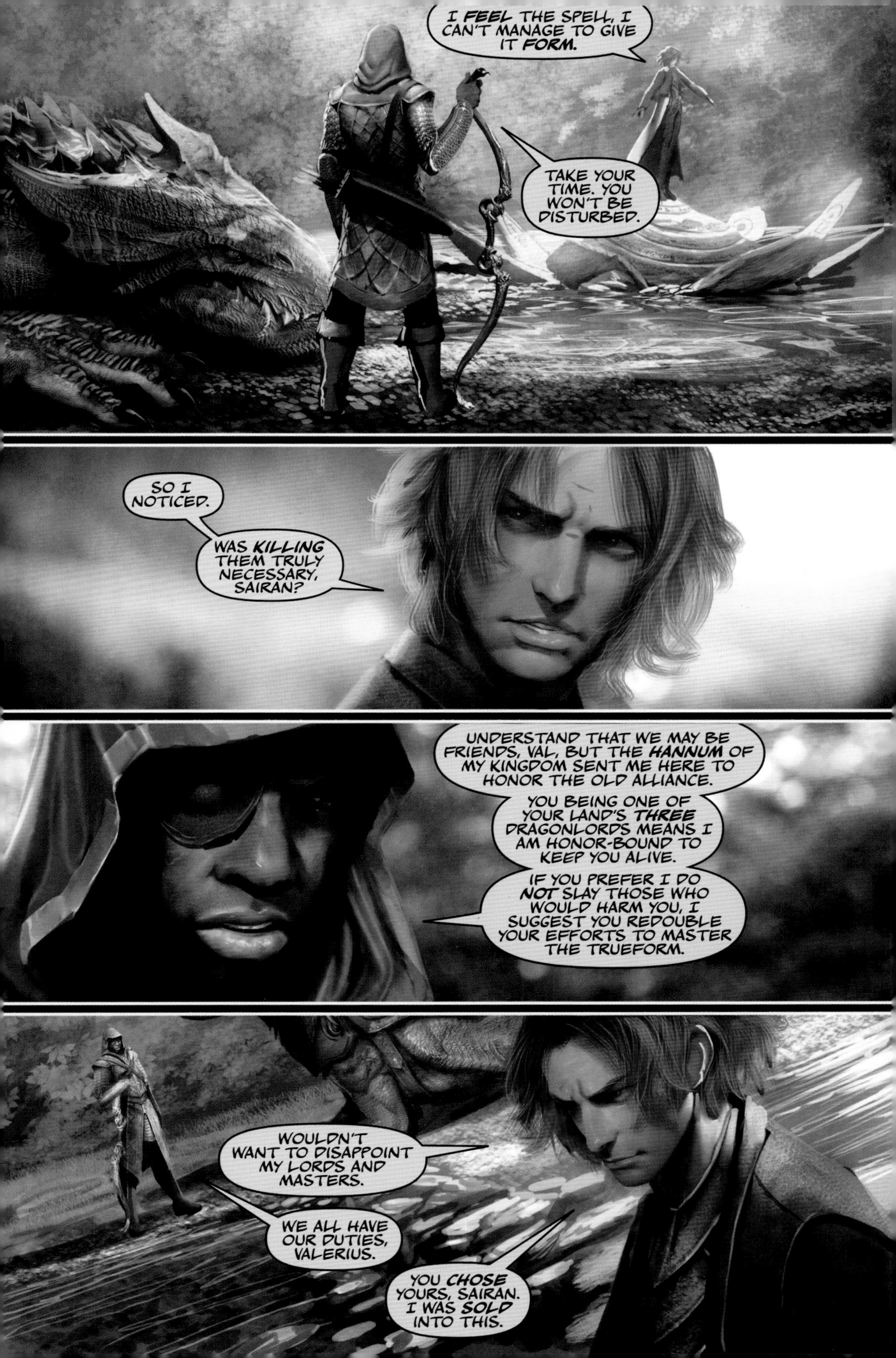
I FEEL THE SPELL, I CAN'T MANAGE TO GIVE IT FORM.
TAKE YOUR TIME. YOU WON'T BE DISTURBED.
SO I NOTICED.
WAS KILLING THEM TRULY NECESSARY, SAIRAN?
UNDERSTAND THAT WE MAY BE FRIENDS, VAL, BUT THE HANNUM OF MY KINGDOM SENT ME HERE TO HONOR THE OLD ALLIANCE.
YOU BEING ONE OF YOUR LAND'S THREE DRAGONLORDS MEANS I AM HONOR-BOUND TO KEEP YOU ALIVE.
IF YOU PREFER I DO NOT SLAY THOSE WHO WOULD HARM YOU, I SUGGEST YOU REDOUBLE YOUR EFFORTS TO MASTER THE TRUEFORM.
WOULDN'T WANT TO DISAPPOINT MY LORDS AND MASTERS.
WE ALL HAVE OUR DUTIES, VALERIUS.
YOU CHOSE YOURS, SAIRAN. I WAS SOLD INTO THIS.

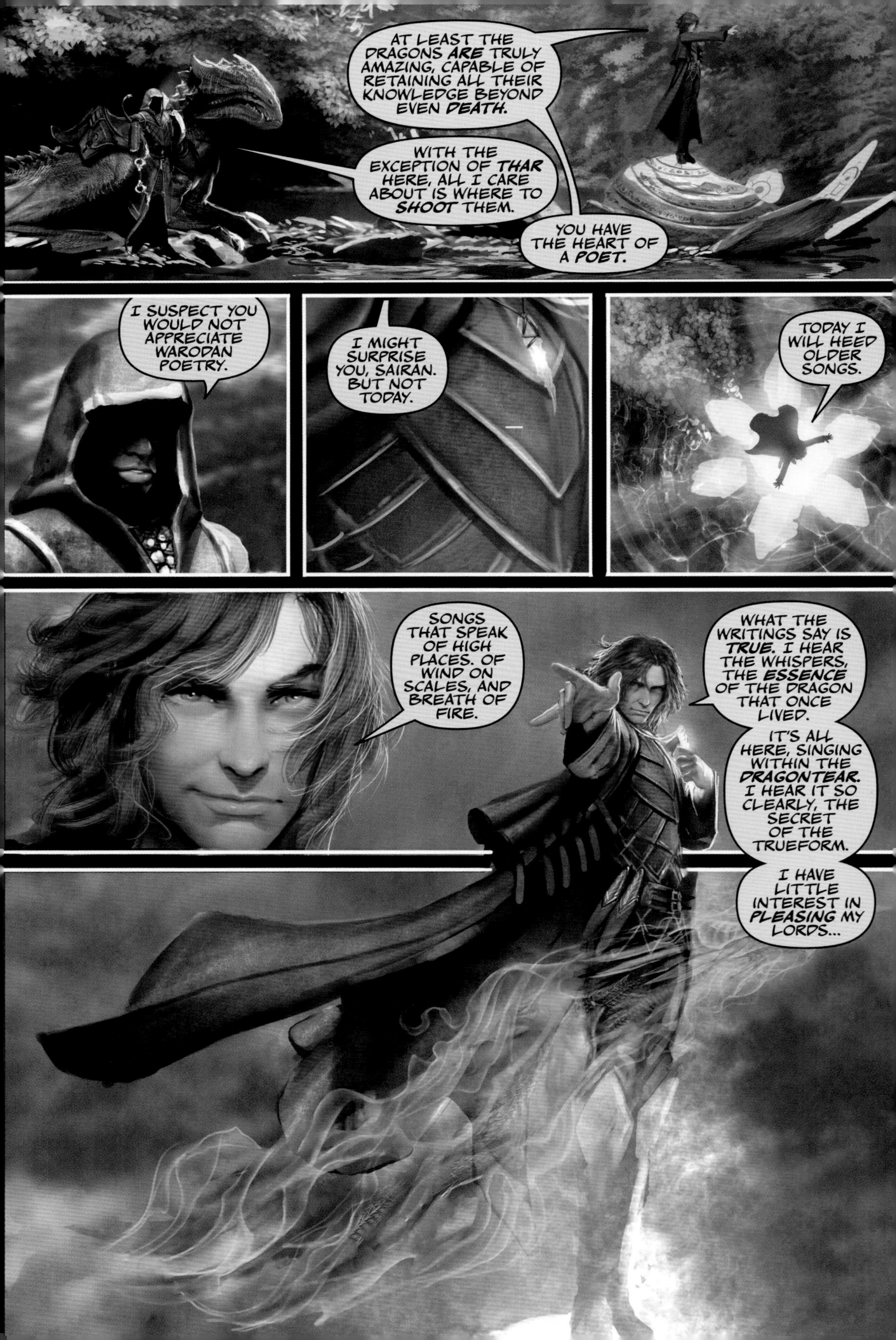
AT LEAST THE DRAGONS ARE TRULY AMAZING, CAPABLE OF RETAINING ALL THEIR KNOWLEDGE BEYOND EVEN DEATH.
WITH THE EXCEPTION OF THAR HERE, ALL I CARE ABOUT IS WHERE TO SHOOT THEM.
YOU HAVE THE HEART OF A POET.
I SUSPECT YOU WOULD NOT APPRECIATE WARODAN POETRY.
I MIGHT SURPRISE YOU, SAIRAN. BUT NOT TODAY.
TODAY I WILL HEED OLDER SONGS.
SONGS THAT SPEAK OF HIGH PLACES. OF WIND ON SCALES, AND BREATH OF FIRE.
WHAT THE WRITINGS SAY IS TRUE. I HEAR THE WHISPERS, THE ESSENCE OF THE DRAGON THAT ONCE LIVED.
IT'S ALL HERE, SINGING WITHIN THE DRAGONTEAR. I HEAR IT SO CLEARLY, THE SECRET OF THE TRUEFORM.
I HAVE LITTLE INTEREST IN PLEASING MY LORDS...

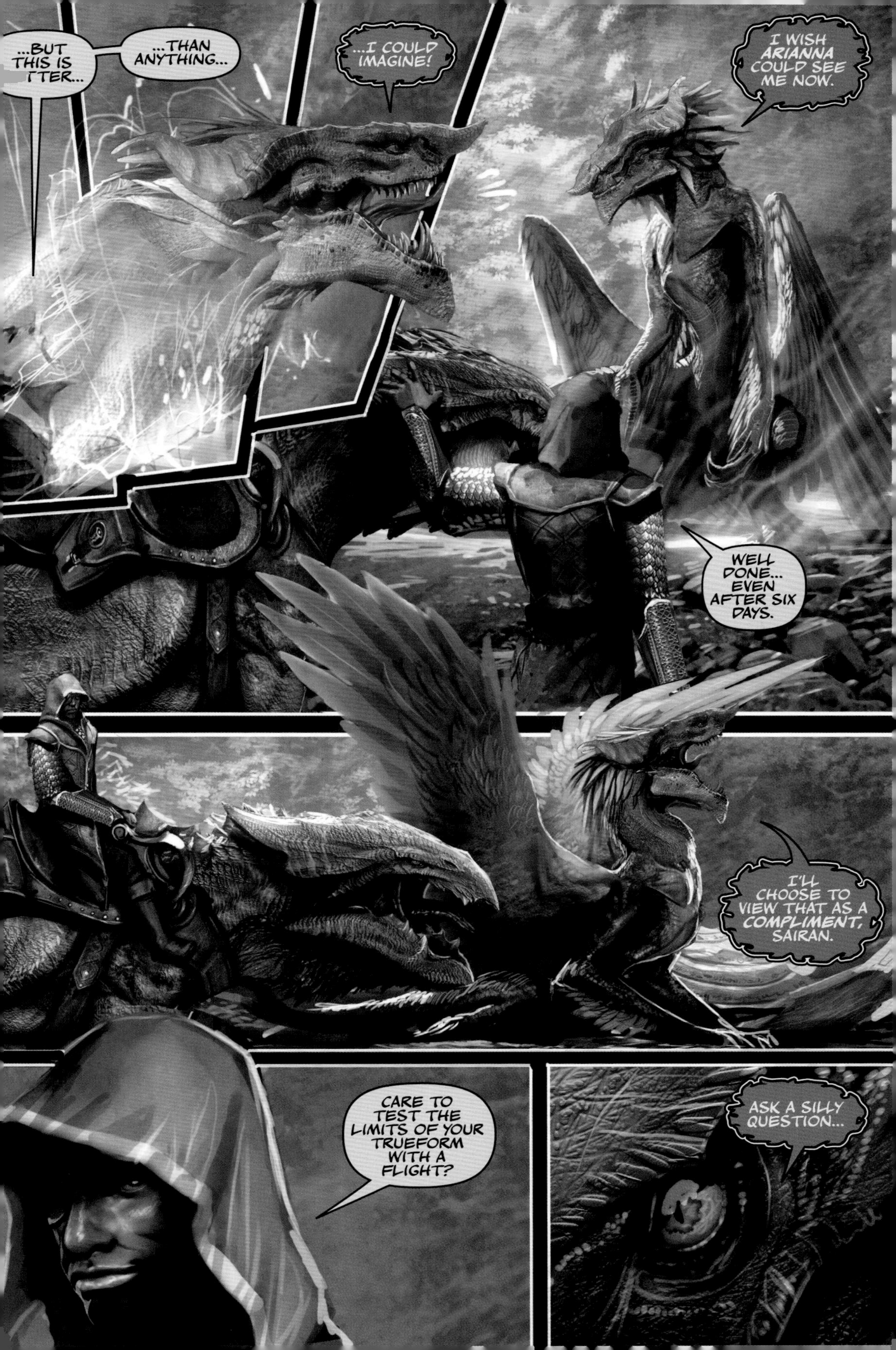
...BUT THIS IS TTER...
...THAN ANYTHING...
...I COULD IMAGINE!
I WISH ARIANNA COULD SEE ME NOW.
WELL DONE... EVEN AFTER SIX DAYS.
I'LL CHOOSE TO VIEW THAT AS A COMPLIMENT, SAIRAN.
CARE TO TEST THE LIMITS OF YOUR TRUEFORM WITH A FLIGHT?
ASK A SILLY QUESTION...

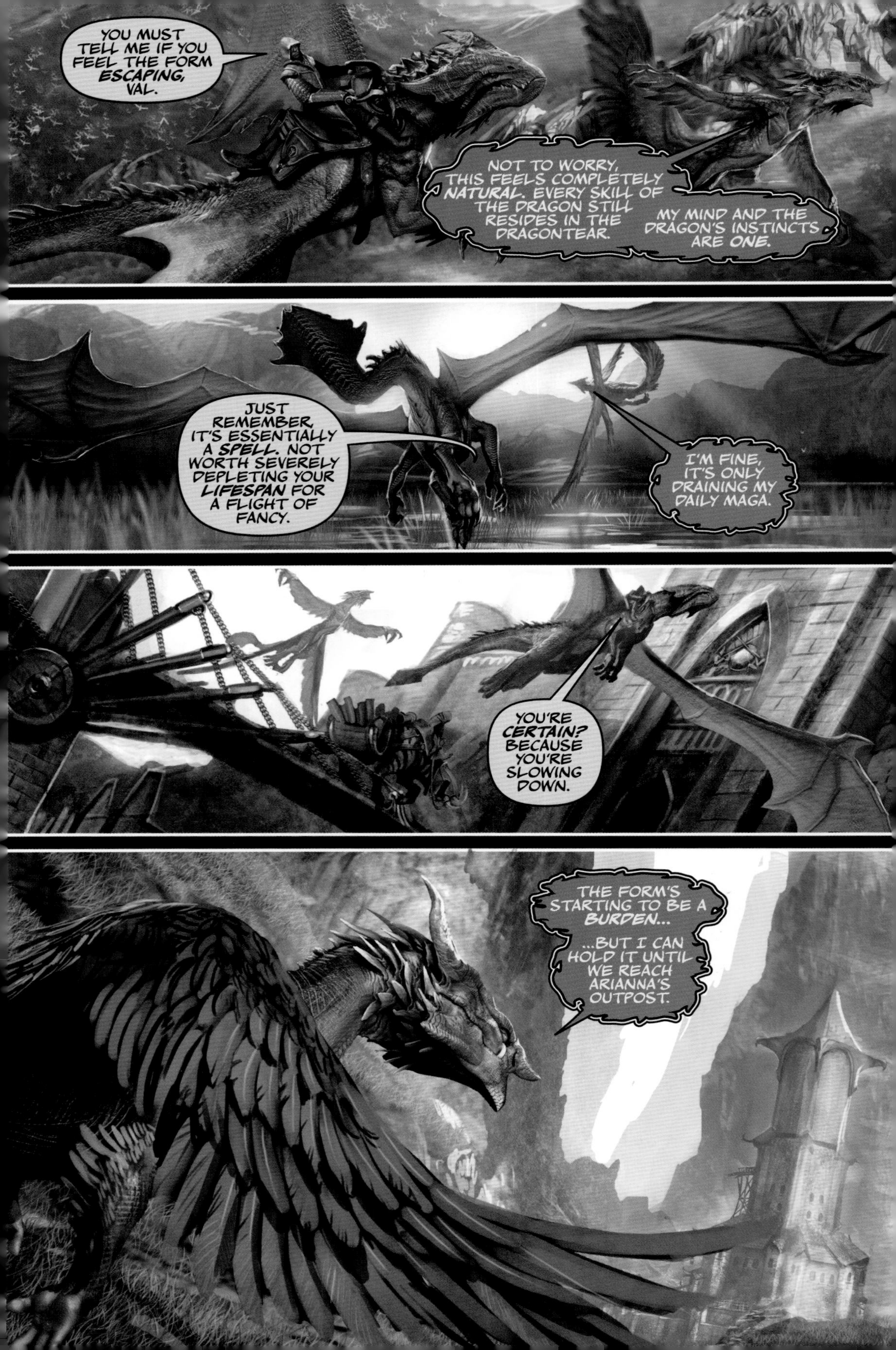
YOU MUST TELL ME IF YOU FEEL THE FORM ESCAPING, VAL.
NOT TO WORRY, THIS FEELS COMPLETELY NATURAL. EVERY SKILL OF THE DRAGON STILL RESIDES IN THE DRAGONTEAR.
MY MIND AND THE DRAGON'S INSTINCTS ARE ONE.
JUST REMEMBER, IT'S ESSENTIALLY A SPELL. NOT WORTH SEVERELY DEPLETING YOUR LIFESPAN FOR A FLIGHT OF FANCY.
I'M FINE, IT'S ONLY DRAINING MY DAILY MAGA.
YOU'RE CERTAIN? BECAUSE YOU'RE SLOWING DOWN.
THE FORM'S STARTING TO BE A BURDEN...
...BUT I CAN HOLD IT UNTIL WE REACH ARIANNA'S OUTPOST.

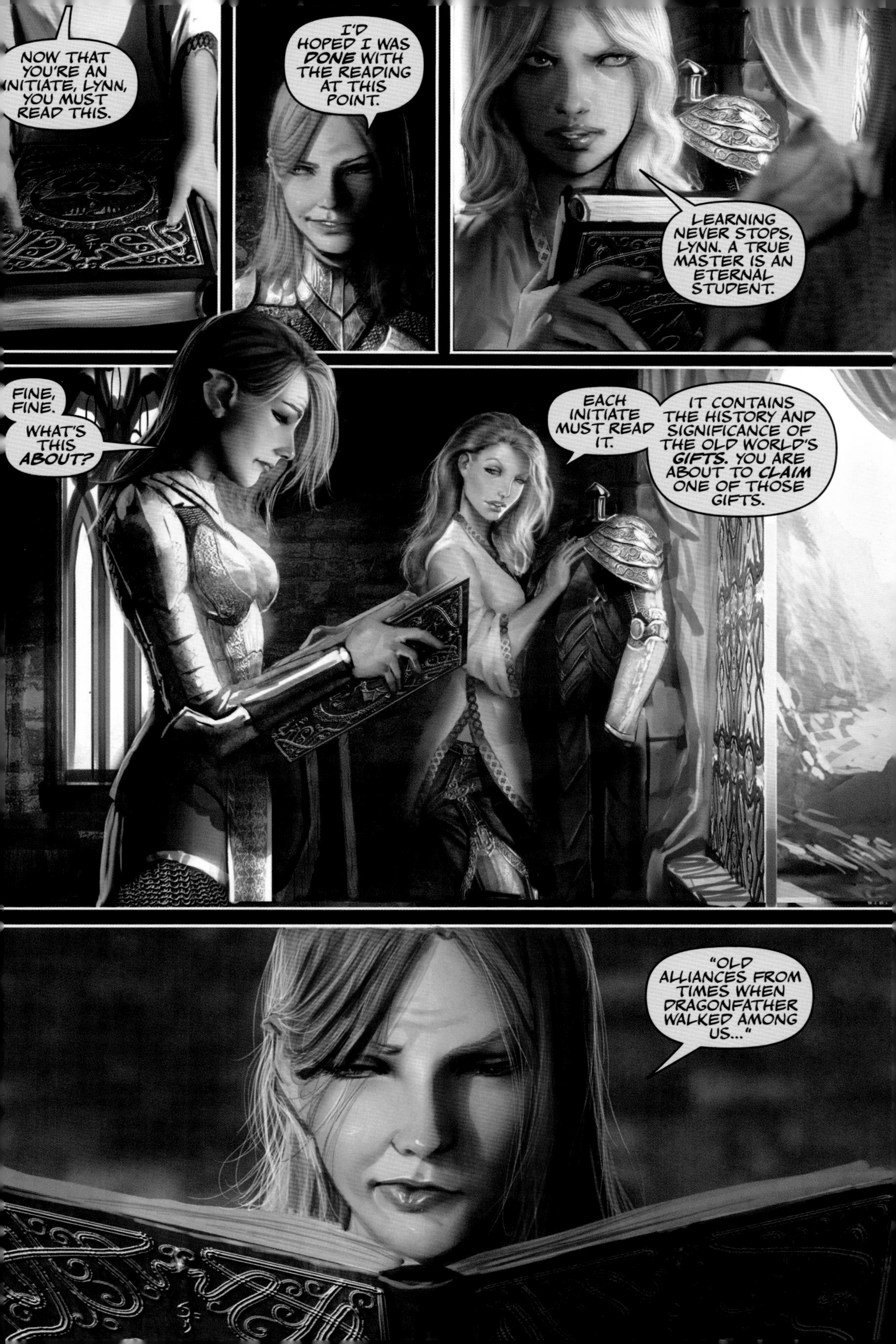
NOW THAT YOU'RE AN INITIATE, LYNN, YOU MUST READ THIS.
I'D HOPED I WAS DONE WITH THE READING AT THIS POINT.
LEARNING NEVER STOPS, LYNN. A TRUE MASTER IS AN ETERNAL STUDENT.
FINE, FINE.
WHAT'S THIS ABOUT?
EACH INITIATE MUST READ IT.
IT CONTAINS THE HISTORY AND SIGNIFICANCE OF THE OLD WORLD'S GIFTS. YOU ARE ABOUT TO CLAIM ONE OF THOSE GIFTS.
"OLD ALLIANCES FROM TIMES WHEN DRAGONFATHER WALKED AMONG US..."

GIFTS OF THE OLD WORLD

OLD ALLIANCES FROM TIMES WHEN DRAGONFATHER WALKED AMONG US RESULTED IN THE ARCANE KNOWLEDGE OF THE OLD WORLD BEING PASSED DOWN TO HUMANITY. FOUR GIFTS STAND ABOVE ALL.

GIFT OF THE WHISPERING FLAME

FIRST WAS THE GIFT OF THE WHISPERING FLAME, GIVEN BY DRAGONMOTHER BARAHEA. THIS RAREST OF ALL GIFTS WAS GIVEN TO THE FIRST TWO PEOPLE WHO WITNESSED THE EXODUS OF THE OLD WORLD. FROM THE BLOODLINE OF TWO MEN, THE FATHER HURRON WORGAL AND THE SON GAMMUR, COMES THE POWERFUL GIFT ENABLING THEIR DESCENDENTS TO COMMUNICATE WITH DRAGONS, EVEN TAKE THEIR FORM.

GIFT OF BLOOD AND POWER

DRAGONFATHER MERGARAND SHARED THE GIFT OF BLOOD AND POWER TO STRENGTHEN THE PEOPLE IN DARK TIMES. A THREAT WHOSE NAME IS LOST TO THE CENTURIES CREATED THE SINNERS OF FORM. VIOLENT AND POWERFUL, THEY WERE HUMANS ONCE, BUT GAVE INTO THE LUST FOR POWER, AND IT WARPED THEM, BODY AND MIND.

MERGARAND COUNTERED THEM BY EMPOWERING THE NORTHERN TRIBES, CHANGING THEM INTO THE FIRST THREE HALFBLOODED RACES. THEY ARE THE CHILDREN OF MERGARAND, THE LINK BETWEEN DRAGONS AND MAN:

THE SHIVAS, DISCIPLINED MASTERS OF BLADES.

THE MESADEE, THE LONG-LIVED.

AND THE SARDAHEIM, SONS OF MAGIC.

GIFT OF LIFE'S FORCE UNBOUND

MERGARAND'S ELDEST SON, BARAN, GAVE THE GIFT OF LIFE'S FORCE UNBOUND. IT IS THE GIFT OF PURE MAGIC, AND THE MEANS TO CONTROL IT. BARAN TAUGHT MANKIND THE MYSTERY OF THE OLD WORLD'S POWER, THE WAY TO GIVE MAGA FORM, AND TO CHANNEL IT.

BARAN ALSO TAUGHT THE PRICE OF MAGIC, FOR NOTHING SO POWERFUL COMES WITHOUT A TOLL. A MAGE PAYS FOR RECKLESS USE OF SUCH POWER WITH HIS OWN LIFESPAN. THE NECRYTE VARDA BALAHAD MADE PLAIN THE DANGER OF UNBOUND MAGIC. IT IS A VIOLENT AND TERRIBLE FORCE, SAVING NONE, DESTROYING ALL.

GIFT OF MIGHT GIVEN PURPOSE, AND DESTINY'S GUIDE

THE GODDESS AERTES, DESTINY'S HERALD, SYMBOL OF OLD WORLD'S POWER, GAVE THE GIFT OF THE EANI OF SILVERDAIN. THE FAETREES OF THE EANI REPRESENTS A PACT BETWEEN THE KINGDOMS OF MAN AND THE STARFOLK EANI. WEAPONS OF GREAT MYSTIC POWER ARE EMBEDDED IN THESE TREES OF THE OLD WORLD. THOSE WHO POSSESS THE POWER CAN CLAIM THESE WEAPONS.

SEVEN SUCH TREES HAVE BEEN GIVEN TO THE KINGDOMS OF PALLADIA, WRANTHORN, SARADRION, APHELION, ARENI AND THE FALLEN KINGDOMS OF ARDESH AND ARDUNAT. THIS GIFT IS PERHAPS OF GREATEST IMPORTANCE, BECAUSE ABOVE THE MANY EMBEDDED WEAPONS ARE THE MIGHTY GRIMLAS, WEAPONS OF THE WANDERERS, DECIDERS OF DESTINIES.

WANDERER'S WEAPONS ARE A GIFT, AND THE PRICE WE PAY FOR THE BOON OF THE FAETREES. OLD LAW DICTATES THAT THOSE WHO BECOME WANDERERS ARE UNBOUND BY LOYALTIES TO ANY LAND OR LORD. INSTEAD, THEIR ACTIONS ARE AS MAELSTROMS, DIVERTING CURRENTS OF DESTINY FOR ALL.

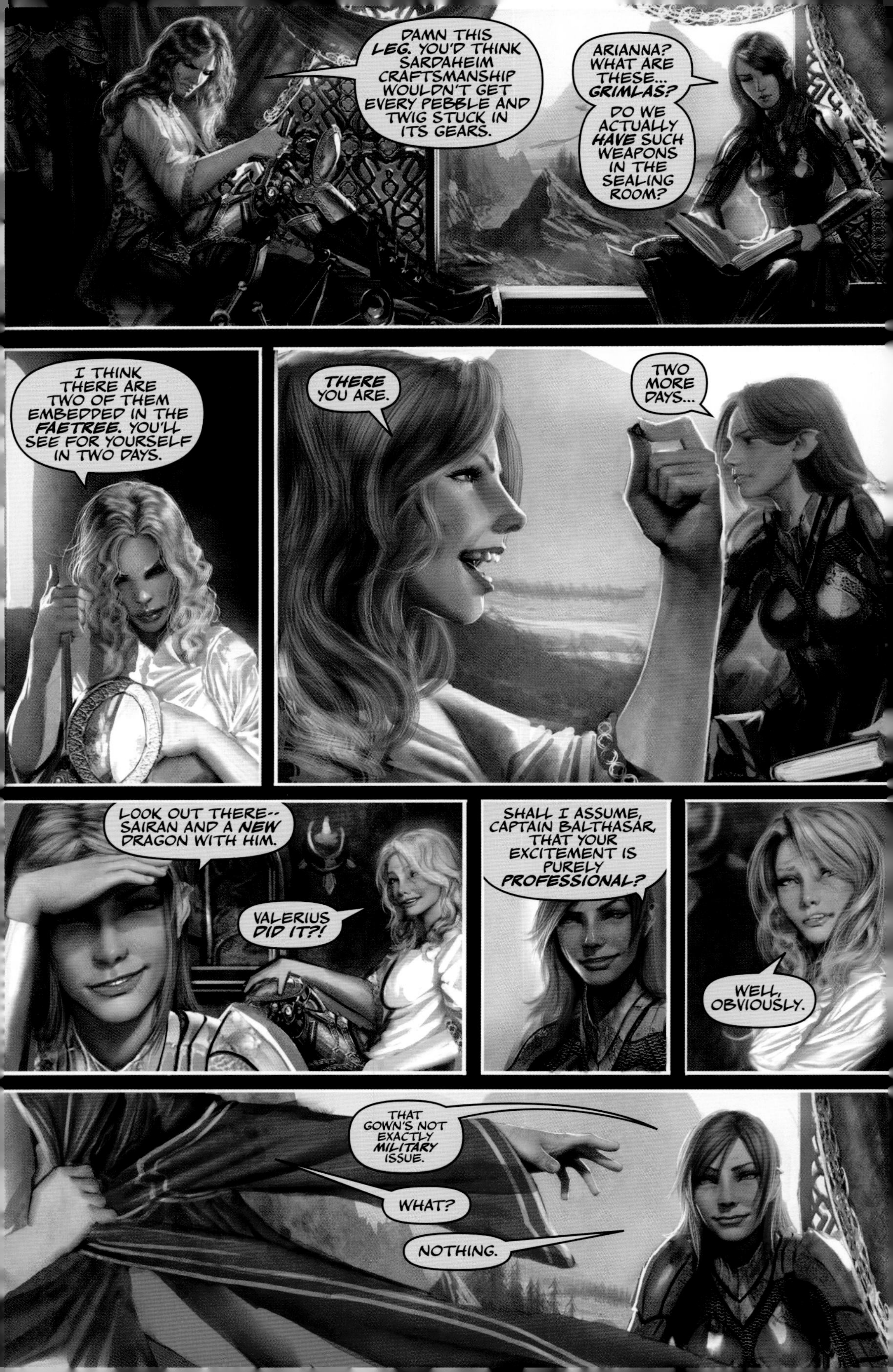
DAMN THIS LEG. YOU'D THINK SARDAHEIM CRAFTSMANSHIP WOULDN'T GET EVERY PEBBLE AND TWIG STUCK IN ITS GEARS.
ARIANNA? WHAT ARE THESE... GRIMLAS?
DO WE ACTUALLY HAVE SUCH WEAPONS IN THE SEALING ROOM?
I THINK THERE ARE TWO OF THEM EMBEDDED IN THE FAETREE. YOU'LL SEE FOR YOURSELF IN TWO DAYS.
THERE YOU ARE.
TWO MORE DAYS...
LOOK OUT THERE-- SAIRAN AND A NEW DRAGON WITH HIM.
VALERIUS DID IT?!
SHALL I ASSUME, CAPTAIN BALTHASAR, THAT YOUR EXCITEMENT IS PURELY PROFESSIONAL?
WELL, OBVIOUSLY.
THAT GOWN'S NOT EXACTLY MILITARY ISSUE.
WHAT?
NOTHING.

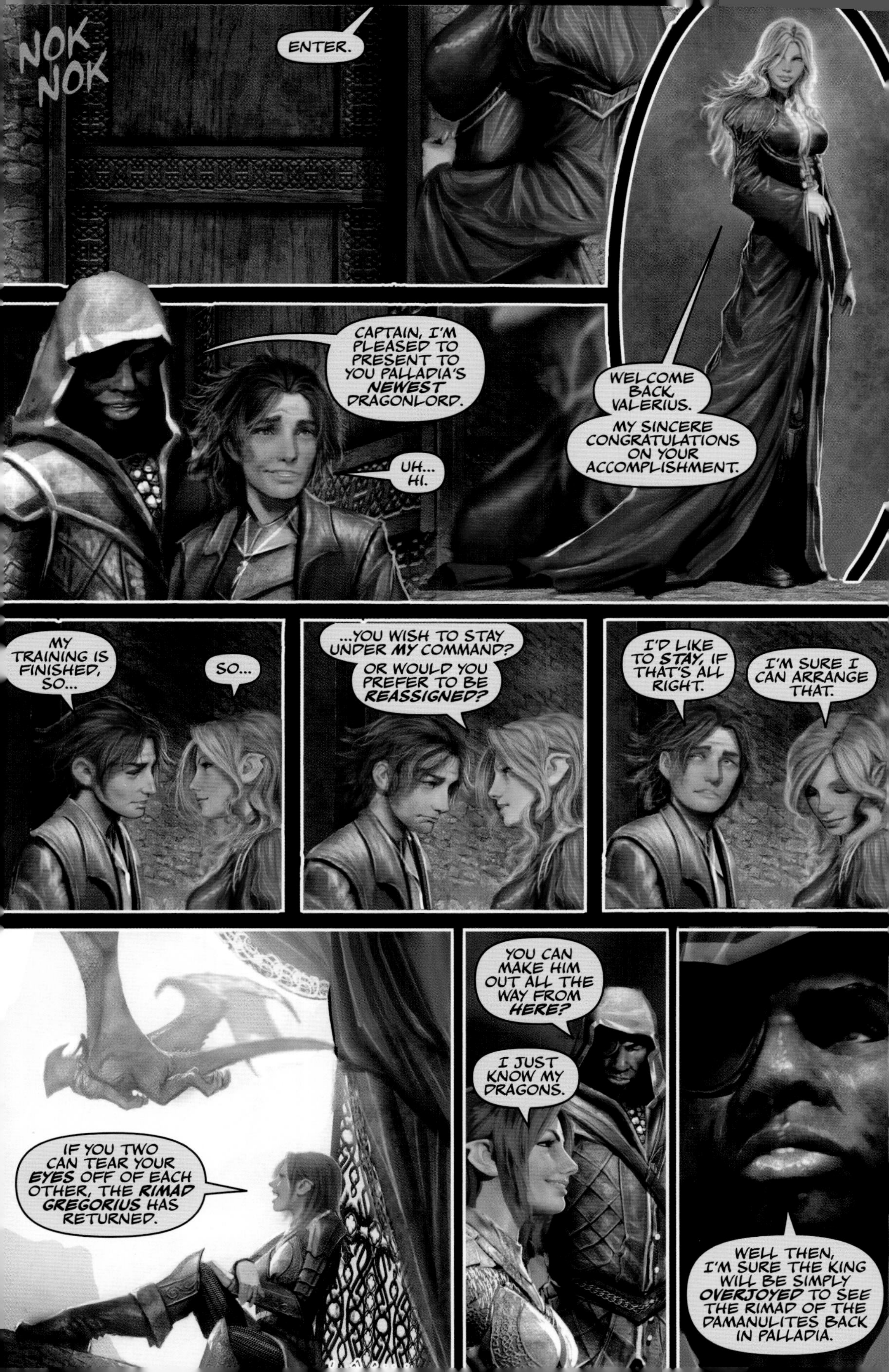
NOK NOK
ENTER.
CAPTAIN, I'M PLEASED TO PRESENT TO YOU PALLADIA'S NEWEST DRAGONLORD.
UH... HI.
WELCOME BACK, VALERIUS.
MY SINCERE CONGRATULATIONS ON YOUR ACCOMPLISHMENT.
MY TRAINING IS FINISHED, SO...
SO...
...YOU WISH TO STAY UNDER MY COMMAND?
OR WOULD YOU PREFER TO BE REASSIGNED?
I'D LIKE TO STAY, IF THAT'S ALL RIGHT.
I'M SURE I CAN ARRANGE THAT.
IF YOU TWO CAN TEAR YOUR EYES OFF OF EACH OTHER, THE RIMAD GREGORIUS HAS RETURNED.
YOU CAN MAKE HIM OUT ALL THE WAY FROM HERE?
I JUST KNOW MY DRAGONS.
WELL THEN, I'M SURE THE KING WILL BE SIMPLY OVERJOYED TO SEE THE RIMAD OF THE DAMANULITES BACK IN PALLADIA.

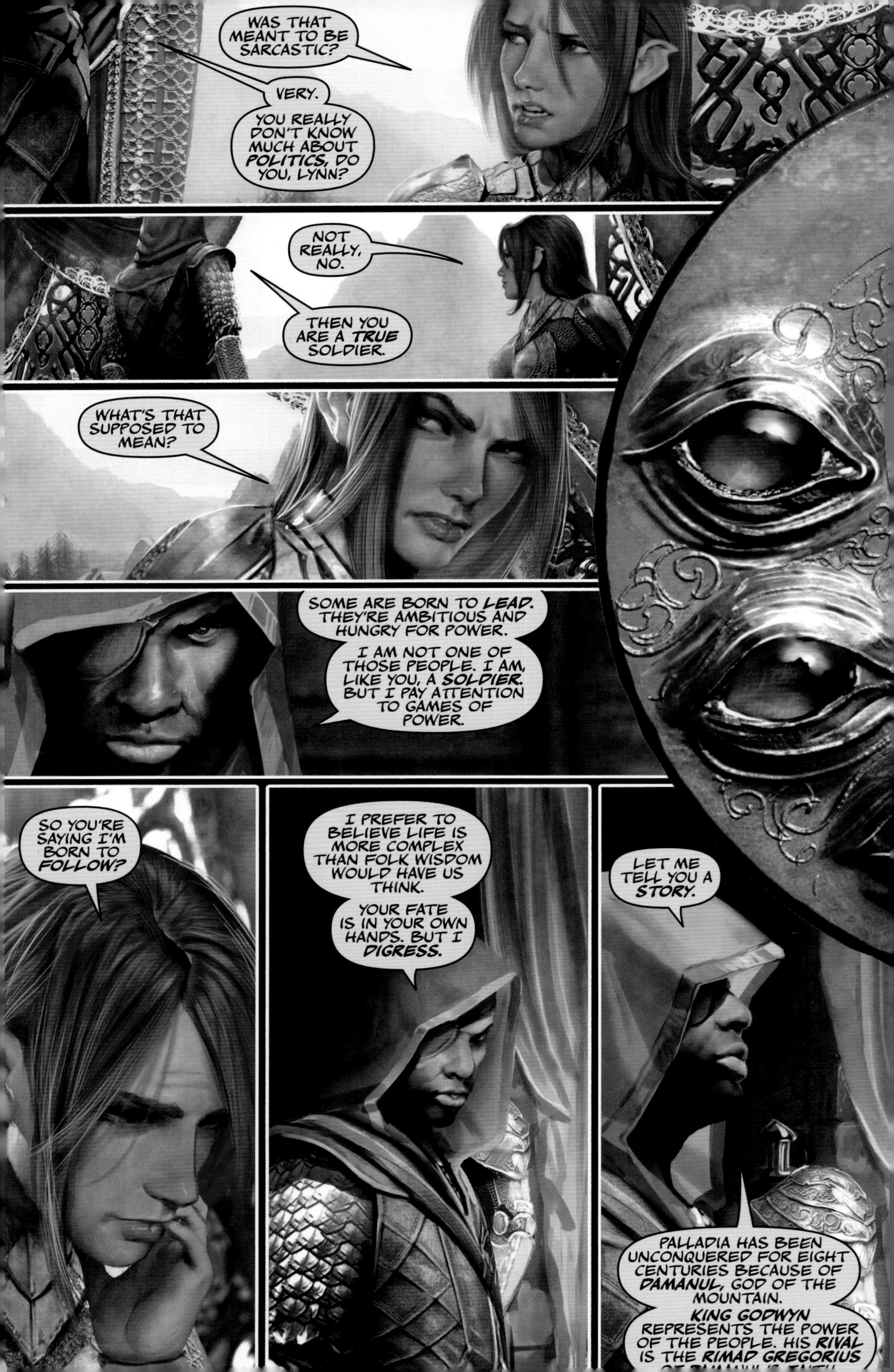
WAS THAT MEANT TO BE SARCASTIC?
VERY.
YOU REALLY DON'T KNOW MUCH ABOUT POLITICS, DO YOU, LYNN?
NOT REALLY, NO.
THEN YOU ARE A TRUE SOLDIER.
WHAT'S THAT SUPPOSED TO MEAN?
SOME ARE BORN TO LEAD. THEY'RE AMBITIOUS AND HUNGRY FOR POWER.
I AM NOT ONE OF THOSE PEOPLE. I AM, LIKE YOU, A SOLDIER. BUT I PAY ATTENTION TO GAMES OF POWER.
SO YOU'RE SAYING I'M BORN TO FOLLOW?
I PREFER TO BELIEVE LIFE IS MORE COMPLEX THAN FOLK WISDOM WOULD HAVE US THINK.
YOUR FATE IS IN YOUR OWN HANDS. BUT I DIGRESS.
LET ME TELL YOU A STORY.
PALLADIA HAS BEEN UNCONQUERED FOR EIGHT CENTURIES BECAUSE OF DAMANUL, GOD OF THE MOUNTAIN.
KING GODWYN REPRESENTS THE POWER OF THE PEOPLE. HIS RIVAL IS THE RIMAD GREGORIUS

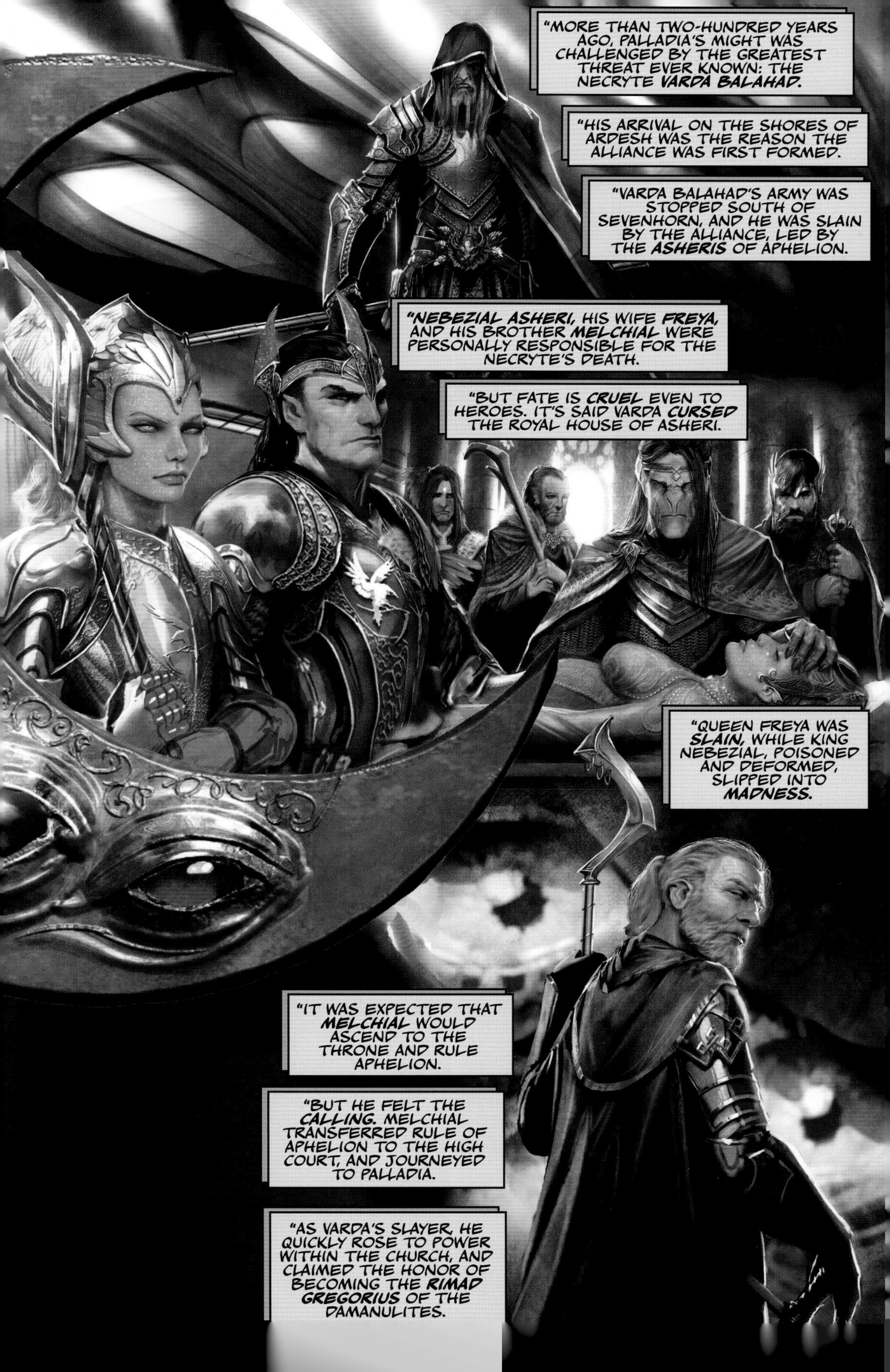
"MORE THAN TWO-HUNDRED YEARS AGO, PALLADIA'S MIGHT WAS CHALLENGED BY THE GREATEST THREAT EVER KNOWN: THE NECRYTE VARDA BALAHAD.
"HIS ARRIVAL ON THE SHORES OF ARDESH WAS THE REASON THE ALLIANCE WAS FIRST FORMED.
"VARDA BALAHAD'S ARMY WAS STOPPED SOUTH OF SEVENHORN, AND HE WAS SLAIN BY THE ALLIANCE, LED BY THE ASHERIS OF APHELION.
"NEBEZIAL ASHERI, HIS WIFE FREYA, AND HIS BROTHER MELCHIAL WERE PERSONALLY RESPONSIBLE FOR THE NECRYTE'S DEATH.
"BUT FATE IS CRUEL EVEN TO HEROES. IT'S SAID VARDA CURSED THE ROYAL HOUSE OF ASHERI.
"QUEEN FREYA WAS SLAIN, WHILE KING NEBEZIAL, POISONED AND DEFORMED, SLIPPED INTO MADNESS.
"IT WAS EXPECTED THAT MELCHIAL WOULD ASCEND TO THE THRONE AND RULE APHELION.
"BUT HE FELT THE CALLING. MELCHIAL TRANSFERRED RULE OF APHELION TO THE HIGH COURT, AND JOURNEYED TO PALLADIA.
"AS VARDA'S SLAYER, HE QUICKLY ROSE TO POWER WITHIN THE CHURCH, AND CLAIMED THE HONOR OF BECOMING THE RIMAD GREGORIUS OF THE DAMANULITES.

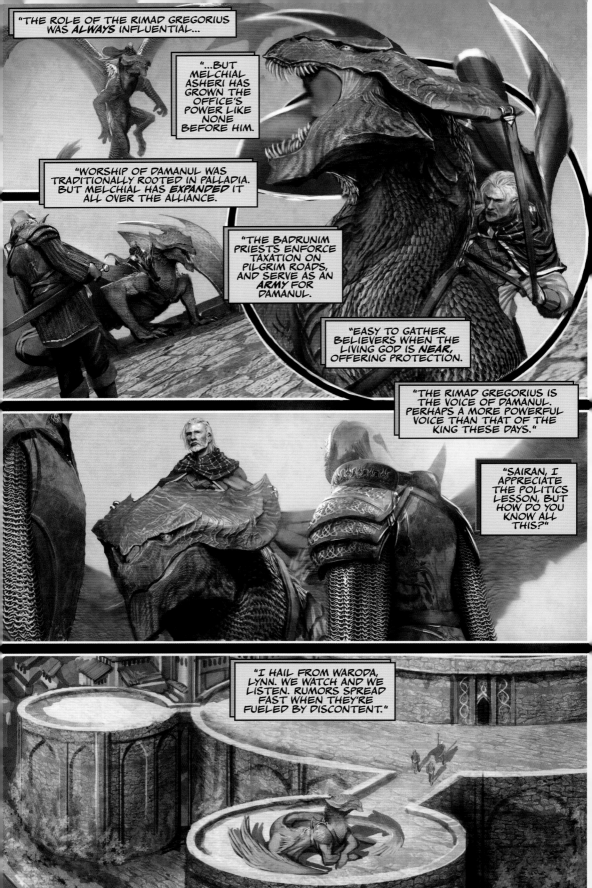

"THE ROLE OF THE RIMAD GREGORIUS WAS *ALWAYS* INFLUENTIAL...

"...BUT MELCHIAL ASHERI HAS GROWN THE OFFICE'S POWER LIKE NONE BEFORE HIM.

"WORSHIP OF DAMANUL WAS TRADITIONALLY ROOTED IN PALLADIA. BUT MELCHIAL HAS *EXPANDED* IT ALL OVER THE ALLIANCE.

"THE BADRUNIM PRIESTS ENFORCE TAXATION ON PILGRIM ROADS, AND SERVE AS AN *ARMY* FOR DAMANUL.

"EASY TO GATHER BELIEVERS WHEN THE LIVING GOD IS *NEAR*, OFFERING PROTECTION.

"THE RIMAD GREGORIUS IS THE VOICE OF DAMANUL. PERHAPS A MORE POWERFUL VOICE THAN THAT OF THE KING THESE DAYS."

"SAIRAN, I APPRECIATE THE POLITICS LESSON, BUT HOW DO YOU KNOW ALL THIS?"

"I HAIL FROM WARODA, LYNN. WE WATCH AND WE LISTEN. RUMORS SPREAD FAST WHEN THEY'RE FUELED BY DISCONTENT."

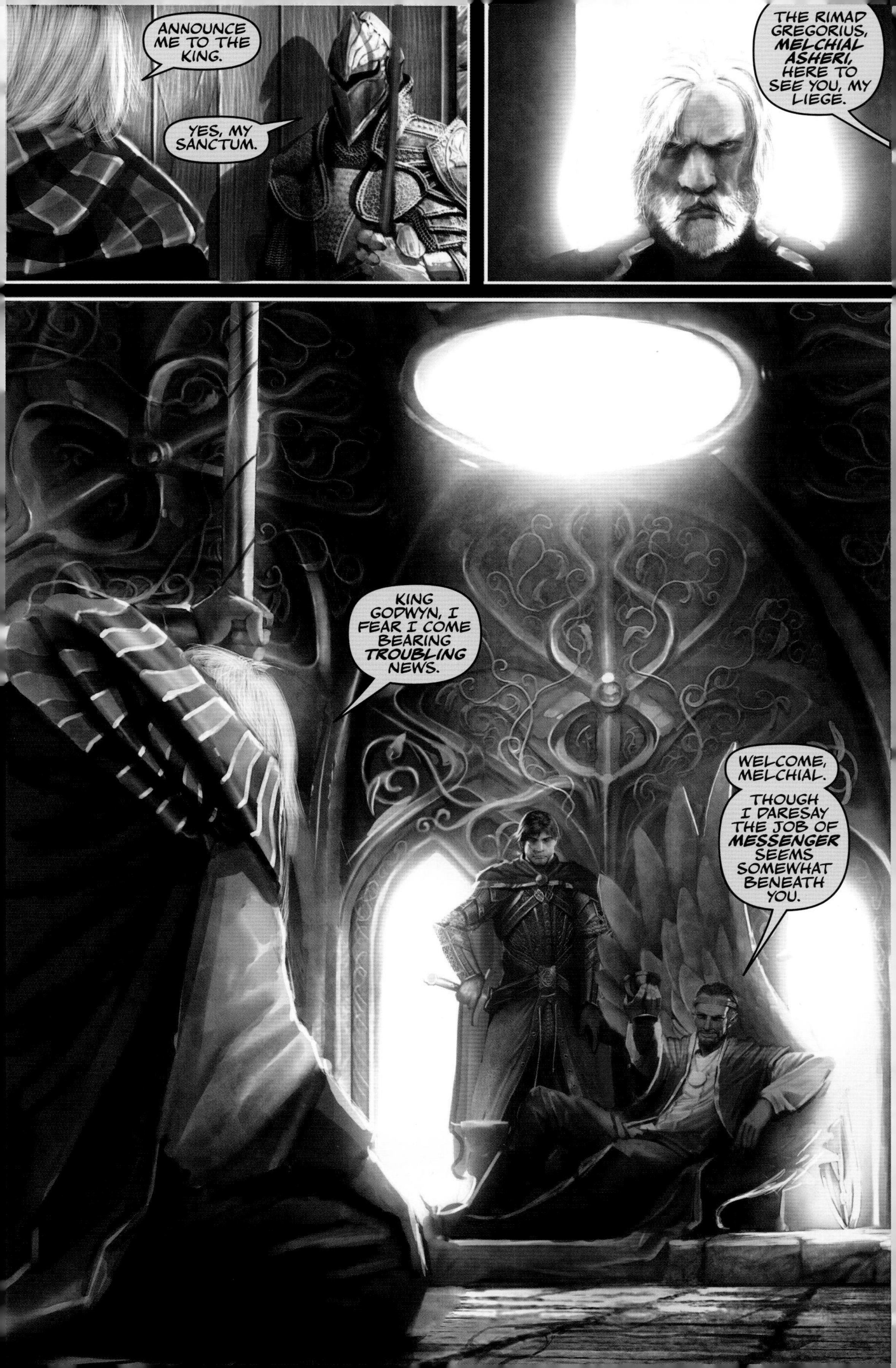
ANNOUNCE ME TO THE KING.
YES, MY SANCTUM.
THE RIMAD GREGORIUS, MELCHIAL ASHERI, HERE TO SEE YOU, MY LIEGE.
KING GODWYN, I FEAR I COME BEARING TROUBLING NEWS.
WELCOME, MELCHIAL.
THOUGH I DARESAY THE JOB OF MESSENGER SEEMS SOMEWHAT BENEATH YOU.

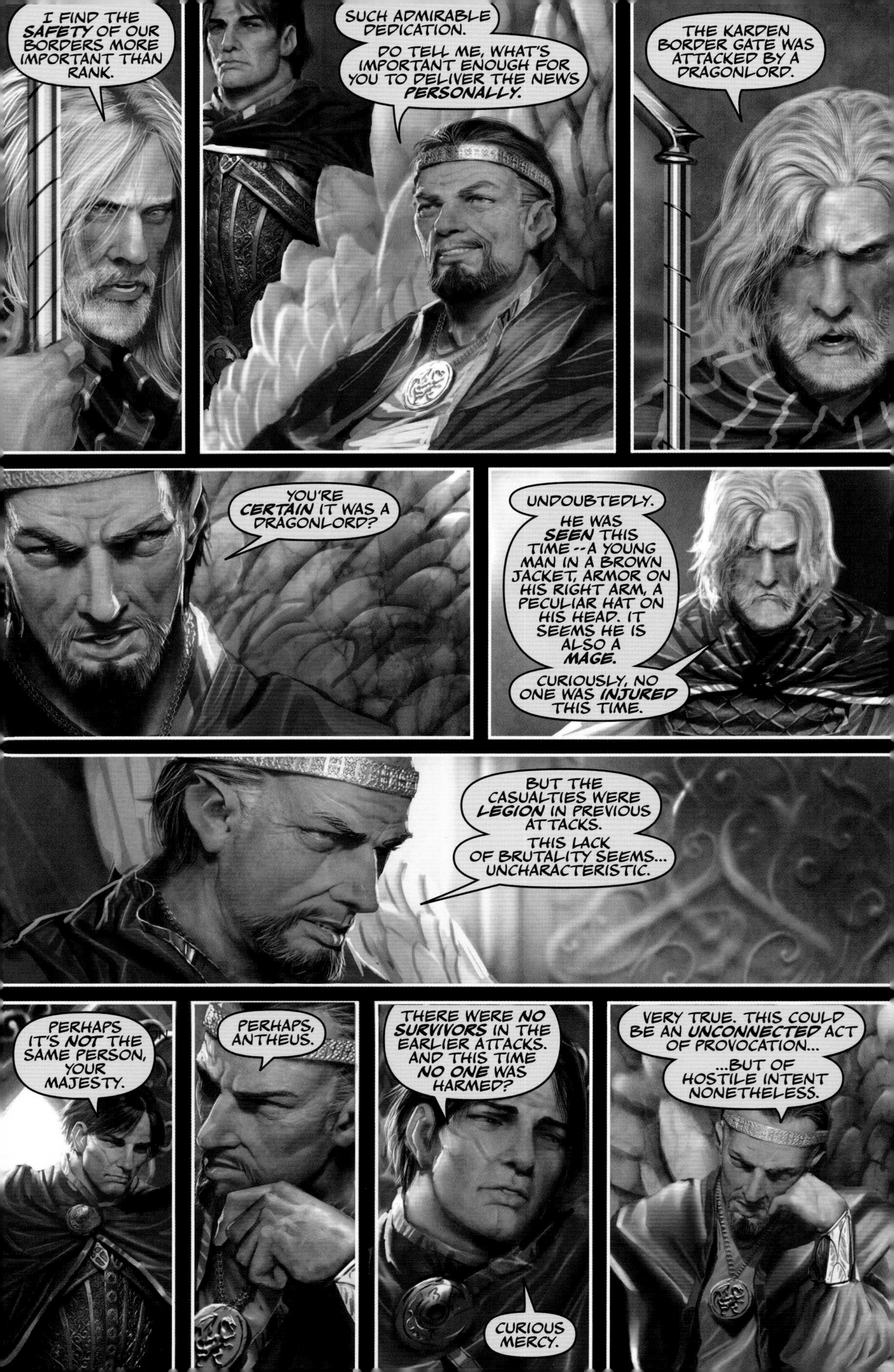
I FIND THE SAFETY OF OUR BORDERS MORE IMPORTANT THAN RANK.
SUCH ADMIRABLE DEDICATION.
DO TELL ME, WHAT'S IMPORTANT ENOUGH FOR YOU TO DELIVER THE NEWS PERSONALLY.
THE KARDEN BORDER GATE WAS ATTACKED BY A DRAGONLORD.
YOU'RE CERTAIN IT WAS A DRAGONLORD?
UNDOUBTEDLY.
HE WAS SEEN THIS TIME--A YOUNG MAN IN A BROWN JACKET, ARMOR ON HIS RIGHT ARM, A PECULIAR HAT ON HIS HEAD. IT SEEMS HE IS ALSO A MAGE.
CURIOUSLY, NO ONE WAS INJURED THIS TIME.
BUT THE CASUALTIES WERE LEGION IN PREVIOUS ATTACKS.
THIS LACK OF BRUTALITY SEEMS... UNCHARACTERISTIC.
PERHAPS IT'S NOT THE SAME PERSON, YOUR MAJESTY.
PERHAPS, ANTHEUS.
THERE WERE NO SURVIVORS IN THE EARLIER ATTACKS. AND THIS TIME NO ONE WAS HARMED?
CURIOUS MERCY.
VERY TRUE. THIS COULD BE AN UNCONNECTED ACT OF PROVOCATION...
...BUT OF HOSTILE INTENT NONETHELESS.

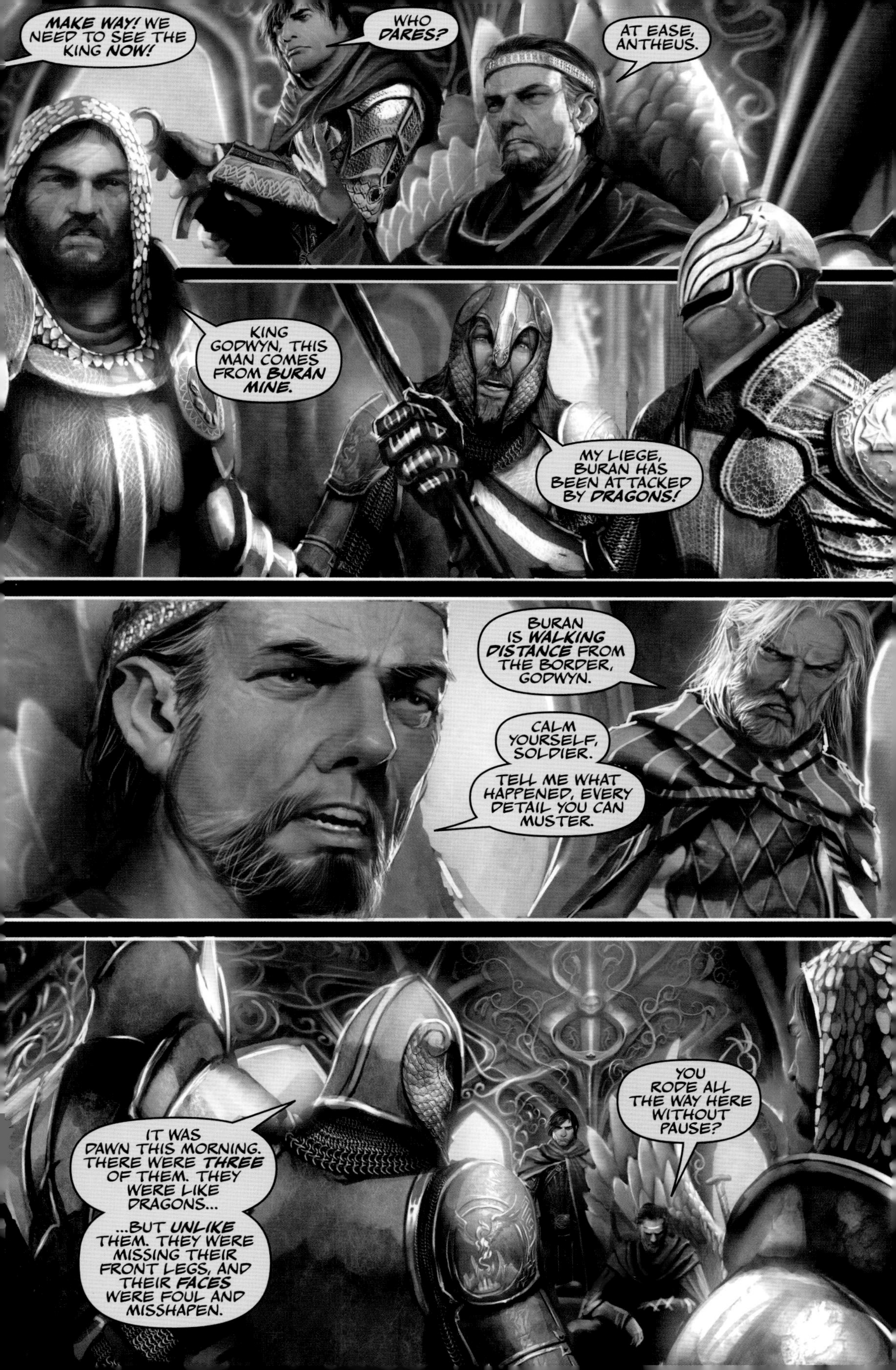
MAKE WAY! WE NEED TO SEE THE KING NOW!
WHO DARES?
AT EASE, ANTHEUS.
KING GODWYN, THIS MAN COMES FROM BURAN MINE.
MY LIEGE, BURAN HAS BEEN ATTACKED BY DRAGONS!
BURAN IS WALKING DISTANCE FROM THE BORDER, GODWYN.
CALM YOURSELF, SOLDIER.
TELL ME WHAT HAPPENED, EVERY DETAIL YOU CAN MUSTER.
IT WAS DAWN THIS MORNING. THERE WERE THREE OF THEM. THEY WERE LIKE DRAGONS...
...BUT UNLIKE THEM. THEY WERE MISSING THEIR FRONT LEGS, AND THEIR FACES WERE FOUL AND MISSHAPEN.
YOU RODE ALL THE WAY HERE WITHOUT PAUSE?

MY PEOPLE NEED *HELP*, MY LIEGE!

THE BEASTS WERE HEAVILY SCALED AND LIGHTNING FAST. MY COMMANDER BADE ME GIVE YOU *THIS*...

...A SCALE SHED BY ONE OF THE CREATURES.

I WONDER, DID YOU SEE A YOUNG MAN IN BROWN LEATHER, ARMOR TO ONE SIDE, AND AN UNUSUAL CAP?

I *DID*. JUST AS WE WERE ESCAPING, WE ENCOUNTERED SOMEONE OF THAT DESCRIPTION IN THE PASS.

HE SCARCELY SEEMED *AFRAID* OF THE DRAGON.

YOU SEE? THE *SAME* MAN WHO ATTACKED THE BORDER GATE!

I'M LEFT WITH LITTLE CHOICE BUT TO PLACE A *BOUNTY* ON THE MAN'S HEAD.

TELL LADY ANDREA TO TAKE HER SQUADRON TO BURAN. *DESTROY* THESE ROGUE DRAGONS, IF THEY'RE STILL PRESENT. THEN I WANT THE WOUNDED EVACUATED.

SOLDIER, YOU HAVE BEEN OF GREAT SERVICE TO THE KINGDOM. WHAT IS YOUR NAME?

ARTHUR, SIRE. ARTHUR FELDENSTROM.

THE KINGDOM IS IN *PERIL*, MAJESTY, JUST AS I WARNED YOU.

LEAVE US NOW, ARTHUR. YOUR RIDE WAS LONG, YOU MUST BE *STARVING*.

GUARD, SHOW HIM TO THE DINING HALL.

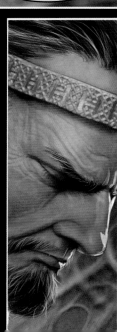

WHAT OF *YOU*, MELCHIAL?

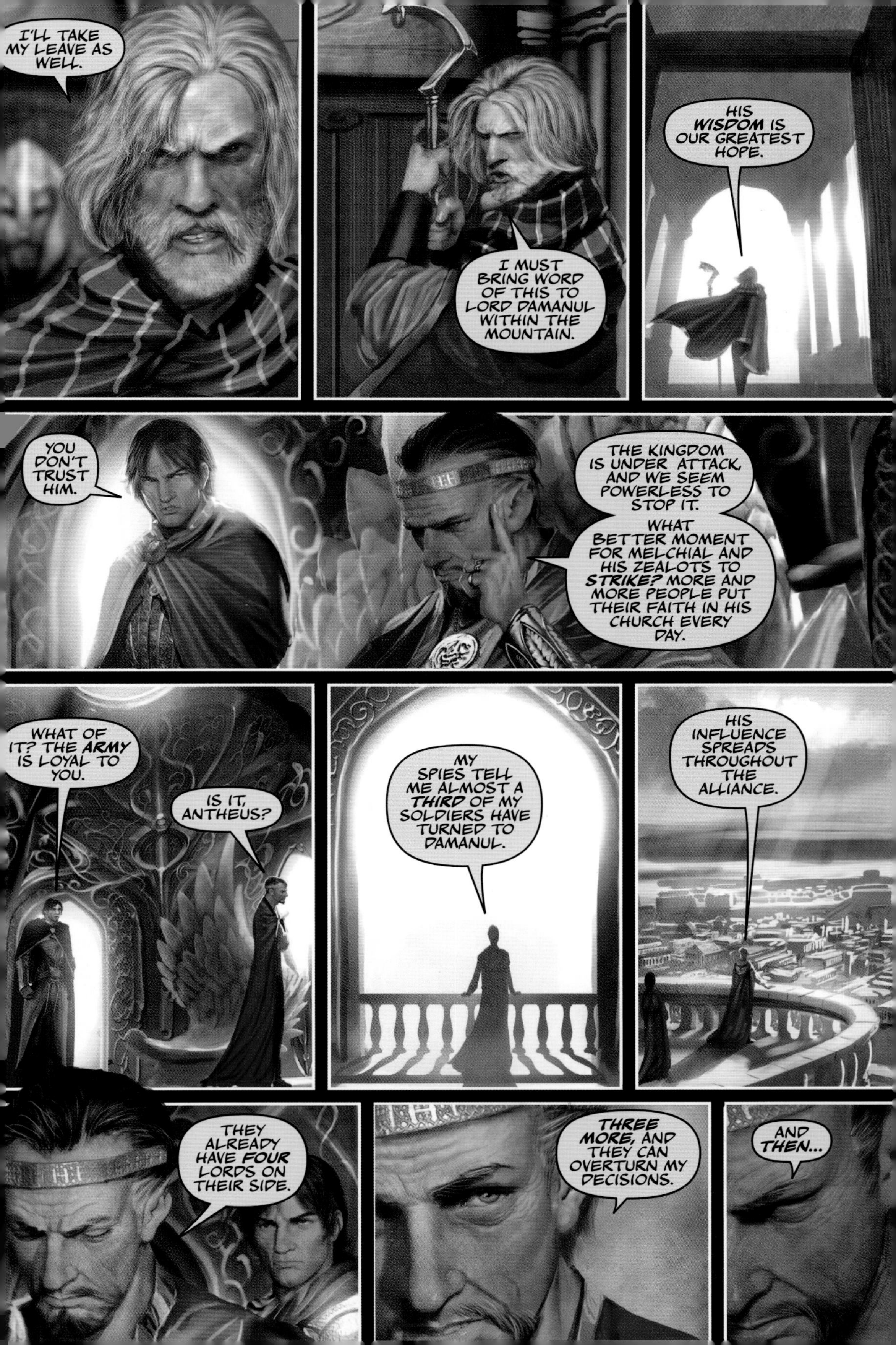
I'LL TAKE MY LEAVE AS WELL.
I MUST BRING WORD OF THIS TO LORD DAMANUL WITHIN THE MOUNTAIN.
HIS WISDOM IS OUR GREATEST HOPE.
YOU DON'T TRUST HIM.
THE KINGDOM IS UNDER ATTACK, AND WE SEEM POWERLESS TO STOP IT.
WHAT BETTER MOMENT FOR MELCHIAL AND HIS ZEALOTS TO STRIKE? MORE AND MORE PEOPLE PUT THEIR FAITH IN HIS CHURCH EVERY DAY.
WHAT OF IT? THE ARMY IS LOYAL TO YOU.
IS IT, ANTHEUS?
MY SPIES TELL ME ALMOST A THIRD OF MY SOLDIERS HAVE TURNED TO DAMANUL.
HIS INFLUENCE SPREADS THROUGHOUT THE ALLIANCE.
THEY ALREADY HAVE FOUR LORDS ON THEIR SIDE.
THREE MORE, AND THEY CAN OVERTURN MY DECISIONS.
AND THEN...

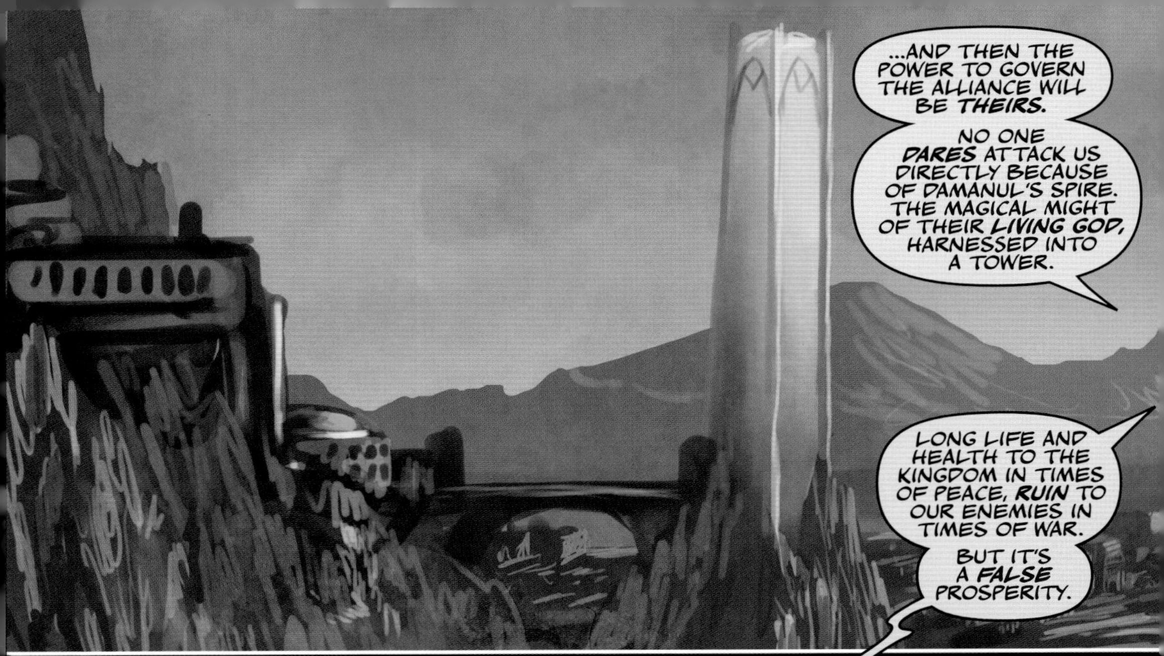
...AND THEN THE POWER TO GOVERN THE ALLIANCE WILL BE THEIRS.
NO ONE DARES ATTACK US DIRECTLY BECAUSE OF DAMANUL'S SPIRE. THE MAGICAL MIGHT OF THEIR LIVING GOD, HARNESSED INTO A TOWER.
LONG LIFE AND HEALTH TO THE KINGDOM IN TIMES OF PEACE, RUIN TO OUR ENEMIES IN TIMES OF WAR.
BUT IT'S A FALSE PROSPERITY.

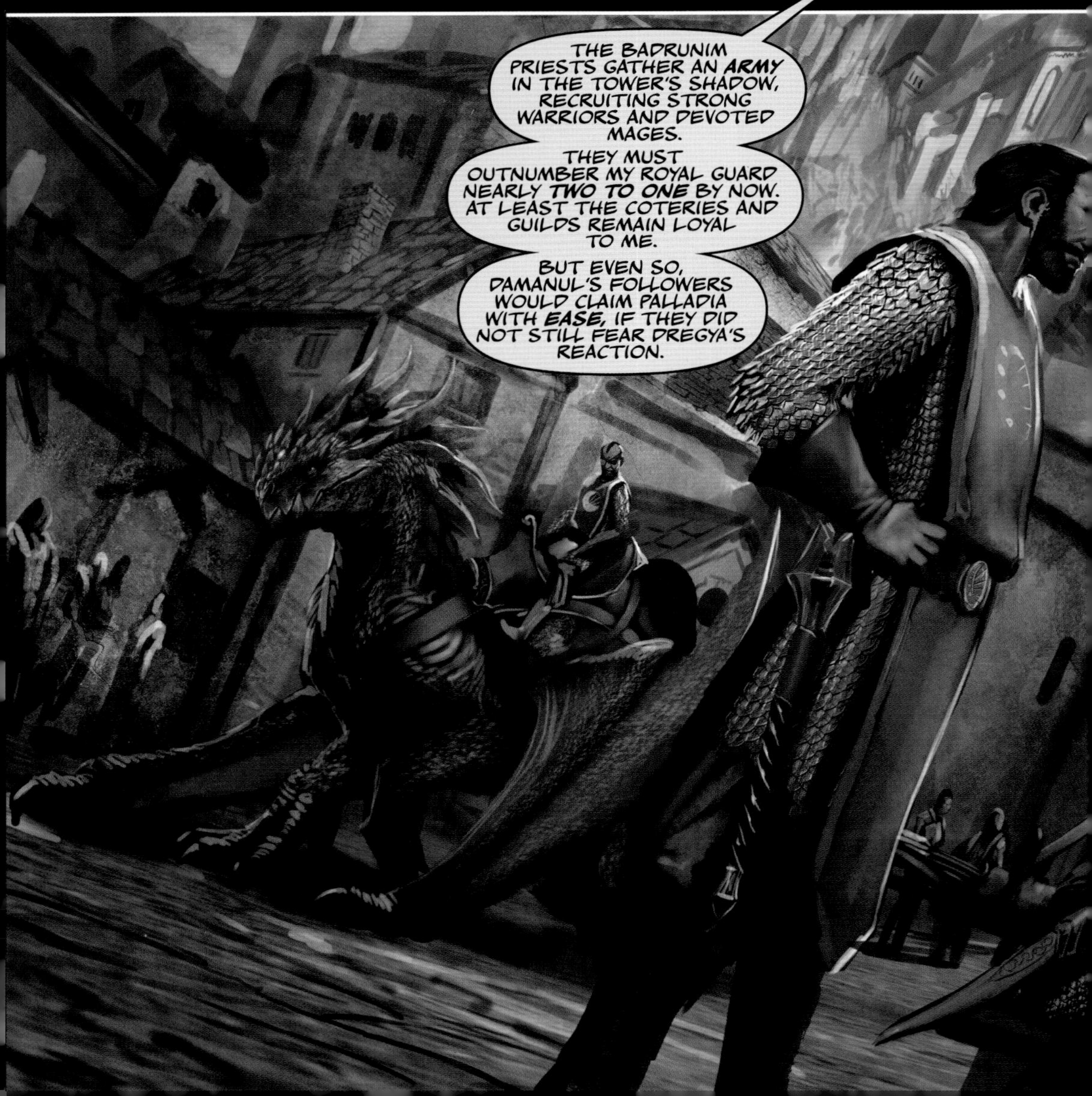
THE BADRUNIM PRIESTS GATHER AN ARMY IN THE TOWER'S SHADOW, RECRUITING STRONG WARRIORS AND DEVOTED MAGES.
THEY MUST OUTNUMBER MY ROYAL GUARD NEARLY TWO TO ONE BY NOW. AT LEAST THE COTERIES AND GUILDS REMAIN LOYAL TO ME.
BUT EVEN SO, DAMANUL'S FOLLOWERS WOULD CLAIM PALLADIA WITH EASE, IF THEY DID NOT STILL FEAR DREGYA'S REACTION.

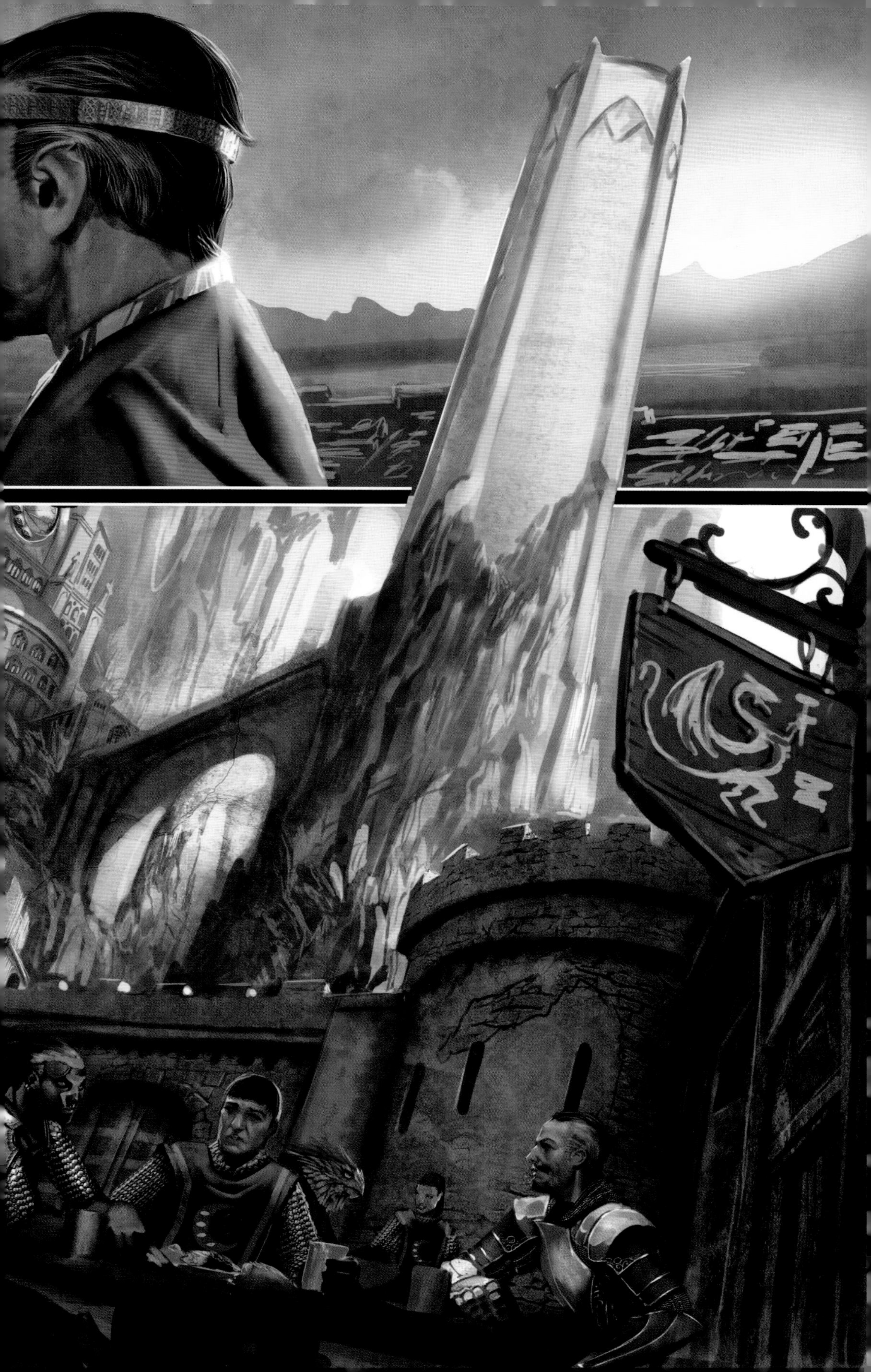

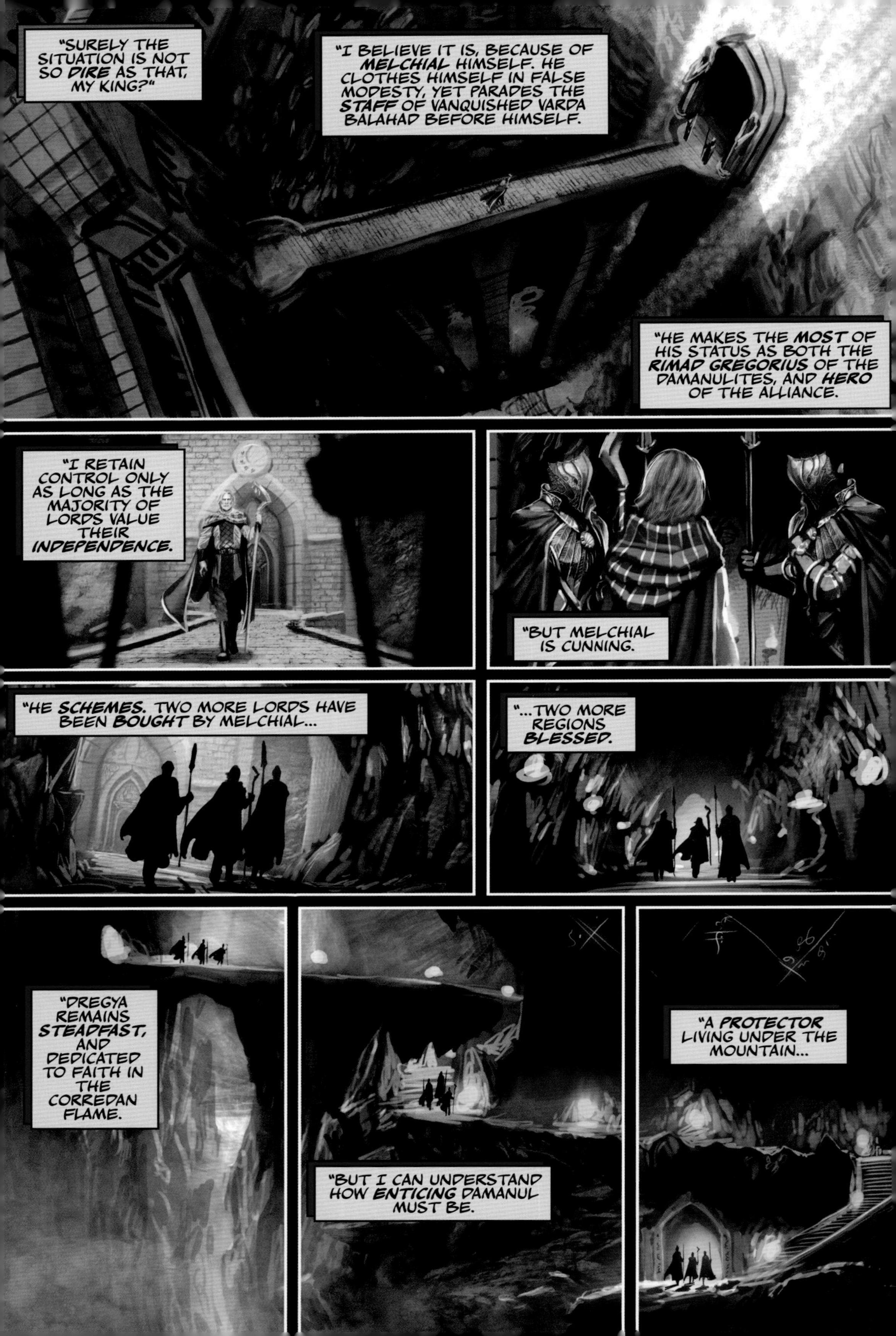

"SURELY THE SITUATION IS NOT SO DIRE AS THAT, MY KING?"
"I BELIEVE IT IS, BECAUSE OF MELCHIAL HIMSELF. HE CLOTHES HIMSELF IN FALSE MODESTY, YET PARADES THE STAFF OF VANQUISHED VARDA BALAHAD BEFORE HIMSELF.
"HE MAKES THE MOST OF HIS STATUS AS BOTH THE RIMAD GREGORIUS OF THE DAMANULITES, AND HERO OF THE ALLIANCE.
"I RETAIN CONTROL ONLY AS LONG AS THE MAJORITY OF LORDS VALUE THEIR INDEPENDENCE.
"BUT MELCHIAL IS CUNNING.
"HE SCHEMES. TWO MORE LORDS HAVE BEEN BOUGHT BY MELCHIAL...
"...TWO MORE REGIONS BLESSED.
"DREGYA REMAINS STEADFAST, AND DEDICATED TO FAITH IN THE CORREDAN FLAME.
"BUT I CAN UNDERSTAND HOW ENTICING DAMANUL MUST BE.
"A PROTECTOR LIVING UNDER THE MOUNTAIN...

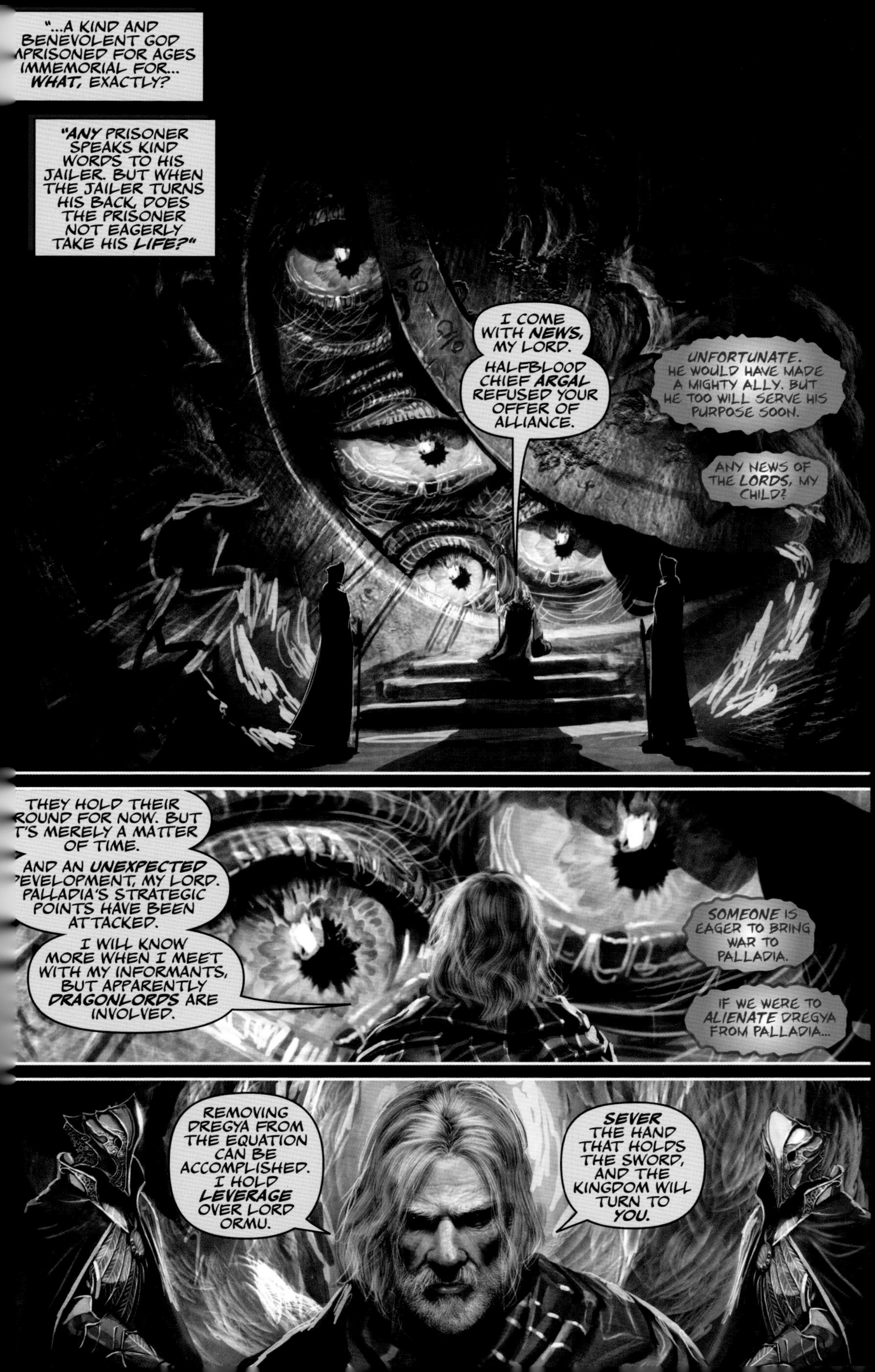
"...A KIND AND BENEVOLENT GOD IMPRISONED FOR AGES IMMEMORIAL FOR... WHAT, EXACTLY?
"ANY PRISONER SPEAKS KIND WORDS TO HIS JAILER. BUT WHEN THE JAILER TURNS HIS BACK, DOES THE PRISONER NOT EAGERLY TAKE HIS LIFE?"
I COME WITH NEWS, MY LORD.
HALFBLOOD CHIEF ARGAL REFUSED YOUR OFFER OF ALLIANCE.
UNFORTUNATE. HE WOULD HAVE MADE A MIGHTY ALLY. BUT HE TOO WILL SERVE HIS PURPOSE SOON.
ANY NEWS OF THE LORDS, MY CHILD?
THEY HOLD THEIR GROUND FOR NOW. BUT IT'S MERELY A MATTER OF TIME.
AND AN UNEXPECTED DEVELOPMENT, MY LORD. PALLADIA'S STRATEGIC POINTS HAVE BEEN ATTACKED.
I WILL KNOW MORE WHEN I MEET WITH MY INFORMANTS, BUT APPARENTLY DRAGONLORDS ARE INVOLVED.
SOMEONE IS EAGER TO BRING WAR TO PALLADIA.
IF WE WERE TO ALIENATE DREGYA FROM PALLADIA...
REMOVING DREGYA FROM THE EQUATION CAN BE ACCOMPLISHED. I HOLD LEVERAGE OVER LORD ORMU.
SEVER THE HAND THAT HOLDS THE SWORD, AND THE KINGDOM WILL TURN TO YOU.

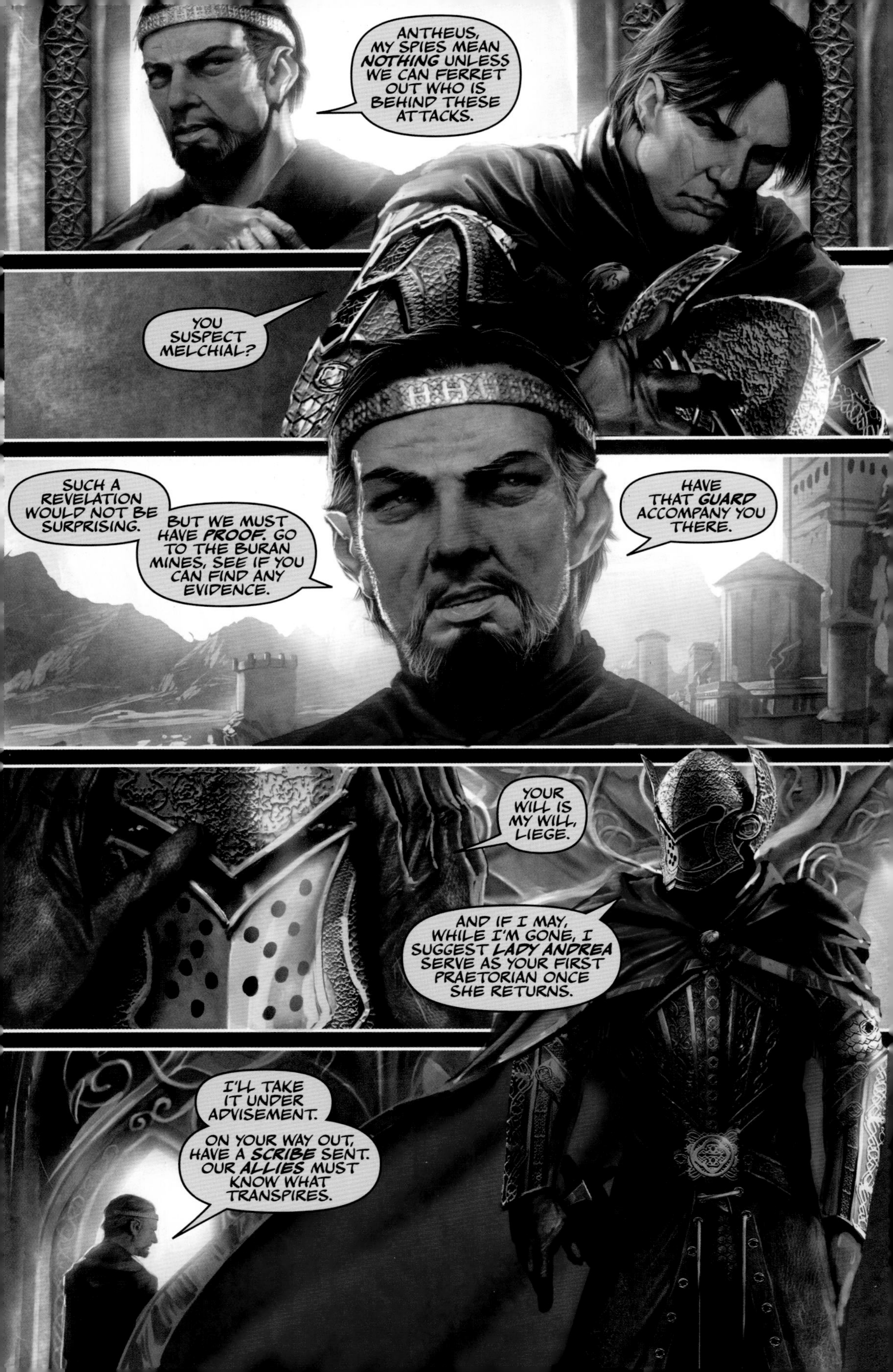
ANTHEUS, MY SPIES MEAN NOTHING UNLESS WE CAN FERRET OUT WHO IS BEHIND THESE ATTACKS.
YOU SUSPECT MELCHIAL?
SUCH A REVELATION WOULD NOT BE SURPRISING.
BUT WE MUST HAVE PROOF. GO TO THE BURAN MINES, SEE IF YOU CAN FIND ANY EVIDENCE.
HAVE THAT GUARD ACCOMPANY YOU THERE.
YOUR WILL IS MY WILL, LIEGE.
AND IF I MAY, WHILE I'M GONE, I SUGGEST LADY ANDREA SERVE AS YOUR FIRST PRAETORIAN ONCE SHE RETURNS.
I'LL TAKE IT UNDER ADVISEMENT.
ON YOUR WAY OUT, HAVE A SCRIBE SENT. OUR ALLIES MUST KNOW WHAT TRANSPIRES.

ANY GOOD NEWS?

ACCORDING TO THIS, I NEED A SARDAHEIM CRAFTER TO REPAIR THE RUNEGLASS, AND I'LL BE BACK ON TRACK.

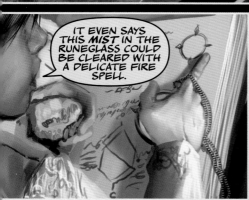

IT EVEN SAYS THIS MIST IN THE RUNEGLASS COULD BE CLEARED WITH A DELICATE FIRE SPELL.

OH, THE SMALL IRONIES OF LIFE.

"DELICATE" IS NOT MY FORTÉ.

SO THE OPTIONS FOR FINDING A SARDAHEIM CRAFTER WOULD SEEM TO BE PUSH ON TO PALLADIA, OR TRY FOR WADE.

JUST... LOVELY.

WHAT TROUBLES YOU?

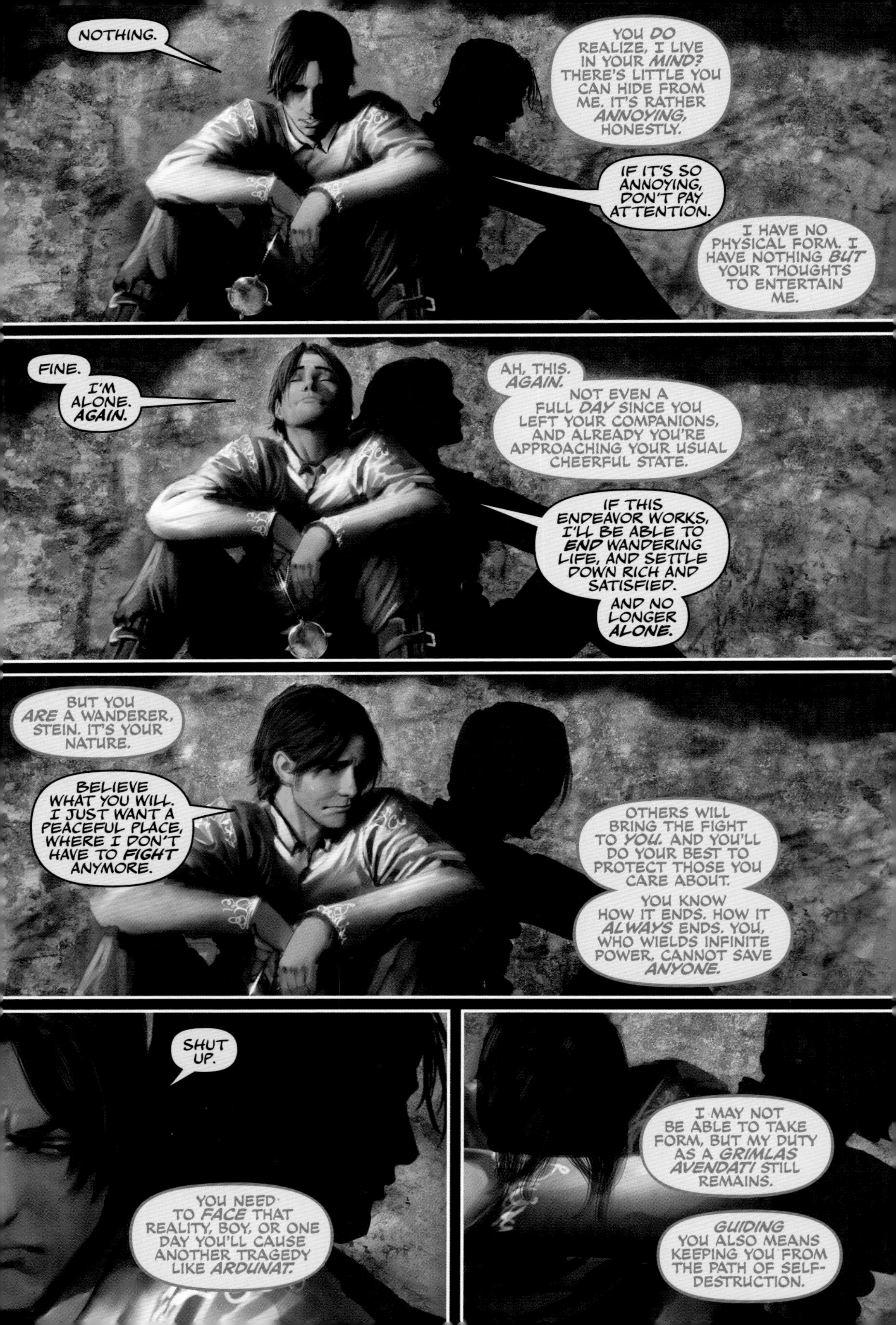
NOTHING.
YOU DO REALIZE, I LIVE IN YOUR MIND? THERE'S LITTLE YOU CAN HIDE FROM ME. IT'S RATHER ANNOYING, HONESTLY.
IF IT'S SO ANNOYING, DON'T PAY ATTENTION.
I HAVE NO PHYSICAL FORM. I HAVE NOTHING BUT YOUR THOUGHTS TO ENTERTAIN ME.
FINE. I'M ALONE. AGAIN.
AH, THIS. AGAIN.
NOT EVEN A FULL DAY SINCE YOU LEFT YOUR COMPANIONS, AND ALREADY YOU'RE APPROACHING YOUR USUAL CHEERFUL STATE.
IF THIS ENDEAVOR WORKS, I'LL BE ABLE TO END WANDERING LIFE, AND SETTLE DOWN RICH AND SATISFIED.
AND NO LONGER ALONE.
BUT YOU ARE A WANDERER, STEIN. IT'S YOUR NATURE.
BELIEVE WHAT YOU WILL. I JUST WANT A PEACEFUL PLACE, WHERE I DON'T HAVE TO FIGHT ANYMORE.
OTHERS WILL BRING THE FIGHT TO YOU. AND YOU'LL DO YOUR BEST TO PROTECT THOSE YOU CARE ABOUT.
YOU KNOW HOW IT ENDS. HOW IT ALWAYS ENDS. YOU, WHO WIELDS INFINITE POWER, CANNOT SAVE ANYONE.
SHUT UP.
YOU NEED TO FACE THAT REALITY, BOY, OR ONE DAY YOU'LL CAUSE ANOTHER TRAGEDY LIKE ARDUNAT.
I MAY NOT BE ABLE TO TAKE FORM, BUT MY DUTY AS A GRIMLAS AVENDATI STILL REMAINS.
GUIDING YOU ALSO MEANS KEEPING YOU FROM THE PATH OF SELF-DESTRUCTION.

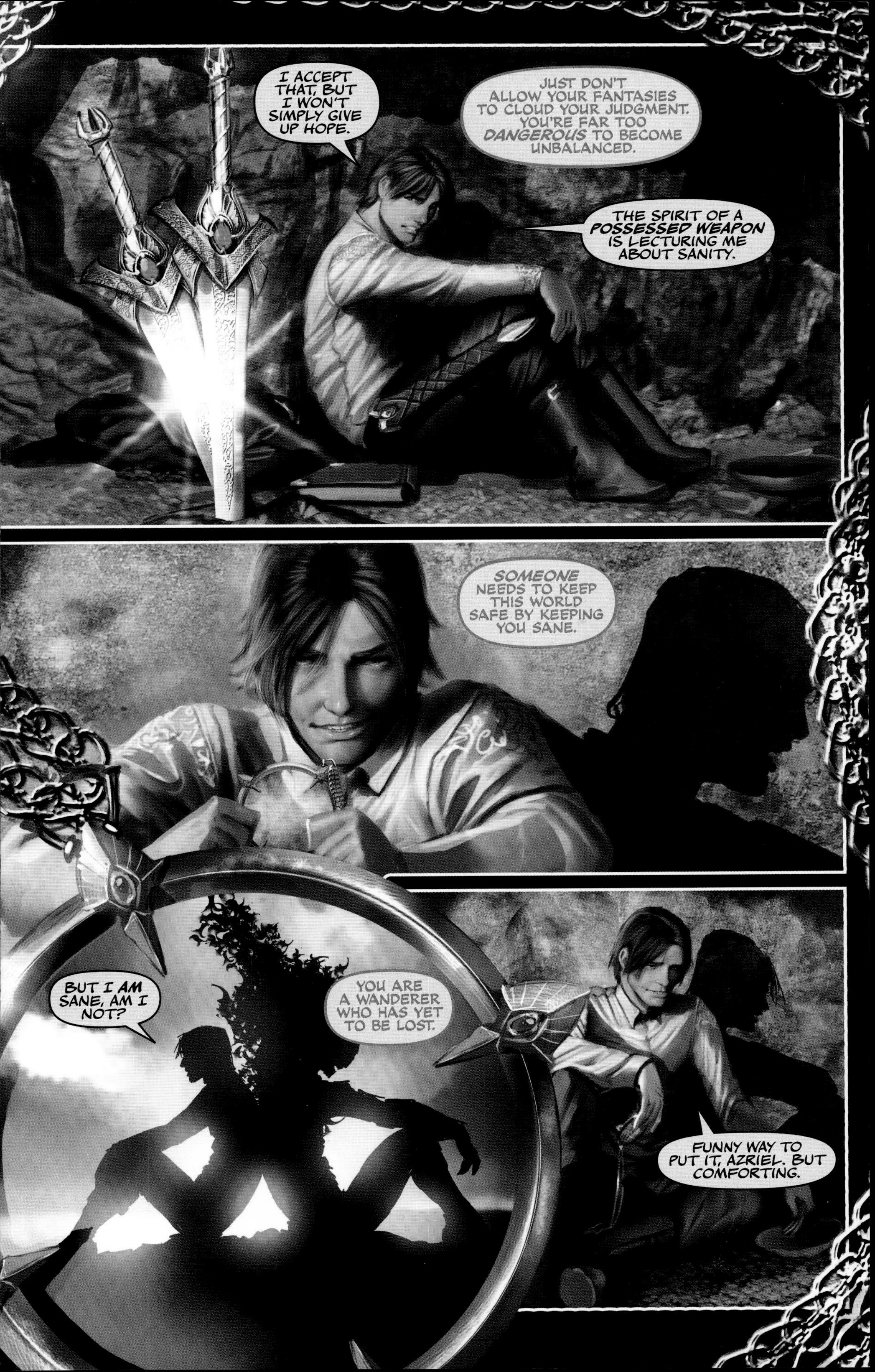
I ACCEPT THAT, BUT I WON'T SIMPLY GIVE UP HOPE.
JUST DON'T ALLOW YOUR FANTASIES TO CLOUD YOUR JUDGMENT. YOU'RE FAR TOO DANGEROUS TO BECOME UNBALANCED.
THE SPIRIT OF A POSSESSED WEAPON IS LECTURING ME ABOUT SANITY.
SOMEONE NEEDS TO KEEP THIS WORLD SAFE BY KEEPING YOU SANE.
BUT I AM SANE, AM I NOT?
YOU ARE A WANDERER WHO HAS YET TO BE LOST.
FUNNY WAY TO PUT IT, AZRIEL. BUT COMFORTING.

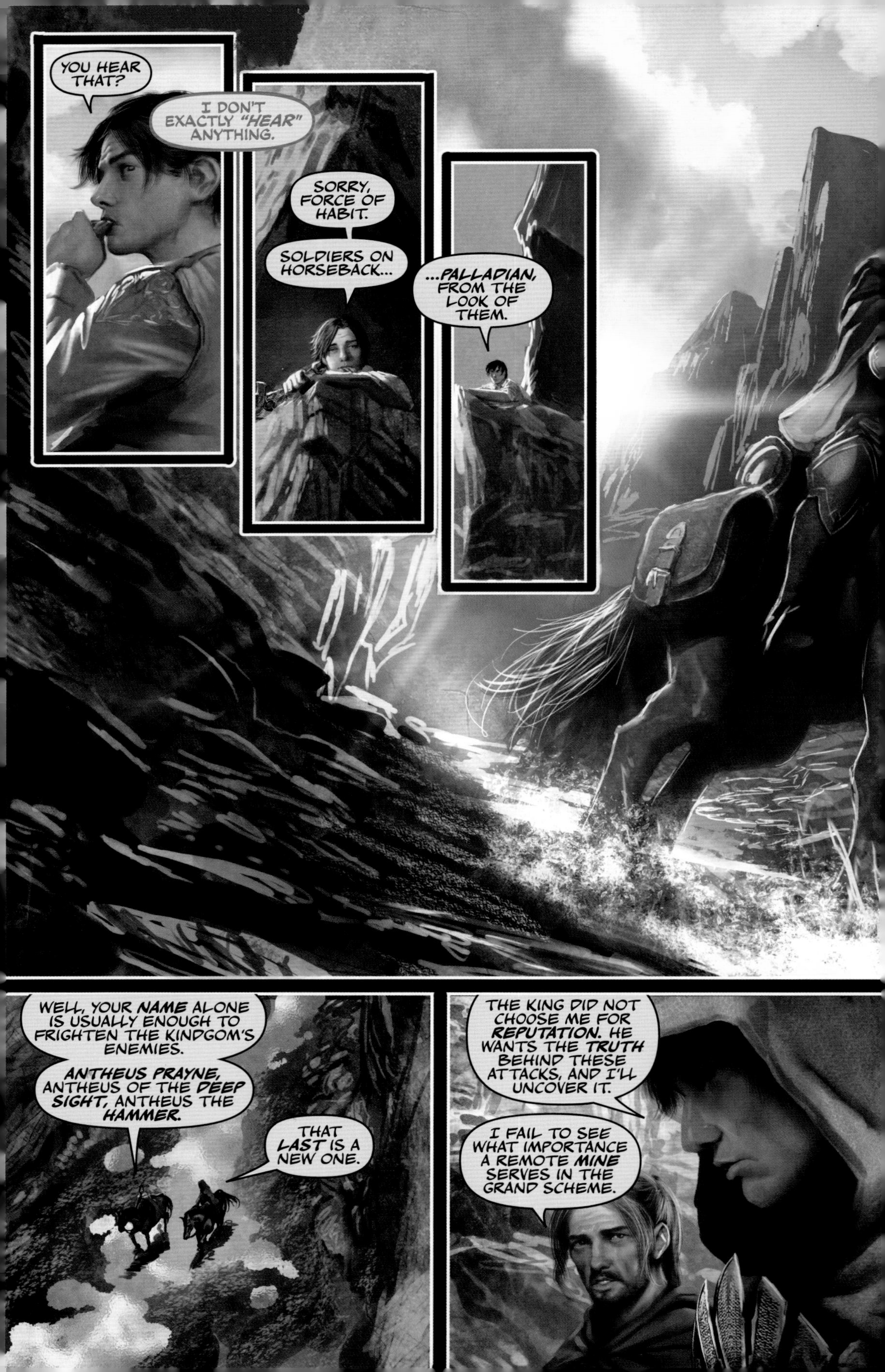
YOU HEAR THAT?
I DON'T EXACTLY "HEAR" ANYTHING.
SORRY, FORCE OF HABIT.
SOLDIERS ON HORSEBACK...
...PALLADIAN, FROM THE LOOK OF THEM.
WELL, YOUR NAME ALONE IS USUALLY ENOUGH TO FRIGHTEN THE KINDGOM'S ENEMIES.
ANTHEUS PRAYNE, ANTHEUS OF THE DEEP SIGHT, ANTHEUS THE HAMMER.
THAT LAST IS A NEW ONE.
THE KING DID NOT CHOOSE ME FOR REPUTATION. HE WANTS THE TRUTH BEHIND THESE ATTACKS, AND I'LL UNCOVER IT.
I FAIL TO SEE WHAT IMPORTANCE A REMOTE MINE SERVES IN THE GRAND SCHEME.

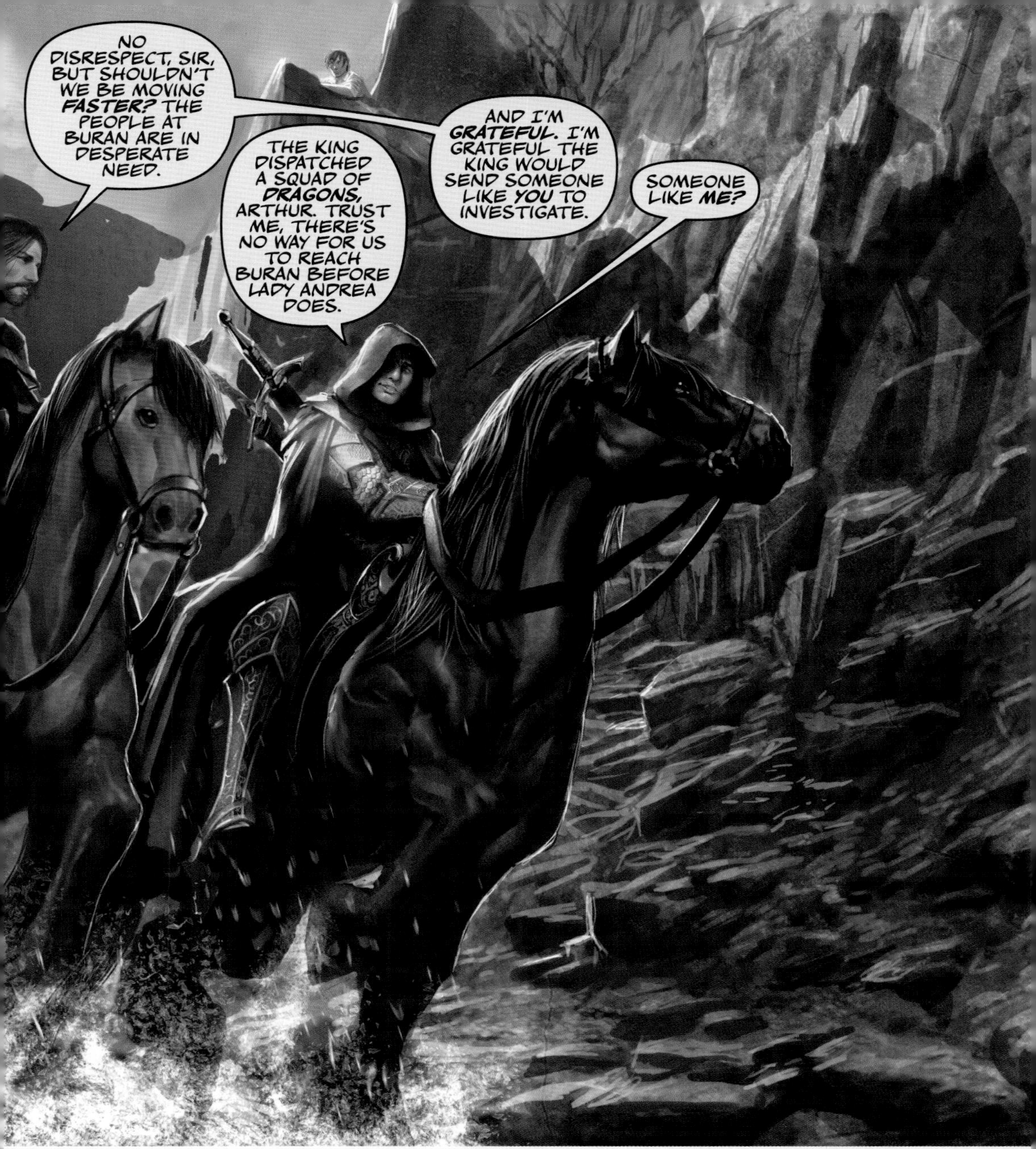
NO DISRESPECT, SIR, BUT SHOULDN'T WE BE MOVING FASTER? THE PEOPLE AT BURAN ARE IN DESPERATE NEED.
THE KING DISPATCHED A SQUAD OF DRAGONS, ARTHUR. TRUST ME, THERE'S NO WAY FOR US TO REACH BURAN BEFORE LADY ANDREA DOES.
AND I'M GRATEFUL. I'M GRATEFUL THE KING WOULD SEND SOMEONE LIKE YOU TO INVESTIGATE.
SOMEONE LIKE ME?

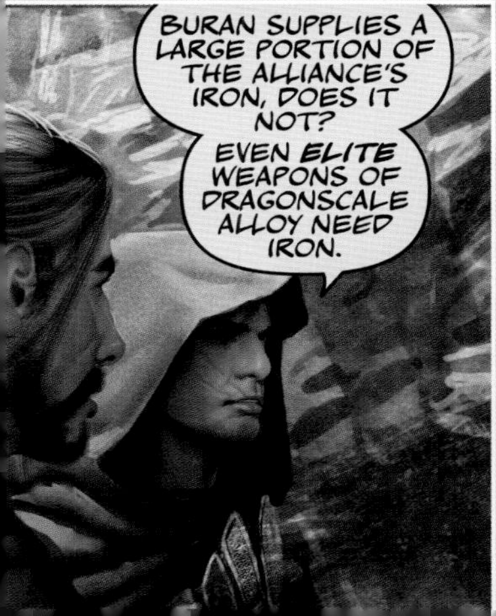
BURAN SUPPLIES A LARGE PORTION OF THE ALLIANCE'S IRON, DOES IT NOT?
EVEN ELITE WEAPONS OF DRAGONSCALE ALLOY NEED IRON.

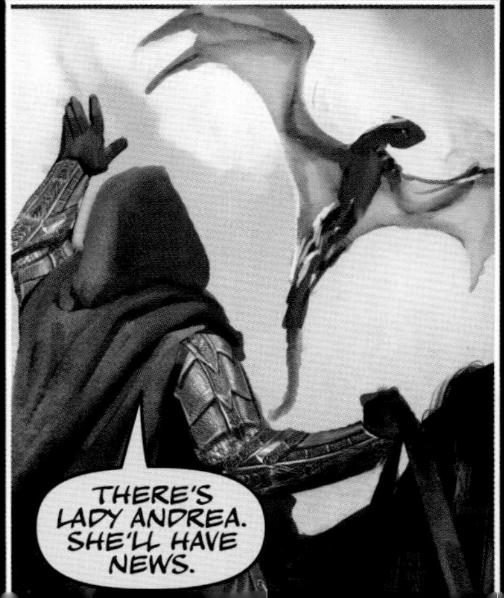
THERE'S LADY ANDREA. SHE'LL HAVE NEWS.

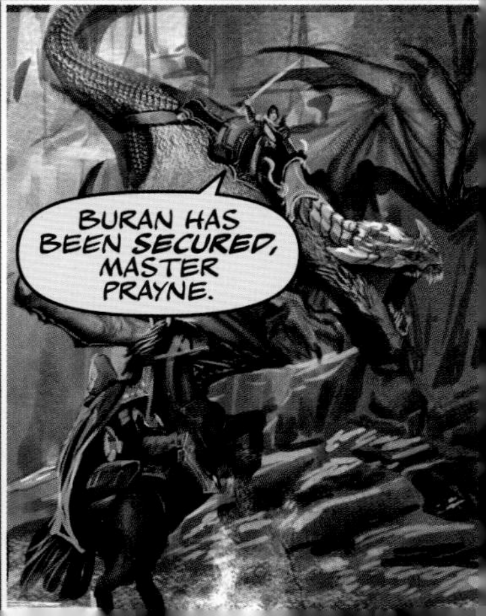
BURAN HAS BEEN SECURED, MASTER PRAYNE.

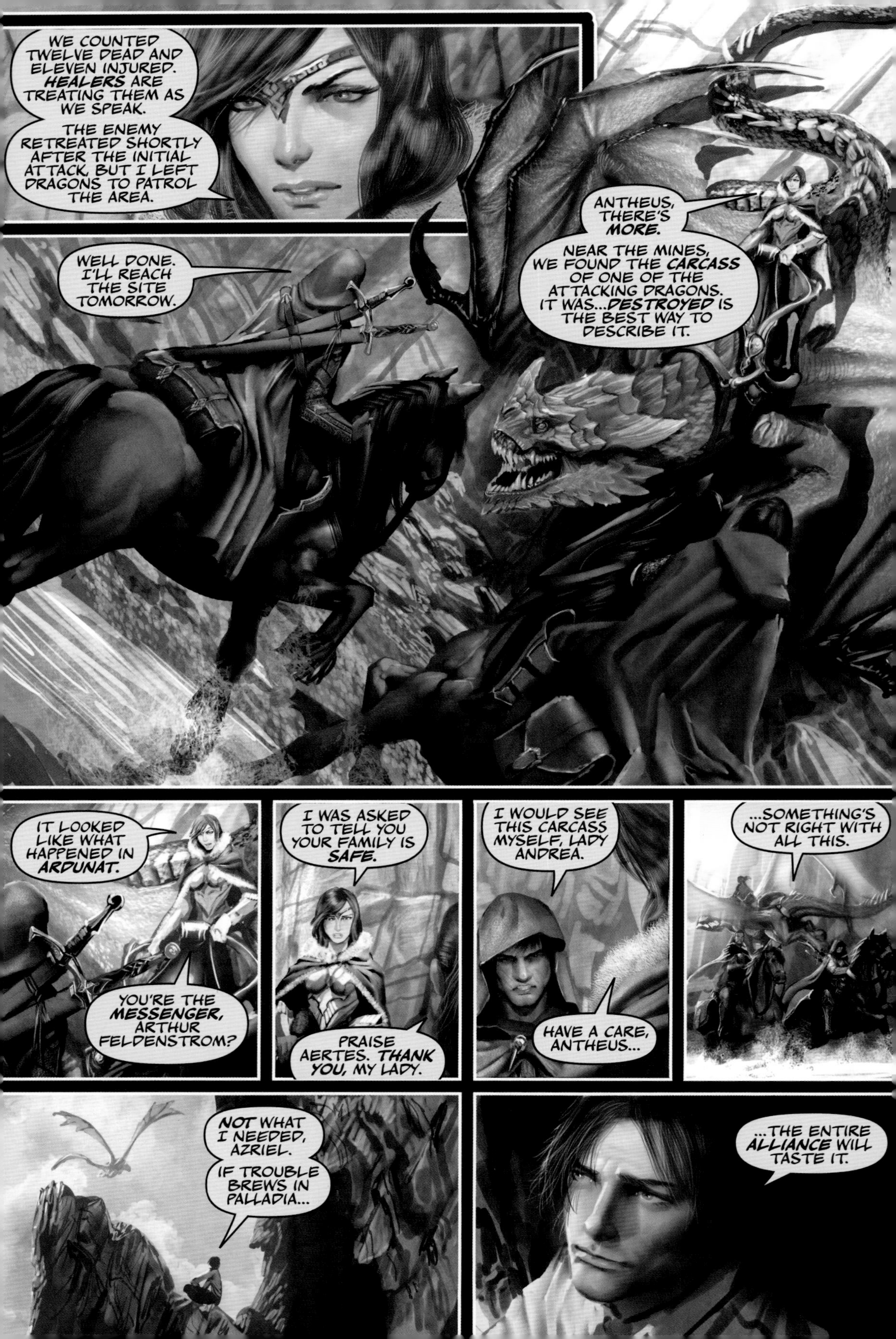
WE COUNTED TWELVE DEAD AND ELEVEN INJURED. HEALERS ARE TREATING THEM AS WE SPEAK.
THE ENEMY RETREATED SHORTLY AFTER THE INITIAL ATTACK, BUT I LEFT DRAGONS TO PATROL THE AREA.
WELL DONE. I'LL REACH THE SITE TOMORROW.
ANTHEUS, THERE'S MORE.
NEAR THE MINES, WE FOUND THE CARCASS OF ONE OF THE ATTACKING DRAGONS. IT WAS...DESTROYED IS THE BEST WAY TO DESCRIBE IT.
IT LOOKED LIKE WHAT HAPPENED IN ARDUNAT.
YOU'RE THE MESSENGER, ARTHUR FELDENSTROM?
I WAS ASKED TO TELL YOU YOUR FAMILY IS SAFE.
PRAISE AERTES. THANK YOU, MY LADY.
I WOULD SEE THIS CARCASS MYSELF, LADY ANDREA.
HAVE A CARE, ANTHEUS...
...SOMETHING'S NOT RIGHT WITH ALL THIS.
NOT WHAT I NEEDED, AZRIEL.
IF TROUBLE BREWS IN PALLADIA...
...THE ENTIRE ALLIANCE WILL TASTE IT.

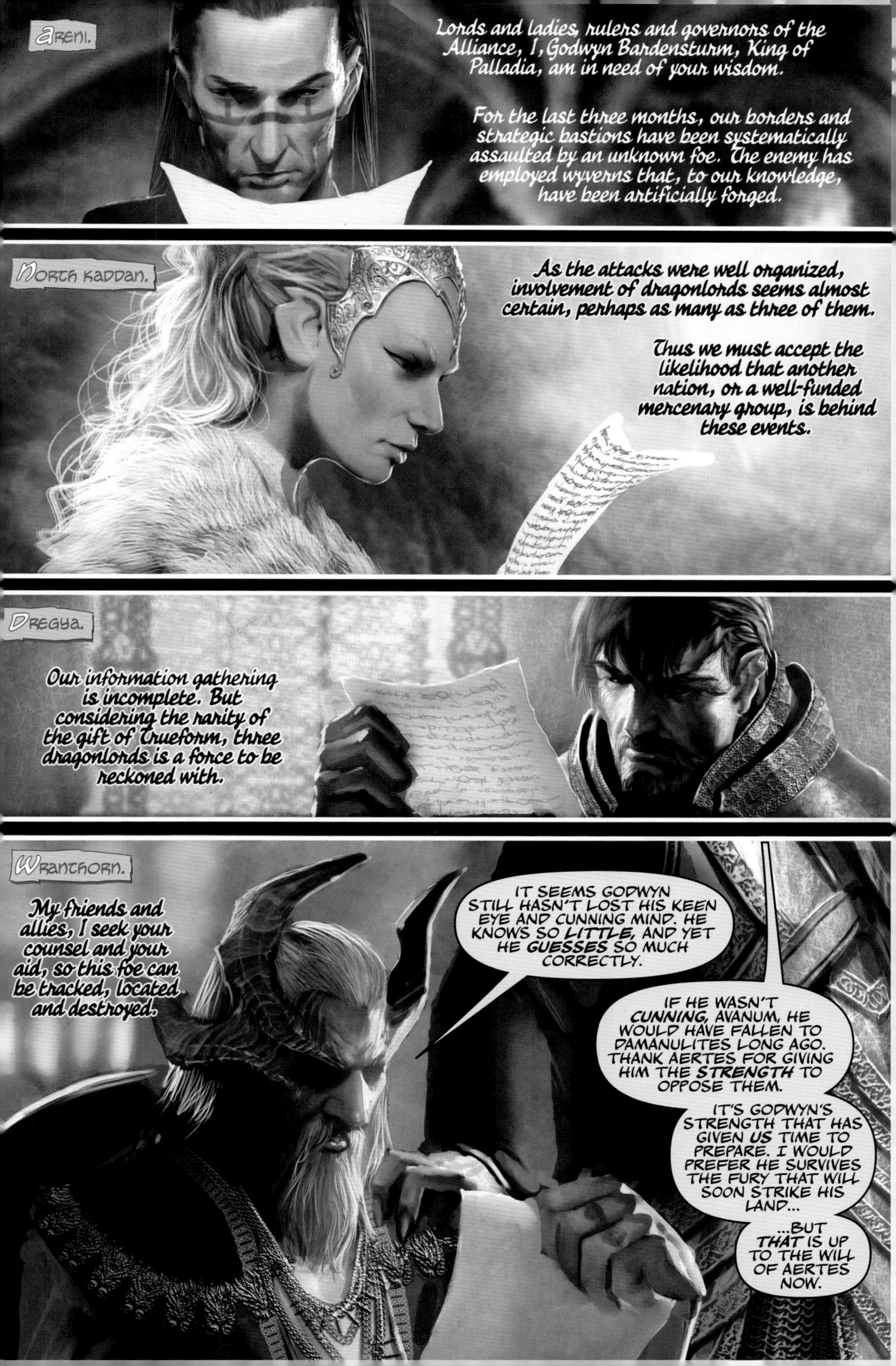
Areni.
Lords and ladies, rulers and governors of the Alliance, I, Godwyn Bardensturm, King of Palladia, am in need of your wisdom.
For the last three months, our borders and strategic bastions have been systematically assaulted by an unknown foe. The enemy has employed wyverns that, to our knowledge, have been artificially forged.
North Kaddan.
As the attacks were well organized, involvement of dragonlords seems almost certain, perhaps as many as three of them.
Thus we must accept the likelihood that another nation, or a well-funded mercenary group, is behind these events.
Dregya.
Our information gathering is incomplete. But considering the rarity of the gift of Trueform, three dragonlords is a force to be reckoned with.
Wranthorn.
My friends and allies, I seek your counsel and your aid, so this foe can be tracked, located and destroyed.
IT SEEMS GODWYN STILL HASN'T LOST HIS KEEN EYE AND CUNNING MIND. HE KNOWS SO LITTLE, AND YET HE GUESSES SO MUCH CORRECTLY.
IF HE WASN'T CUNNING, AVANUM, HE WOULD HAVE FALLEN TO DAMANULITES LONG AGO. THANK AERTES FOR GIVING HIM THE STRENGTH TO OPPOSE THEM.
IT'S GODWYN'S STRENGTH THAT HAS GIVEN US TIME TO PREPARE. I WOULD PREFER HE SURVIVES THE FURY THAT WILL SOON STRIKE HIS LAND...
...BUT THAT IS UP TO THE WILL OF AERTES NOW.

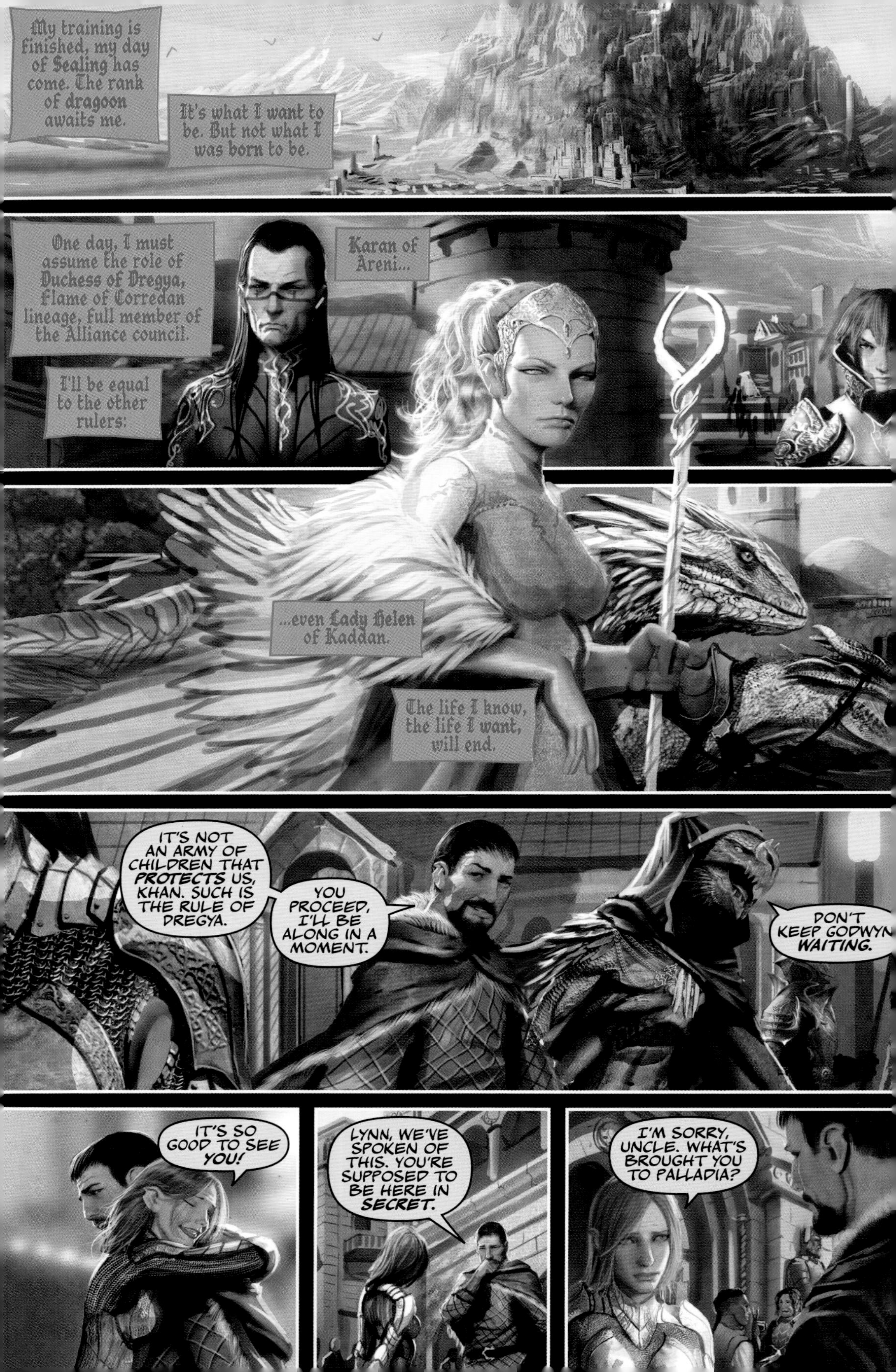
My training is finished, my day of Sealing has come. The rank of dragoon awaits me.
It's what I want to be. But not what I was born to be.
One day, I must assume the role of Duchess of Dregya, Flame of Corredan lineage, full member of the Alliance council.
Karan of Areni...
I'll be equal to the other rulers:
...even Lady Helen of Kaddan.
The life I know, the life I want, will end.
IT'S NOT AN ARMY OF CHILDREN THAT PROTECTS US, KHAN. SUCH IS THE RULE OF DREGYA.
YOU PROCEED, I'LL BE ALONG IN A MOMENT.
DON'T KEEP GODWYN WAITING.
IT'S SO GOOD TO SEE YOU!
LYNN, WE'VE SPOKEN OF THIS. YOU'RE SUPPOSED TO BE HERE IN SECRET.
I'M SORRY, UNCLE. WHAT'S BROUGHT YOU TO PALLADIA?

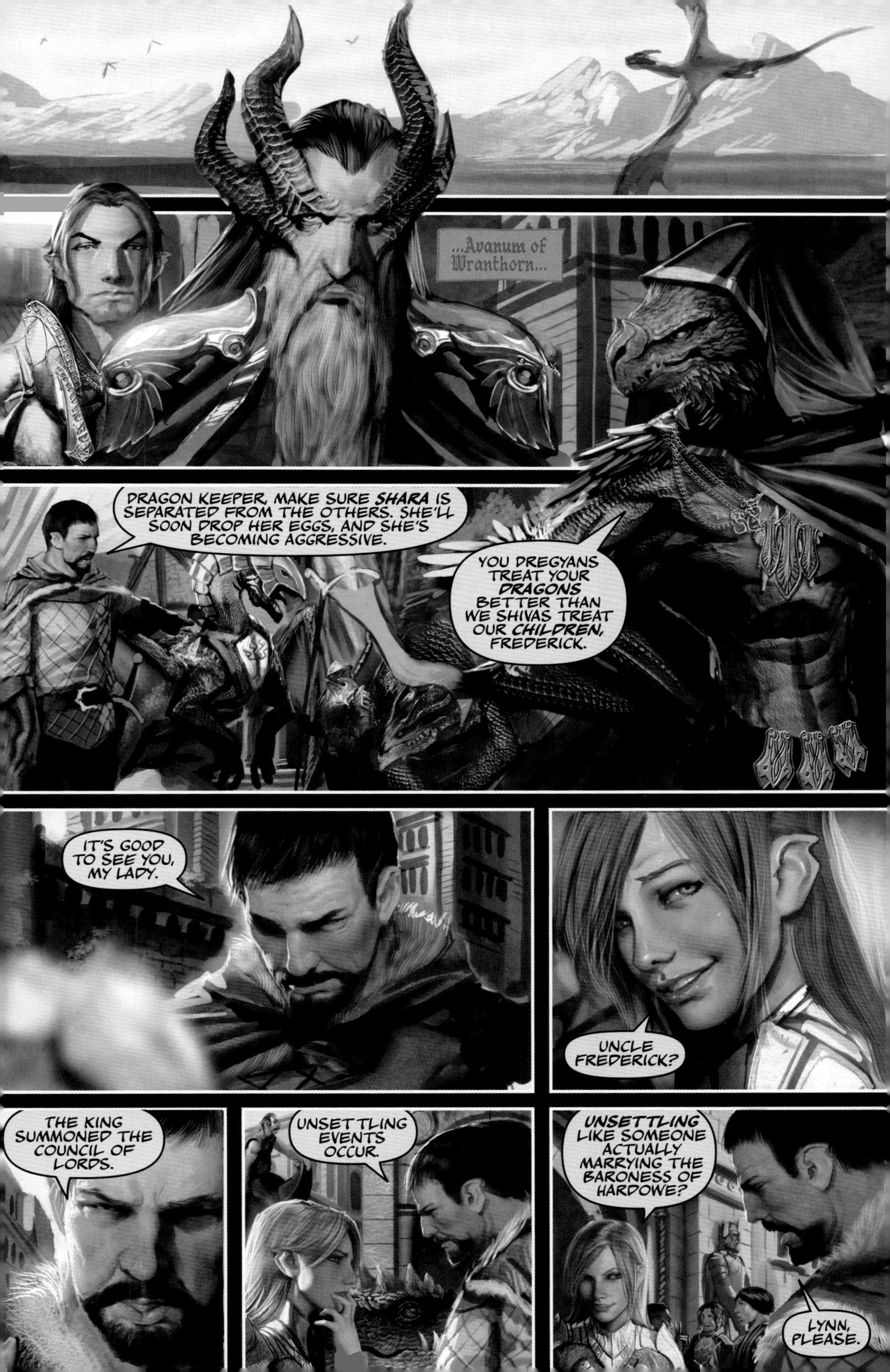
...Avanum of Wranthorn...
DRAGON KEEPER, MAKE SURE SHARA IS SEPARATED FROM THE OTHERS. SHE'LL SOON DROP HER EGGS, AND SHE'S BECOMING AGGRESSIVE.
YOU DREGYANS TREAT YOUR DRAGONS BETTER THAN WE SHIVAS TREAT OUR CHILDREN, FREDERICK.
IT'S GOOD TO SEE YOU, MY LADY.
UNCLE FREDERICK?
THE KING SUMMONED THE COUNCIL OF LORDS.
UNSETTLING EVENTS OCCUR.
UNSETTLING LIKE SOMEONE ACTUALLY MARRYING THE BARONESS OF HARDOWE?
LYNN, PLEASE.

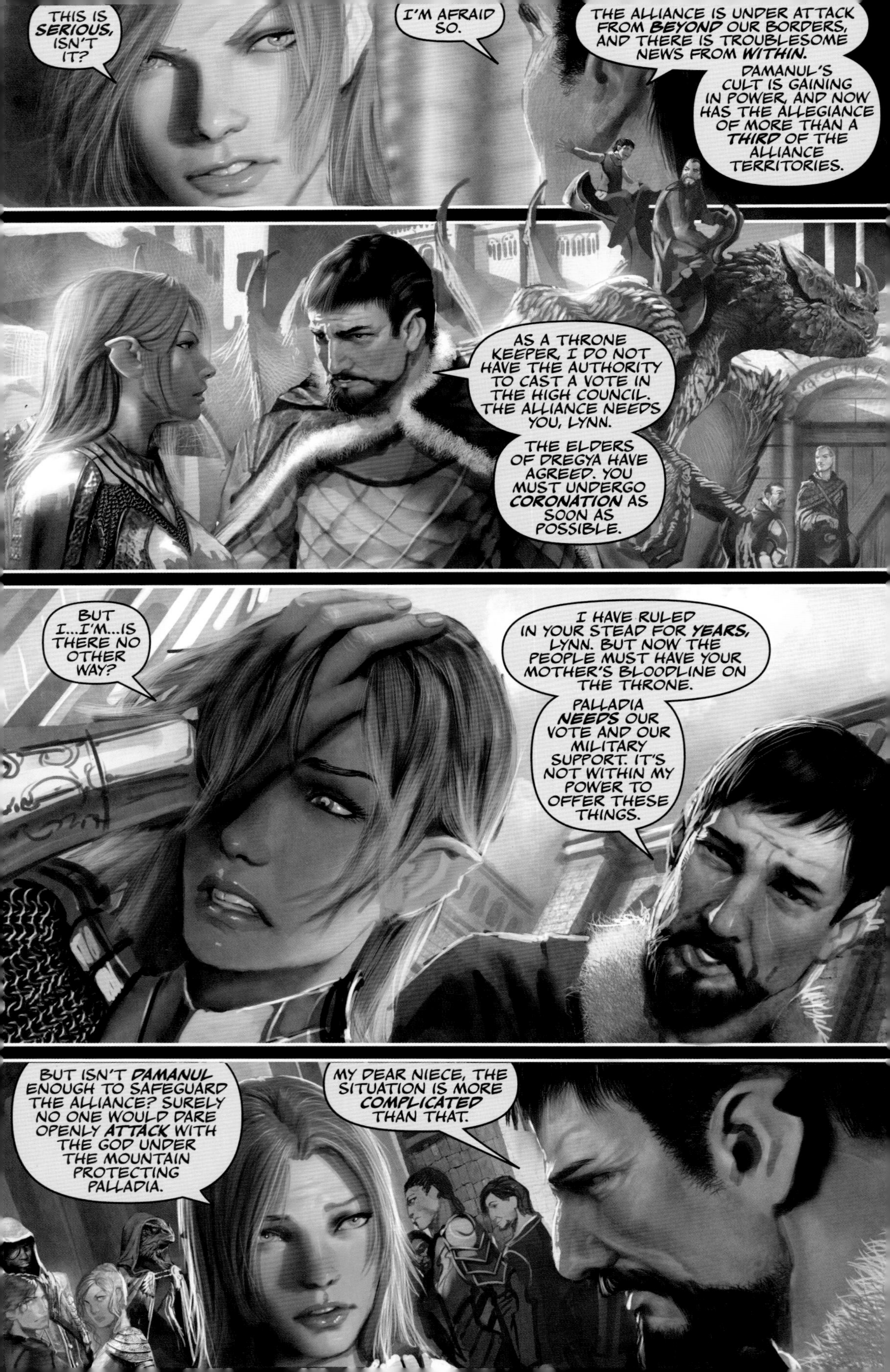
THIS IS SERIOUS, ISN'T IT?
I'M AFRAID SO.
THE ALLIANCE IS UNDER ATTACK FROM BEYOND OUR BORDERS, AND THERE IS TROUBLESOME NEWS FROM WITHIN.
DAMANUL'S CULT IS GAINING IN POWER, AND NOW HAS THE ALLEGIANCE OF MORE THAN A THIRD OF THE ALLIANCE TERRITORIES.
AS A THRONE KEEPER, I DO NOT HAVE THE AUTHORITY TO CAST A VOTE IN THE HIGH COUNCIL. THE ALLIANCE NEEDS YOU, LYNN.
THE ELDERS OF DREGYA HAVE AGREED. YOU MUST UNDERGO CORONATION AS SOON AS POSSIBLE.
BUT I...I'M...IS THERE NO OTHER WAY?
I HAVE RULED IN YOUR STEAD FOR YEARS, LYNN. BUT NOW THE PEOPLE MUST HAVE YOUR MOTHER'S BLOODLINE ON THE THRONE.
PALLADIA NEEDS OUR VOTE AND OUR MILITARY SUPPORT. IT'S NOT WITHIN MY POWER TO OFFER THESE THINGS.
BUT ISN'T DAMANUL ENOUGH TO SAFEGUARD THE ALLIANCE? SURELY NO ONE WOULD DARE OPENLY ATTACK WITH THE GOD UNDER THE MOUNTAIN PROTECTING PALLADIA.
MY DEAR NIECE, THE SITUATION IS MORE COMPLICATED THAN THAT.

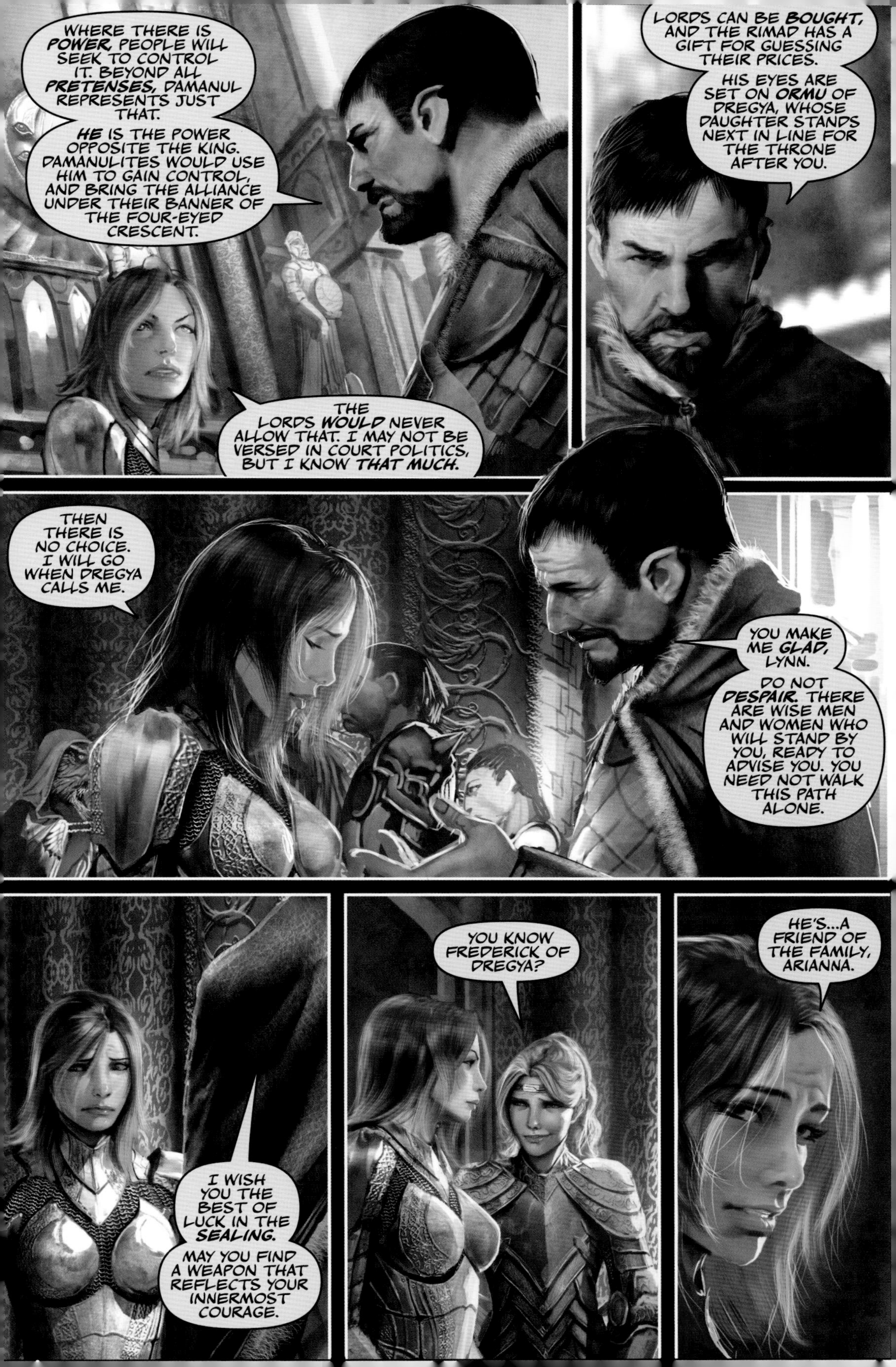
WHERE THERE IS POWER, PEOPLE WILL SEEK TO CONTROL IT. BEYOND ALL PRETENSES, DAMANUL REPRESENTS JUST THAT.
HE IS THE POWER OPPOSITE THE KING. DAMANULITES WOULD USE HIM TO GAIN CONTROL, AND BRING THE ALLIANCE UNDER THEIR BANNER OF THE FOUR-EYED CRESCENT.
THE LORDS WOULD NEVER ALLOW THAT. I MAY NOT BE VERSED IN COURT POLITICS, BUT I KNOW THAT MUCH.
LORDS CAN BE BOUGHT, AND THE RIMAD HAS A GIFT FOR GUESSING THEIR PRICES.
HIS EYES ARE SET ON ORMU OF DREGYA, WHOSE DAUGHTER STANDS NEXT IN LINE FOR THE THRONE AFTER YOU.
THEN THERE IS NO CHOICE. I WILL GO WHEN DREGYA CALLS ME.
YOU MAKE ME GLAD, LYNN.
DO NOT DESPAIR. THERE ARE WISE MEN AND WOMEN WHO WILL STAND BY YOU, READY TO ADVISE YOU. YOU NEED NOT WALK THIS PATH ALONE.
I WISH YOU THE BEST OF LUCK IN THE SEALING.
MAY YOU FIND A WEAPON THAT REFLECTS YOUR INNERMOST COURAGE.
YOU KNOW FREDERICK OF DREGYA?
HE'S...A FRIEND OF THE FAMILY, ARIANNA.

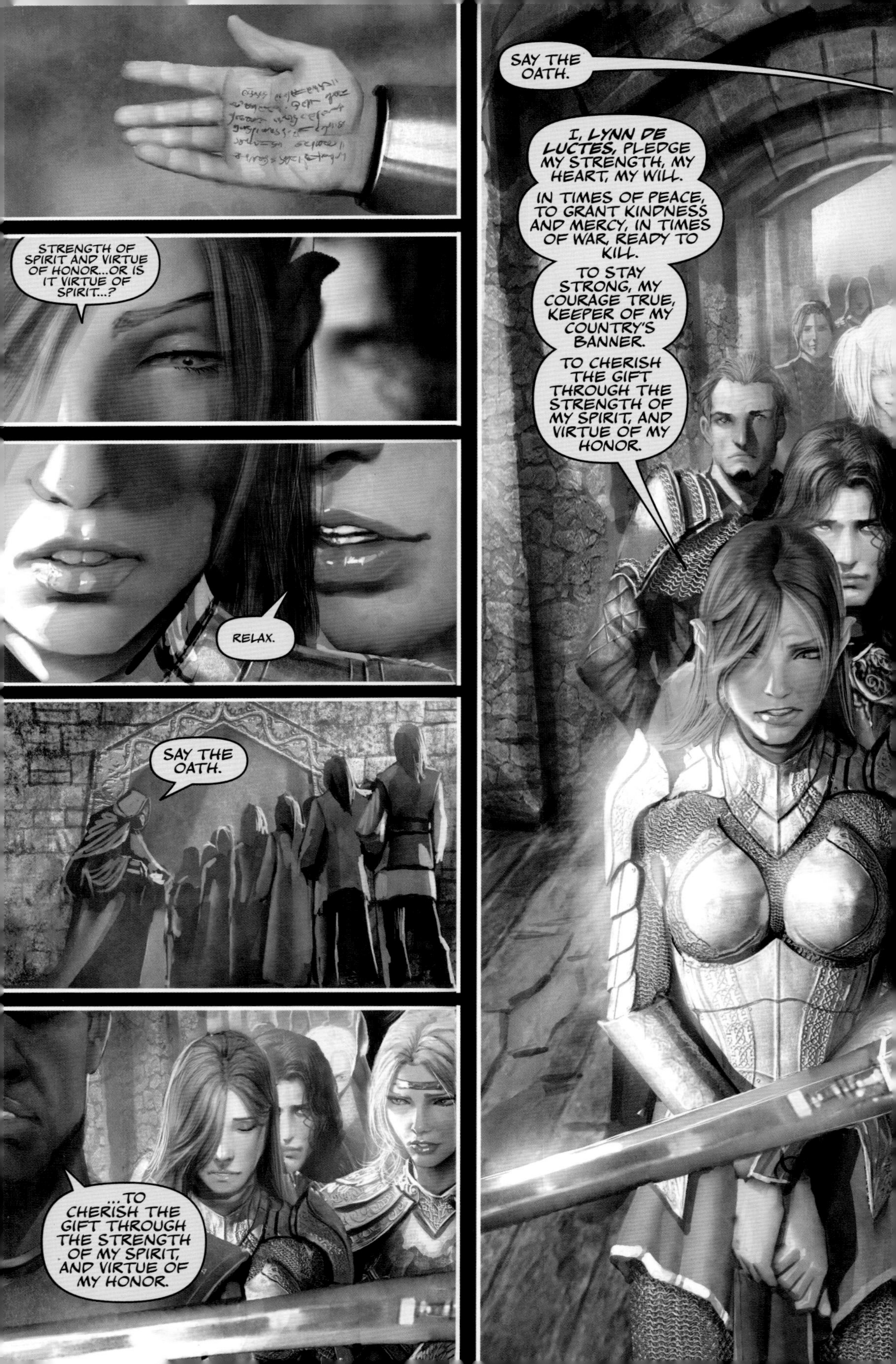
STRENGTH OF SPIRIT AND VIRTUE OF HONOR...OR IS IT VIRTUE OF SPIRIT...?
RELAX.
SAY THE OATH.
...TO CHERISH THE GIFT THROUGH THE STRENGTH OF MY SPIRIT, AND VIRTUE OF MY HONOR.
SAY THE OATH.
I, *LYNN DE LUCTES,* PLEDGE MY STRENGTH, MY HEART, MY WILL.
IN TIMES OF PEACE, TO GRANT KINDNESS AND MERCY, IN TIMES OF WAR, READY TO KILL.
TO STAY STRONG, MY COURAGE TRUE, KEEPER OF MY COUNTRY'S BANNER.
TO CHERISH THE GIFT THROUGH THE STRENGTH OF MY SPIRIT, AND VIRTUE OF MY HONOR.

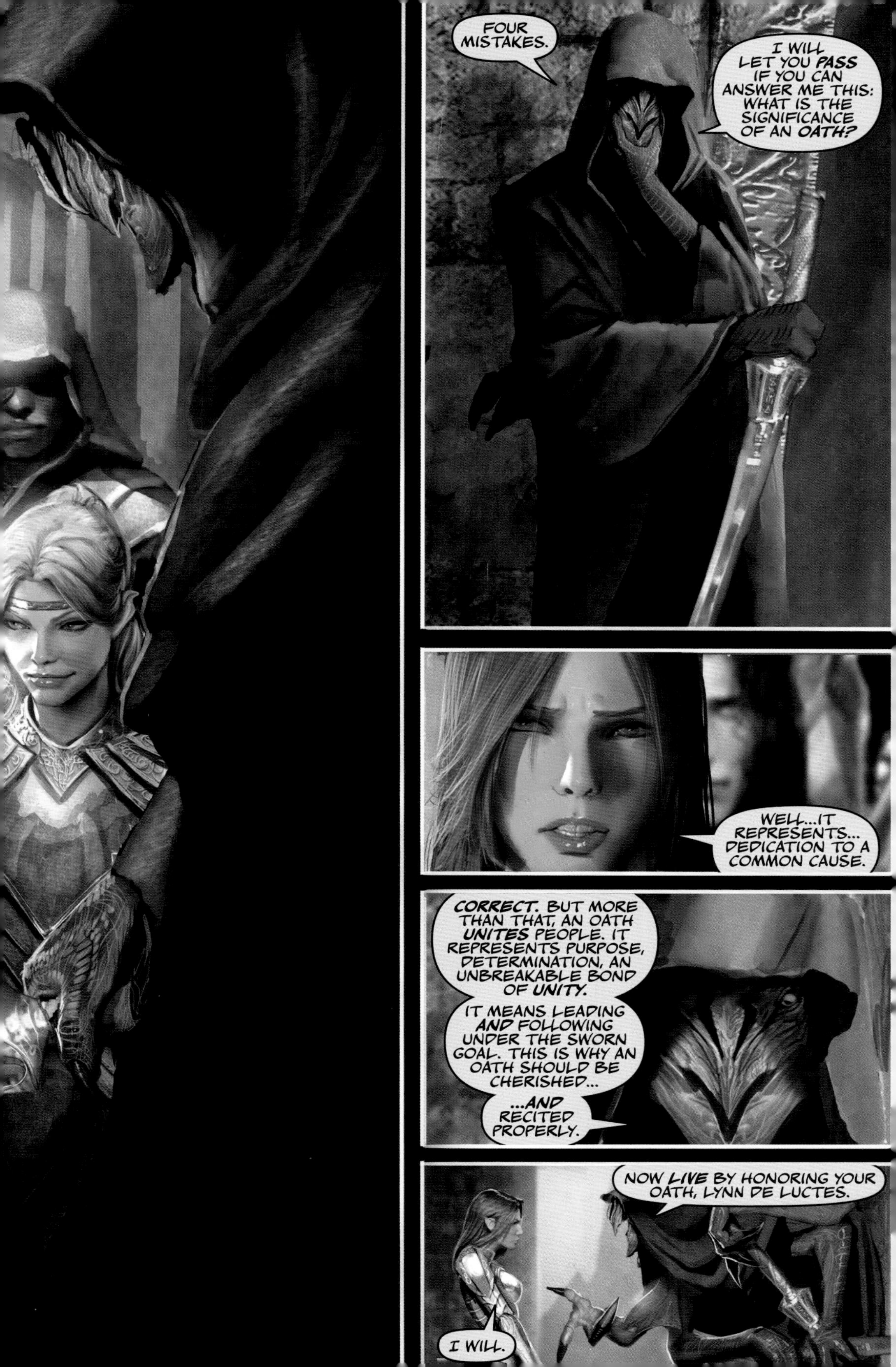
FOUR MISTAKES.
I WILL LET YOU PASS IF YOU CAN ANSWER ME THIS: WHAT IS THE SIGNIFICANCE OF AN OATH?
WELL...IT REPRESENTS... DEDICATION TO A COMMON CAUSE.
CORRECT. BUT MORE THAN THAT, AN OATH UNITES PEOPLE. IT REPRESENTS PURPOSE, DETERMINATION, AN UNBREAKABLE BOND OF UNITY.
IT MEANS LEADING AND FOLLOWING UNDER THE SWORN GOAL. THIS IS WHY AN OATH SHOULD BE CHERISHED...
...AND RECITED PROPERLY.
NOW LIVE BY HONORING YOUR OATH, LYNN DE LUCTES.
I WILL.

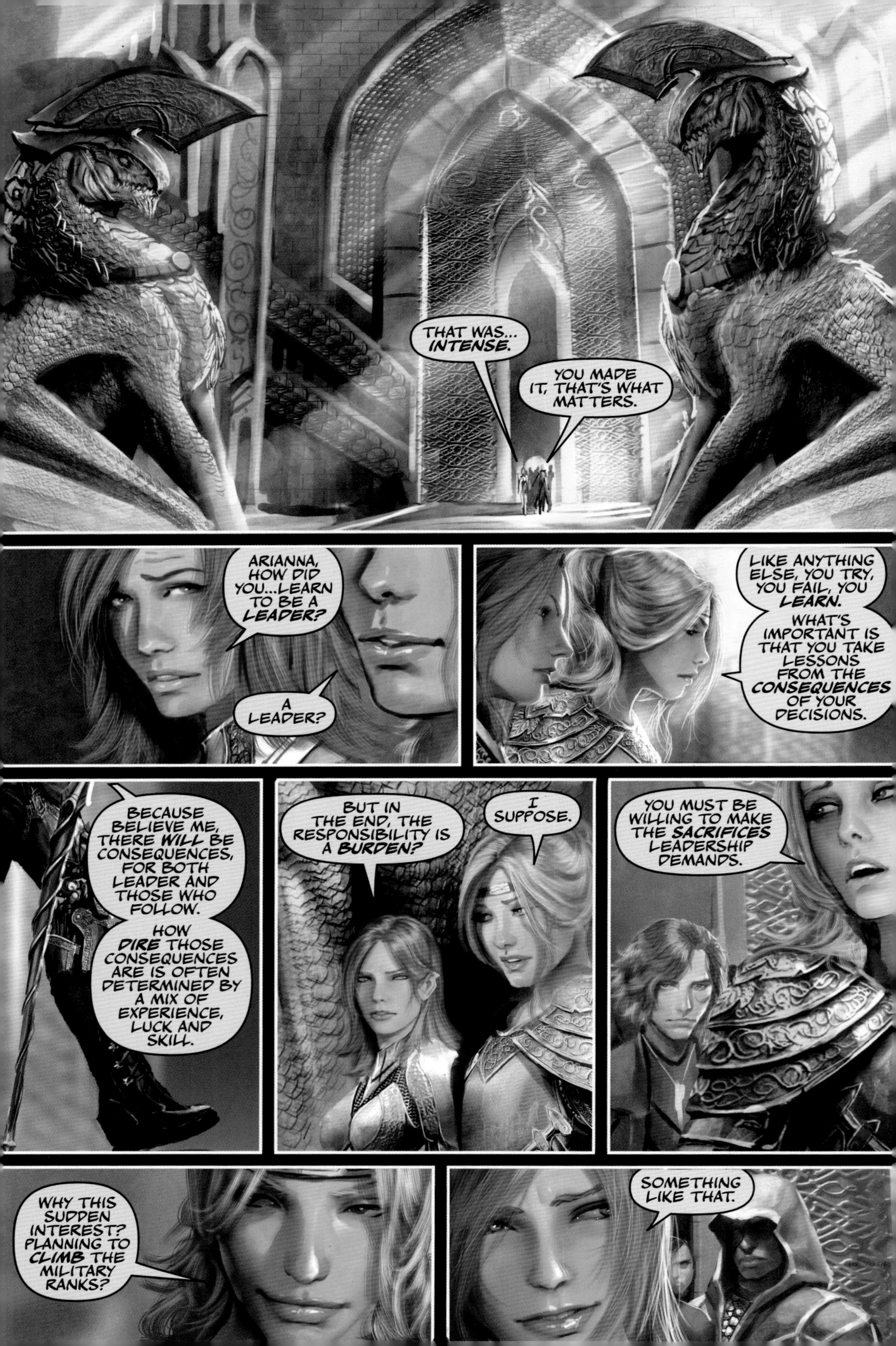
THAT WAS... *INTENSE*.
YOU MADE IT, THAT'S WHAT MATTERS.
ARIANNA, HOW DID YOU...LEARN TO BE A *LEADER*?
A LEADER?
LIKE ANYTHING ELSE, YOU TRY, YOU FAIL, YOU *LEARN*.
WHAT'S IMPORTANT IS THAT YOU TAKE LESSONS FROM THE *CONSEQUENCES* OF YOUR DECISIONS.
BECAUSE BELIEVE ME, THERE *WILL* BE CONSEQUENCES, FOR BOTH LEADER AND THOSE WHO FOLLOW.
HOW *DIRE* THOSE CONSEQUENCES ARE IS OFTEN DETERMINED BY A MIX OF EXPERIENCE, LUCK AND SKILL.
BUT IN THE END, THE RESPONSIBILITY IS A *BURDEN*?
I SUPPOSE.
YOU MUST BE WILLING TO MAKE THE *SACRIFICES* LEADERSHIP DEMANDS.
WHY THIS SUDDEN INTEREST? PLANNING TO *CLIMB* THE MILITARY RANKS?
SOMETHING LIKE THAT.

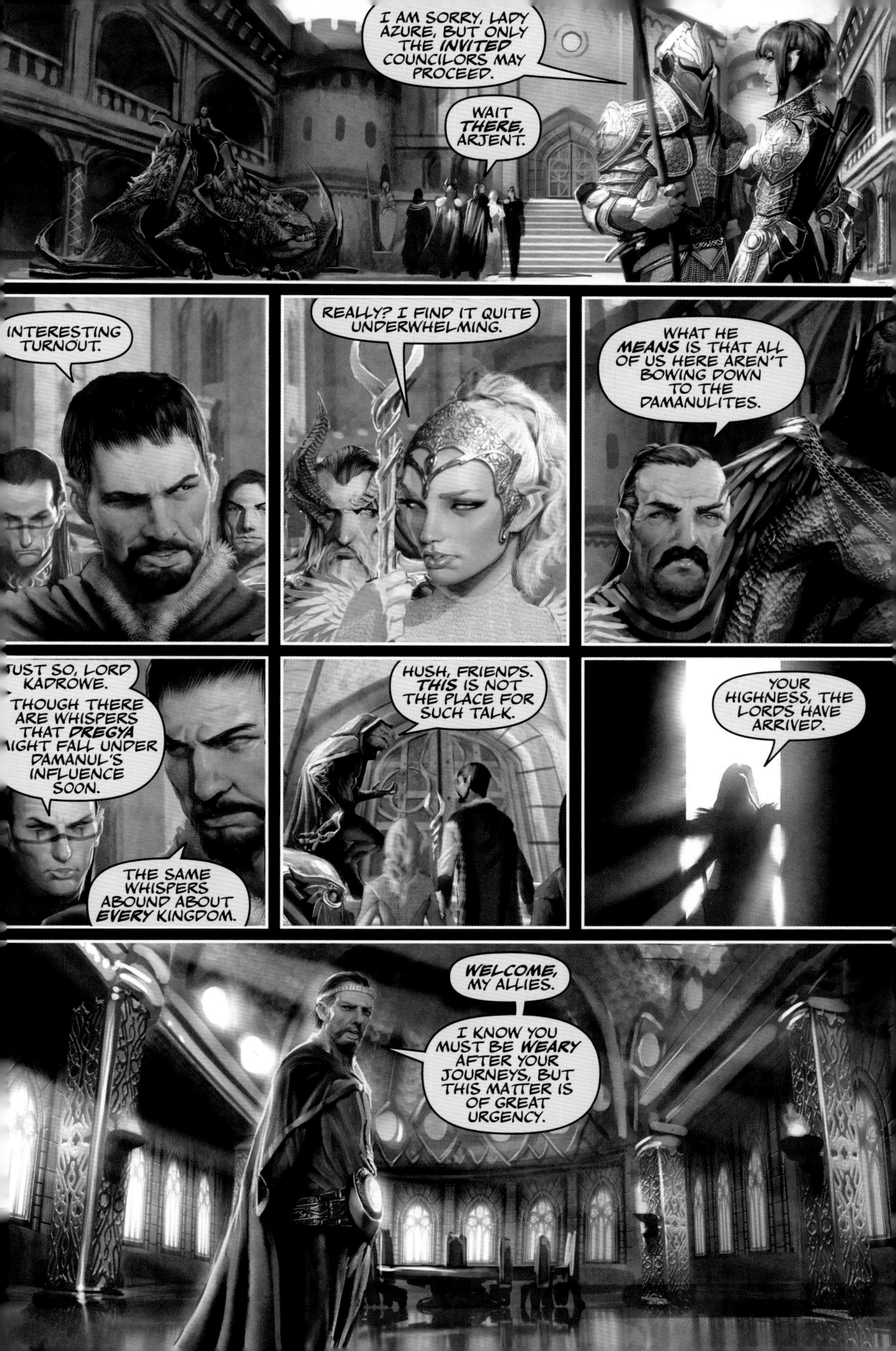
I AM SORRY, LADY AZURE, BUT ONLY THE INVITED COUNCILORS MAY PROCEED.
WAIT THERE, ARJENT.
INTERESTING TURNOUT.
REALLY? I FIND IT QUITE UNDERWHELMING.
WHAT HE MEANS IS THAT ALL OF US HERE AREN'T BOWING DOWN TO THE DAMANULITES.
JUST SO, LORD KADROWE.
THOUGH THERE ARE WHISPERS THAT DREGYA MIGHT FALL UNDER DAMANUL'S INFLUENCE SOON.
THE SAME WHISPERS ABOUND ABOUT EVERY KINGDOM.
HUSH, FRIENDS. THIS IS NOT THE PLACE FOR SUCH TALK.
YOUR HIGHNESS, THE LORDS HAVE ARRIVED.
WELCOME, MY ALLIES.
I KNOW YOU MUST BE WEARY AFTER YOUR JOURNEYS, BUT THIS MATTER IS OF GREAT URGENCY.

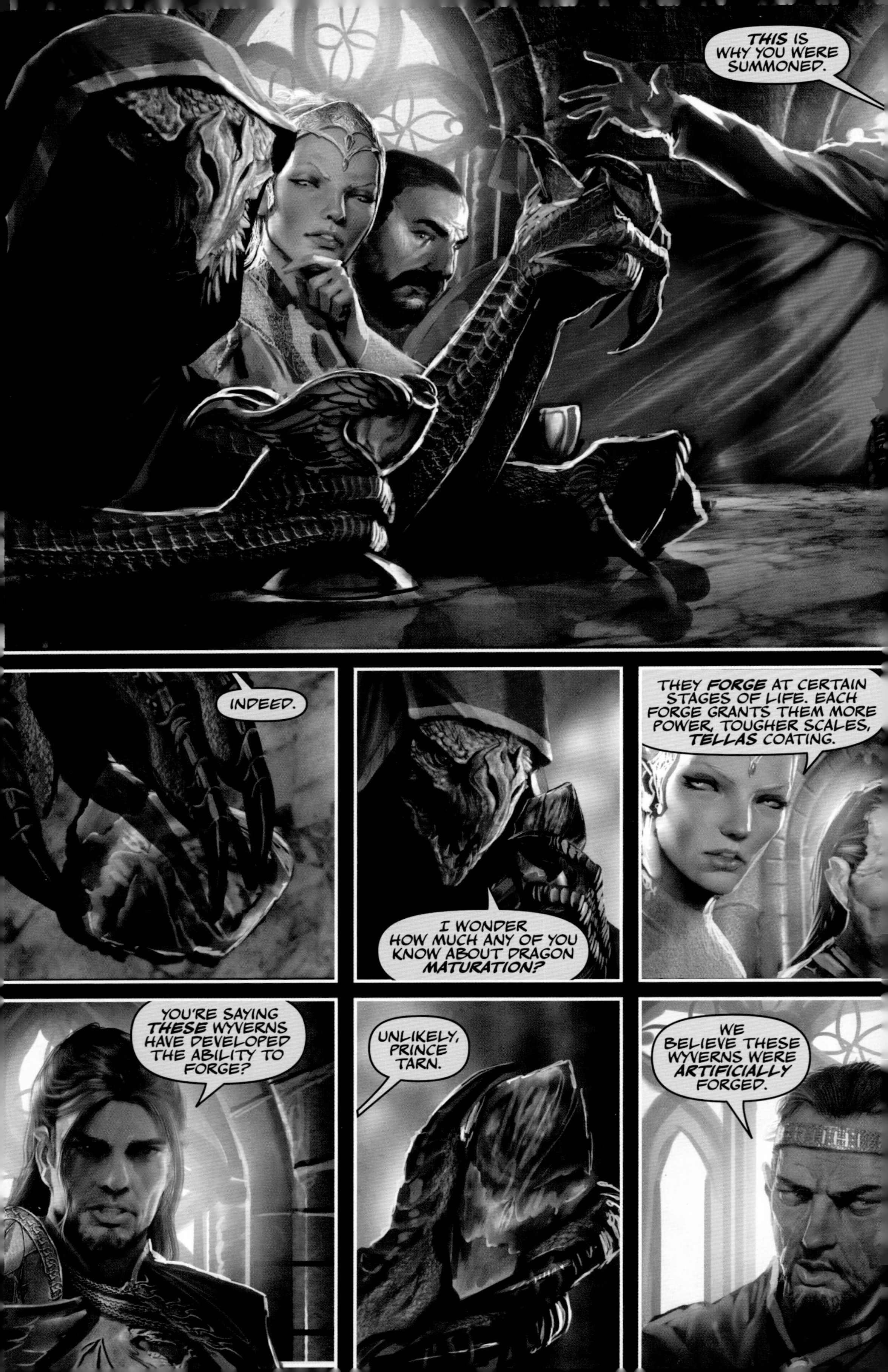
THIS IS WHY YOU WERE SUMMONED.
INDEED.
I WONDER HOW MUCH ANY OF YOU KNOW ABOUT DRAGON MATURATION?
THEY FORGE AT CERTAIN STAGES OF LIFE. EACH FORGE GRANTS THEM MORE POWER, TOUGHER SCALES, TELLAS COATING.
YOU'RE SAYING THESE WYVERNS HAVE DEVELOPED THE ABILITY TO FORGE?
UNLIKELY, PRINCE TARN.
WE BELIEVE THESE WYVERNS WERE ARTIFICIALLY FORGED.

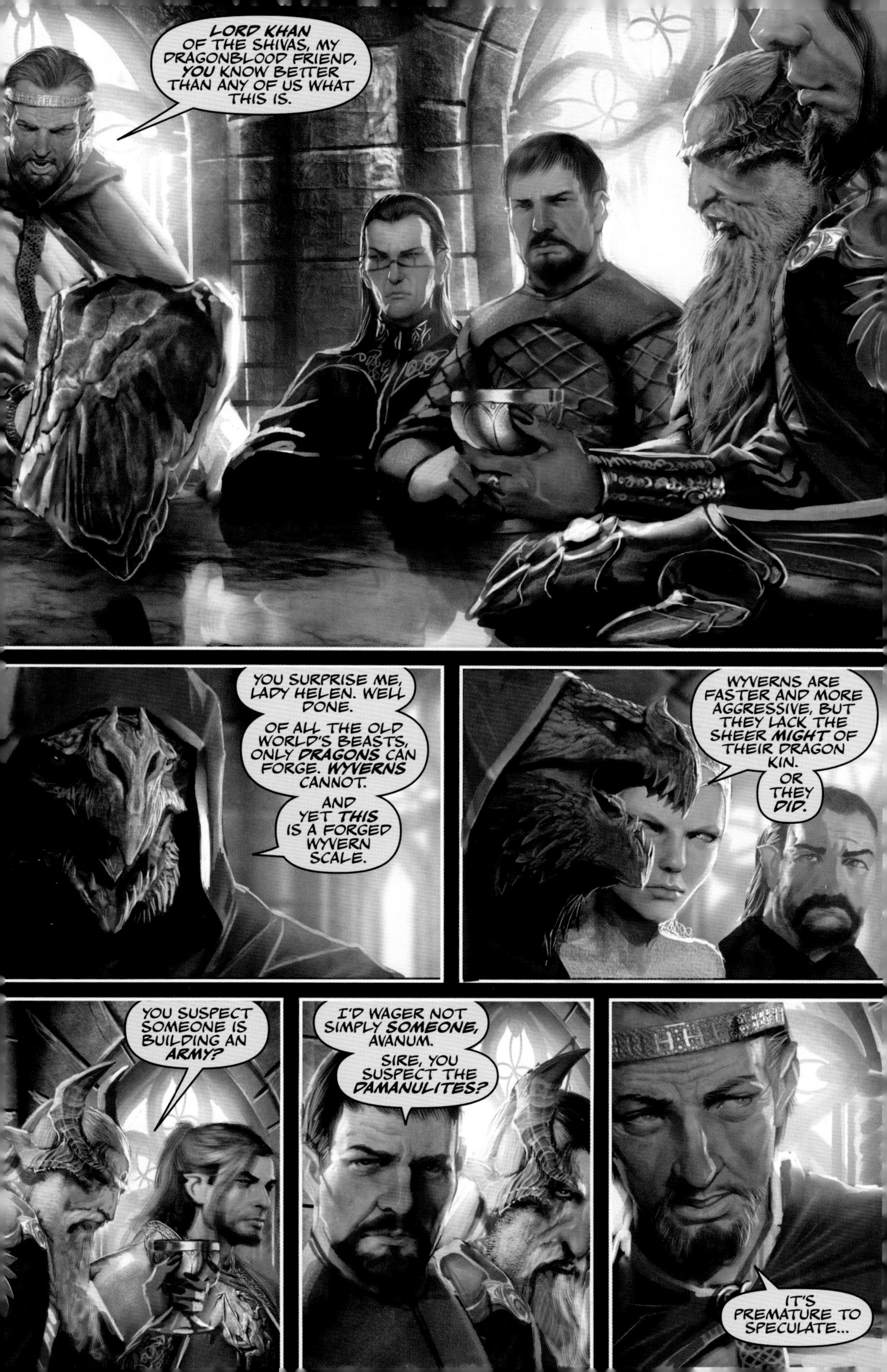
LORD KHAN OF THE SHIVAS, MY DRAGONBLOOD FRIEND, YOU KNOW BETTER THAN ANY OF US WHAT THIS IS.
YOU SURPRISE ME, LADY HELEN. WELL DONE.
OF ALL THE OLD WORLD'S BEASTS, ONLY DRAGONS CAN FORGE. WYVERNS CANNOT.
AND YET THIS IS A FORGED WYVERN SCALE.
WYVERNS ARE FASTER AND MORE AGGRESSIVE, BUT THEY LACK THE SHEER MIGHT OF THEIR DRAGON KIN.
OR THEY DID.
YOU SUSPECT SOMEONE IS BUILDING AN ARMY?
I'D WAGER NOT SIMPLY SOMEONE, AVANUM.
SIRE, YOU SUSPECT THE DAMANULITES?
IT'S PREMATURE TO SPECULATE...

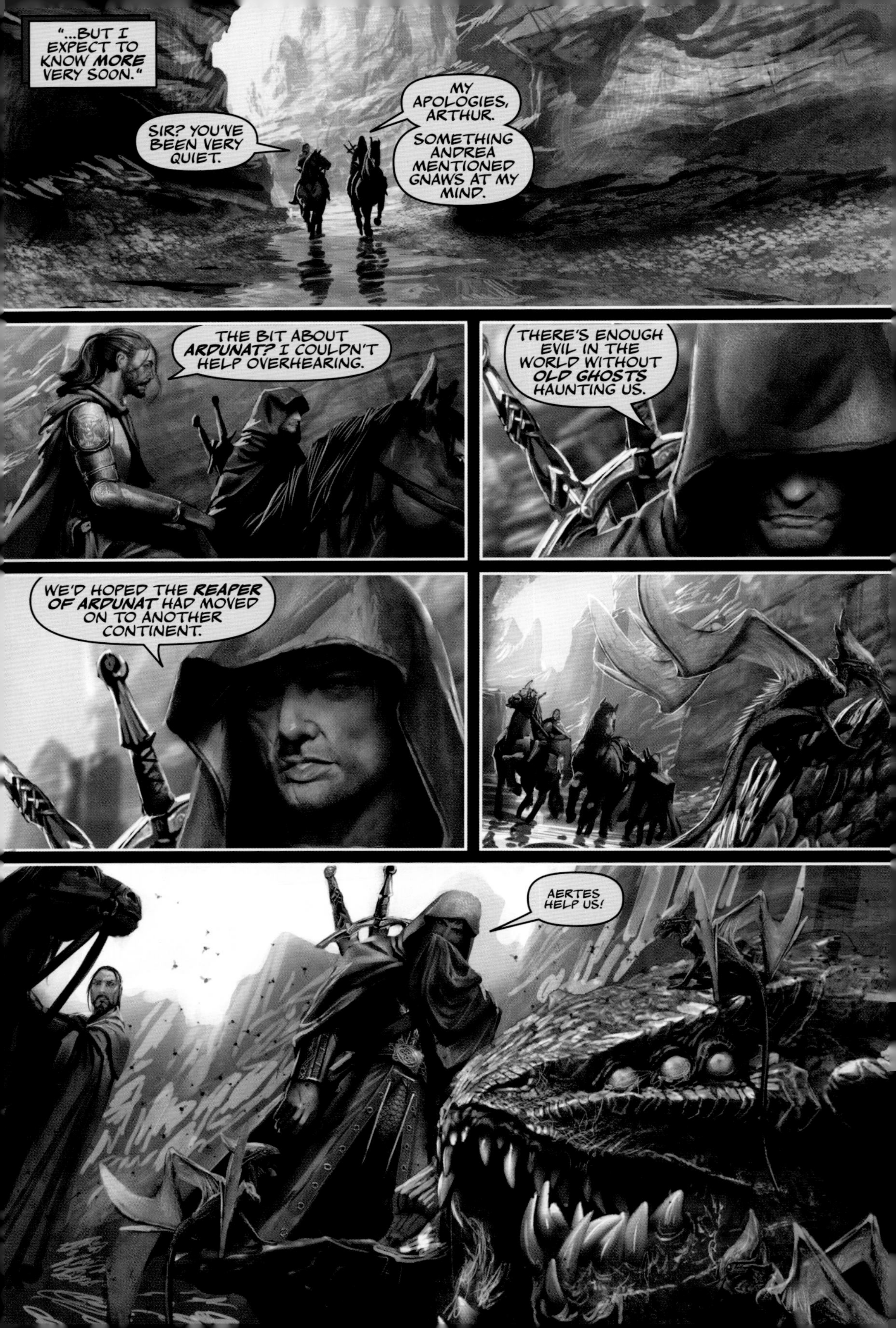
"...BUT I EXPECT TO KNOW MORE VERY SOON."
SIR? YOU'VE BEEN VERY QUIET.
MY APOLOGIES, ARTHUR.
SOMETHING ANDREA MENTIONED GNAWS AT MY MIND.
THE BIT ABOUT ARDUNAT? I COULDN'T HELP OVERHEARING.
THERE'S ENOUGH EVIL IN THE WORLD WITHOUT OLD GHOSTS HAUNTING US.
WE'D HOPED THE REAPER OF ARDUNAT HAD MOVED ON TO ANOTHER CONTINENT.
AERTES HELP US!

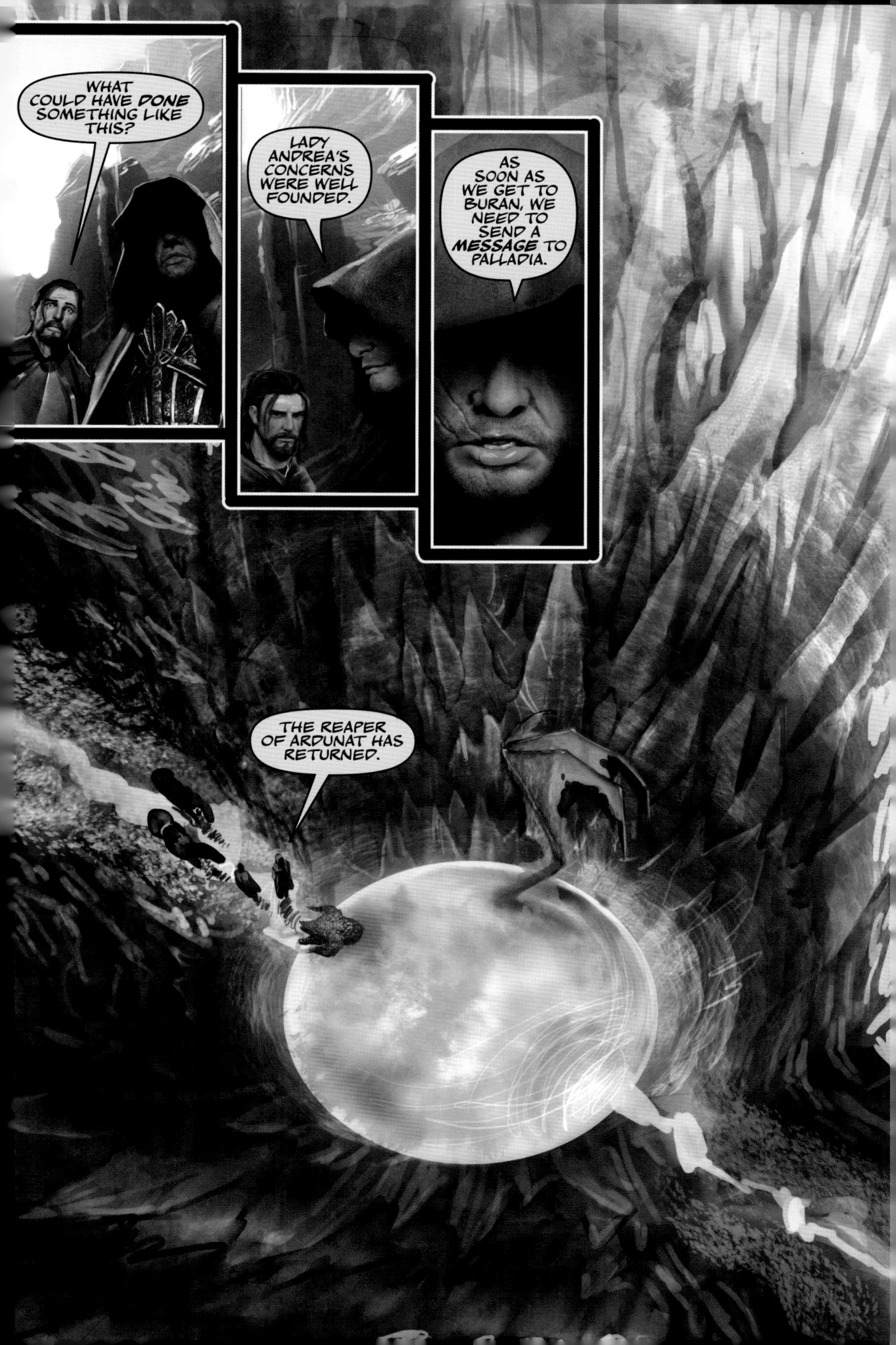
WHAT COULD HAVE DONE SOMETHING LIKE THIS?
LADY ANDREA'S CONCERNS WERE WELL FOUNDED.
AS SOON AS WE GET TO BURAN, WE NEED TO SEND A MESSAGE TO PALLADIA.
THE REAPER OF ARDUNAT HAS RETURNED.

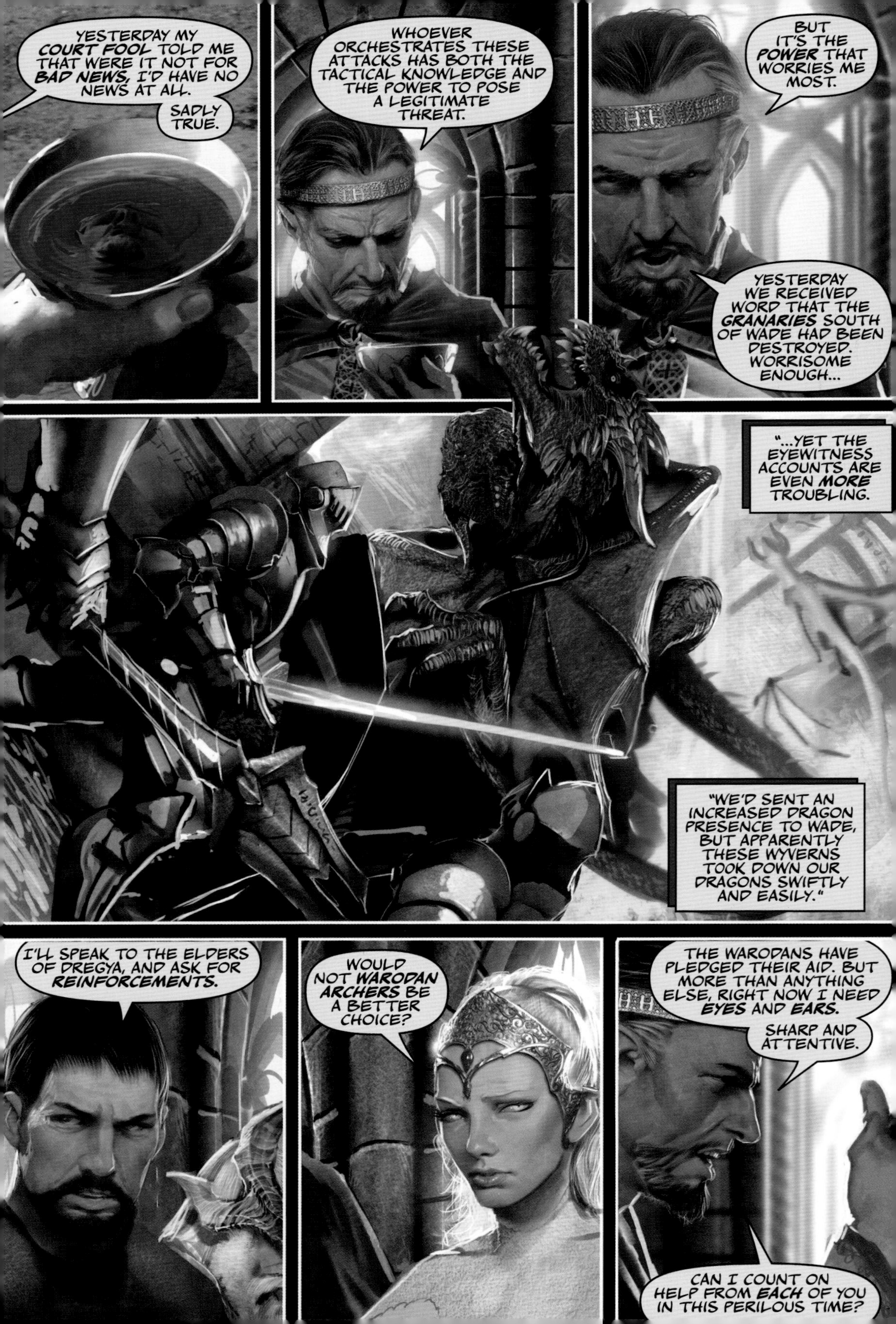
YESTERDAY MY COURT FOOL TOLD ME THAT WERE IT NOT FOR BAD NEWS, I'D HAVE NO NEWS AT ALL.
SADLY TRUE.
WHOEVER ORCHESTRATES THESE ATTACKS HAS BOTH THE TACTICAL KNOWLEDGE AND THE POWER TO POSE A LEGITIMATE THREAT.
BUT IT'S THE POWER THAT WORRIES ME MOST.
YESTERDAY WE RECEIVED WORD THAT THE GRANARIES SOUTH OF WADE HAD BEEN DESTROYED. WORRISOME ENOUGH...
"...YET THE EYEWITNESS ACCOUNTS ARE EVEN MORE TROUBLING.
"WE'D SENT AN INCREASED DRAGON PRESENCE TO WADE, BUT APPARENTLY THESE WYVERNS TOOK DOWN OUR DRAGONS SWIFTLY AND EASILY."
I'LL SPEAK TO THE ELDERS OF DREGYA, AND ASK FOR REINFORCEMENTS.
WOULD NOT WARODAN ARCHERS BE A BETTER CHOICE?
THE WARODANS HAVE PLEDGED THEIR AID. BUT MORE THAN ANYTHING ELSE, RIGHT NOW I NEED EYES AND EARS.
SHARP AND ATTENTIVE.
CAN I COUNT ON HELP FROM EACH OF YOU IN THIS PERILOUS TIME?

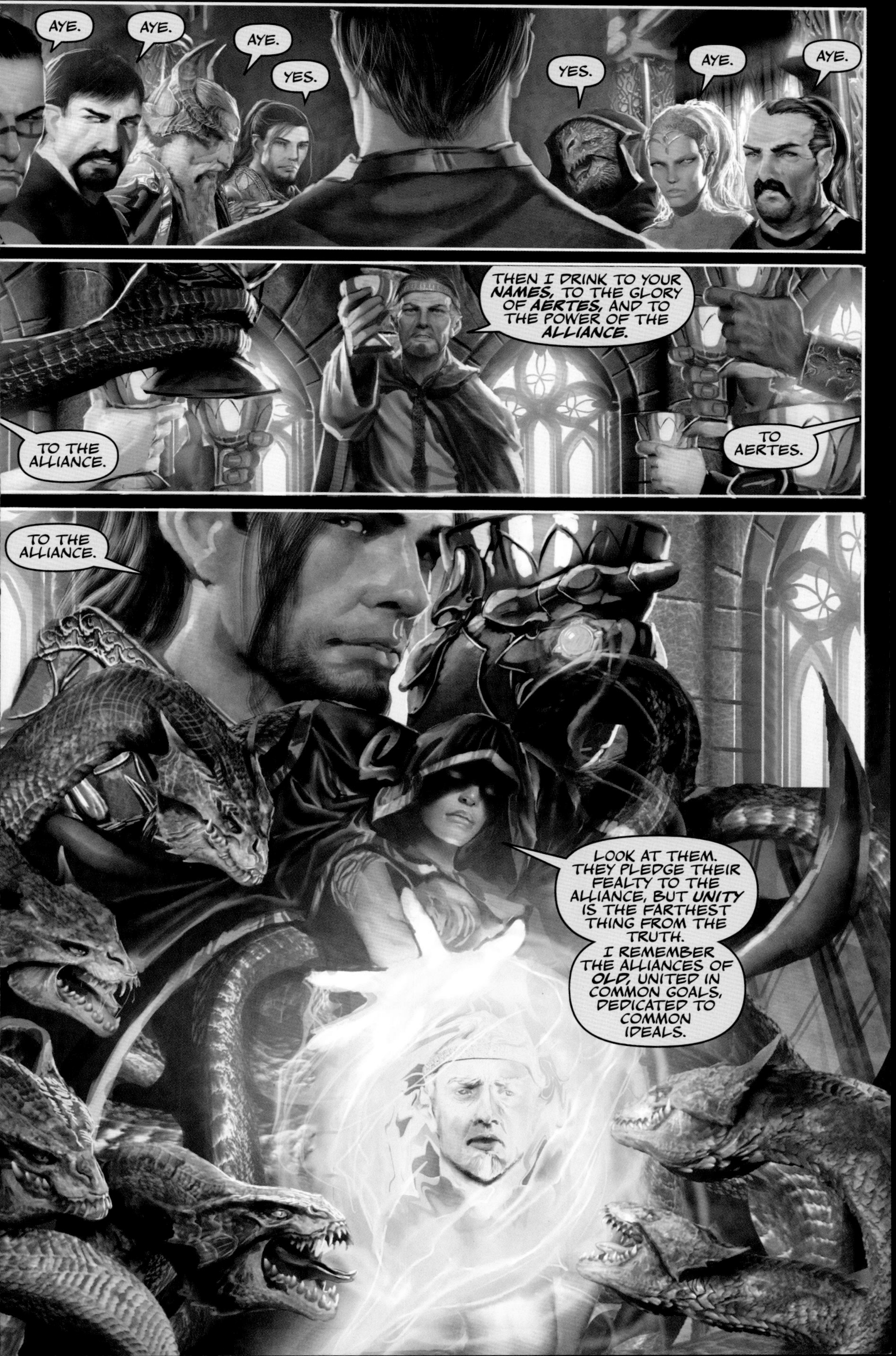
AYE.
AYE.
AYE.
YES.
YES.
AYE.
AYE.
THEN I DRINK TO YOUR NAMES, TO THE GLORY OF AERTES, AND TO THE POWER OF THE ALLIANCE.
TO THE ALLIANCE.
TO AERTES.
TO THE ALLIANCE.
LOOK AT THEM. THEY PLEDGE THEIR FEALTY TO THE ALLIANCE, BUT UNITY IS THE FARTHEST THING FROM THE TRUTH.
I REMEMBER THE ALLIANCES OF OLD, UNITED IN COMMON GOALS, DEDICATED TO COMMON IDEALS.

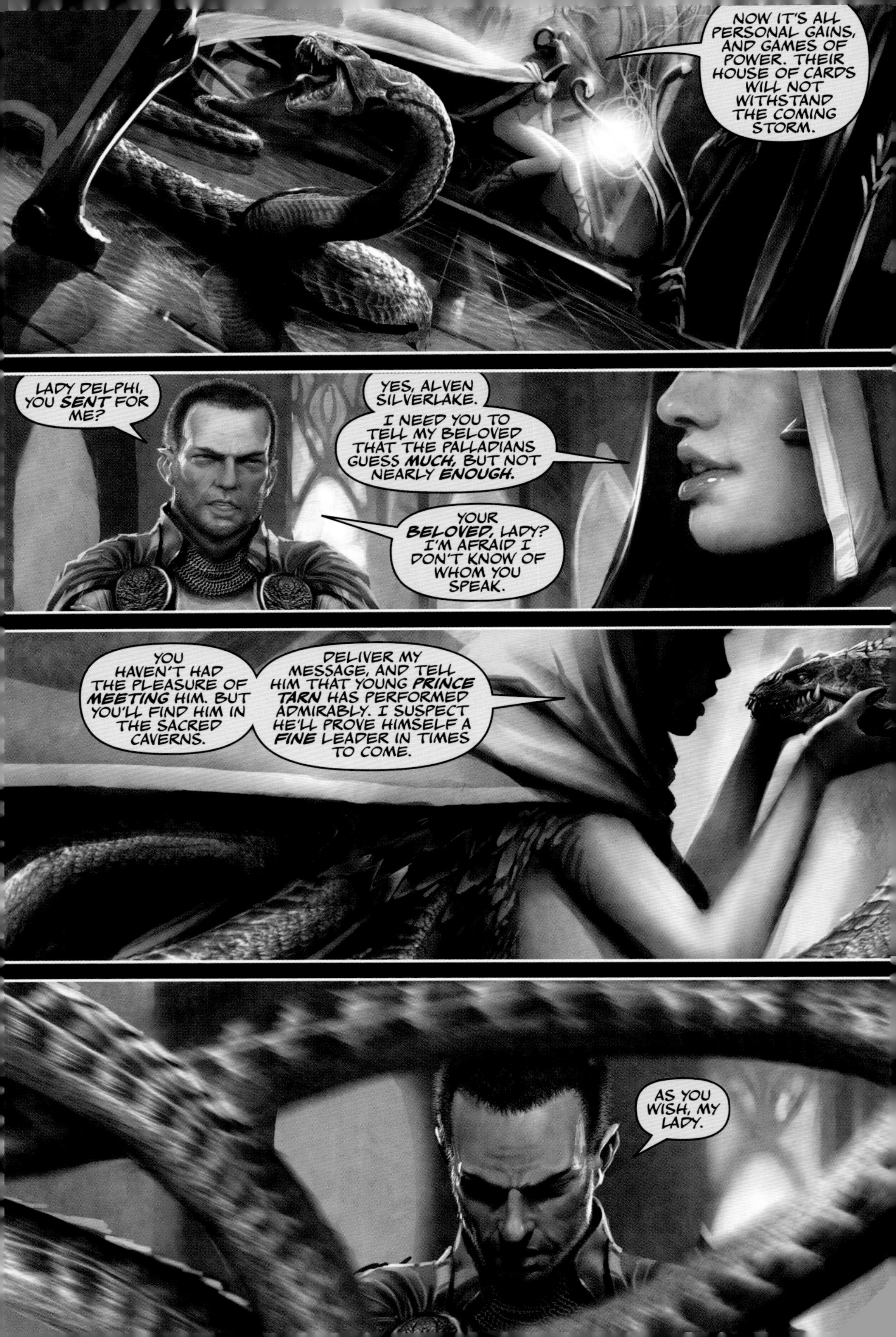
NOW IT'S ALL PERSONAL GAINS, AND GAMES OF POWER. THEIR HOUSE OF CARDS WILL NOT WITHSTAND THE COMING STORM.
LADY DELPHI, YOU SENT FOR ME?
YES, ALVEN SILVERLAKE.
I NEED YOU TO TELL MY BELOVED THAT THE PALLADIANS GUESS MUCH, BUT NOT NEARLY ENOUGH.
YOUR BELOVED, LADY? I'M AFRAID I DON'T KNOW OF WHOM YOU SPEAK.
YOU HAVEN'T HAD THE PLEASURE OF MEETING HIM. BUT YOU'LL FIND HIM IN THE SACRED CAVERNS.
DELIVER MY MESSAGE, AND TELL HIM THAT YOUNG PRINCE TARN HAS PERFORMED ADMIRABLY. I SUSPECT HE'LL PROVE HIMSELF A FINE LEADER IN TIMES TO COME.
AS YOU WISH, MY LADY.

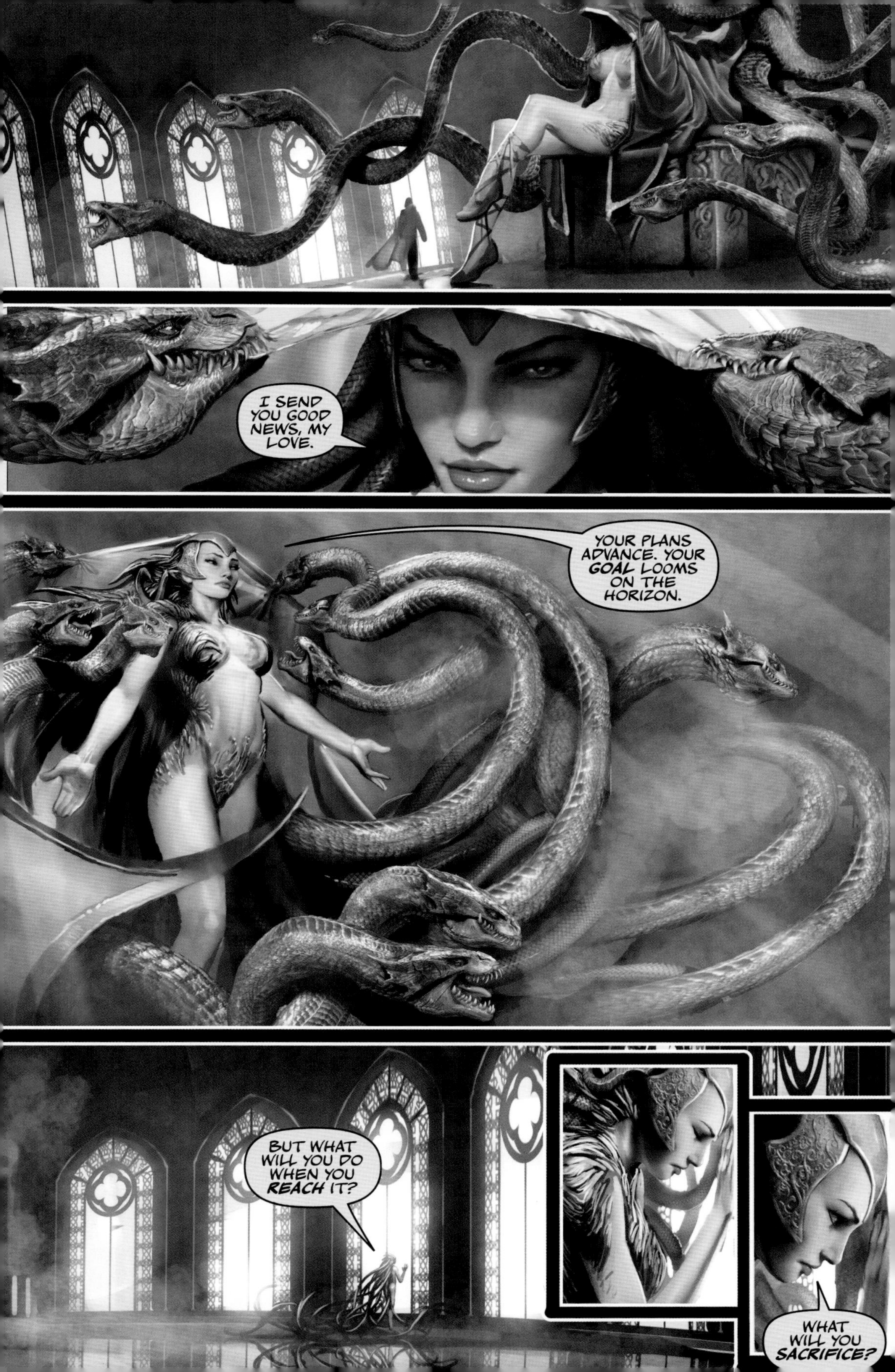
I SEND YOU GOOD NEWS, MY LOVE.
YOUR PLANS ADVANCE. YOUR GOAL LOOMS ON THE HORIZON.
BUT WHAT WILL YOU DO WHEN YOU REACH IT?
WHAT WILL YOU SACRIFICE?

I AM THE KEEPER OF WEAPONS.

TODAY YOU WILL STAND BEFORE THE *GIFT OF AERTES.*

YOU WILL BE *JUDGED* BY YOUR POWER, AND BY ITS WORTH SHALL YOU BE REWARDED.

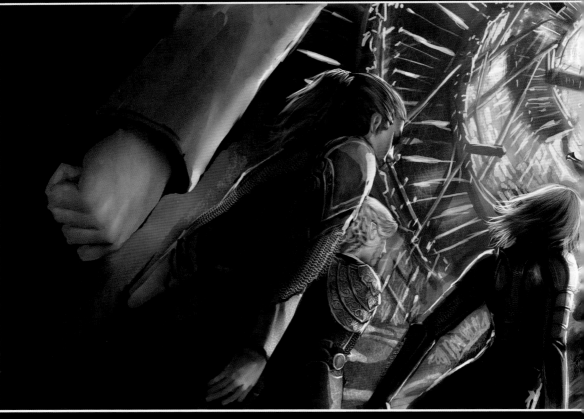

SO THOSE TWO AT THE *TOP* ARE THE STRONGEST?

YES, THOUGH REST ASSURED THAT'S OF LITTLE CONCERN TO *YOU.*

THE TWO WEAPONS AT THE TOP HAVE BEEN THERE SINCE BEFORE I BECAME KEEPER OF WEAPONS, ALMOST FORTY YEARS AGO.

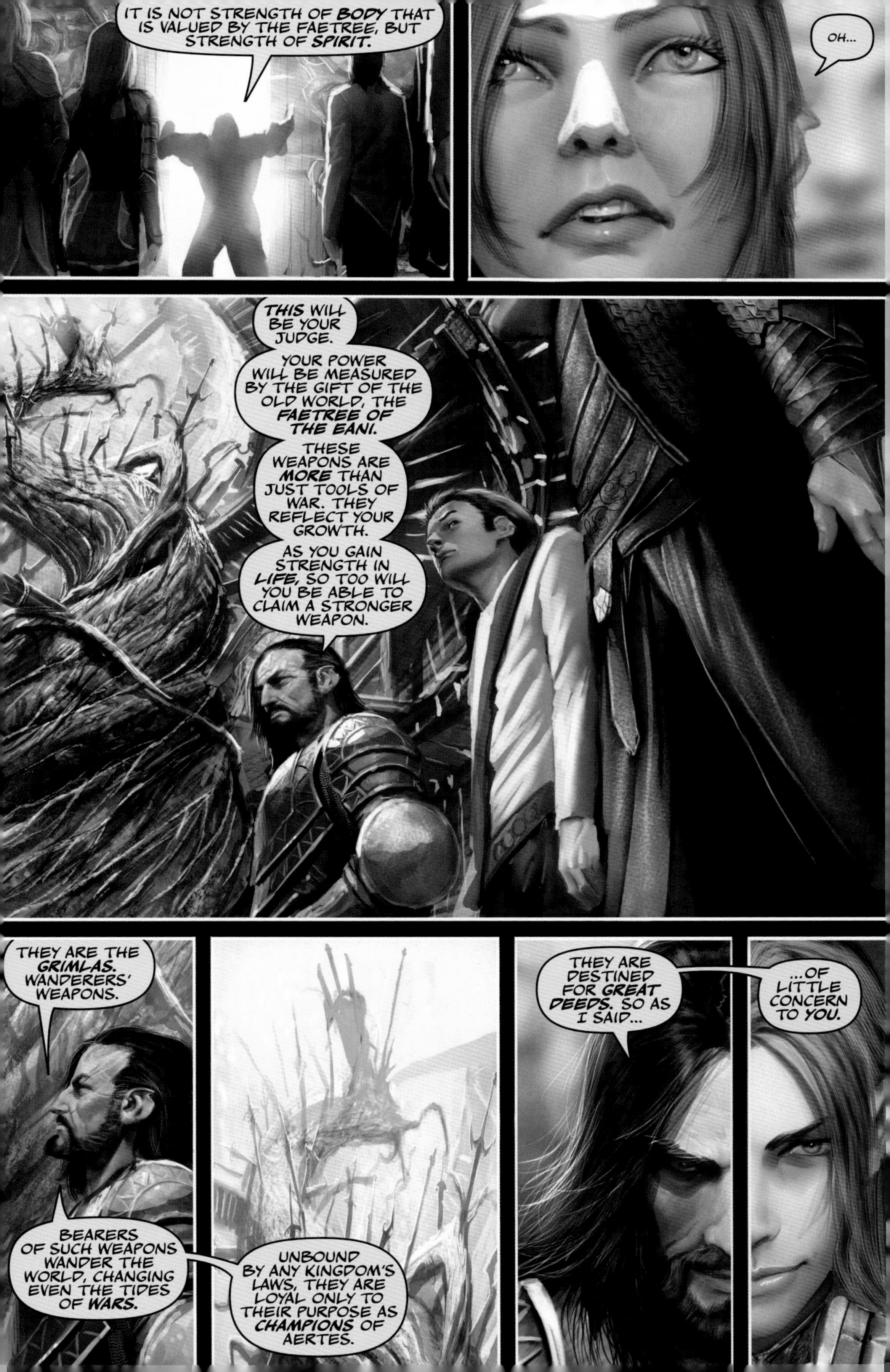
IT IS NOT STRENGTH OF BODY THAT IS VALUED BY THE FAETREE, BUT STRENGTH OF SPIRIT.
OH...
THIS WILL BE YOUR JUDGE.
YOUR POWER WILL BE MEASURED BY THE GIFT OF THE OLD WORLD, THE FAETREE OF THE EANI.
THESE WEAPONS ARE MORE THAN JUST TOOLS OF WAR. THEY REFLECT YOUR GROWTH.
AS YOU GAIN STRENGTH IN LIFE, SO TOO WILL YOU BE ABLE TO CLAIM A STRONGER WEAPON.
THEY ARE THE GRIMLAS. WANDERERS' WEAPONS.
BEARERS OF SUCH WEAPONS WANDER THE WORLD, CHANGING EVEN THE TIDES OF WARS.
UNBOUND BY ANY KINGDOM'S LAWS, THEY ARE LOYAL ONLY TO THEIR PURPOSE AS CHAMPIONS OF AERTES.
THEY ARE DESTINED FOR GREAT DEEDS. SO AS I SAID...
...OF LITTLE CONCERN TO YOU.

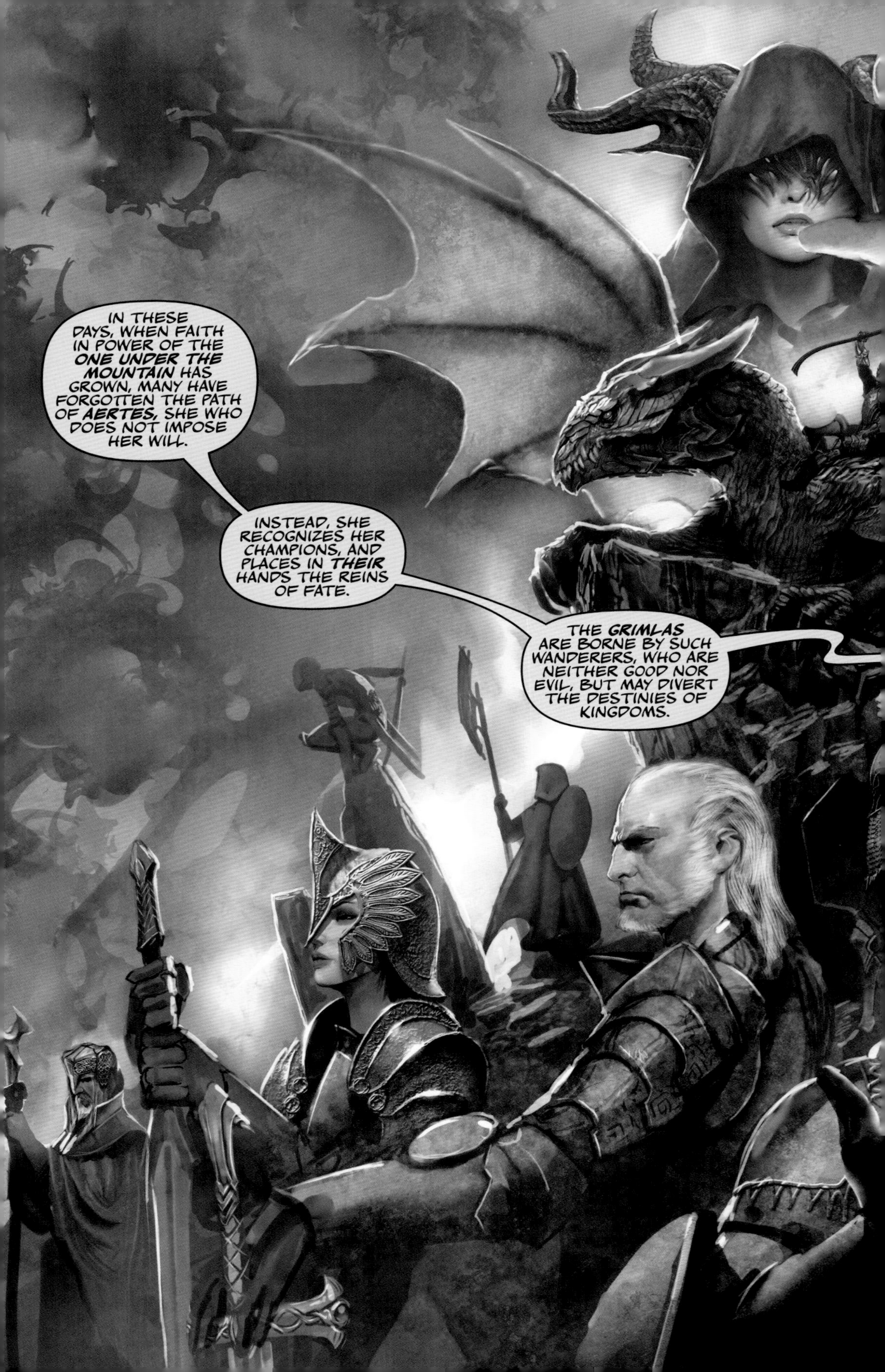
IN THESE DAYS, WHEN FAITH IN POWER OF THE ONE UNDER THE MOUNTAIN HAS GROWN, MANY HAVE FORGOTTEN THE PATH OF AERTES, SHE WHO DOES NOT IMPOSE HER WILL.
INSTEAD, SHE RECOGNIZES HER CHAMPIONS, AND PLACES IN THEIR HANDS THE REINS OF FATE.
THE GRIMLAS ARE BORNE BY SUCH WANDERERS, WHO ARE NEITHER GOOD NOR EVIL, BUT MAY DIVERT THE DESTINIES OF KINGDOMS.

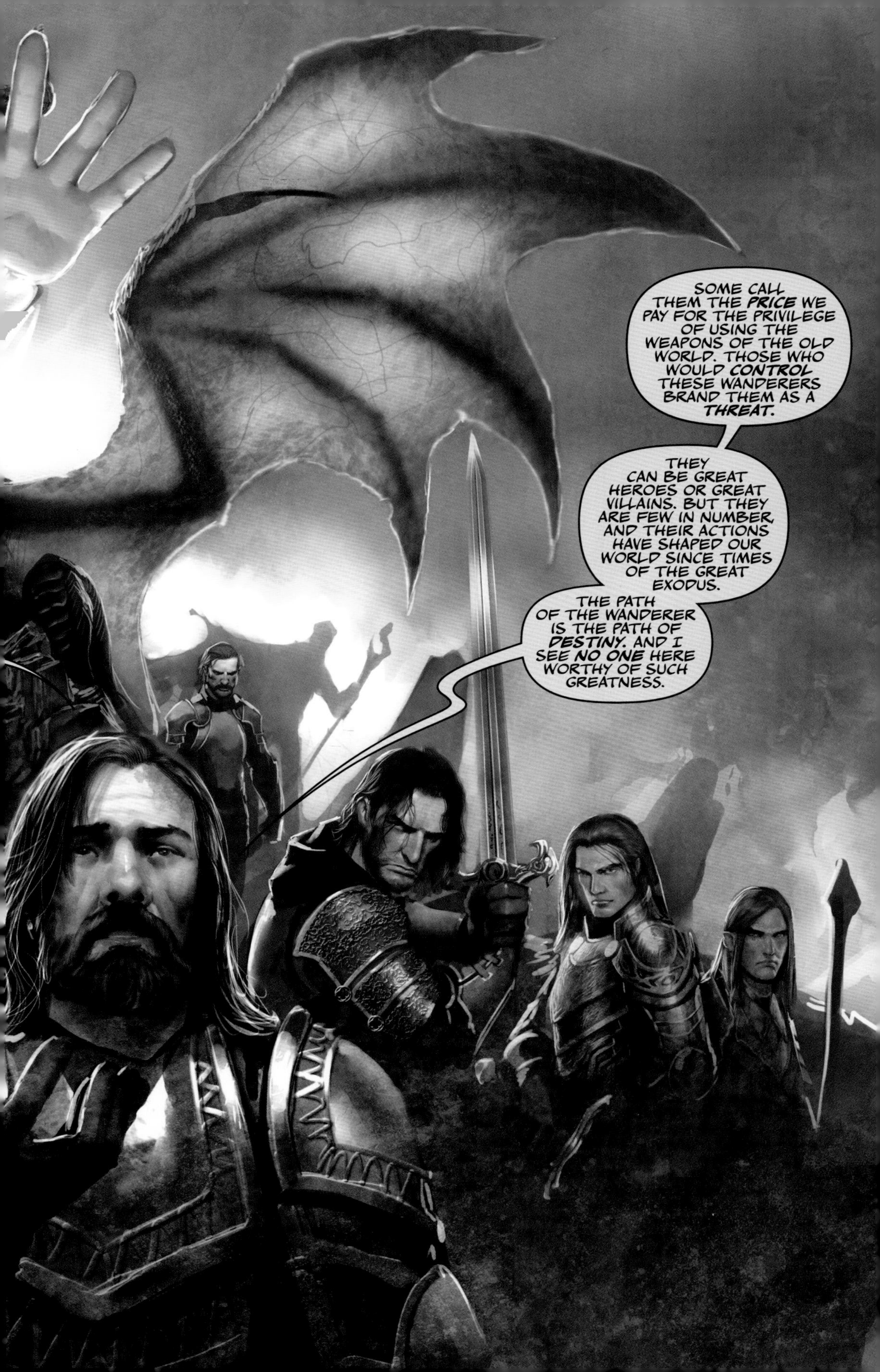
SOME CALL THEM THE PRICE WE PAY FOR THE PRIVILEGE OF USING THE WEAPONS OF THE OLD WORLD. THOSE WHO WOULD CONTROL THESE WANDERERS BRAND THEM AS A THREAT.
THEY CAN BE GREAT HEROES OR GREAT VILLAINS. BUT THEY ARE FEW IN NUMBER, AND THEIR ACTIONS HAVE SHAPED OUR WORLD SINCE TIMES OF THE GREAT EXODUS.
THE PATH OF THE WANDERER IS THE PATH OF DESTINY. AND I SEE NO ONE HERE WORTHY OF SUCH GREATNESS.

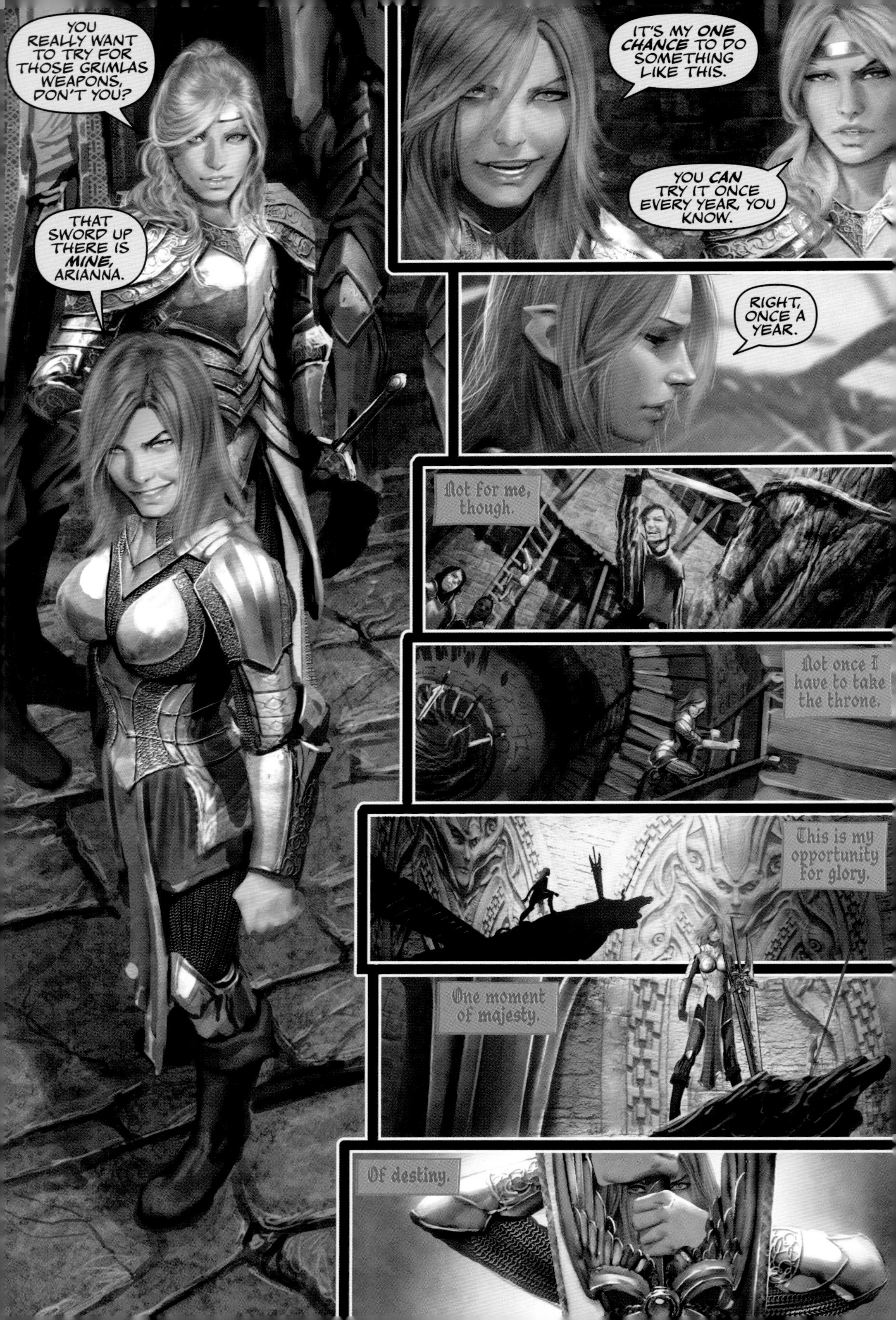

YOU REALLY WANT TO TRY FOR THOSE GRIMLAS WEAPONS, DON'T YOU?
THAT SWORD UP THERE IS MINE, ARIANNA.
IT'S MY ONE CHANCE TO DO SOMETHING LIKE THIS.
YOU CAN TRY IT ONCE EVERY YEAR, YOU KNOW.
RIGHT, ONCE A YEAR.
Not for me, though.
Not once I have to take the throne.
This is my opportunity for glory.
One moment of majesty.
Of destiny.

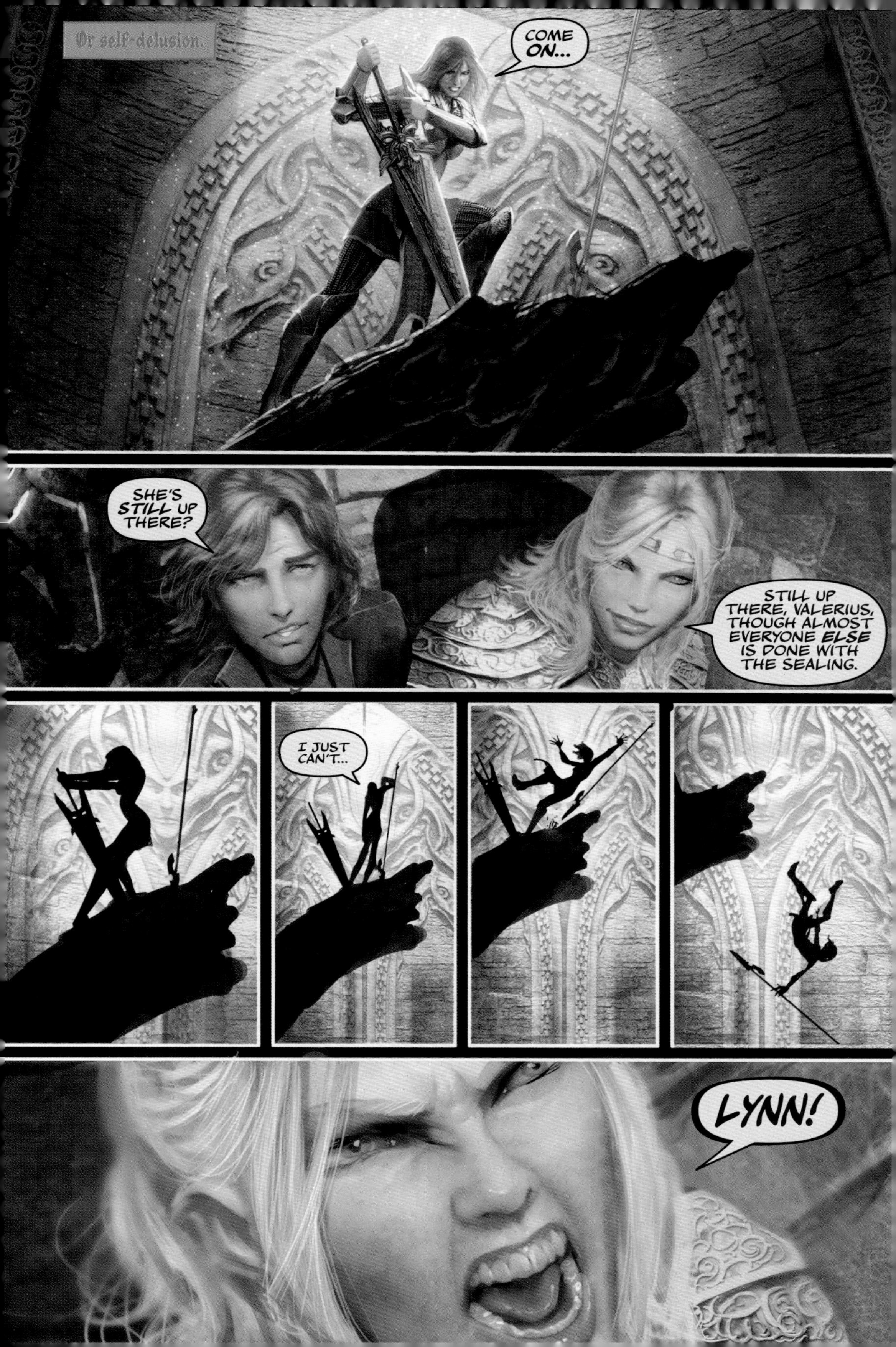
Or self-delusion.
COME ON...
SHE'S STILL UP THERE?
STILL UP THERE, VALERIUS, THOUGH ALMOST EVERYONE ELSE IS DONE WITH THE SEALING.
I JUST CAN'T...
LYNN!

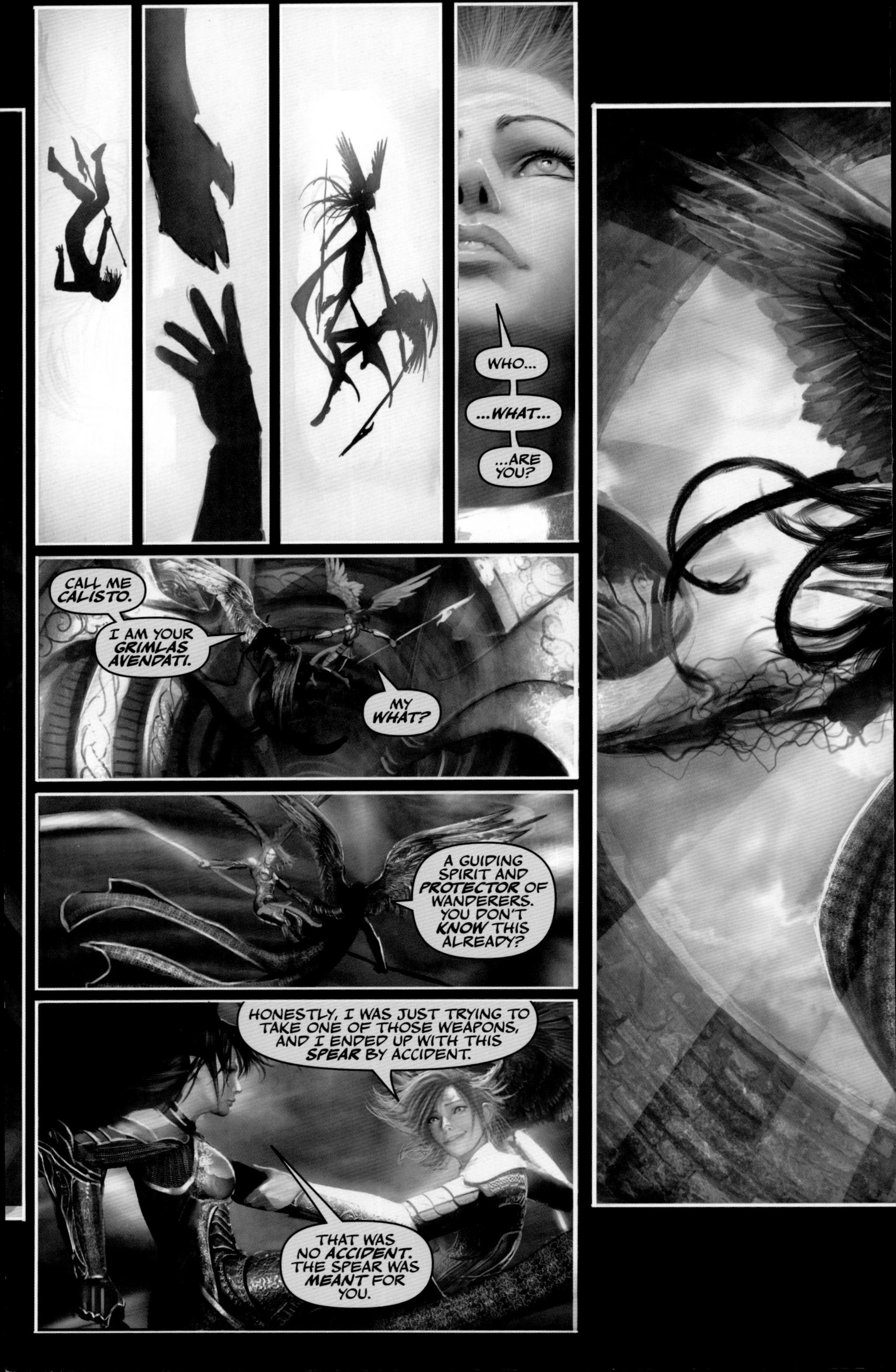
WHO...
...WHAT...
...ARE YOU?
CALL ME CALISTO.
I AM YOUR GRIMLAS AVENDATI.
MY WHAT?
A GUIDING SPIRIT AND PROTECTOR OF WANDERERS. YOU DON'T KNOW THIS ALREADY?
HONESTLY, I WAS JUST TRYING TO TAKE ONE OF THOSE WEAPONS, AND I ENDED UP WITH THIS SPEAR BY ACCIDENT.
THAT WAS NO ACCIDENT. THE SPEAR WAS MEANT FOR YOU.

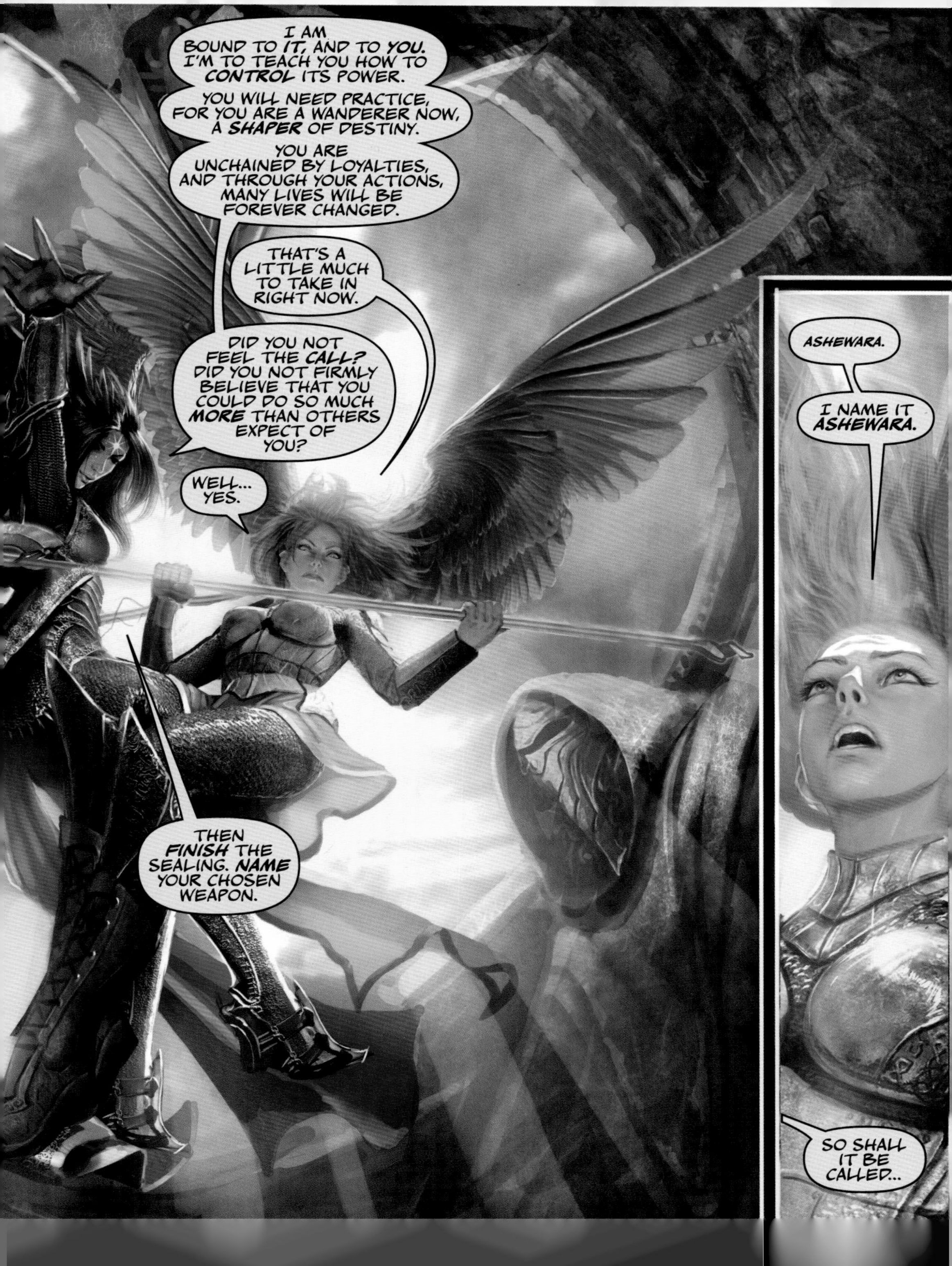
I AM BOUND TO IT, AND TO YOU. I'M TO TEACH YOU HOW TO CONTROL ITS POWER.
YOU WILL NEED PRACTICE, FOR YOU ARE A WANDERER NOW, A SHAPER OF DESTINY.
YOU ARE UNCHAINED BY LOYALTIES, AND THROUGH YOUR ACTIONS, MANY LIVES WILL BE FOREVER CHANGED.
THAT'S A LITTLE MUCH TO TAKE IN RIGHT NOW.
DID YOU NOT FEEL THE CALL? DID YOU NOT FIRMLY BELIEVE THAT YOU COULD DO SO MUCH MORE THAN OTHERS EXPECT OF YOU?
WELL... YES.
THEN FINISH THE SEALING. NAME YOUR CHOSEN WEAPON.
ASHEWARA.
I NAME IT ASHEWARA.
SO SHALL IT BE CALLED...

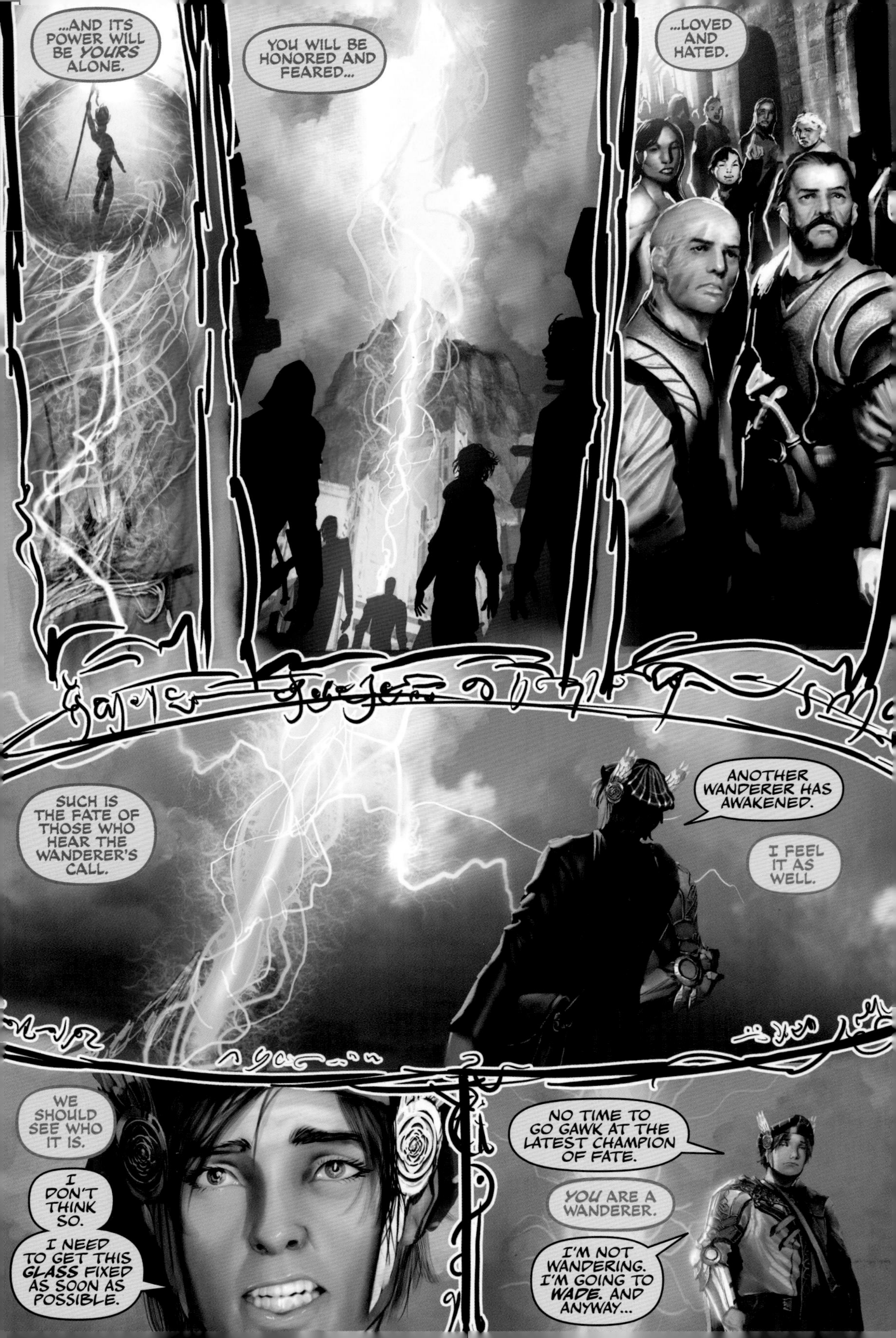
...AND ITS POWER WILL BE *YOURS* ALONE.
YOU WILL BE HONORED AND FEARED...
...LOVED AND HATED.
SUCH IS THE FATE OF THOSE WHO HEAR THE WANDERER'S CALL.
ANOTHER WANDERER HAS AWAKENED.
I FEEL IT AS WELL.
WE SHOULD SEE WHO IT IS.
I DON'T THINK SO.
I NEED TO GET THIS *GLASS* FIXED AS SOON AS POSSIBLE.
NO TIME TO GO GAWK AT THE LATEST CHAMPION OF FATE.
YOU ARE A WANDERER.
I'M NOT WANDERING. I'M GOING TO *WADE*. AND ANYWAY...

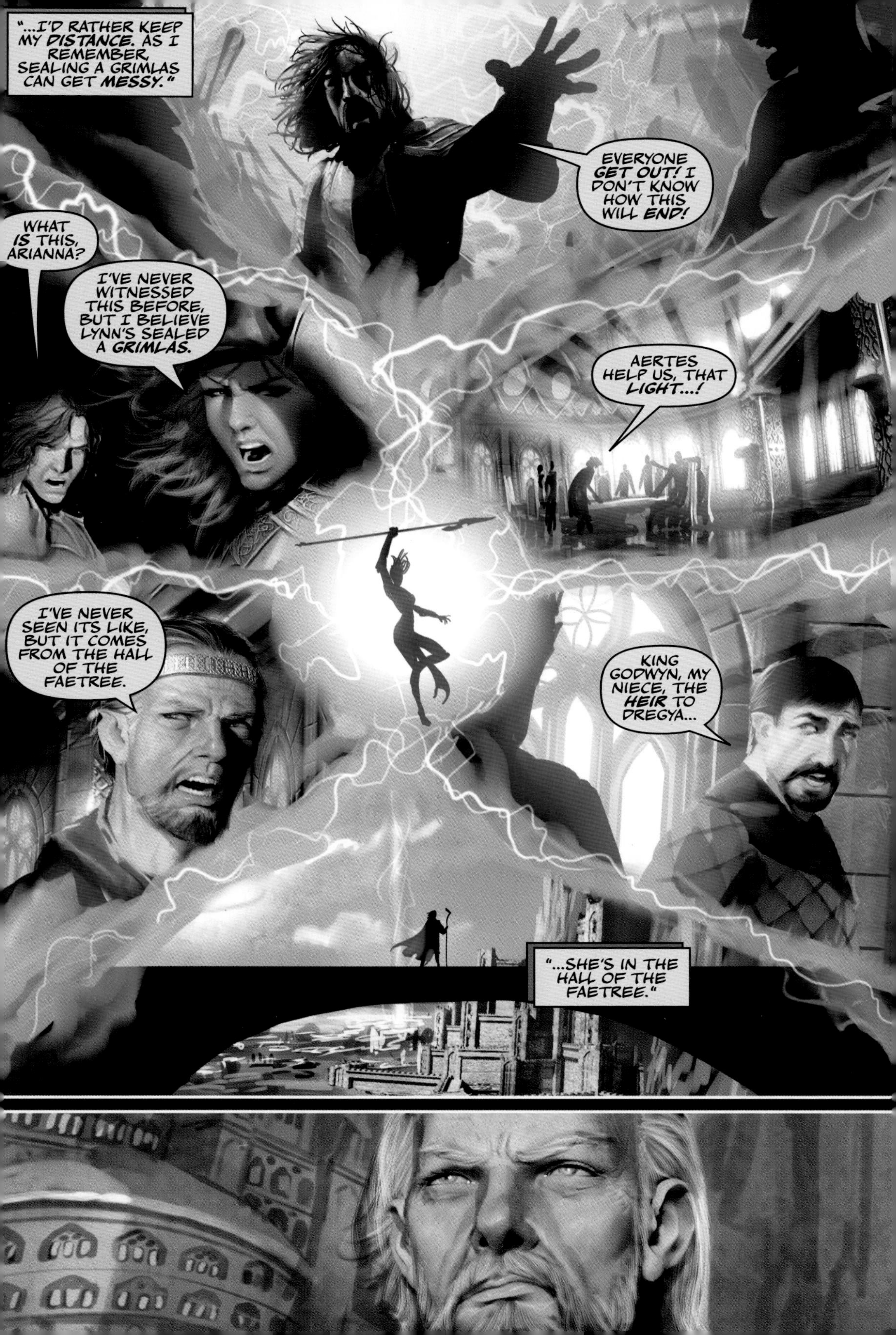
"...I'D RATHER KEEP MY DISTANCE. AS I REMEMBER, SEALING A GRIMLAS CAN GET MESSY."
EVERYONE GET OUT! I DON'T KNOW HOW THIS WILL END!
WHAT IS THIS, ARIANNA?
I'VE NEVER WITNESSED THIS BEFORE, BUT I BELIEVE LYNN'S SEALED A GRIMLAS.
AERTES HELP US, THAT LIGHT...!
I'VE NEVER SEEN ITS LIKE, BUT IT COMES FROM THE HALL OF THE FAETREE.
KING GODWYN, MY NIECE, THE HEIR TO DREGYA...
"...SHE'S IN THE HALL OF THE FAETREE."

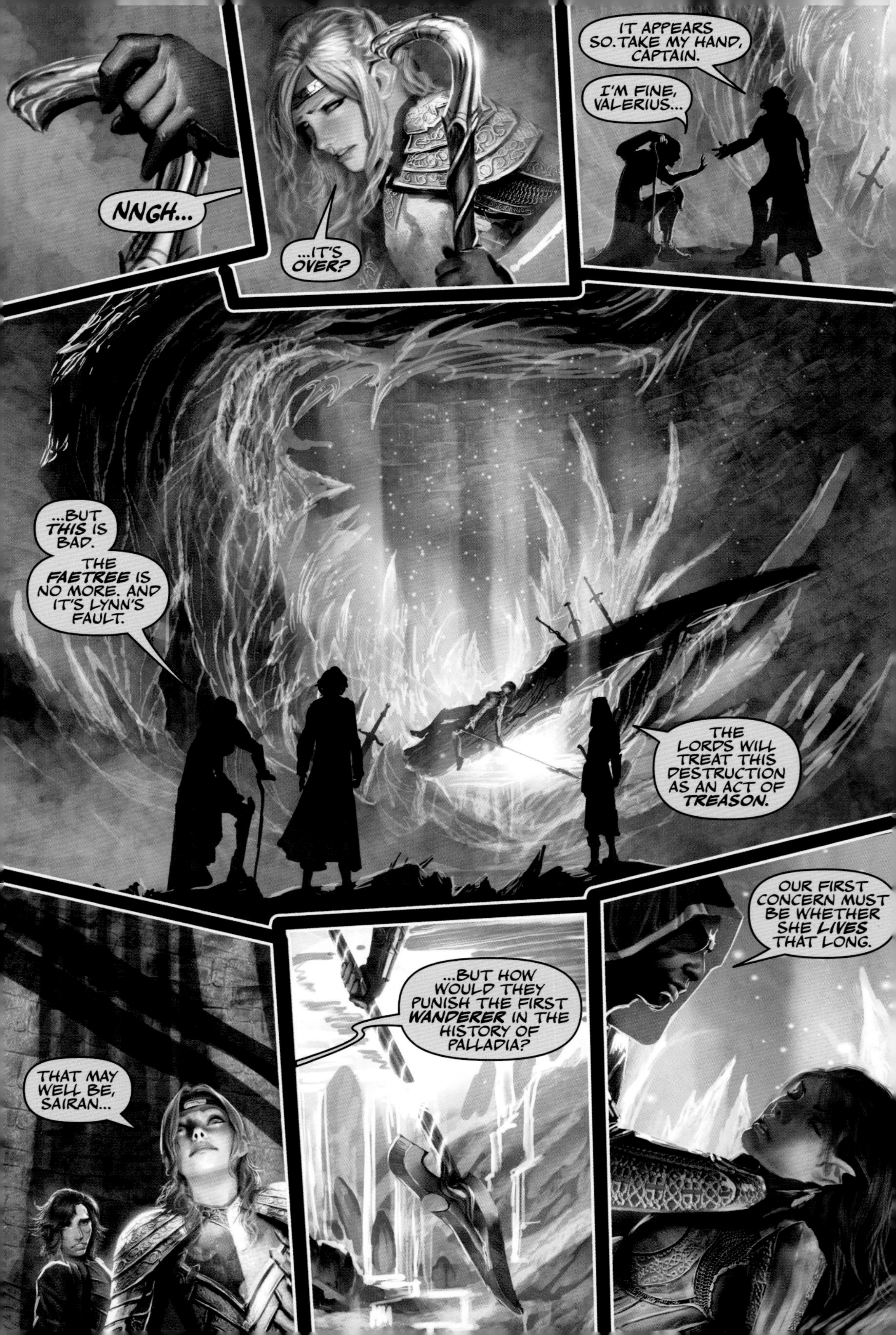
NNGH...
...IT'S OVER?
IT APPEARS SO. TAKE MY HAND, CAPTAIN.
I'M FINE, VALERIUS...
...BUT THIS IS BAD.
THE FAETREE IS NO MORE. AND IT'S LYNN'S FAULT.
THE LORDS WILL TREAT THIS DESTRUCTION AS AN ACT OF TREASON.
THAT MAY WELL BE, SAIRAN...
...BUT HOW WOULD THEY PUNISH THE FIRST WANDERER IN THE HISTORY OF PALLADIA?
OUR FIRST CONCERN MUST BE WHETHER SHE LIVES THAT LONG.

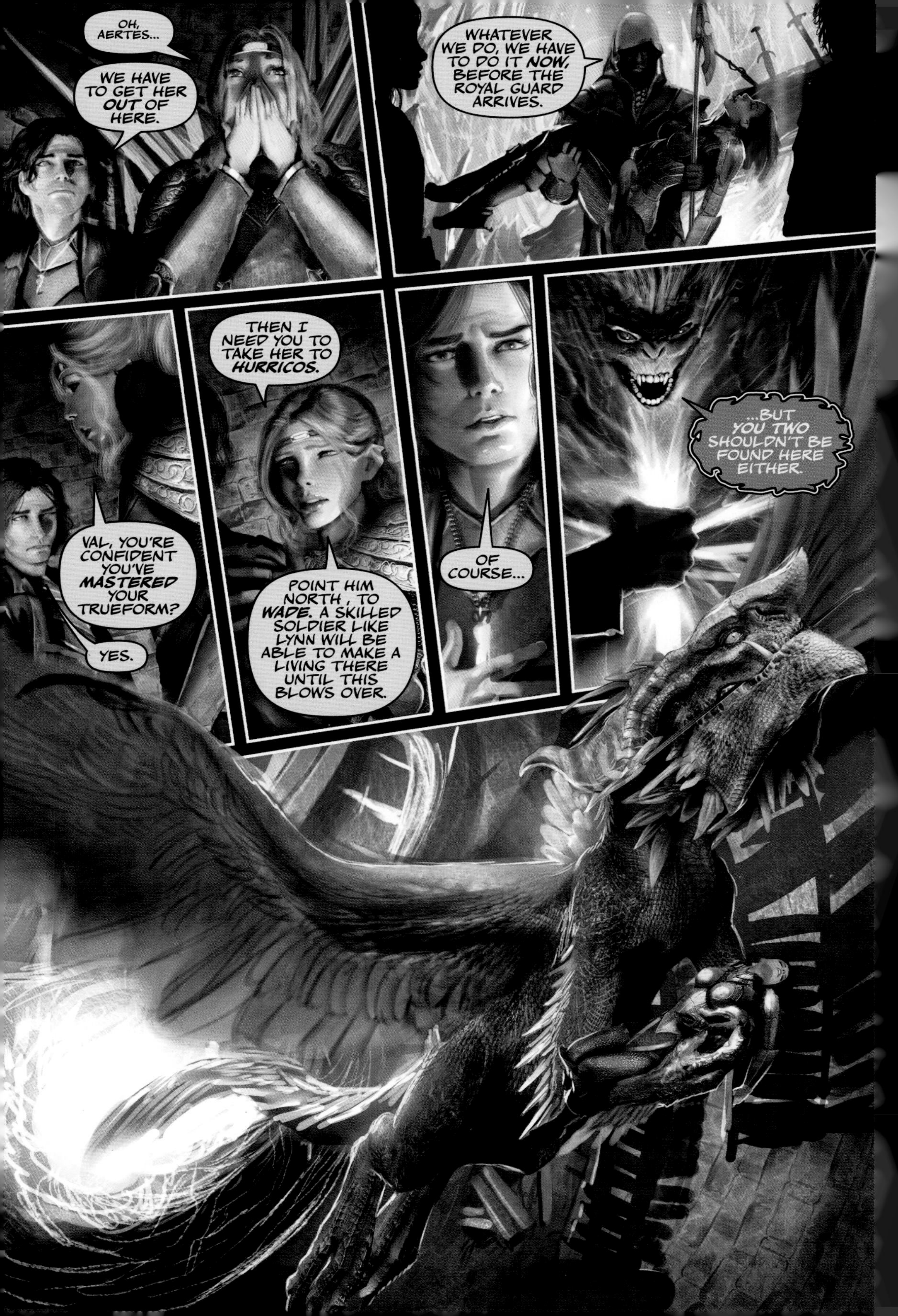

OH, AERTES...
WE HAVE TO GET HER OUT OF HERE.
WHATEVER WE DO, WE HAVE TO DO IT NOW, BEFORE THE ROYAL GUARD ARRIVES.
VAL, YOU'RE CONFIDENT YOU'VE MASTERED YOUR TRUEFORM?
YES.
THEN I NEED YOU TO TAKE HER TO HURRICOS.
POINT HIM NORTH , TO WADE. A SKILLED SOLDIER LIKE LYNN WILL BE ABLE TO MAKE A LIVING THERE UNTIL THIS BLOWS OVER.
OF COURSE...
...BUT YOU TWO SHOULDN'T BE FOUND HERE EITHER.

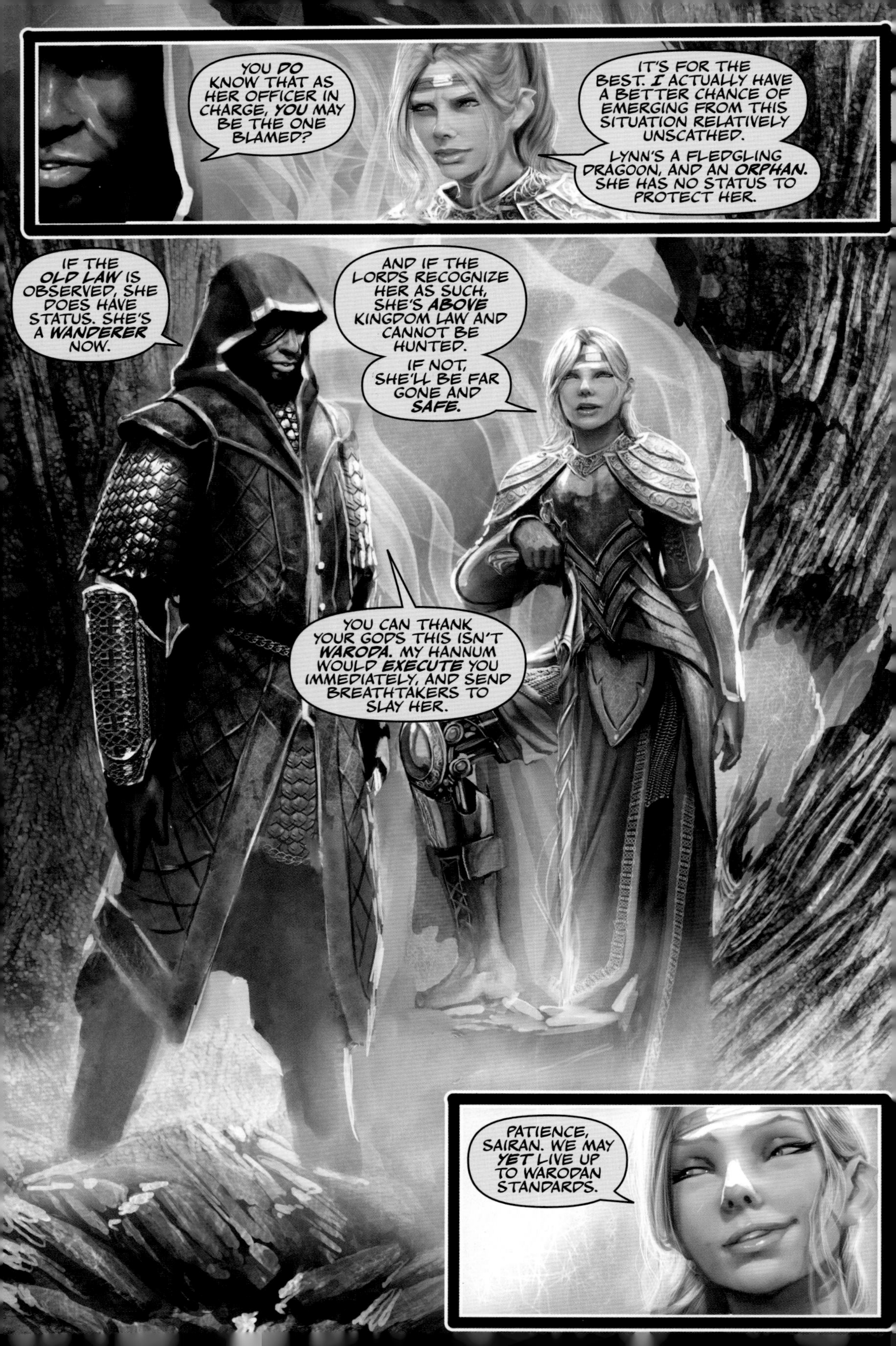
YOU DO KNOW THAT AS HER OFFICER IN CHARGE, YOU MAY BE THE ONE BLAMED?
IT'S FOR THE BEST. I ACTUALLY HAVE A BETTER CHANCE OF EMERGING FROM THIS SITUATION RELATIVELY UNSCATHED.
LYNN'S A FLEDGLING DRAGOON, AND AN ORPHAN. SHE HAS NO STATUS TO PROTECT HER.
IF THE OLD LAW IS OBSERVED, SHE DOES HAVE STATUS. SHE'S A WANDERER NOW.
AND IF THE LORDS RECOGNIZE HER AS SUCH, SHE'S ABOVE KINGDOM LAW AND CANNOT BE HUNTED.
IF NOT, SHE'LL BE FAR GONE AND SAFE.
YOU CAN THANK YOUR GODS THIS ISN'T WARODA. MY HANNUM WOULD EXECUTE YOU IMMEDIATELY, AND SEND BREATHTAKERS TO SLAY HER.
PATIENCE, SAIRAN. WE MAY YET LIVE UP TO WARODAN STANDARDS.

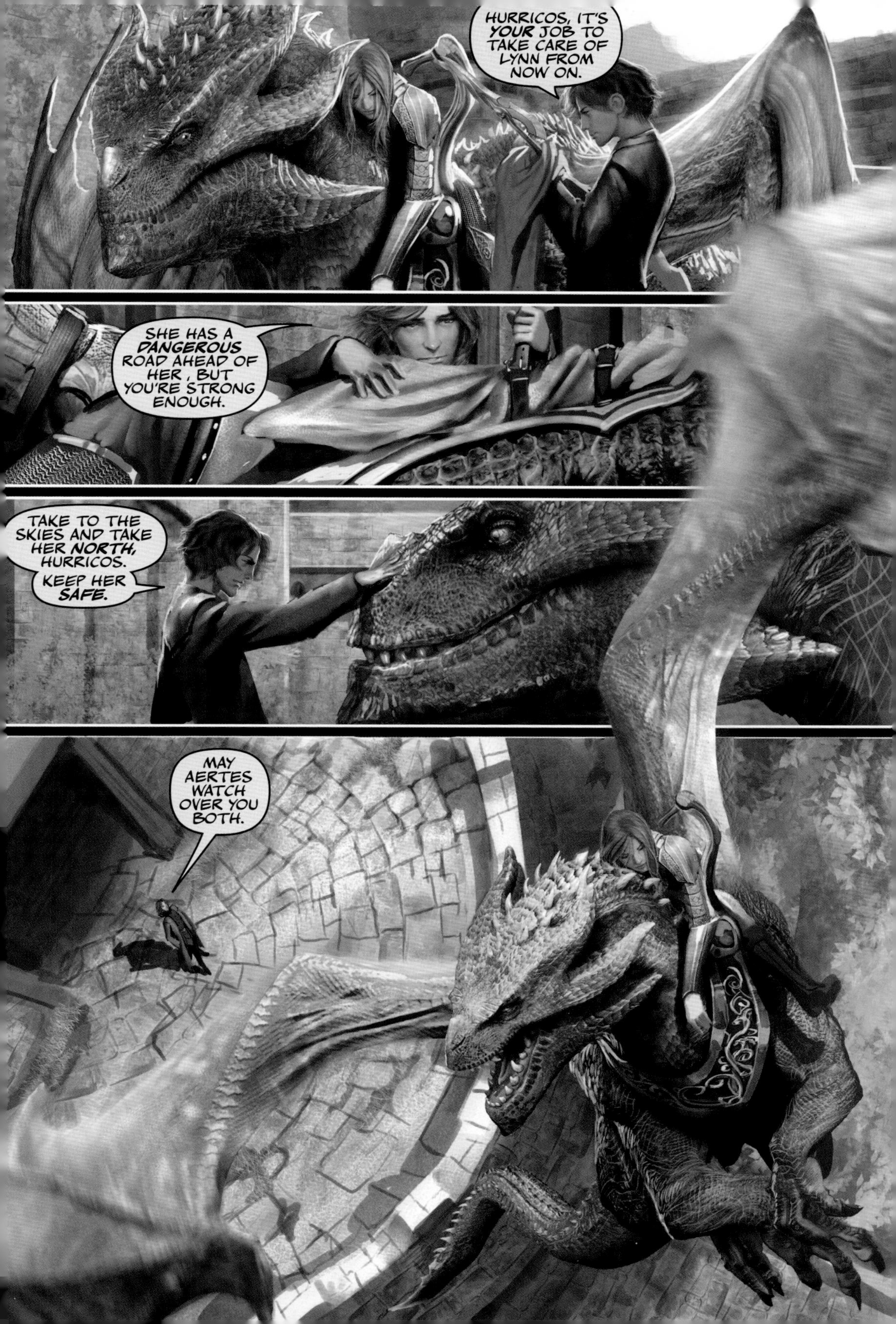
HURRICOS, IT'S YOUR JOB TO TAKE CARE OF LYNN FROM NOW ON.
SHE HAS A DANGEROUS ROAD AHEAD OF HER, BUT YOU'RE STRONG ENOUGH.
TAKE TO THE SKIES AND TAKE HER NORTH, HURRICOS. KEEP HER SAFE.
MAY AERTES WATCH OVER YOU BOTH.

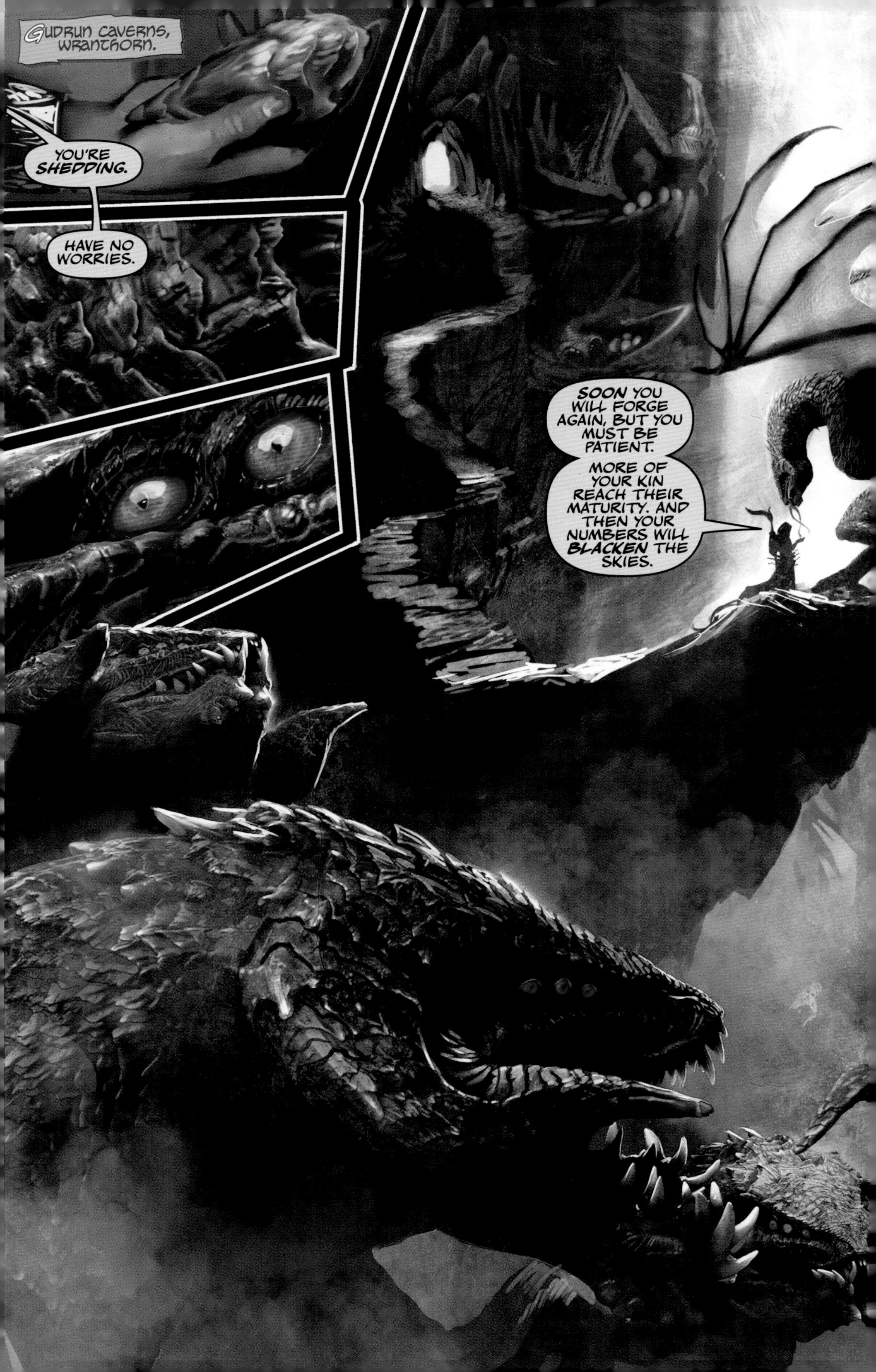
GUDRUN CAVERNS, WRANTHORN.
YOU'RE SHEDDING.
HAVE NO WORRIES.
SOON YOU WILL FORGE AGAIN, BUT YOU MUST BE PATIENT.
MORE OF YOUR KIN REACH THEIR MATURITY. AND THEN YOUR NUMBERS WILL BLACKEN THE SKIES.

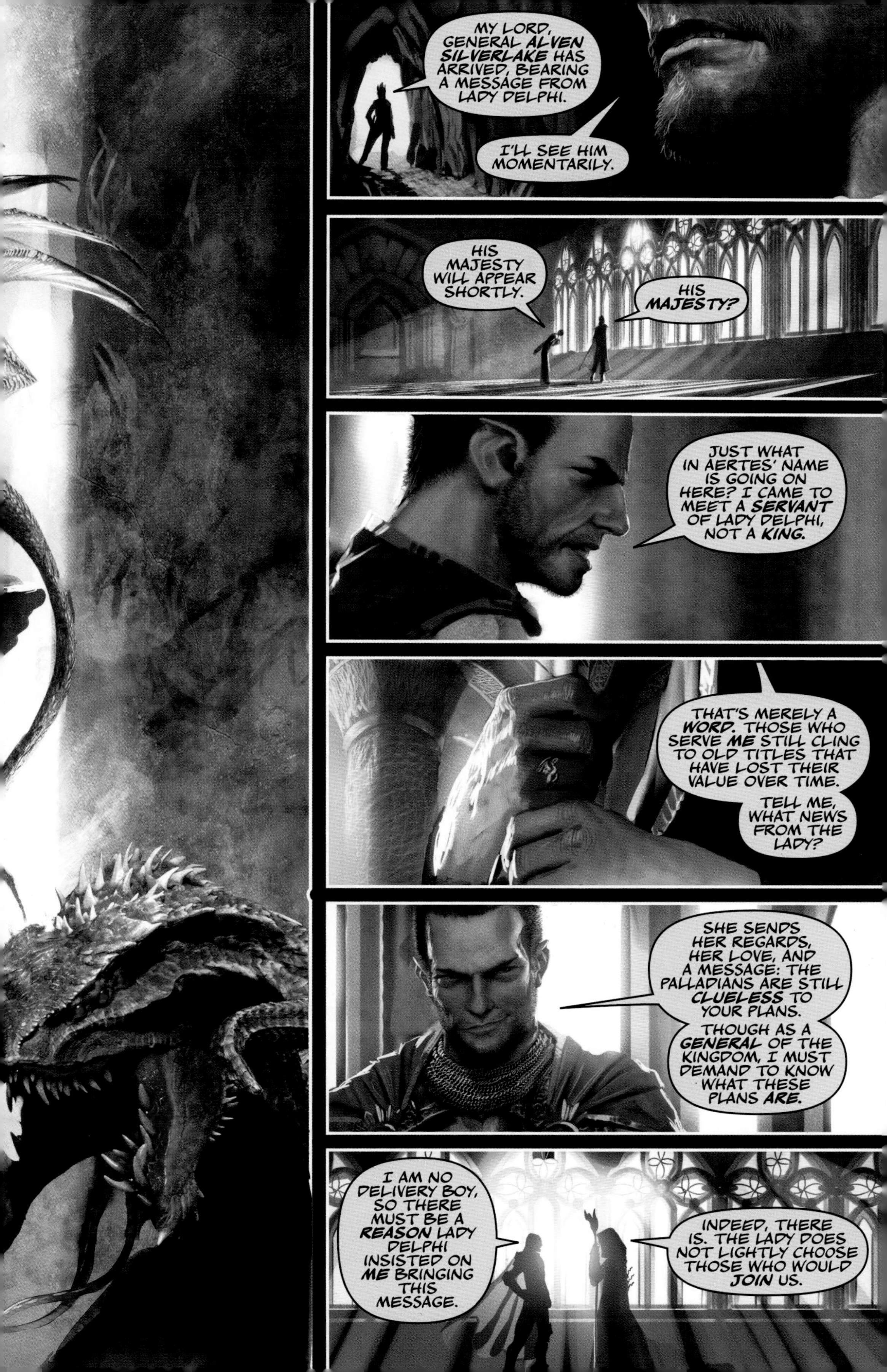
MY LORD, GENERAL ALVEN SILVERLAKE HAS ARRIVED, BEARING A MESSAGE FROM LADY DELPHI.
I'LL SEE HIM MOMENTARILY.
HIS MAJESTY WILL APPEAR SHORTLY.
HIS MAJESTY?
JUST WHAT IN AERTES' NAME IS GOING ON HERE? I CAME TO MEET A SERVANT OF LADY DELPHI, NOT A KING.
THAT'S MERELY A WORD. THOSE WHO SERVE ME STILL CLING TO OLD TITLES THAT HAVE LOST THEIR VALUE OVER TIME.
TELL ME, WHAT NEWS FROM THE LADY?
SHE SENDS HER REGARDS, HER LOVE, AND A MESSAGE: THE PALLADIANS ARE STILL CLUELESS TO YOUR PLANS.
THOUGH AS A GENERAL OF THE KINGDOM, I MUST DEMAND TO KNOW WHAT THESE PLANS ARE.
I AM NO DELIVERY BOY, SO THERE MUST BE A REASON LADY DELPHI INSISTED ON ME BRINGING THIS MESSAGE.
INDEED, THERE IS. THE LADY DOES NOT LIGHTLY CHOOSE THOSE WHO WOULD JOIN US.

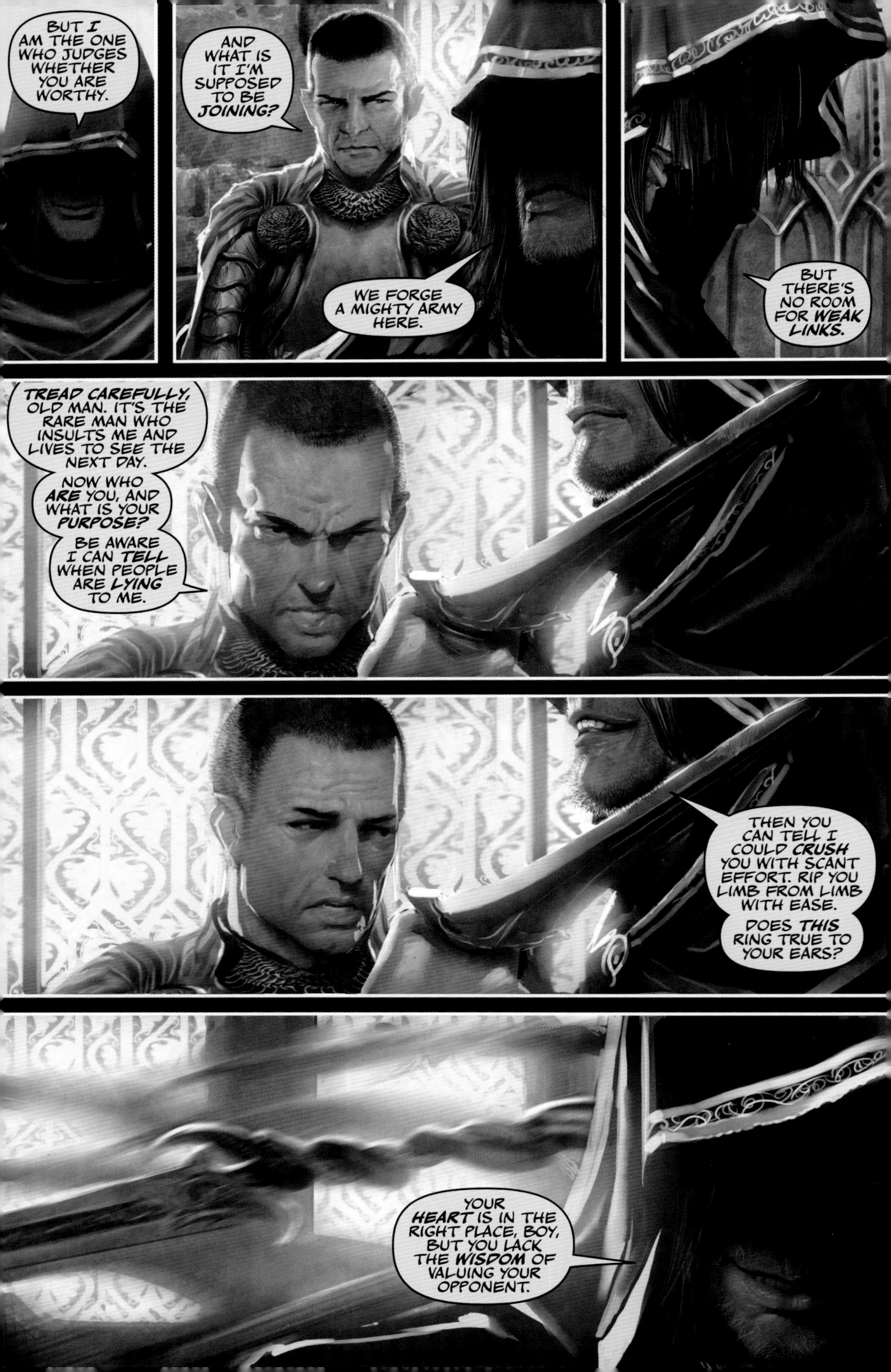
BUT I AM THE ONE WHO JUDGES WHETHER YOU ARE WORTHY.
AND WHAT IS IT I'M SUPPOSED TO BE JOINING?
WE FORGE A MIGHTY ARMY HERE.
BUT THERE'S NO ROOM FOR WEAK LINKS.
TREAD CAREFULLY, OLD MAN. IT'S THE RARE MAN WHO INSULTS ME AND LIVES TO SEE THE NEXT DAY.
NOW WHO ARE YOU, AND WHAT IS YOUR PURPOSE?
BE AWARE I CAN TELL WHEN PEOPLE ARE LYING TO ME.
THEN YOU CAN TELL I COULD CRUSH YOU WITH SCANT EFFORT. RIP YOU LIMB FROM LIMB WITH EASE.
DOES THIS RING TRUE TO YOUR EARS?
YOUR HEART IS IN THE RIGHT PLACE, BOY, BUT YOU LACK THE WISDOM OF VALUING YOUR OPPONENT.

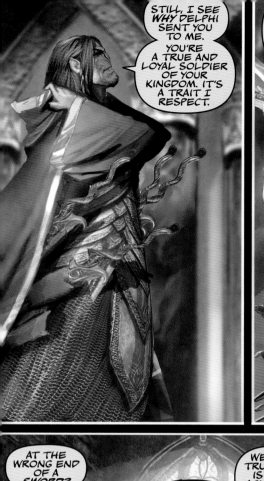

STILL, I SEE WHY DELPHI SENT YOU TO ME. YOU'RE A TRUE AND LOYAL SOLDIER OF YOUR KINGDOM. IT'S A TRAIT I RESPECT.

LISTEN WELL, ALVEN SILVERLAKE. I AM A *FRIEND* TO YOUR KING, AND OUR DEEDS HERE ARE FOR THE *GOOD* OF THIS KINGDOM.

FOR THE GOOD OF THE ENTIRE CONTINENT.

I'M TO TAKE YOU AT YOUR WORD?

AT THE WRONG END OF A SWORD?

WELL SAID. TRUE *TRUST* IS RARELY ACHIEVED AT POINT OF A BLADE.

LET'S *START OVER,* SHALL WE?

THAT SOUNDS... REASONABLE.

EXCELLENT! THEN ALLOW ME TO INTRODUCE MYSELF...

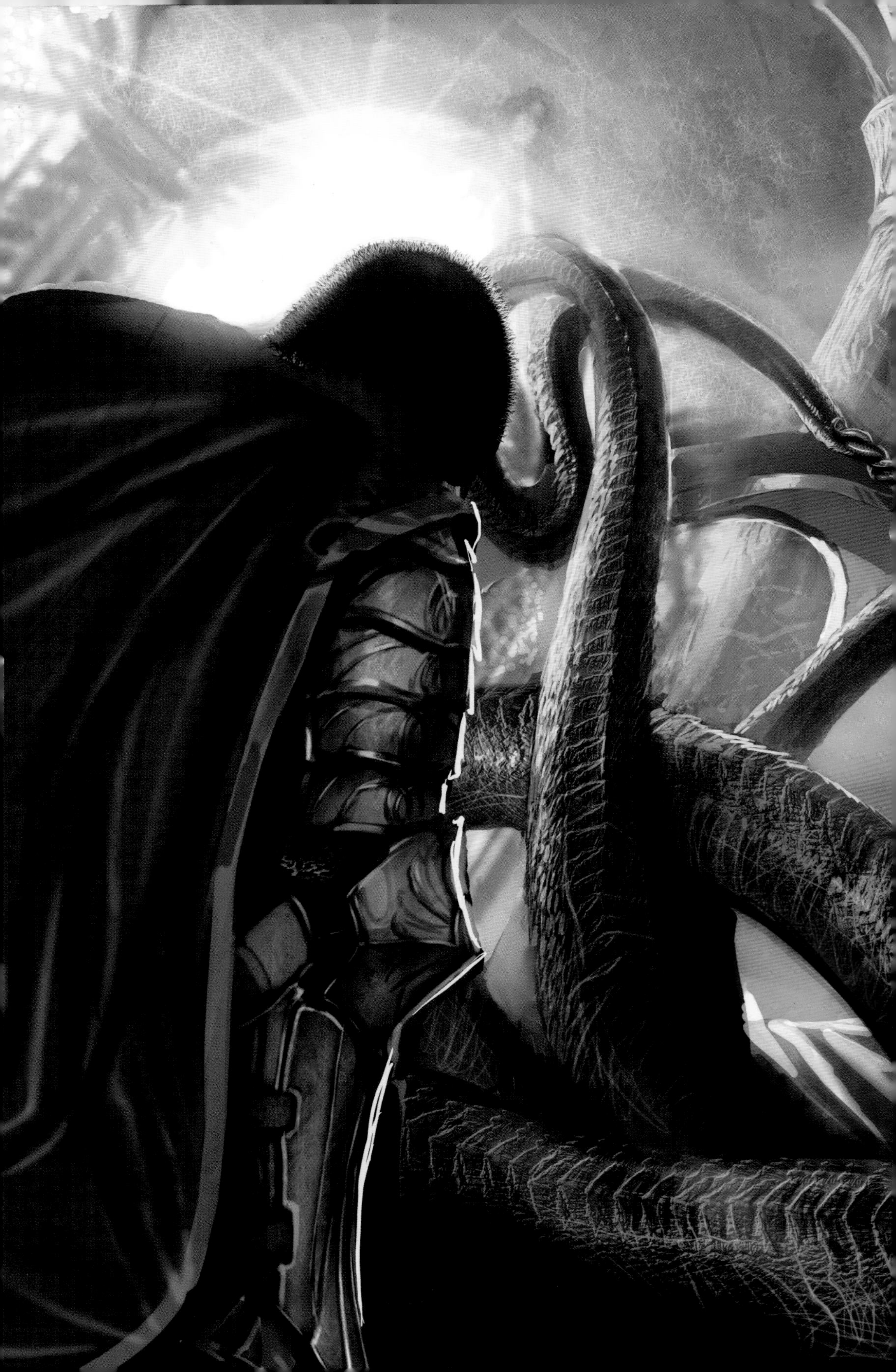

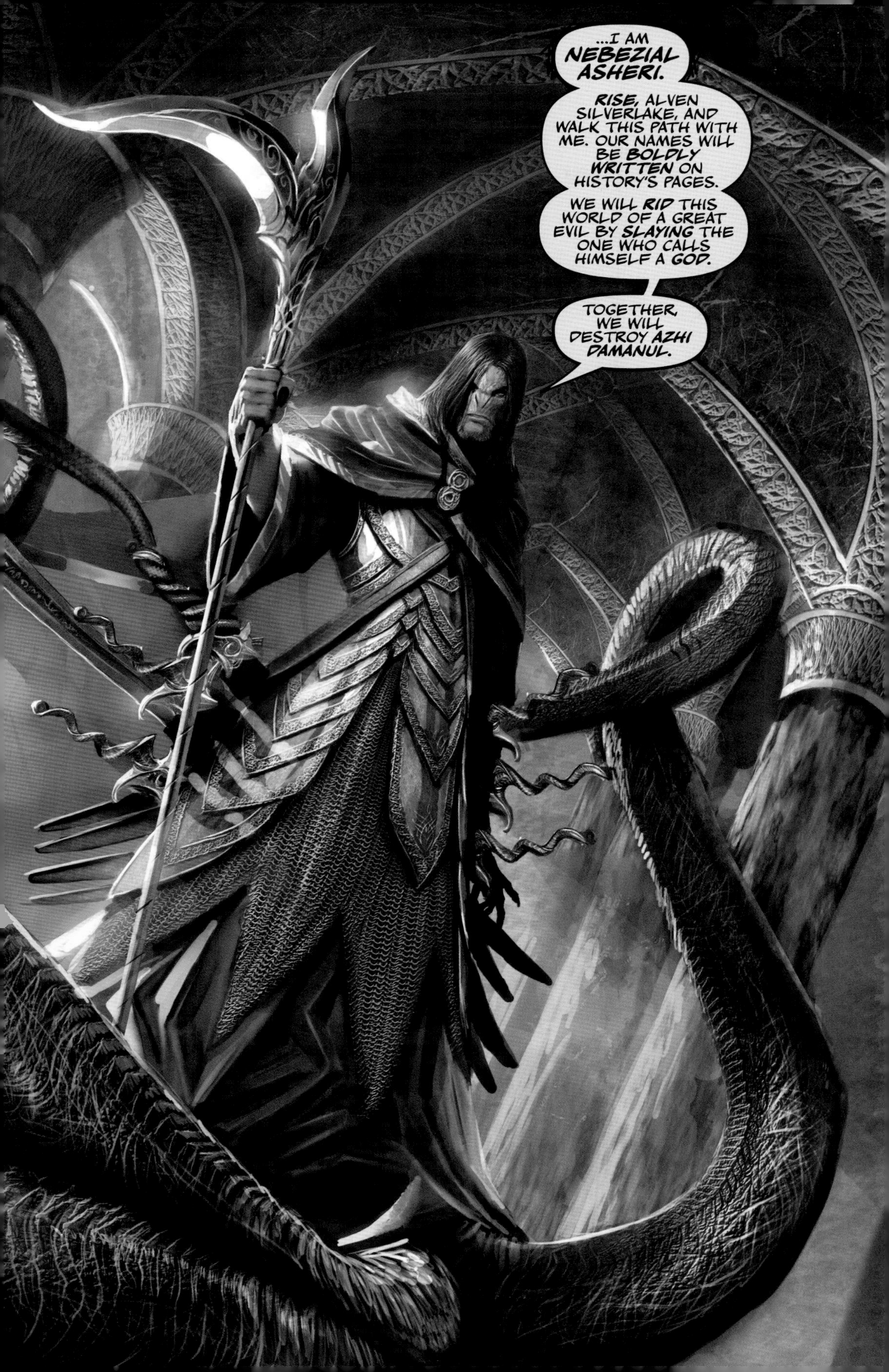
...I AM NEBEZIAL ASHERI.
RISE, ALVEN SILVERLAKE, AND WALK THIS PATH WITH ME. OUR NAMES WILL BE BOLDLY WRITTEN ON HISTORY'S PAGES.
WE WILL RID THIS WORLD OF A GREAT EVIL BY SLAYING THE ONE WHO CALLS HIMSELF A GOD.
TOGETHER, WE WILL DESTROY AZHI DAMANUL.

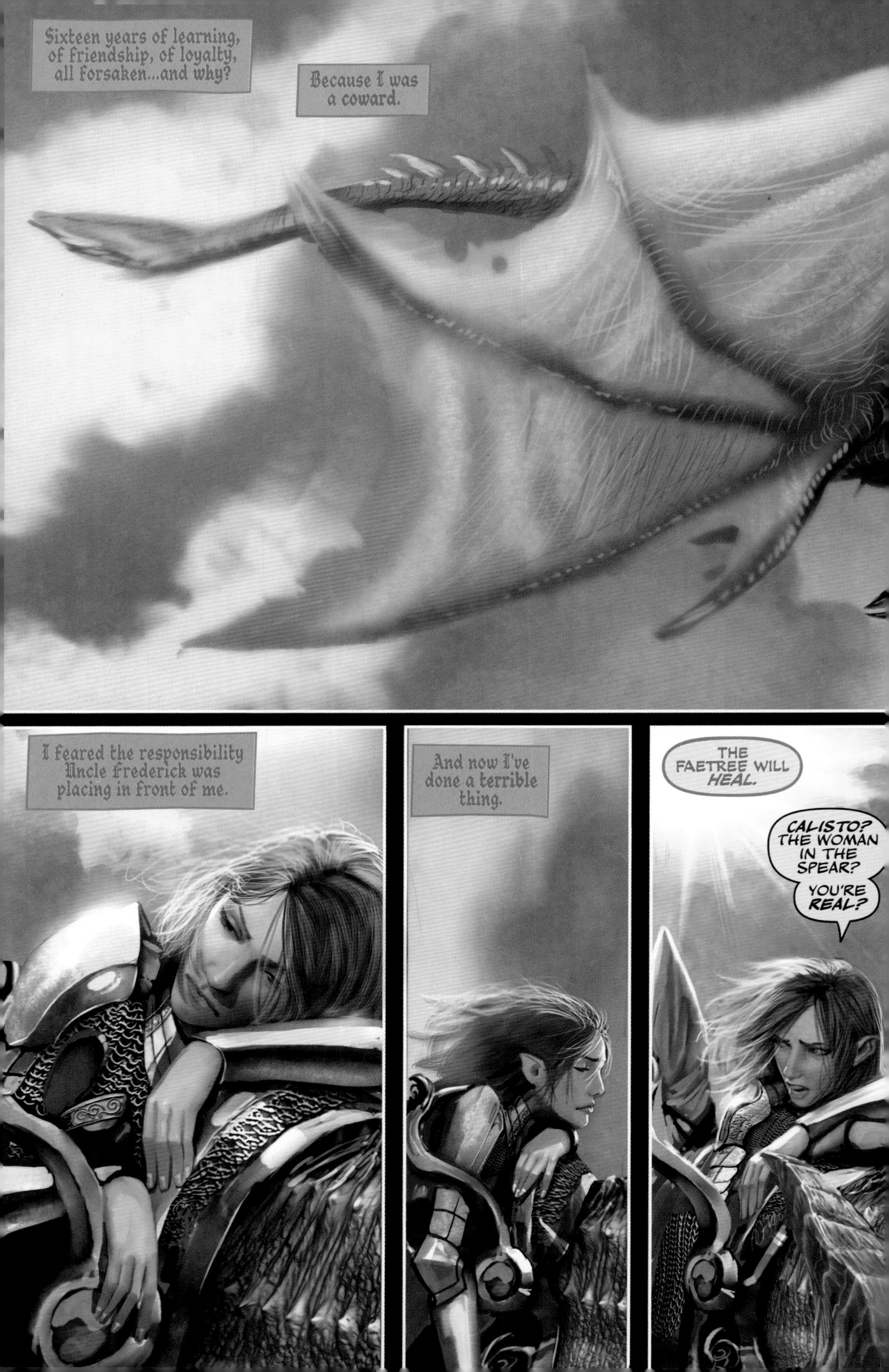
Sixteen years of learning, of friendship, of loyalty, all forsaken...and why?
Because I was a coward.
I feared the responsibility Uncle Frederick was placing in front of me.
And now I've done a terrible thing.
THE FAETREE WILL HEAL.
CALISTO? THE WOMAN IN THE SPEAR?
YOU'RE REAL?

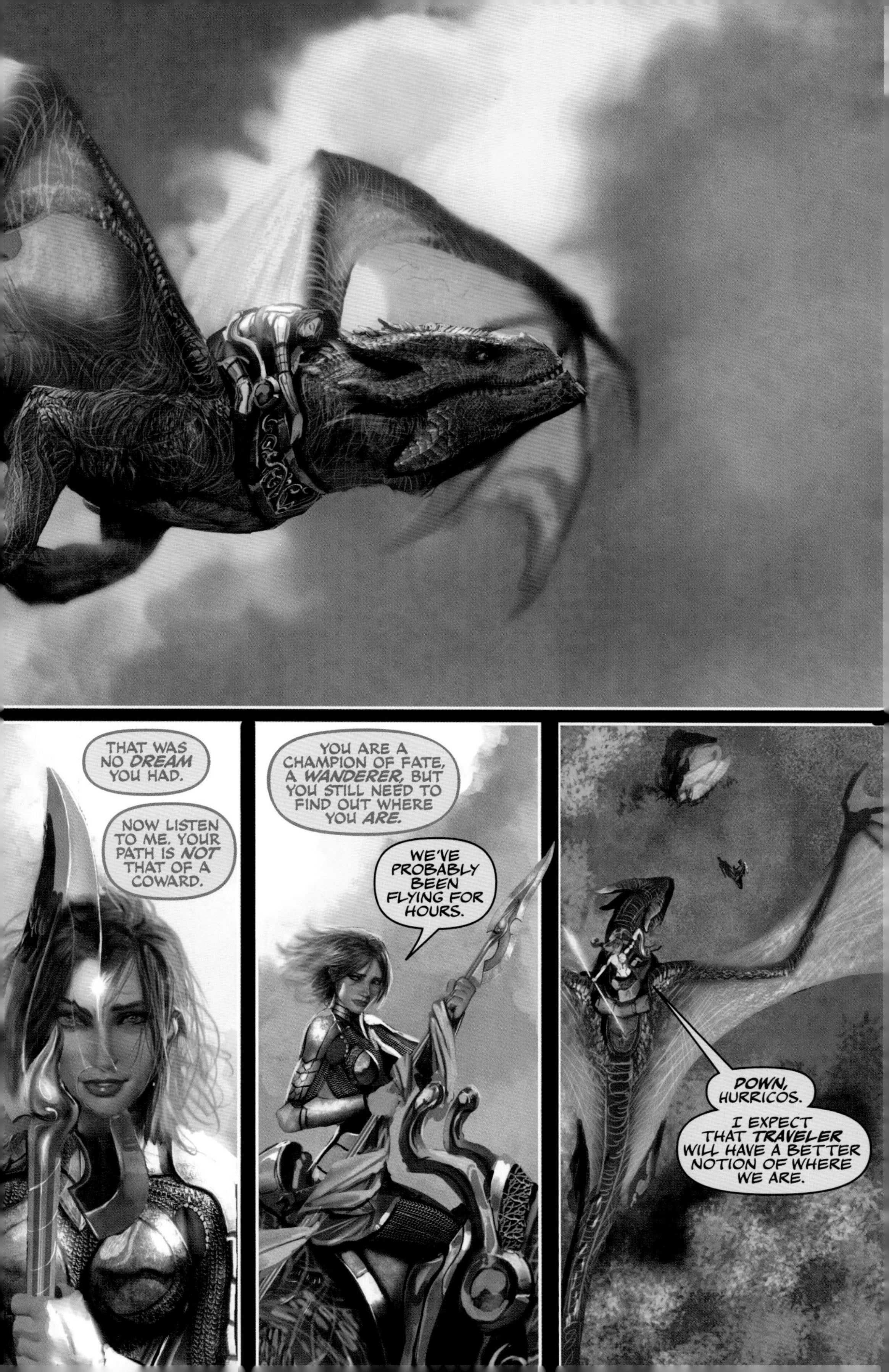
THAT WAS NO *DREAM* YOU HAD.
NOW LISTEN TO ME. YOUR PATH IS *NOT* THAT OF A COWARD.
YOU ARE A CHAMPION OF FATE, A *WANDERER,* BUT YOU STILL NEED TO FIND OUT WHERE YOU *ARE.*
WE'VE PROBABLY BEEN FLYING FOR HOURS.
DOWN, HURRICOS.
I EXPECT THAT *TRAVELER* WILL HAVE A BETTER NOTION OF WHERE WE ARE.

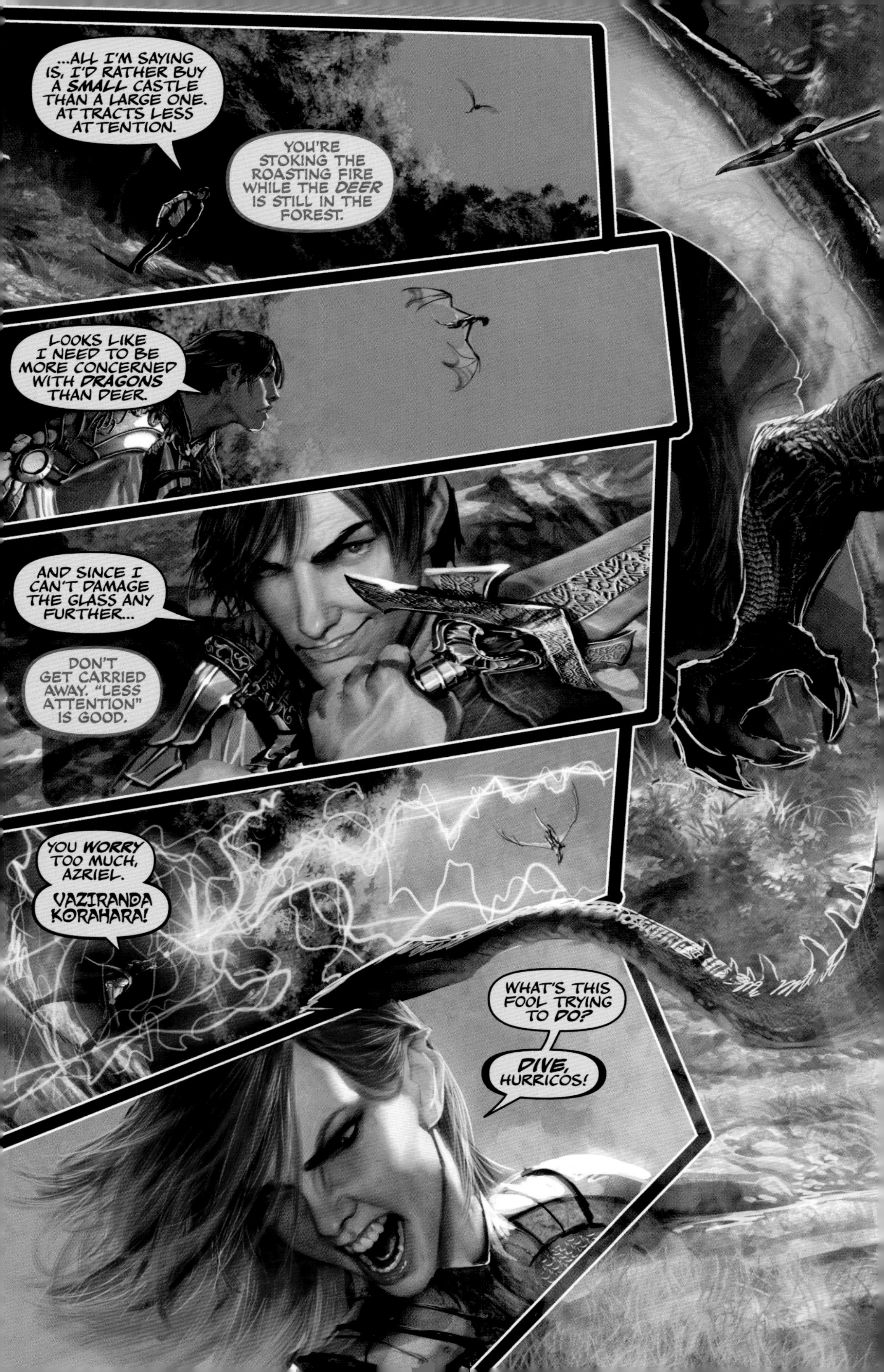
...ALL I'M SAYING IS, I'D RATHER BUY A SMALL CASTLE THAN A LARGE ONE. ATTRACTS LESS ATTENTION.
YOU'RE STOKING THE ROASTING FIRE WHILE THE DEER IS STILL IN THE FOREST.
LOOKS LIKE I NEED TO BE MORE CONCERNED WITH DRAGONS THAN DEER.
AND SINCE I CAN'T DAMAGE THE GLASS ANY FURTHER...
DON'T GET CARRIED AWAY. "LESS ATTENTION" IS GOOD.
YOU WORRY TOO MUCH, AZRIEL.
VAZIRANDA KORAHARA!
WHAT'S THIS FOOL TRYING TO DO?
DIVE, HURRICOS!

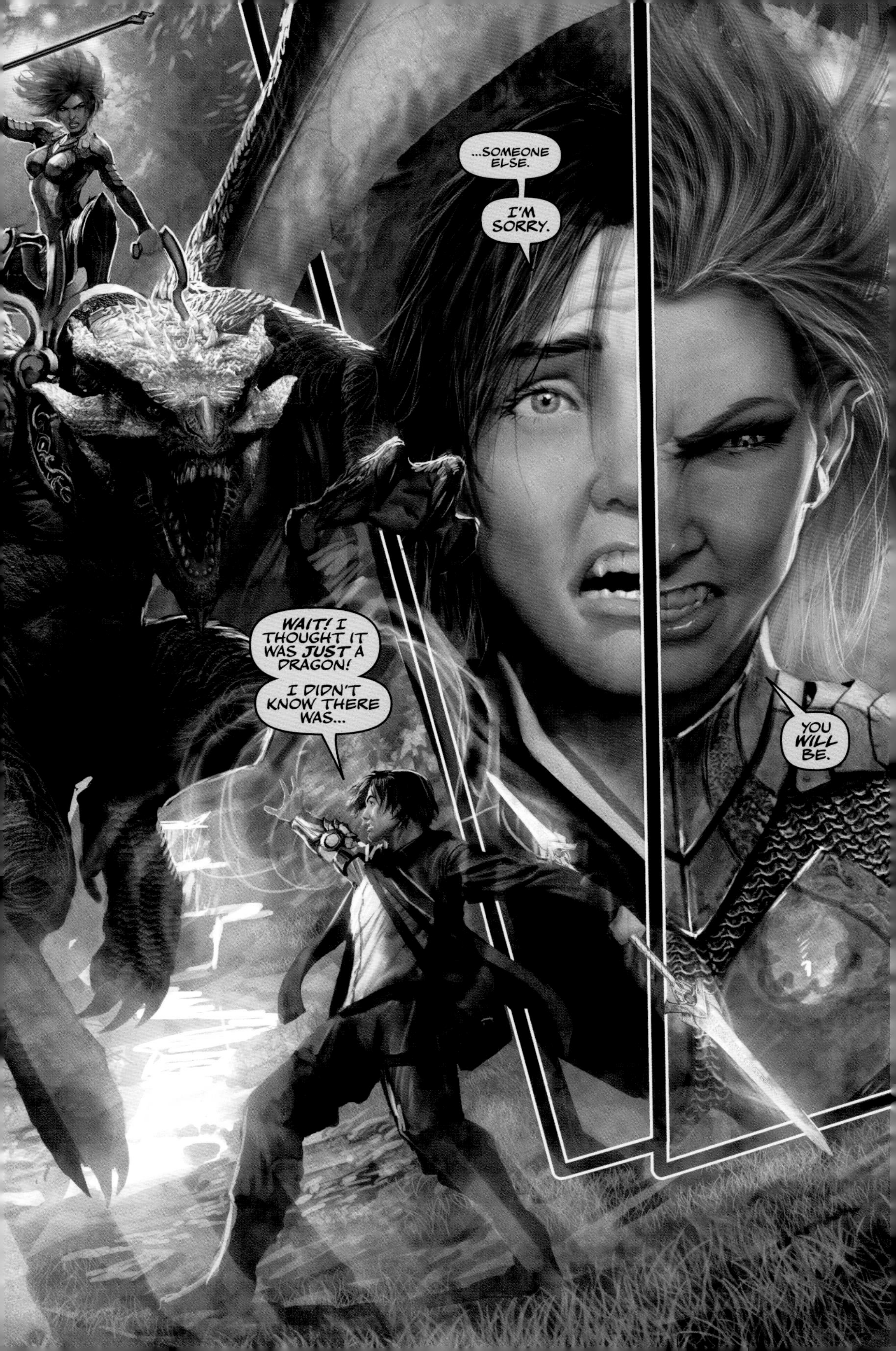
...SOMEONE ELSE.
I'M SORRY.
WAIT! I THOUGHT IT WAS JUST A DRAGON!
I DIDN'T KNOW THERE WAS...
YOU WILL BE.

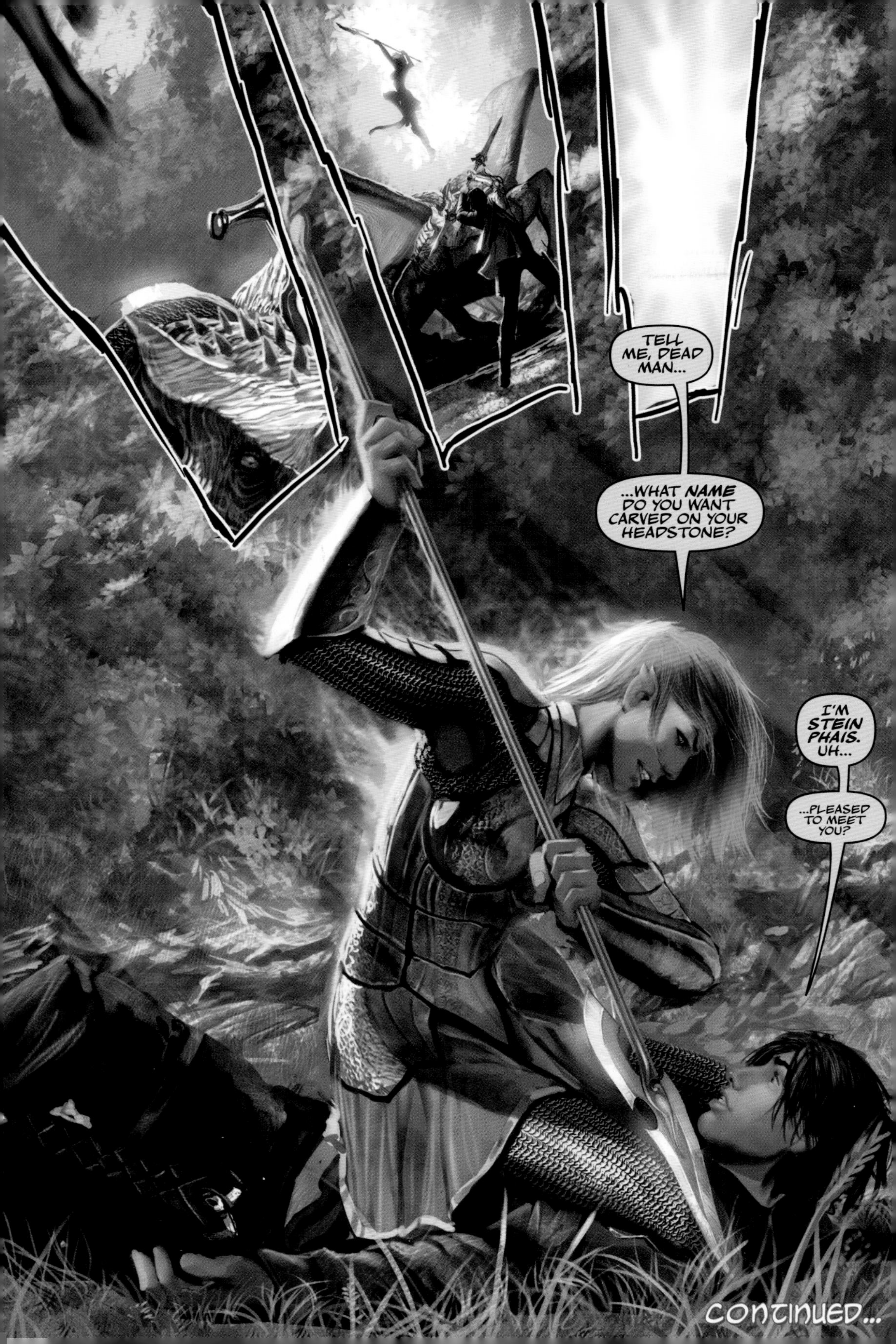
TELL ME, DEAD MAN...
...WHAT NAME DO YOU WANT CARVED ON YOUR HEADSTONE?
I'M STEIN PHAIS. UH...
...PLEASED TO MEET YOU?
CONTINUED...

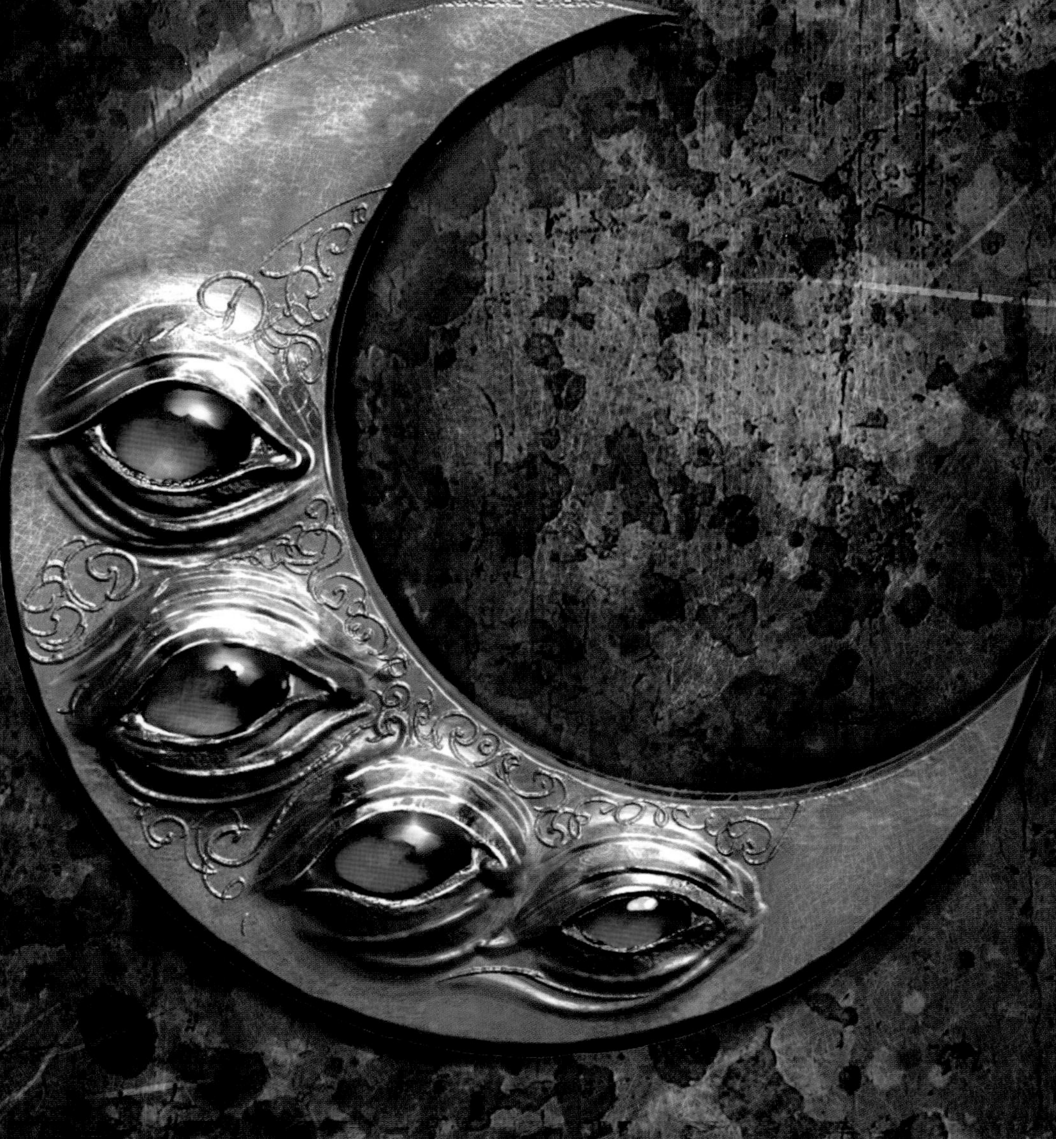

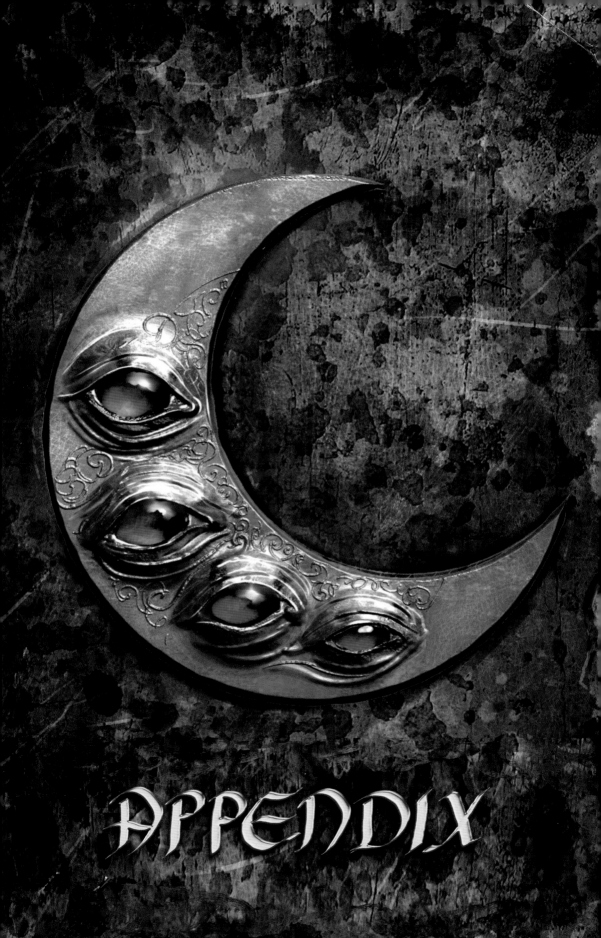

APPENDIX

Glossary

Aertes: Called Aertes of the Fates, goddess and servant of destiny. She is referred to by Damanulites as the deaf goddess, as she is unlikely to answer prayers.

Ardunat: One of the two fallen kingdoms of Ravine, destroyed by the second Necryte, known only as the Reaper of Ardunat.

Badrunim Priest: High-ranking warrior priest in the service of Azhi Damanul.

Casta Palladia: Kingdom and fortress bearing the same name since the time of the Muraman barbarian kings. Considered unconquerable because of the presence of the god under the mountain. Muraman translation: unbroken star.

Damanul: Living god of the mountain, sealed under Mount Palladron. He protects Palladia, and is considered the hidden power of the Alliance.

Dragonlord: Of the bloodline of Worgal, gifted with the ability of dragonmind, enabling them to give simple orders to dragons, and organize their actions in battle.

Dragontear: A crystalline formation within a dragon's throat, used to generate the firebreath. It grows stronger with a dragon's forging. In time, other traits have been discovered.

Dragoon: Dragon rider. The kingdom of Dregya is know for producing the best dragoons.

Eani: Also called starfolk, people of the old world who followed the great exodus of dragons. Immortal, though weaker in spellcasting than people of Ravine.

Faetree: Massive tree in Palladia that judges those who would seal the weapons embedded in it. It's said the roots reach to the heart of all worlds.

Forging: Natural process of dragon maturation. The first forge gives dragons their breath, and layers their scales with tellas. It also gives them stronger bones, enabling them to wingwalk.

Grimlas: Weapon of another world, those who seal it become wanderers. Muraman translation: fated.

Grimlas Avendati: Spirit chosen by fates to serve as a wanderer's guide. Muraman translation: fated spirit.

Hannum: Official title of the ruler of Waroda, most technologically-developed kingdom of the Alliance.

Maga: Muraman translation: life force.

Magic: Manipulation of necra through use of one's life force.

Necra: That of which all is made. Muraman translation: matter.

Necryte: An abberation of magic, a mage who neither pays for spells with life force, nor can aim spells. The lonely nature of their existence makes them prone to madness.

Palladian Alliance: Formed to oppose the threat of the Necryte, Varda Ballahad, it originally included the kingdoms of Palladia, Wranthorn, Waroda , Dregya, Areni, Kaddan and Ardunat.

Praetorian Guard: Elite guard to King Godwyn of Palladia, led by High Praetorean Antheus Prayne.

Ravine: Name by which most call the continent of Harrak. Thus renamed because of the ravine in the Saradrion Empire, through which the old world's denizens first entered.

Rimad Gregorius: Leader of the church of Damanul. Muraman translation: mountain blessed.

Runeglass: Originally a Sardaheim creation, but copied by many. A tracker that is used in combination with maga branding, also called a tracking rune.

Runenos: Long rumored to be the location of dragon tombs, but never found. Dragons jealously guard their dead.

Sealing: The act of marking a weapon with one's own life force. It synchronizes the user and the weapon for balanced spellwork.

Tellas: Metallic substance derived from dragon scales, strengthened each time a dragon forges. Tellas of fifth rank (forging) is more valuable than any other metal. Harvested from molting dragons, it's said that the Runenos tomb holds the greatest concentration of tellas.

Trueform: The ability of a dragonlord to use the dragontear of a dead dragon to claim the beast's form.

Wanderer: Paragon of fate, changer of destinies, who bears the grimlas weapon.

Wyvern: Lesser dragonkin. They are savage, faster than dragons, but unable to forge. They are born with a static dragontear, which means their firebreath does not gain power with age.

CAST OF CHARACTERS

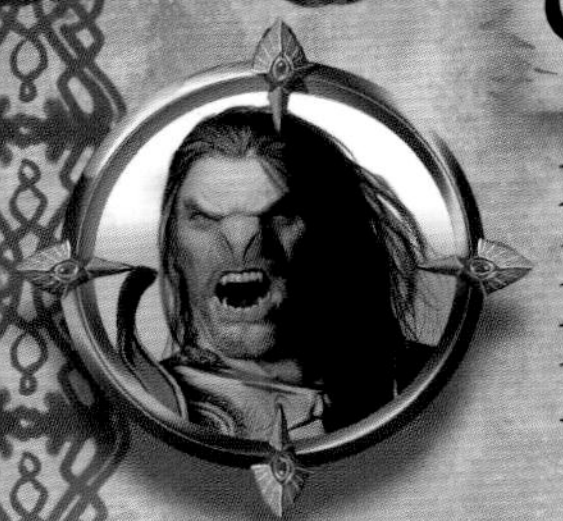

Nebezial Asheri: Husband to Freya, brother to Melchial, father to Calisto, once called Raven of the North and hero of the Alliance. He is now often referred to as the cursed or mad king.

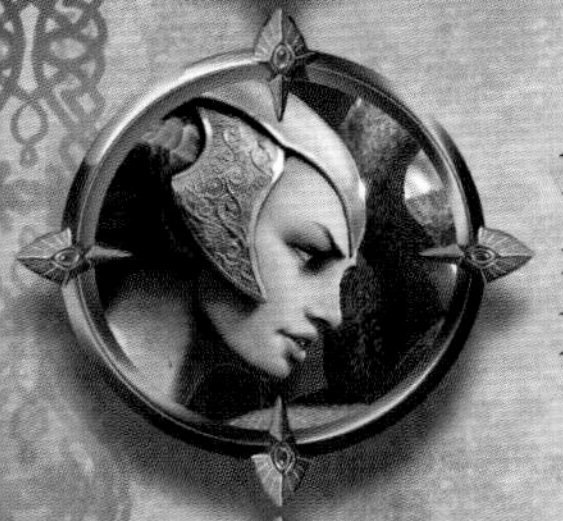

Delphi Bellarya: Once of the Eani, her history is veiled in mystery. She is currently bound in marriage to Nebezial, who set her free.

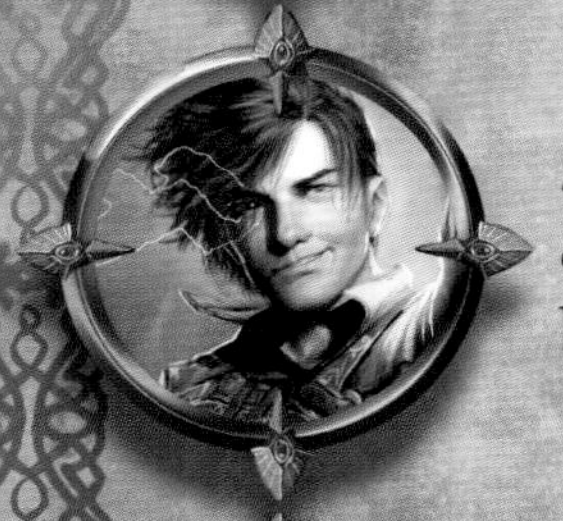

Stein Phais: A wanderer, whose grimlas weapon contains the spirit of Azriel Sanreya. Stein is also known by the terrible name of Reaper of Ardunat.

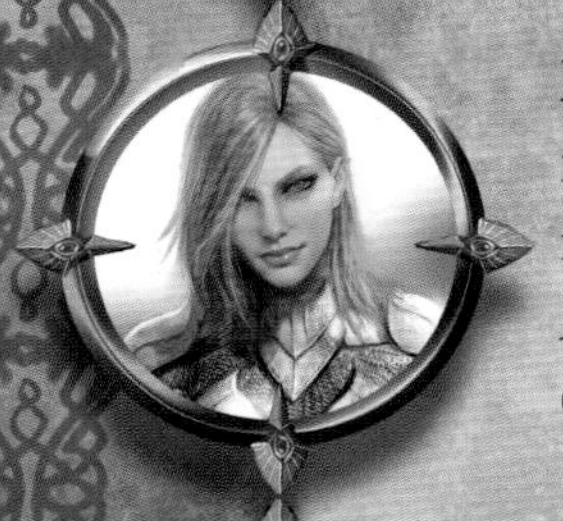

Lynn de Luctes: Real name Evelynn de Corredan, she is the future ruler of the dragoon capital of Dregya. She is a wanderer in whose spear resides the spirit of Calisto Asheri, and in whose blood burns the legacy of the Corredan flame.

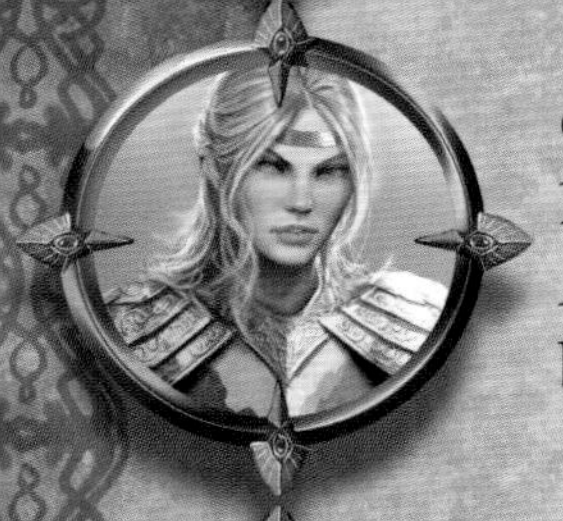

Captain Arianna Balthasar: A tactical mage from Palladia, and a proud member of the Sisterhood of Anya. A dragon attack left her severely scarred and crippled, but she carries on.

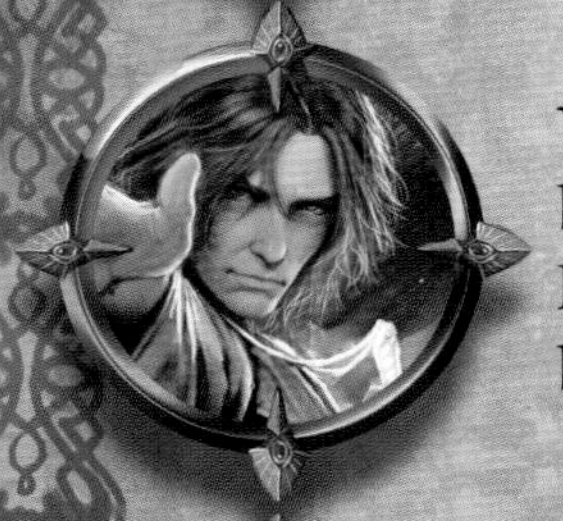

Valerius Mordine: A young dragonmaster who was sold by his family to Palladia, where he was trained in the legacy of his rare gift. His loyalty to Palladia is reluctant, but he has strong affection for Captain Arianna.

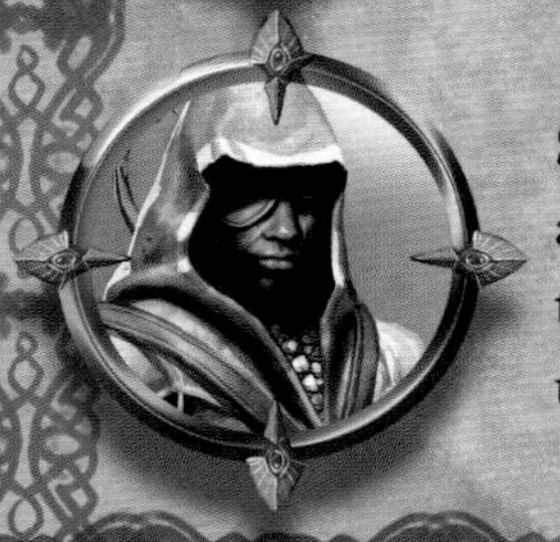

Sairan Aradee: A member of the elite ranks of Warodan assassins, known as Breathtakers. He was sent to Palladia to serve as a guard to Valerius Mordine, whom he ultimately befriended.

Antheus Prayne: Praetorean Guard to King Godwyn, also known as Antheus of the Deep Sight, due to his mastery of Shivas swordsmanship.

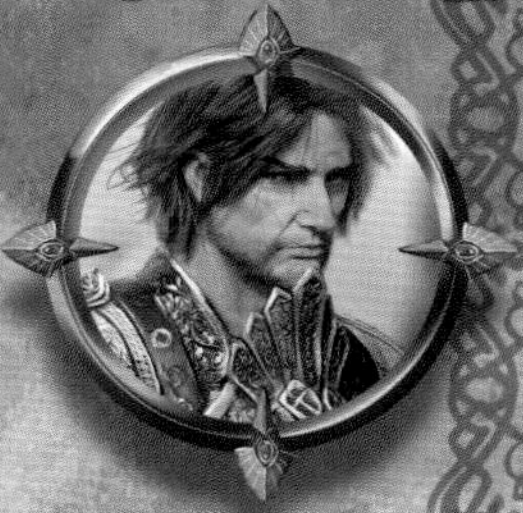

King Godwyn Bardensturm: Ruler of Palladia, former general to King Ardan. He was chosen by the Council of Lords to take the throne of Palladia.

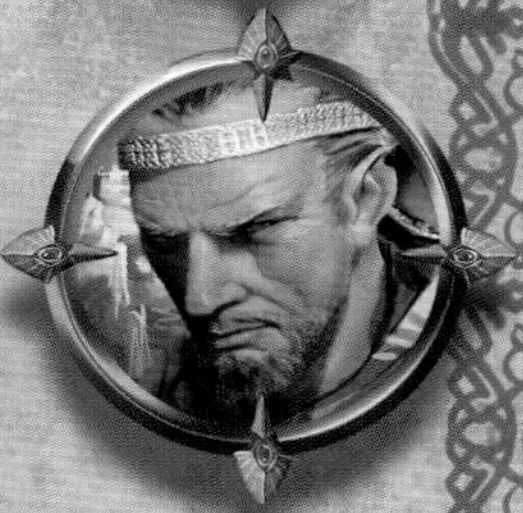

Melchial Asheri: Brother to Nebezial, slayer of the Necryte Varda Balahad, and current leader or Rimad Gregorius of the Church of Damanul.

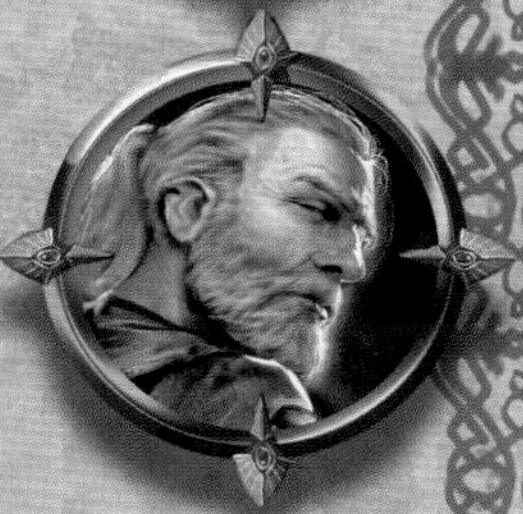

Frederick de Ruddan of Dregya: Uncle to Lynn de Luctes, and lord and throne keeper of Dregya.

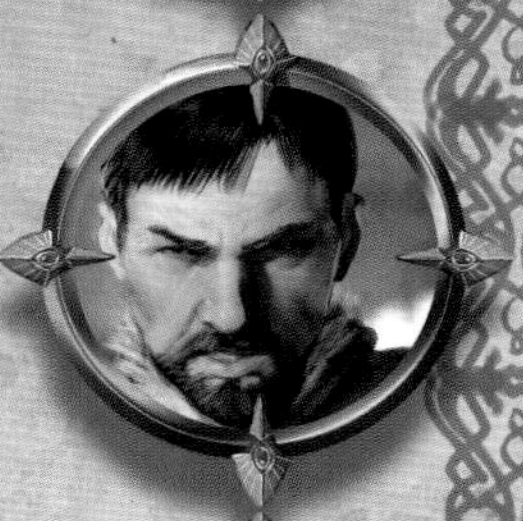

Calisto Asheri: Daughter of Nebezial and Freya, princess of Aphelion, half-Eani on her mother's side, fiancee to Azriel. After death, she was chosen as grimlas avendati, guiding spirit to Lynn de Luctes.

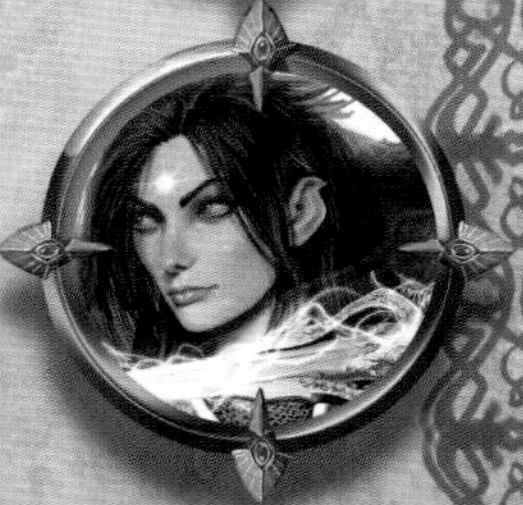

Azriel Sanreya: General for the armies of Aphelion, fiance to Calisto Asheri, a pureblood Eani of the old world. After death, he was granted a chance for redemption by becoming grimlas avendati to Stein Phais.

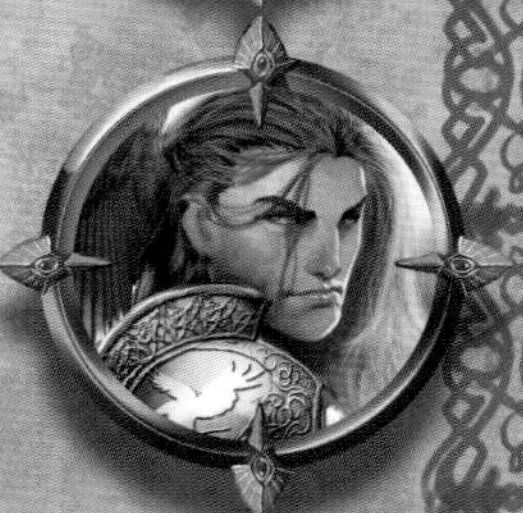

Alven Silverlake: Following the fall of the lordship of Lochenburg, Alven has faithfully served the Shinreyus family of Wranthorn. For this loyalty, Alven is included in their most secret councils.

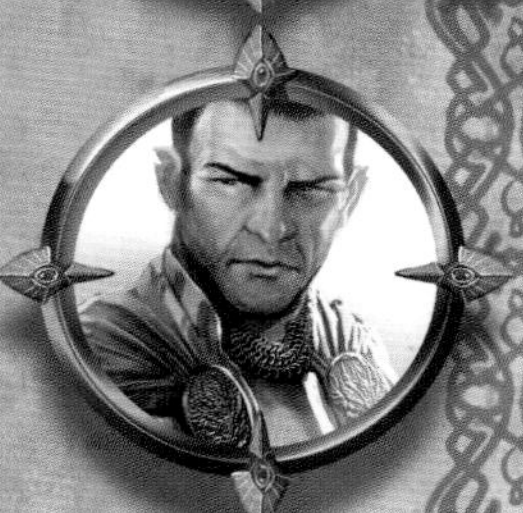

Hurron's Tale

The bear, the wolf, the eagle. Any of these beasts could turn the hunter into prey. Hurron knew this, it was knowledge his father taught him well on his first bleeding of the snow. Up in the cold, you keep the three rulers in mind at all times, especially at winter's end. The wolf is still rabid with winter's hunger. The bear awakens from its slumber, sharing the same thought as the wolf. And northern eagles, who have learned to wound their prey and watch it bleed to death, are always a threat. Yes, three ruled the mountains, but on the day of the bleeding of the snow, they were all prey.

Hurron pretended to be sleeping while he watched his son standing guard by the fire. The boy had grown strong, stronger than the old wives of the village had foreseen. Not surprising. Hurron never looked kindly on the self-proclaimed prophets. Fate is what one makes of it, and his son was the living, breathing proof.

Hurron watched as his son grabbed his sword when a noise sounded beyond fire's reach. The boy was scared. Fear is good, thought Hurron. It keeps your eyes open in the dark of night. Panic is what will end your life. Hurron was pleased to see his son's face bore a determined look.

Winter was at its end in the mountains, but its bite was still in the air. Even a hunter as old as Hurron felt its grasp. No matter. Dawn was fast approaching, and a brilliant light framed the peaks of Rurda. Bear peaks, they called them, for hunters saw in Rurda a giant bear's claw. It was there that Gammur will bleed the snow, there that he will slay a black bear of his own, and be named a hunter.

Still, Rurda was two days away on foot, and there was still the steep path by the abyss, the Ravine of the old times. The legends said old things live at the bottom. Whispers of the old world can be heard by those who learn to listen. Hurron had walked along the abyss that seemed to split the world in two, but all he ever heard was the relentless howling of the wind echoing in the deep. Spirits and gods never answered his calls. Hurron learned long ago that the dangers of the world came in flesh and blood, bearing claws, fangs and blades. These he knew how to deal with, and soon, so would Gammur.

The light of dawn reached the valley and Hurron stretched noisily, startling Gammur. Hurron noticed the speed with which his son turned toward him, sword slightly drawn from its sheath.

Hurron smiled. "You have a hunter's speed, boy. Good. You'll need it when you face your bear."

Gammur looked down at his sword

thoughtfully. "Volkan was a better swordsman that I am, and he died last year," he said, with the air of someone who had carried a burden for some time. Hurron was silent. He cut a piece of dried meat, then held it over the fire upon his knife. Then he spoke. "Volkan was an arrogant fool, he may have been good with a sword, but he lacked the most important weapon of the hunter."

Gammur gazed back at his father with a questioning look. Hurron chewed the meat in silence for a moment. "Volkan took Idro and Taru to the cave, but instead of being smart and luring the bear out, or setting a trap, they decided to fight the bear in his territory," Hurron said. "Three idiots entered that cave, and only one made it out. They deserved their fate, Gammur. They were fools. The most important weapon a hunter has is a keen mind."

He went on: "Now, listen well, Gammur. A hunter must never underestimate the animal. Respect it. Be aware of its strength, its speed, its cunning. You're dueling centuries of the beast's ancestry. They're wise. Never forget that. It is primal knowledge, wisdom of the high places, deep places and dark places. You are entering the animal's ground, and there you must respect your opponent, or die by your own foolishness."

Gammur looked down at his sword once more in silence, then looked resolutely at his father and smiled a bit. They ate the rest of their breakfast in silence.

Night had fully retreated by the time they packed up their makeshift camp and carried on towards the Ravine path that followed the east side of the abyss. They walked for hours, until the forest retreated before grim wasteland. The land was barren, plains of spare color waiting for the spring that was fast approaching.

Soon food would be plentiful. The hunters would fill the ice pits with meat. Work to do, Hurron thought, and Gammur would join him then as a man of the tribe.

They walked the plains for hours more, and the moon was behind them when they reached the abyss. It stood before them, gaping, bottomless. Old tales call it Cleave of the First, for this was the place where The First planted his axe and let loose all the life that was resting in the deeps.

Hurron never placed much worth in the old tales. A hunter must keep his legs firmly planted on the ground, his mind must be clear of all distractions. One who thinks too much of spirits, hags and whispers from the deep will start seeing such things where none exist. There are enough real dangers in this world.

Hurron and Gammur walked down the winding path along the edge of the Ravine in silence, listening to the wind howling in the deep. Gammur glanced at his father nervously. Hurron laughed suddenly. "Your mother has been filling your ears with old tales, I reckon." Gammur said nothing.

Hurron looked at his son for a moment, then continued in a playful mood. "Come, boy, let's have a look into the abyss, and see if the spirits of the deep look back at us." Gammur hesitated a moment, then reluctantly joined his father at the edge.

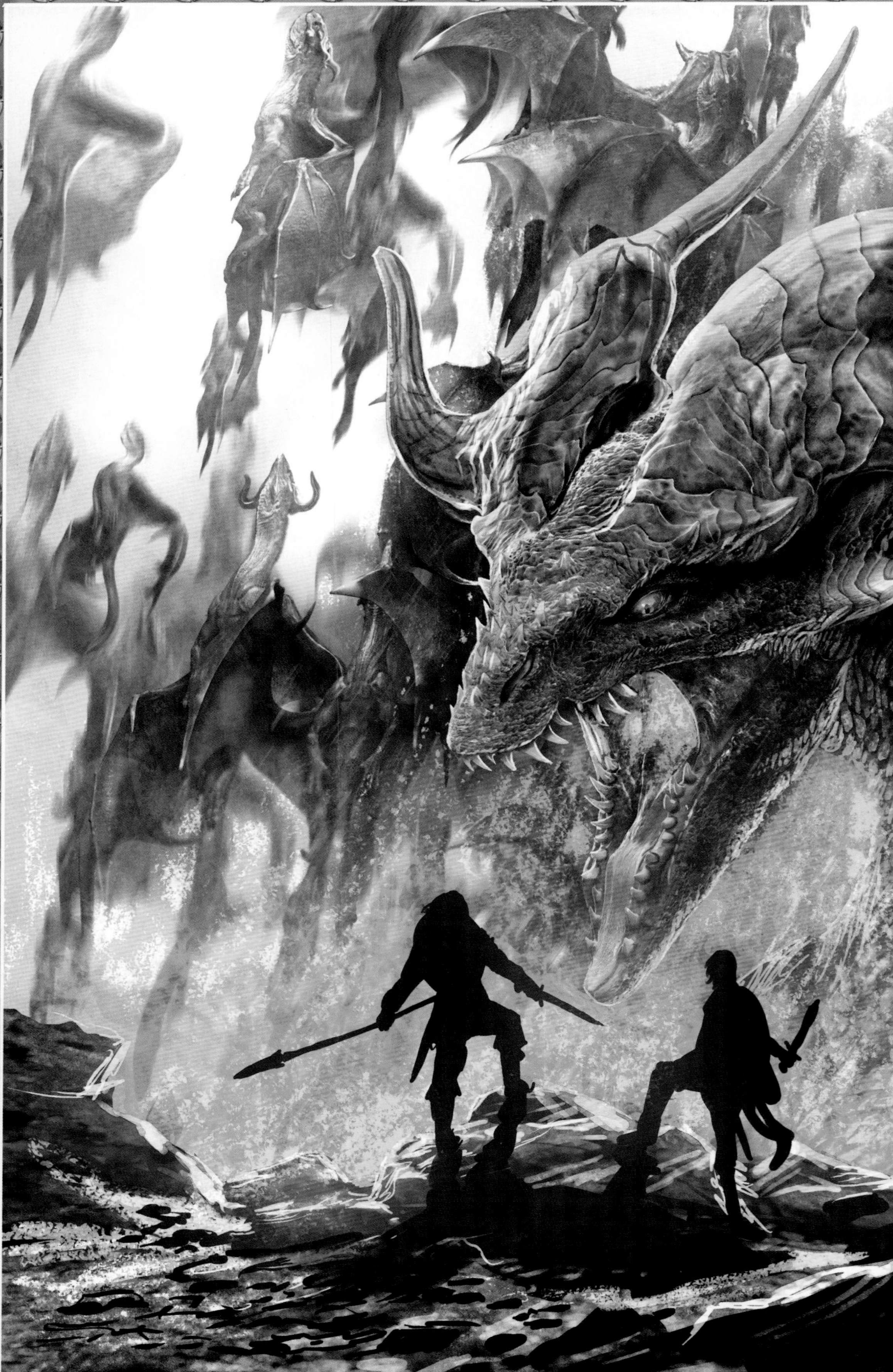

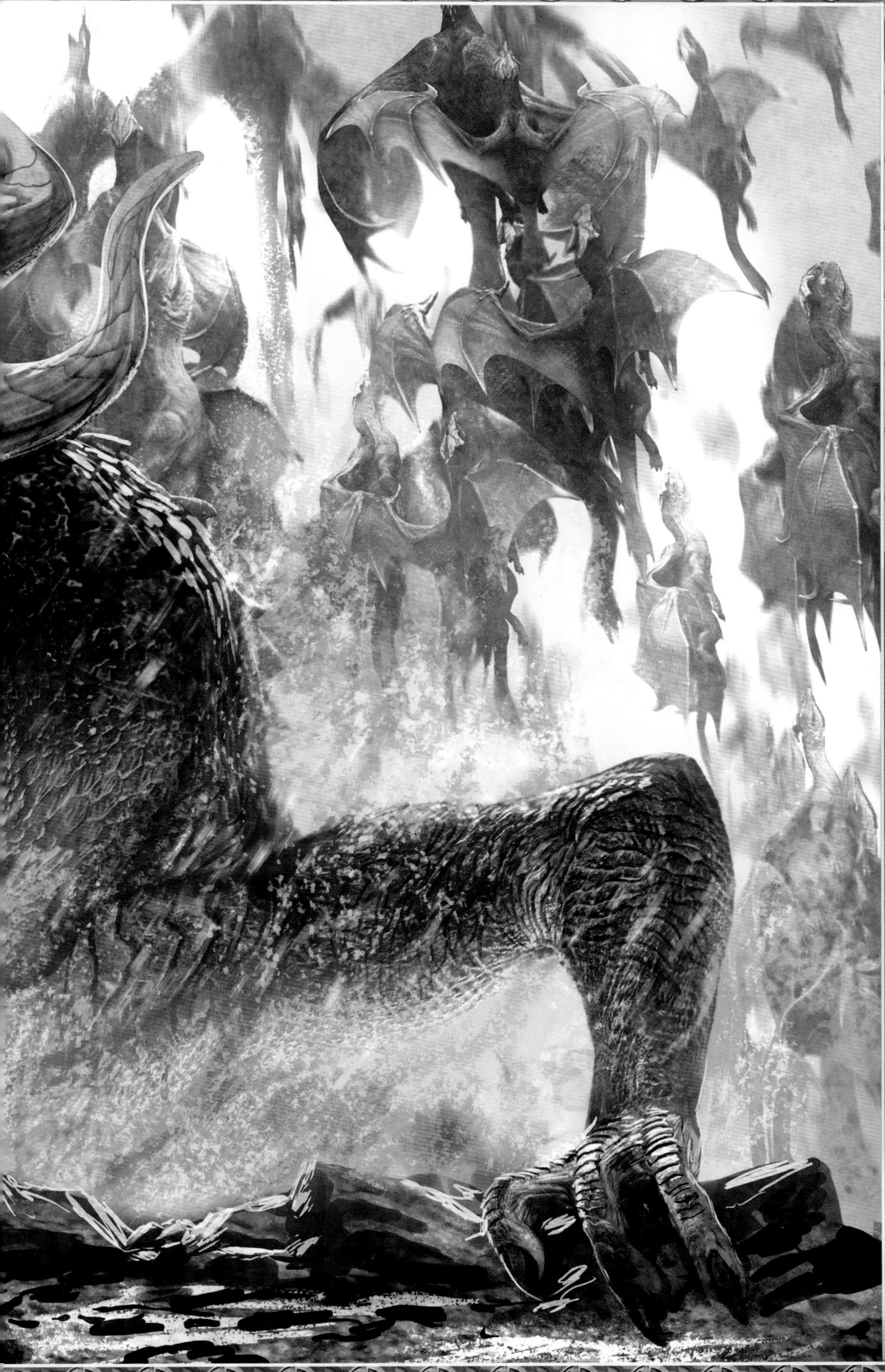

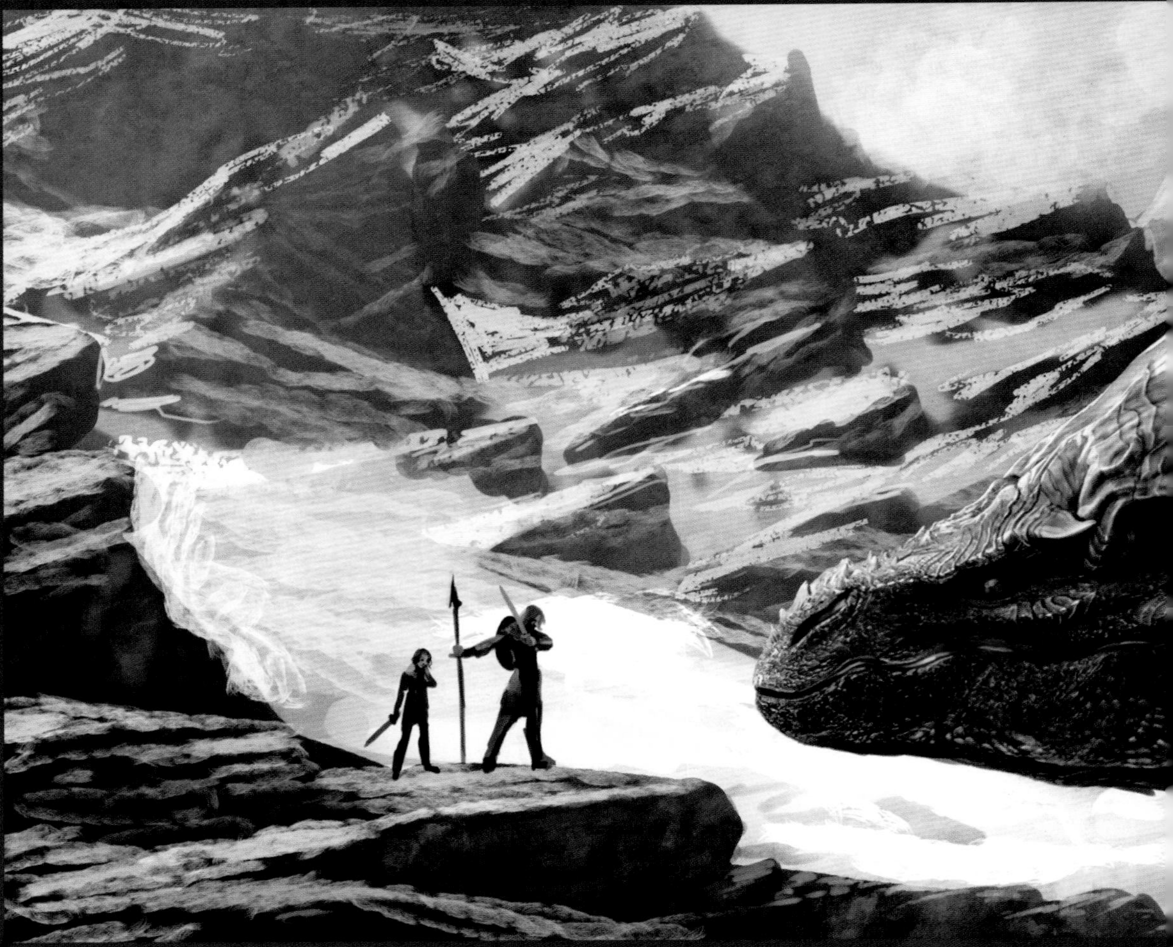

The smile drained from Hurron's face as he realized that the birds, quite loud until then, had grown silent. He regained his courage and peered over the edge.

The world exploded, and the skies went dark with flying things. Not eagles. These were things not of this world, and huge, most far larger than bears. They swarmed, seemingly infinite in number, all different.

Hurron looked at his son, who stood unblinking. Even at this moment, with legends come to life, Gammur wore an expression of amazement, not fear. Hurron felt a twinge of pride. To hell with the bleeding of the snow, Hurron thought. His son was a brave man, and no ritual of old could prove it more than this moment.

As Hurron and Gammur stood at the edge, fire bloomed in the deep. A beast of unimaginable size rose before them, a red monster crowned with horns, skin glistening like jewels. The scaly terror watched them. No, it studied them.

Father and son stood at world's end, looking into the eyes of the dragon. Then Gammur, driven by some deep understanding, bowed before the beast. Hurron followed his son's example. The dragon observed them in

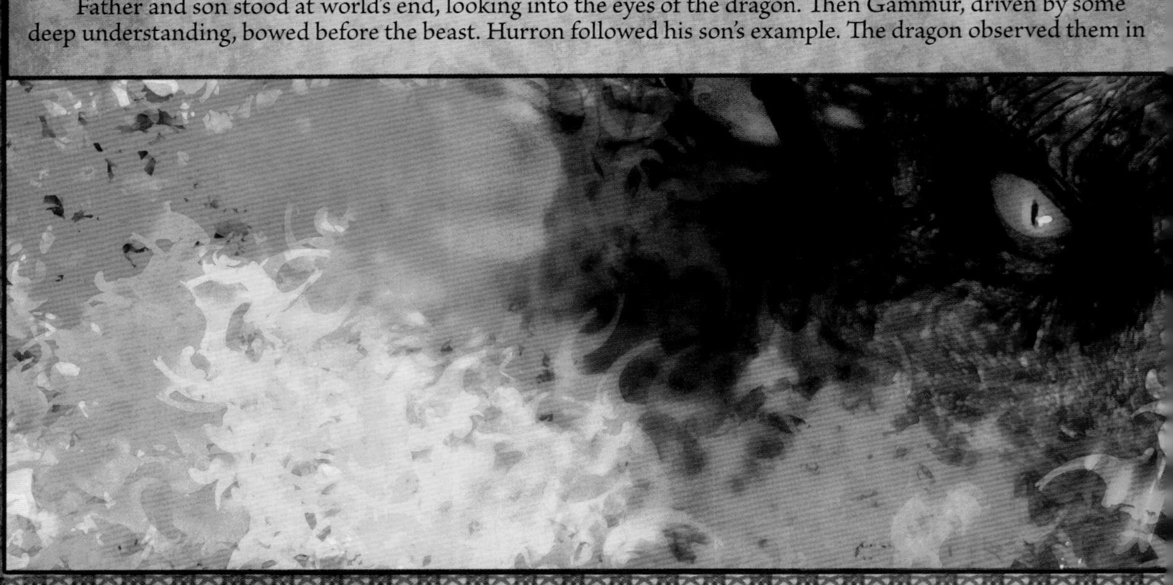

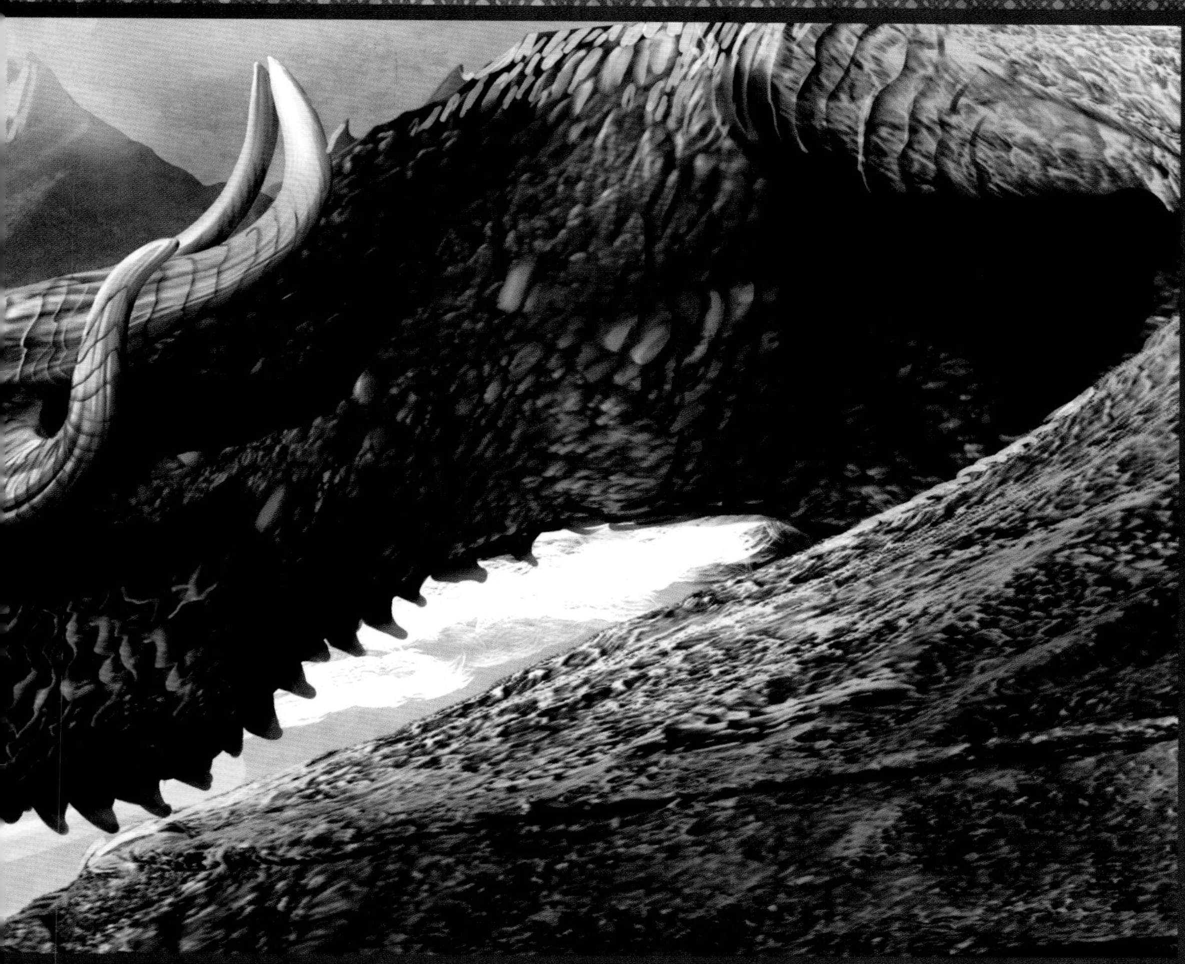

silence, as the smaller beasts, mere children in comparison, darkened the skies.

The dragon opened its massive jaws and an elegant blaze of fire surrounded Hurron and Gammur. It was flame, but did not burn them. They dared not breathe, for fear of the fire all around them, but soon their lungs screamed for air. Hurron inhaled the flames first, his son mere seconds after.

With the fire came knowledge of old things, older than the world of man, an old world of fire and power. They heard the words of the dragon. Simple speech, the speech of a child, but rife with ageless wisdom.

Hurron understood. It was not that dragon spoke as a child. It was that their minds could not comprehend more. The dragon was called Barahea, the mother. Hurron knew this, because the fire had whispered to him. The fire had blessed them as dragonlords, the first of their kind. They would be the bridge between the old world and new world. Everything had changed.

Magic had entered the world.

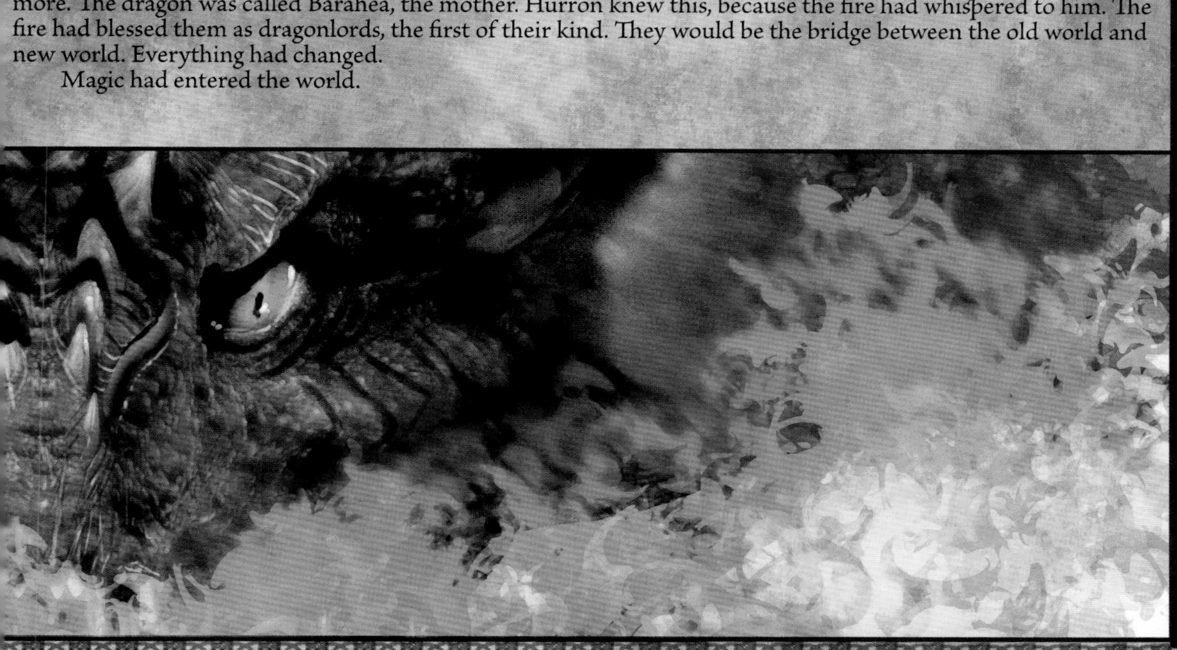

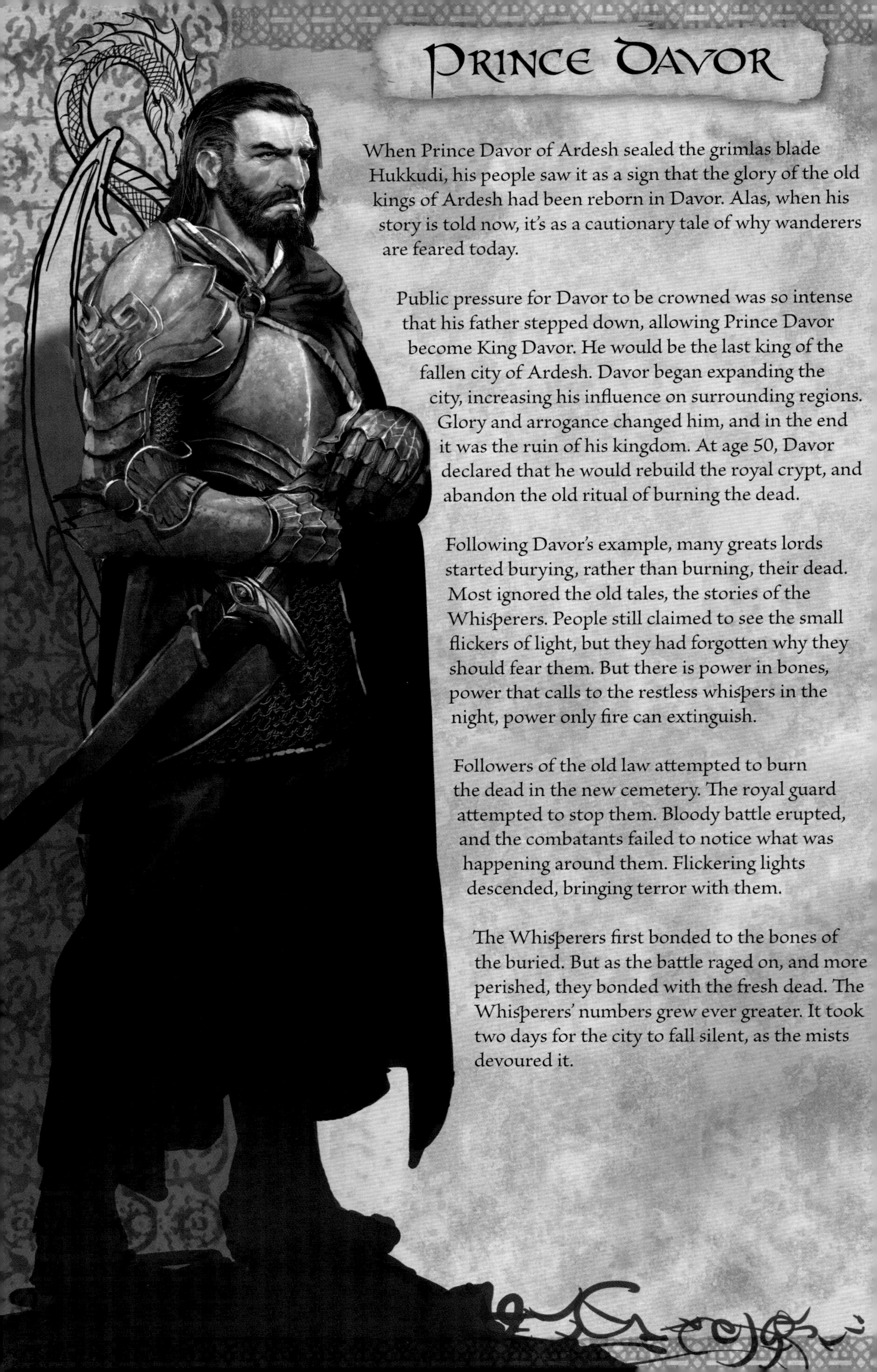

Prince Davor

When Prince Davor of Ardesh sealed the grimlas blade Hukkudi, his people saw it as a sign that the glory of the old kings of Ardesh had been reborn in Davor. Alas, when his story is told now, it's as a cautionary tale of why wanderers are feared today.

Public pressure for Davor to be crowned was so intense that his father stepped down, allowing Prince Davor become King Davor. He would be the last king of the fallen city of Ardesh. Davor began expanding the city, increasing his influence on surrounding regions. Glory and arrogance changed him, and in the end it was the ruin of his kingdom. At age 50, Davor declared that he would rebuild the royal crypt, and abandon the old ritual of burning the dead.

Following Davor's example, many greats lords started burying, rather than burning, their dead. Most ignored the old tales, the stories of the Whisperers. People still claimed to see the small flickers of light, but they had forgotten why they should fear them. But there is power in bones, power that calls to the restless whispers in the night, power only fire can extinguish.

Followers of the old law attempted to burn the dead in the new cemetery. The royal guard attempted to stop them. Bloody battle erupted, and the combatants failed to notice what was happening around them. Flickering lights descended, bringing terror with them.

The Whisperers first bonded to the bones of the buried. But as the battle raged on, and more perished, they bonded with the fresh dead. The Whisperers' numbers grew ever greater. It took two days for the city to fall silent, as the mists devoured it.

ERIN VARTHE

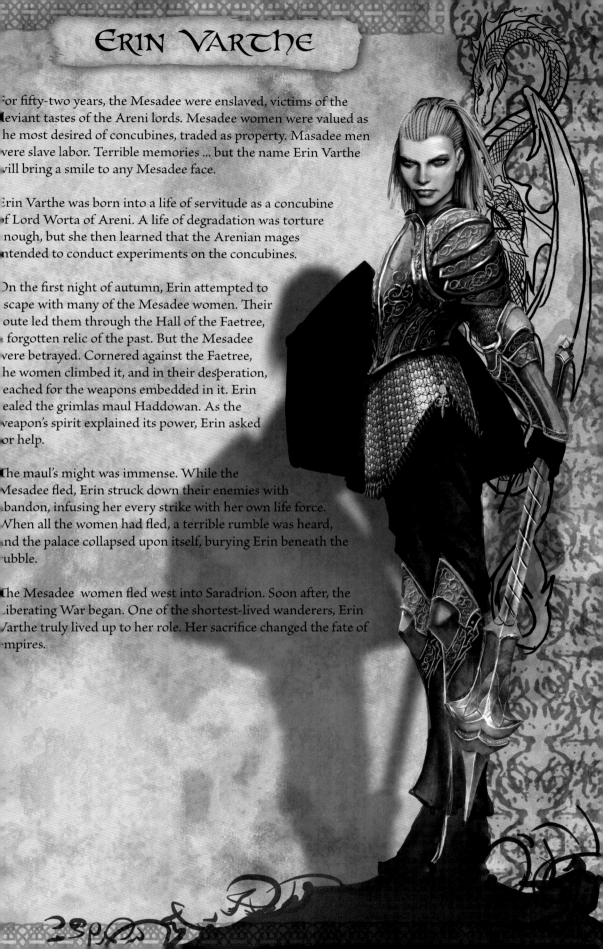

For fifty-two years, the Mesadee were enslaved, victims of the deviant tastes of the Areni lords. Mesadee women were valued as the most desired of concubines, traded as property. Masadee men were slave labor. Terrible memories ... but the name Erin Varthe will bring a smile to any Mesadee face.

Erin Varthe was born into a life of servitude as a concubine of Lord Worta of Areni. A life of degradation was torture enough, but she then learned that the Arenian mages intended to conduct experiments on the concubines.

On the first night of autumn, Erin attempted to escape with many of the Mesadee women. Their route led them through the Hall of the Faetree, a forgotten relic of the past. But the Mesadee were betrayed. Cornered against the Faetree, the women climbed it, and in their desperation, reached for the weapons embedded in it. Erin sealed the grimlas maul Haddowan. As the weapon's spirit explained its power, Erin asked for help.

The maul's might was immense. While the Mesadee fled, Erin struck down their enemies with abandon, infusing her every strike with her own life force. When all the women had fled, a terrible rumble was heard, and the palace collapsed upon itself, burying Erin beneath the rubble.

The Mesadee women fled west into Saradrion. Soon after, the Liberating War began. One of the shortest-lived wanderers, Erin Varthe truly lived up to her role. Her sacrifice changed the fate of empires.

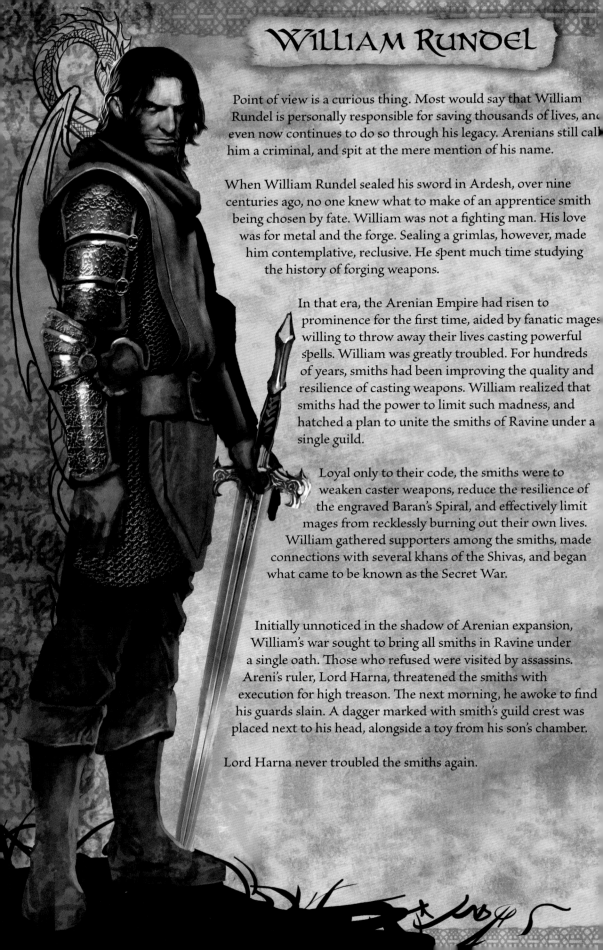

WILLIAM RUNDEL

Point of view is a curious thing. Most would say that William Rundel is personally responsible for saving thousands of lives, and even now continues to do so through his legacy. Arenians still call him a criminal, and spit at the mere mention of his name.

When William Rundel sealed his sword in Ardesh, over nine centuries ago, no one knew what to make of an apprentice smith being chosen by fate. William was not a fighting man. His love was for metal and the forge. Sealing a grimlas, however, made him contemplative, reclusive. He spent much time studying the history of forging weapons.

In that era, the Arenian Empire had risen to prominence for the first time, aided by fanatic mages willing to throw away their lives casting powerful spells. William was greatly troubled. For hundreds of years, smiths had been improving the quality and resilience of casting weapons. William realized that smiths had the power to limit such madness, and hatched a plan to unite the smiths of Ravine under a single guild.

Loyal only to their code, the smiths were to weaken caster weapons, reduce the resilience of the engraved Baran's Spiral, and effectively limit mages from recklessly burning out their own lives. William gathered supporters among the smiths, made connections with several khans of the Shivas, and began what came to be known as the Secret War.

Initially unnoticed in the shadow of Arenian expansion, William's war sought to bring all smiths in Ravine under a single oath. Those who refused were visited by assassins. Areni's ruler, Lord Harna, threatened the smiths with execution for high treason. The next morning, he awoke to find his guards slain. A dagger marked with smith's guild crest was placed next to his head, alongside a toy from his son's chamber.

Lord Harna never troubled the smiths again.

Anya Cerdunna

Magic truly is the great equalizer. None repeat this
more often than the Sisters of Anya.

Anya Cerdunna was the first known wanderer of
Ardunat. Sadly, the same city that birthed a wanderer
as legendary as Anya ultimately fell to the power of its
first wanderer.

Before Anya became a wanderer, she was a daughter
of a lesser lord. Her fate, as with most women of her
time, was an arranged marriage and servitude. Even
though the old laws insisted that everyone had the
right to claim a weapon from the Faetree, rarely were
women afforded the opportunity.

However, Anya seized her moment and sealed the great
sword Valentia. Always envied for masterful control
over her spellwork, Anya claimed a perfect conduit in
Valentia. Women soon gathered around her for training,
and it became apparent that their contemplative nature
might be a superior frame for spellwork.

The Sisterhood of Anya steadily grew in power, and the
men of Arduant steadily grew discontent. They decided
to eradicate the Sisterhood, and hundreds of men, many
of them trained mages, gathered to end Anya's influence.
But their bravado was snuffed out by Anya, as she
released her grimlas avendati. The battle was brief and
decisive.

Victory sparked change on the continent of Ravine.
Anya and her Sisterhood made pilgrimages across
Ravine, growing their numbers and influence. Today the
Sisterhood's influence is on par with that of the smiths
guild. Even Khedira, first Khali of the Shivas, is among its
members.

DRAGONS

Of all the creatures that crossed into the new world, dragons might be the most fascinating. Even after more than two millennia, we are still uncovering some of their secrets.

Dragons are mostly social creatures, usually living in flights of more than ten individuals. They are very protective of their young, and females tend to be aggressive for weeks before their eggs hatch. Hatchlings often stay with the same flight for life.

The ability to form firebreath occurs after a dragon's first forge, which is the natural process of maturation. The same is true for all the subspecies, with exception of wyverns and wyrims, which ar born with their dragontear already formed.

Forging is repeated several times during the life of a dragon, resulting in the strengthening of tellas, the metallic substance found in dragonscales. Forging also results in empowering the dragontear, a natural crystalline formation in a dragon's throat. The dragontear acts as a conductor of magical force, and enables a dragon to perform a raw form of breath-based spellcasting.

Dragontears were once greatly coveted by both dragonmasters and mages. Dragontears are capable c containing the essence of a dragon, enabling a dragonmaster to perform the unique spell of trueform Dragontears also are capable of storing life force, a quality that led to the Traitor's War during the Arenian Empire's first expansion.

Arenian mages saw the potential in dragontears, and began mercilessly harvesting dragons. The hunt resulted in the return of the elder dragon Baran, who united his kind with those opposed to the Arenian Empire, which suffered sound defeat. The dragons were enraged, clamoring for human blood. But Baran calmed them, and made a pact.

Baran offered the last gift of the elder dragons: the fire of alliance, the Corredan Flame. That blessing has been carried by the Corredans of Dregya for centuries, and has kept the dragons allied with them ever since. In return, the Corredans are sworn to protect dragons and dragonkin.

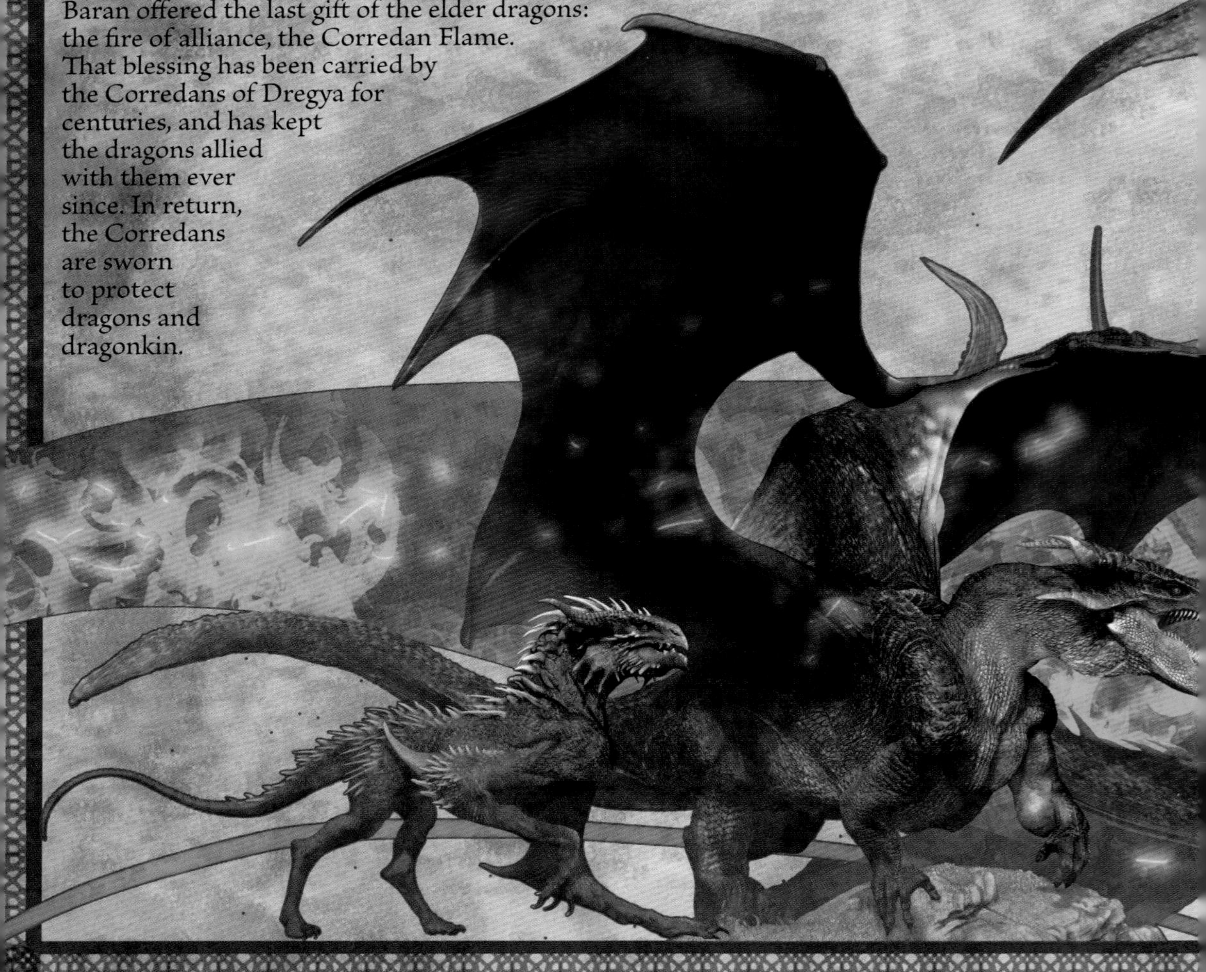

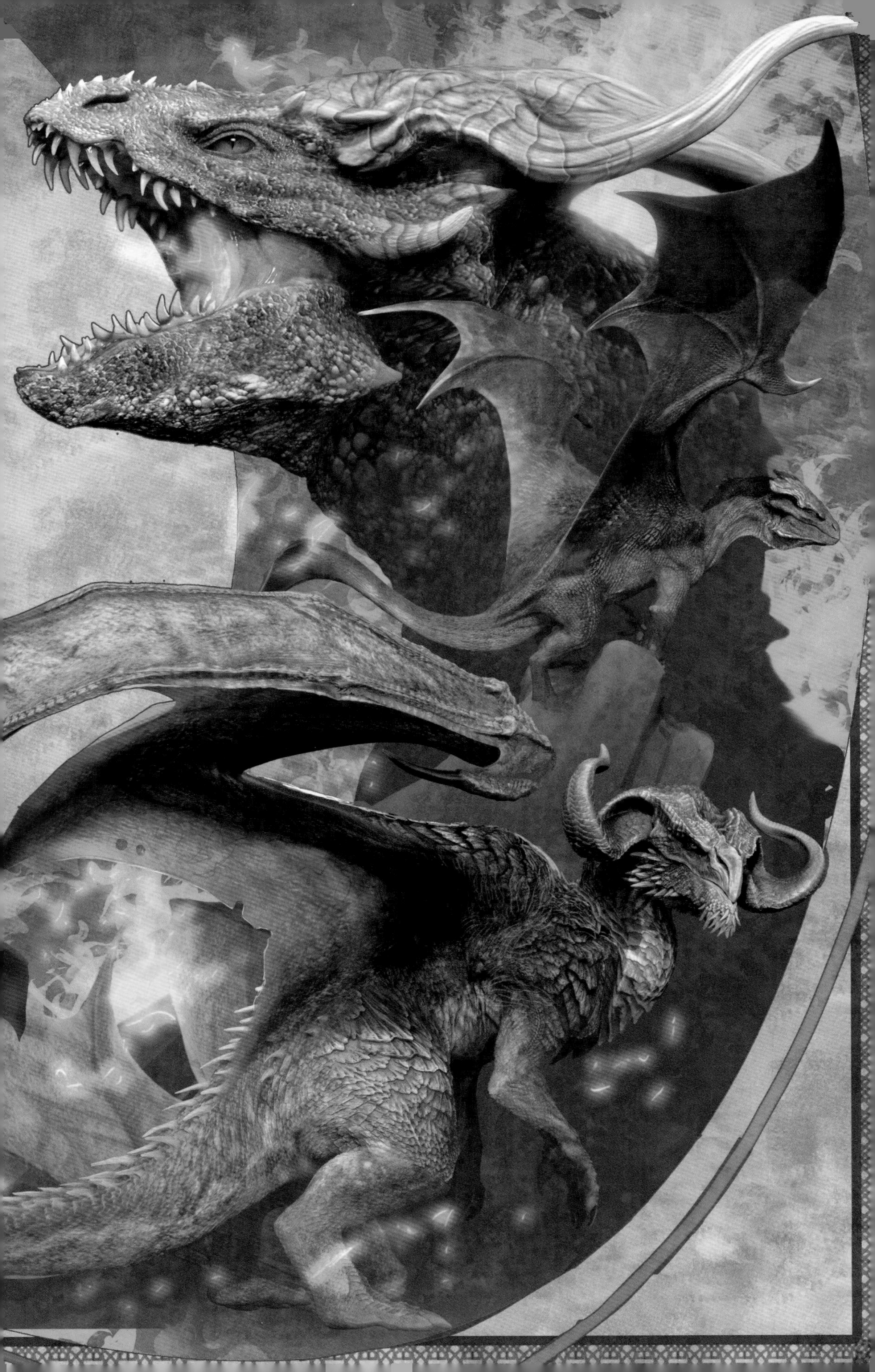

The Shivas

History tells us that two thousand years ago, the Shivas were normal humans. Believed to have originated from the northern regions of what is now Areni, Shivas are a wandering people, consisting of many tribes united under the Harrakkhan.

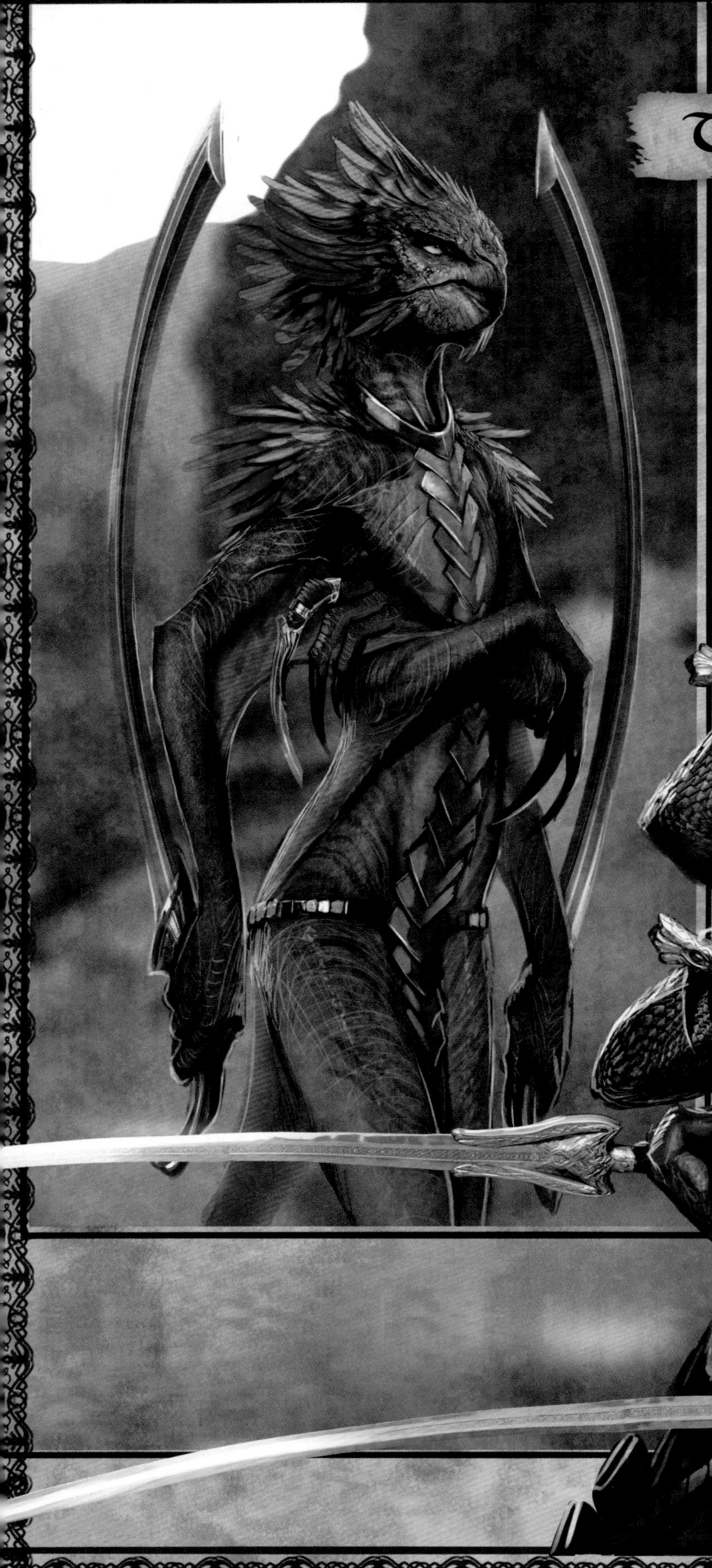

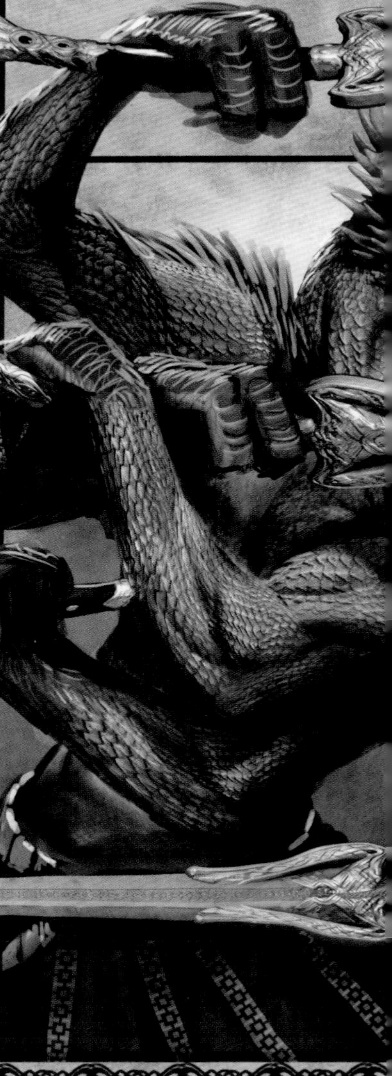

The Harakkhan is the high council of twenty-three Khans and one Khali. As the ruling body, the Harakkhan concerns itself with the chief export product of the Shivas: mercenary forces. Half-blooded blademasters, Shivas are held in high regard as fighters by all the lands of the Alliance. Their blade-wielding techniques make them a force of nature on any battlefield.

Currently there are two schools of combat among the Shivas. The first is the traditional "Five Talons," a five-blade fighting style that is more than a thousand years old. It relies heavily upon powerful strikes combined with quick footwork, and an almost scorpion-like use of the tailblade.

The second is a recently-developed "Five Circles" technique. It became popular after its creator, Chedira, a Khali of the Harrakkhan, proved its efficiency by training a human, who then proceeded to gain the rank of Khadi among the Shivas. Five Circles relies upon fluid circular motions, and transferring the momentum of an opponent's attack for the purpose of unbalancing the opponent.

Shivas take great pride in their combat skills, and are considered mage-banes. By using deep sight, Shivas are capable of disrupting spell formation. It's also believed they can see their opponent's trail of the dead.

Shivas wear less armor as they gain higher rank. This peculiar tradition was used to great strategic advantage by Khan Khazran.

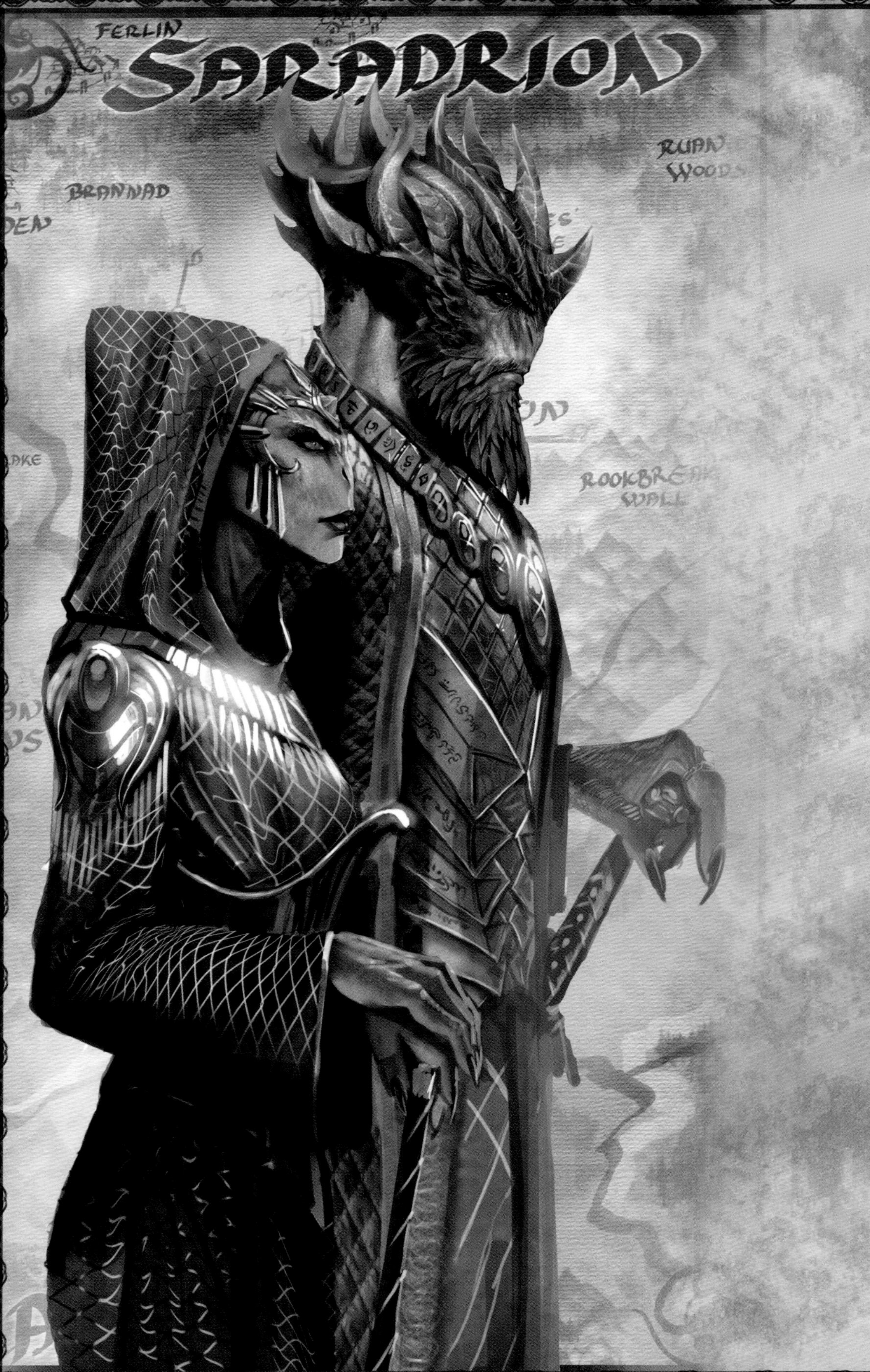
SARADRION
FERLIN
BRANNAD
RUAN WOODS
WALL

THE SARDAHEIM

Trust, once lost, is difficult to reclaim.

It's difficult to specify exactly when and why the Saradrion Empire lost its trust in humanity. Most scholars agree that the first expansion of the Arenians played a major role in the alienation of the Sardaheims. Unlike the Shivas, the Sardaheims have a firm hold on their regions, which today are united under the banner of the Saradrion Empire.

Long ago, the Sardaheims were brave men and women who made a blood pact with the oldest dragons. The bloodgift of the dragon Barahea manifested itself as refined magic potential, and the formation of rudimentary dragontears.

The most coveted gift of the Sardaheims, though, is their tolerance for the otherwise toxic brew mirrodian. It is the only known substance capable of drastically increasing the available amount of one's maga. Consumption of this brew has ensured the survival of their empire.

The Saradrion Empire is ruled by Emperor Kuzak Han-Bardu and Empress Ranna. Saradrion rule is determined by nine rakshas, the governing bodies of nine influential schools of craft. They are known for creating the finest tools for channeling maga. The capital city of the empire is Saradrion Upon the Cleave, now a rich metropolis. The Saradrion Empire today has established trading relationships with most regions of the Alliance.

As trading routes were established, Saradrion flourished, becoming one of the great pilgrimage destinations for followers of Aertes of the Fates. Saradrion is situated upon the Ravine of the Beginning, the gate of the old world. Pilgrims frequently visit to listen for whispers of Aertes. Even though Saradrion is officially a friend to the Alliance, old mistrusts remain.

Pilgrim quarters are strictly separate, and a mood of hidden hostility often can be felt, or even glimpsed in the eyes of elder Sardaheims. Old sins, like the suffering of the Mesadee and the burnings of border villages, are not easily forgotten.

The Mesadee

The tragedy of the Mesadee is the greatest stain on the Alliance's honor. Even though their plight occurred before the formation of the Alliance, the fact that it was known, yet willingly ignored to preserve peace with the Arenians, has forever sown the seeds of mistrust.

The suffering of the Mesadee began with a scurrilous rumor, whispers that Mesadee women possessed unparalleled lovemaking prowess. In that time, the, Mesadee lived in the city of Davana, situated on the border of the Arenian expanse. The Mesadee were skilled artisans, but inexperienced in the art of war. They stood no chance when the Arenians descended, and many Mesadee women were kidnapped and enslaved. Davana was left in ruins. Ridden with corruption, the Council of Saradrion was bribed by the Arenians to turn a blind eye.

The Mesadee suffered for decades, and hatred grew in their hearts. So as they grew in numbers, they plotted against their oppressors, and waited. Their opportunity arrived in unexpected form, when a wanderer unleashed fury upon the palace of Lord Worta of Areni. Many of the captured Mesadee women escaped, and in the ensuing chaos, the Mesadee resistance attacked and captured the capital.

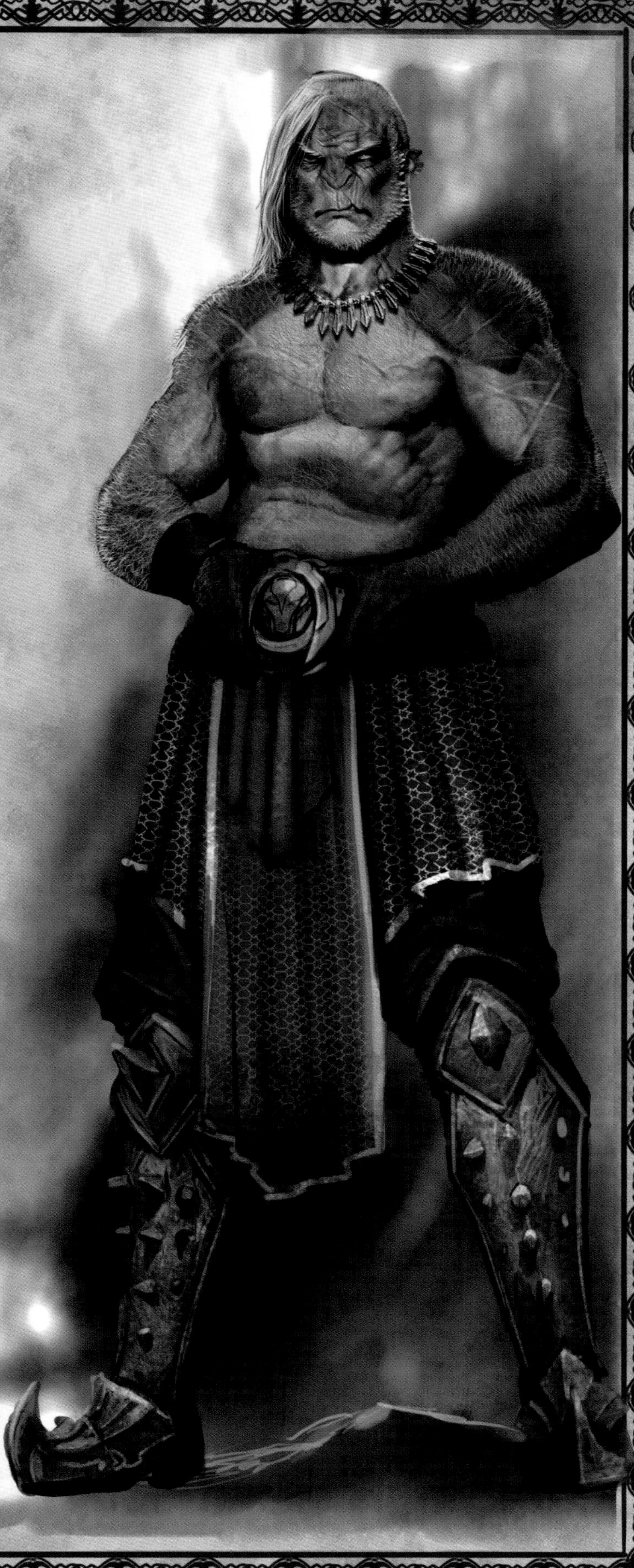

Some of the escaped women reached the Sardaheim court, and revealed to the Emperor the truth of their degradation. Enraged, the Emperor purged his corrupt council by his own sword and spell. Sardaheim invaded Areni, and the battle that followed brought an end to the Arenian expansion.

Now free, the Mesadee had been changed by their suffering. The cruelty of others had taught them harsh lessons. Artisans no longer, they were now feared fighters, swift and silent and merciless. They had become Rippers, and served the Emperor of the Saradrion Protectorate.

The Masadee right of blood vengeance is accepted across all territories of the Alliance. Should any Mesadee man or woman or child be taken against their will, the perpetrator and all his family are captured. The family is slain as the perpetrator watches, and then his hands, feet, ears, eyes, lips and tongue are severed. Once his wounds are healed, the perpetrator is left to die of starvation. There have been only four known cases of Mesadee abduction since.

Casta Palladia, the Unbroken Star

"Unbroken Star" is a rather clumsy translation of the city's old name, dating from the age of the Muraman barbarian kings. Still, it's a fitting title, as Casta Palladia remains unconquered since its founding. Those who called Mount Palladron home always felt safe and protected.

Four hundred years ago, the people of Palladia discovered the source of this strange power: the living god, Damanul, was sealed within the mountain. Who had trapped him, and why, remain unanswered. If Damanul himself knows, he will not say. The only clue was an ancient book, found in the rubble, written in what is presumably the language of the Eani. All attempts at translation have failed, and the last of the Eani remaining in Ravine refuse to speak of it.

Today, Damanul is the source of a Palladia-centric faith that has spread rapidly. Palladia is governed by a king who is chosen after the prior king's passing. The process is a grueling testing of the candidate's body and mind, culling the weak and dimwitted from the strong and wise. King Godwynn earned his crown, a worthy successor to his father. Sovereignty in Palladia is not an inherited right, but Godwyn Bardensturm has proven himself time and again.

The might of Palladia is maintained through a balance of power between the king, representing the secular rule, and the Rimad Gregorius, highest-ranking priest of Damanul. The office of Rimad Gregorius is presently held by Melchial Asheri of Aphelion, hero of the alliance, and the slayer of the Necryte.

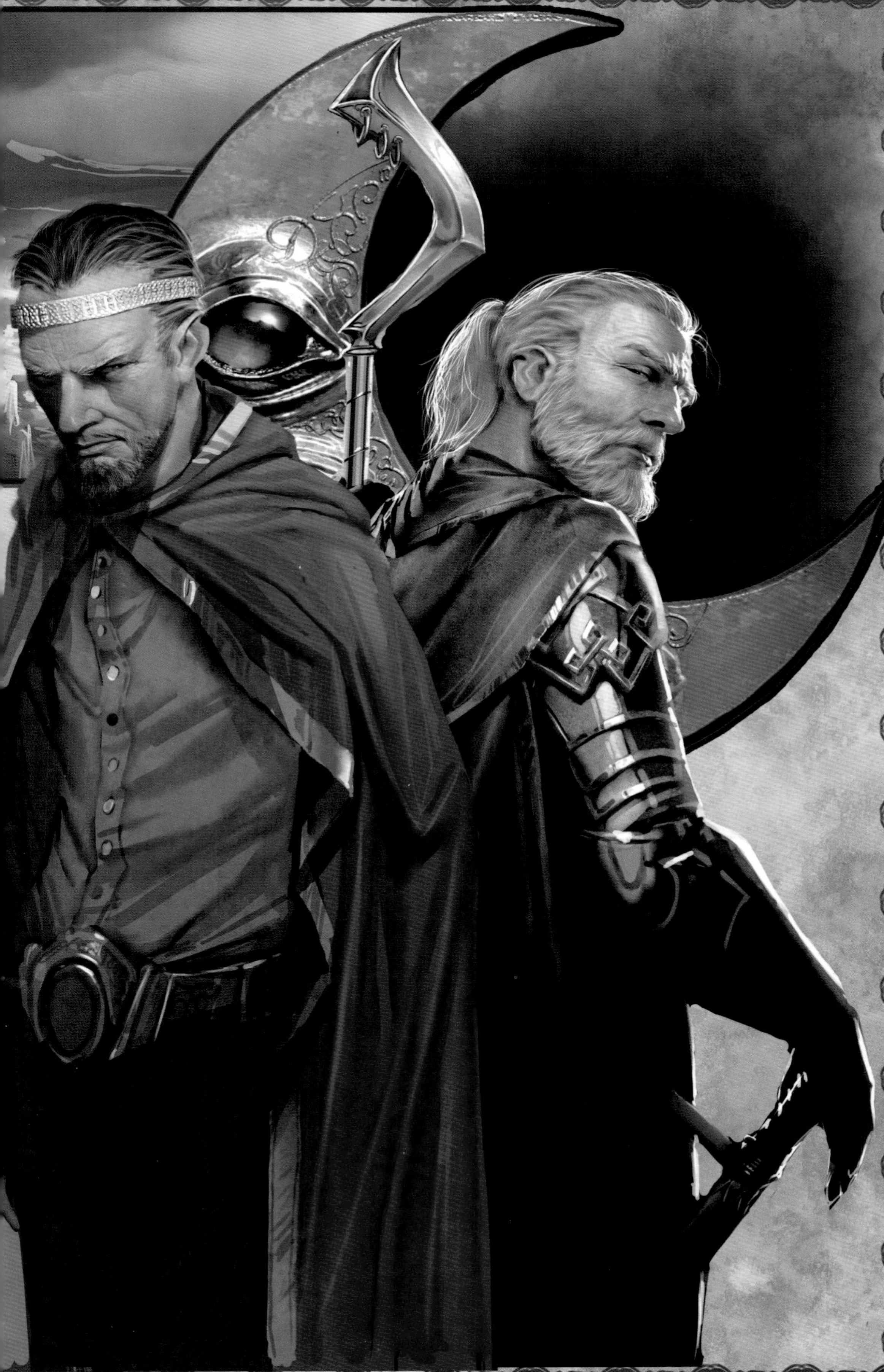

THE FAETREE

The peculiar gift that is a Faetree has been
studied for centuries. Historical records claim
the Faetrees were gifts of the Eani, while also
indicating they are not of the old world.

Ancient knowledge tells us of the root of all
worlds. The faithful hold that the goddess Aertes
resides there. She who serves the fates supposedly uses the
Faetree to grant mystical weapons, known as geos, to those who
are worthy. Above the geos stand the grimlas, weapons of the
wanderers who serve as the right hand of fate.

The Faetree represents a fascinating riddle for the scholars who study it:
why weapons? Could fate not have branded its champions in some other
way? A crown, a necklace, a bracelet? But the gift of fate is a means to end
another's fate. Does this imply the madness of the receiver, or the inherent
cruelty of the giver?

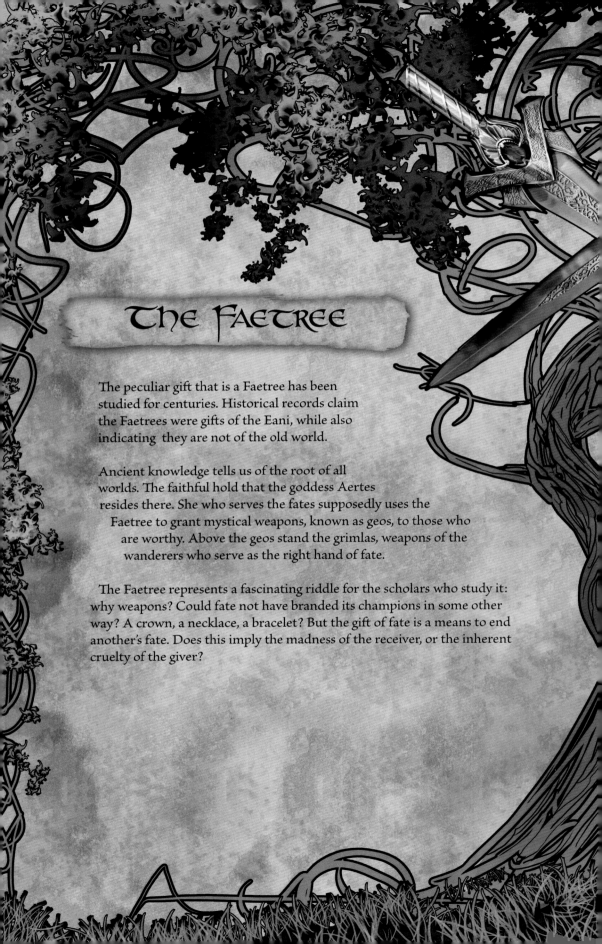

The question has long been debated in
the halls of the University of Ardunat. Most
support the position that fate wishes us to take
our destiny into our own hands, and bravely carve a
path through the dangers we face. But not all agree. There
remains the ominous possibility that in the heart of the world
resides not fate, but chaos.

Chaos abhors peace, which by its very definition is static. Peace is the
dream of farmers and families, bards and settlers. But war is upheaval.
It shapes kingdoms and changes destinies. Weapons are tools of war,
and above all weapons stand the grimlas, borne by those deemed
paragons of fate.

Of Magic

The world is made of necra. This is the wisdom given to us by the Eani. Necra is non-living matter, static by nature. It is the building block of all we see around us. This much we know.

Maga is the opposite of necra. Maga is life. It is the life force, the energy that keeps the universe in motion. Before Baran's gift, we had no knowledge of the vast potential of maga. Any means of controlling this energy was beyond us.

Then dragons appeared, and the three eldest each presented us with a gift. Barahea granted us the whispering flame, and through the gift of her blood, Sardaheim was created. Mergarand gave us the bloodgift of the Mesadee and Shivas. And Baran gave us the Corredan flame, and the power that is magic.

The key to forming spells was in tellas, a metal found in dragon scales. Tellas is highly reactive to energy agitation. When used to create a spiral on a casting weapon, tellas channels the caster's maga, or life force, through the weapon's core. The necra around the weapon becomes agitated, and can be molded. The spellcaster imposes will through life force. Thus a spell is formed.

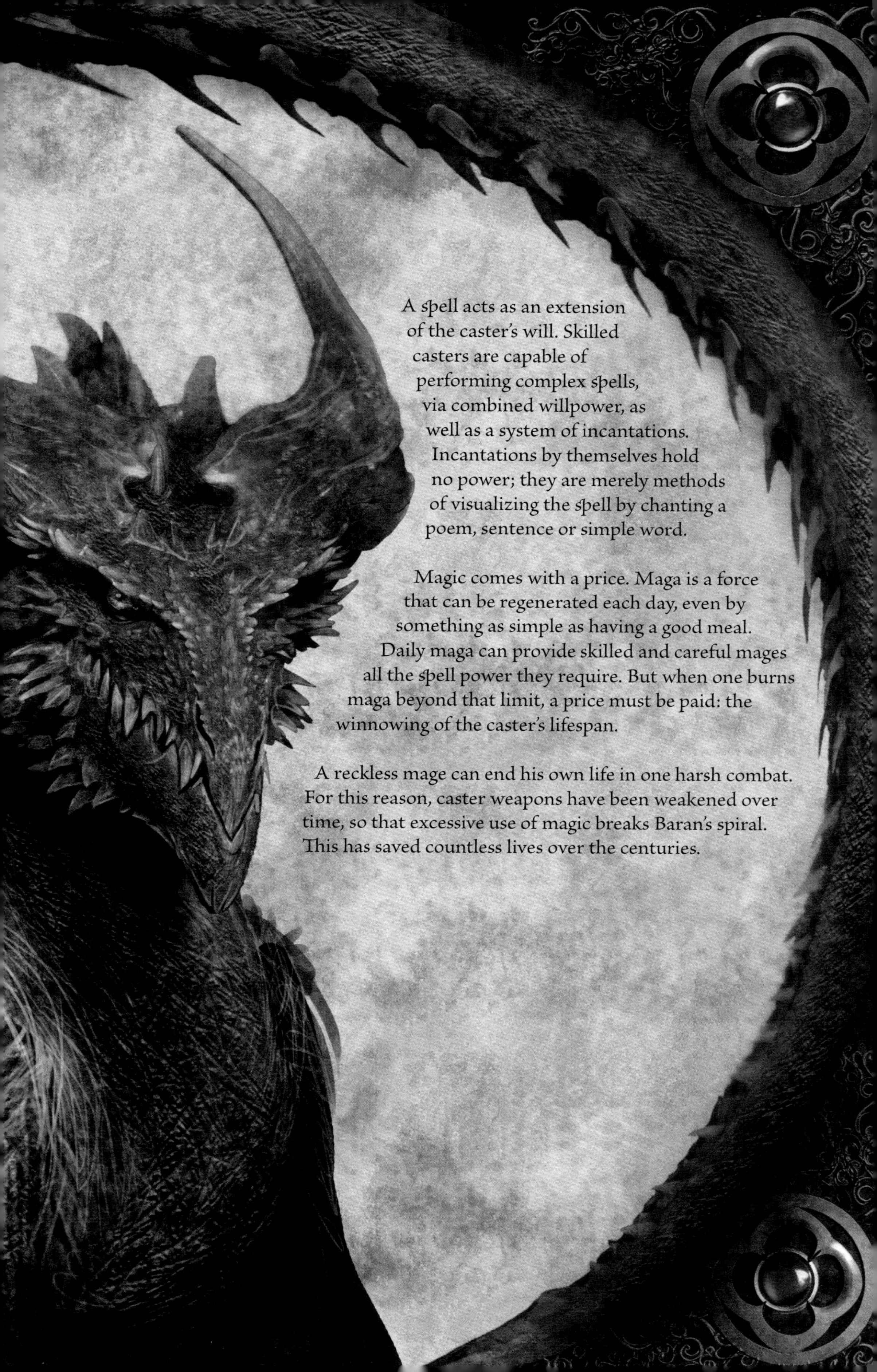

A spell acts as an extension of the caster's will. Skilled casters are capable of performing complex spells, via combined willpower, as well as a system of incantations. Incantations by themselves hold no power; they are merely methods of visualizing the spell by chanting a poem, sentence or simple word.

Magic comes with a price. Maga is a force that can be regenerated each day, even by something as simple as having a good meal. Daily maga can provide skilled and careful mages all the spell power they require. But when one burns maga beyond that limit, a price must be paid: the winnowing of the caster's lifespan.

A reckless mage can end his own life in one harsh combat. For this reason, caster weapons have been weakened over time, so that excessive use of magic breaks Baran's spiral. This has saved countless lives over the centuries.

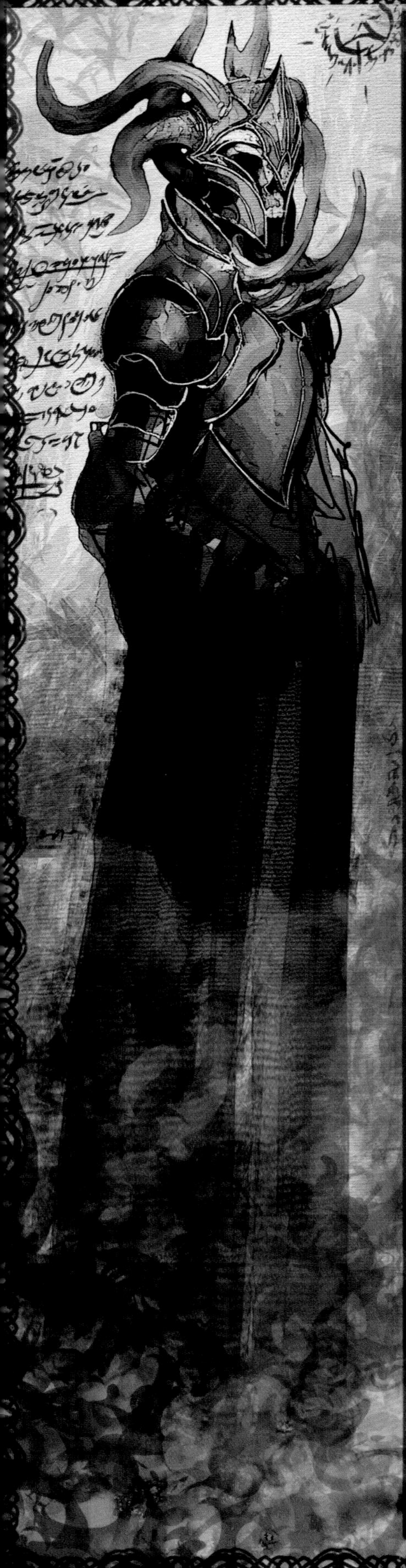

The Whisperers

“There is power in the bones, and it calls to the restless that whisper in the night.” In some form or another, these words have warned of the old terrors for millennia.

As scholars, we question the when, the why, the how. When did the Whisperers first realize they could bind to bones? This may be hardest to answer, for the turbulent history of the continent has a way of twisting facts, obscuring truth with fanciful legend.

We do know the poems of Eldest Three mention the dead rising to claim the living. So some believe that Whisperers are of the old world, arriving at the tail end of the Exodus. Another popular belief is that the Exodus of the old world changed something in our world, and the spirits became restless.

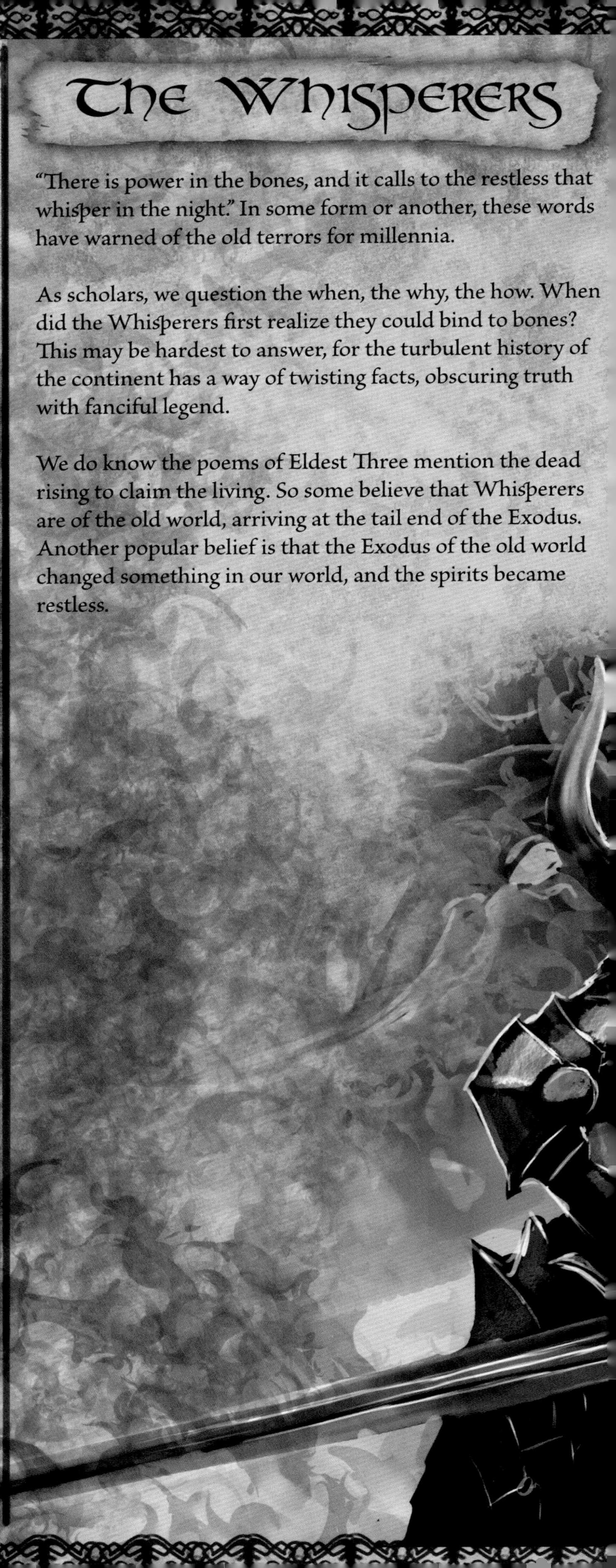

Why bones? Many scholars have come to see bones as the anchors of the soul. The soul binds to the bones, a trait that remains even after death.

The origin of the Whisperers remains a mystery. In their natural form, they are mere wisps of light and mist; harmless, if a bit eerie. The first significant gathering of Whisperers was at the fallen city of Ardesh. The incident taught us that if enough Whisperers are present, the resulting mist becomes thick enough to dampen and even disable spellcasting. This effect, combined with the increasing number of Whisperers, makes them a formidable danger.

The Whisperers' alliance with the Necryte Varda Balahad marked the height of their power. Even after Varda's defeat, the sheer number of Whisperers in Ardesh made the region uninhabitable. Today, Wranthorn's army vigilantly guards the border to Ardesh. However, since the Necryte's defeat, the Whisperers have shown little interest in leaving Ardesh.

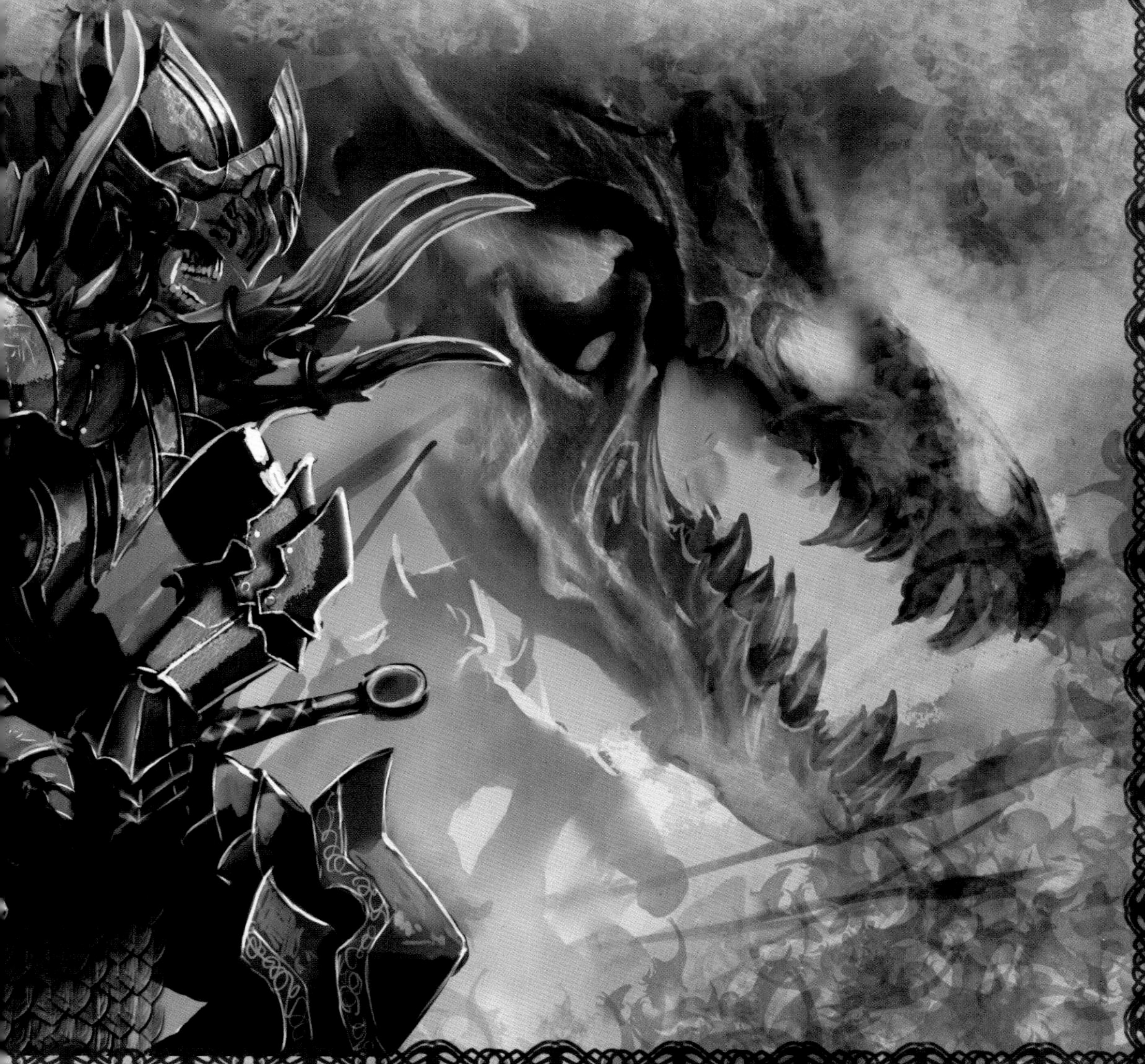

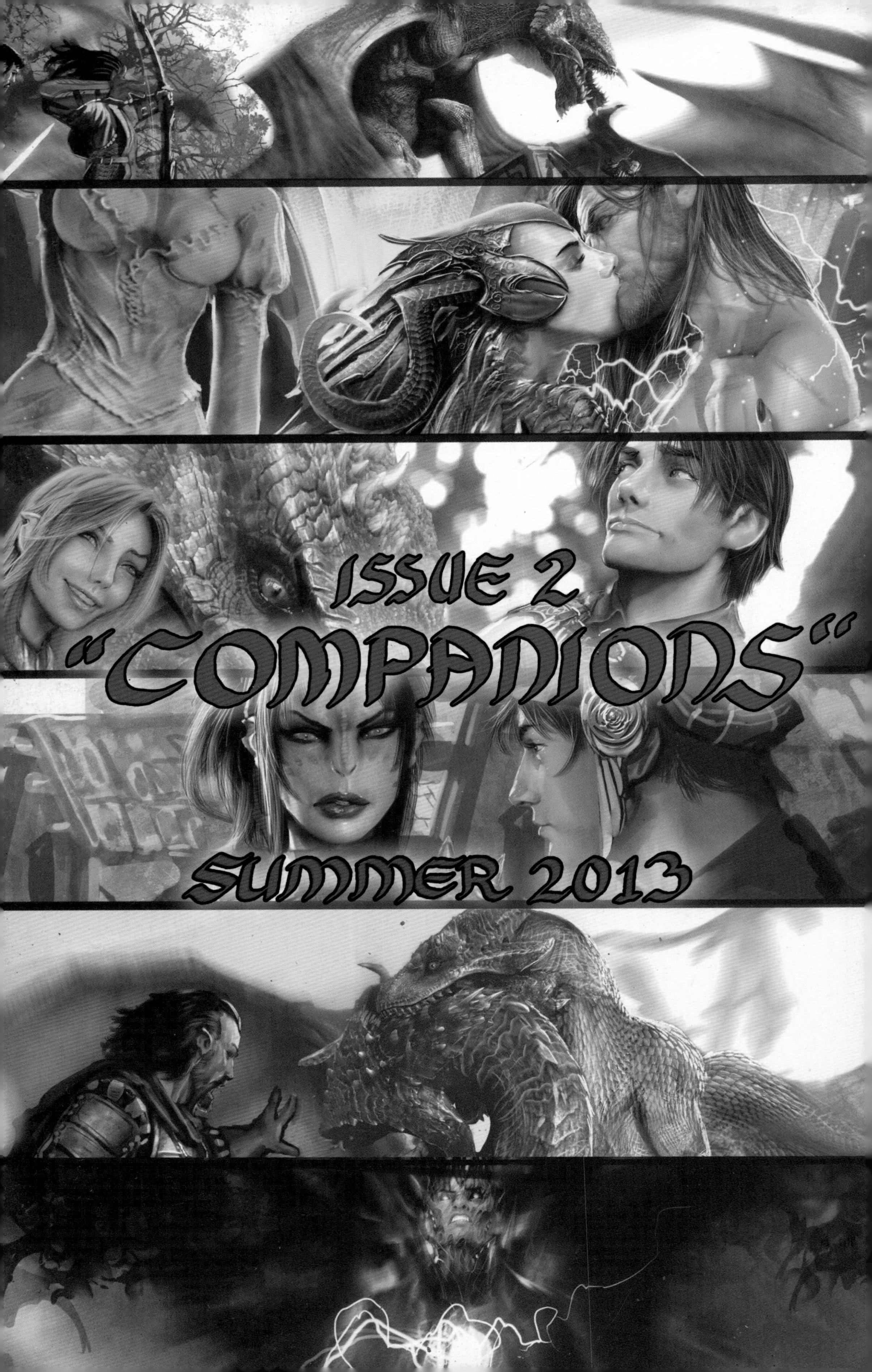
ISSUE 2
"COMPANIONS"
SUMMER 2013